D1603720

Attack
of the
Airacobras

Attack

of the

Airacobras

Soviet Aces,

American P-39s,

and the Air War

against Germany

Dmitriy Loza

Translated and Edited by

James F. Gebhardt

with an Introduction by

Von Hardesty

University Press of Kansas

Photos courtesy of Gennadiy Petrov, Truman A. Partridge, Sr., E. F. Furler, Jr., and National Air and Space Museum, Smithsonian Institution

Published by the University Press of Kansas (Lawrence, Kansas 66049), which was organized by the Kansas Board of Regents and is operated and funded by Emporia State University, Fort Hays State University, Kansas State University, Pittsburg State University, the University of Kansas, and Wichita State University

The paper used in this publication meets the minimum requirements of the American National Standard for Permanence of Paper for Printed Library Materials Z39.48-1984.

Library of Congress
Cataloging-in-Publication Data

Loza, D. F. (Dmitriy Fedorovich)
    Attack of the Airacobras : Soviet aces, American P-39s and the air war against Germany / Dimitriy Loza ; translated and edited by James F. Gebhardt ; with a foreword by Frank Borman and an introduction by Von Hardesty.
        p. cm. — (Modern war studies)
Includes index.
    ISBN 0-7006-1140-1 (alk. paper)
    1. Soviet Union. Raboche-Krest'yanskaya Krasnaya Armiya. Fighter Division, 216th—History. 2. Airacobra (Fighter plane) 3. World War, 1939–1945—Aerial operations, Soviet. 4. World War, 1939–1945 —Regimental histories--Soviet Union. I. Title. II. Series.
    D792.S65 L69 2001
    940.54'4947--dc21   2001002619
British Library Cataloguing in Publication Data is available.

Printed in the United States of America

10   9   8   7   6   5   4   3   2   1

CONTENTS

FOREWORD

The editorial board of the University Press of Kansas was wise in selecting *Attack of the Airacobras: Soviet Aces, American P-39s, and the Air War against Germany* for publication. Excellent histories have been written about the P-39 Airacobra and Bell Aircraft, the company that manufactured it. But none of these works contain as detailed an account of the use of this aircraft by the Red Air Force, which received almost 5,000 Airacobras (approximately 50 percent of the 9,584 produced) through the Lend-Lease program during World War II.

By the time the Soviet Union began to receive them in quantity in mid-1942, the Airacobra's shortcomings were well known to American pilots. The P-39 was a short-range fighter that did not perform well at altitude (above 15,000 feet). It was difficult for an inexperienced pilot to fly and was not easily recovered from a spin. Some pilots went so far as to claim that the aircraft "tumbled in flight." The 37mm cannon, while large in caliber, was slow in velocity and rate of fire and had a limited ammunition supply. With its V-12 Allison engine mounted behind the cockpit, the aircraft was not particularly user-friendly for maintenance personnel. In sum, the P-39 did not endear itself to American fighter pilots, who throughout the war showed a definite preference for the higher performance P-38, P-47, and P-51.

For reasons made clear in this account, none of the P-39 Airacobra's heralded faults deterred the Red Air Force from achieving great combat success with it. Its marginal high-altitude performance was of little consequence in an air war fought largely below 15,000 feet. Range was not an issue in a theater where Soviet aviation units regularly displaced forward to keep pace with advancing ground units. So satisfied was the Soviet government with the firepower of the early-model P-39's nose-mounted cannon and two machine guns that it requested removal of the wing-mounted guns on models subsequently delivered. As for the difficulty of controlling the aircraft in aerobatic flight, this issue was resolved by thorough pilot training. Maintenance of the aircraft would always be a problem, if only because spare parts were in short supply from a line that stretched all the way back to the factory in Buffalo, New York. Like good maintenance personnel everywhere, Soviet mechanics resorted to cannibalization of combat- or accident-damaged aircraft.

This book follows the combat path of a single Airacobra-equipped Red Air Force unit, the 216th Fighter Division, which later was redesignated as the 9th Guards Fighter Division. This unit stood down in the fall of 1942 at a small airfield north of Baku on the Caspian Sea. Over the next several months, as P-39 Airacobras were ferried in from Iran, the division's young and veteran pilots transitioned to this new (to them) American fighter. The division's regiments reentered the fight against the Luftwaffe in the spring of 1943 on the east shore of the Black Sea and over the next two years fought all the way to Berlin.

It may surprise the reader, as it did me, to learn that the top-scoring Airacobra ace in World War II was Guards Major Grigoriy Rechkalov, who shot down fifty German aircraft while flying the P-39. Rechkalov finished the war as the overall number-four Soviet ace, with fifty-six individual and six shared kills. He flew a total of 450 missions and participated in 122 aerial engagements, several of which are described in these pages. By war's end Rechkalov had twice received the coveted award and title Hero of the Soviet Union.

A central figure in this book is Guards Captain Aleksandr Pokryshkin, who is credited with forty-eight kills while flying the P-39. Pokryshkin was a member of and later commanded the 9th Guards Fighter Division, the unit around which this narrative is constructed. Pokryshkin was a tactical innovator whose formula, "altitude, speed, maneuver, fire," transformed his 16th Guards Fighter Regiment into the third-most productive regiment in the Red Air Force. Guards Colonel Pokryshkin finished the war as the Soviet Union's number-two ace, with fifty-nine individual and six shared kills in approximately 650 missions and 156 aerial engagements. Pokryshkin received the award Hero of the Soviet Union on three separate occasions, one of only two pilots to be so honored (the other was Ivan Kozhedub, the leading Soviet ace, with sixty-two individual kills).

This is a story not only of air combat but also of the ground support personnel who refueled and maintained the aircraft, cleaned and reloaded the guns, packed the parachutes, treated the wounded, guarded the airfield at night, and commanded the fighter squadrons and regiments. Seldom have we had such an opportunity to see inside a Soviet combat aviation unit in war.

What stands out above all else is their courage and determination to win. Soviet pilots, like all other Soviet military personnel during the war, had only two choices—win or die. There was no magic number of missions flown that permitted a pilot to return "home" to a war bond tour or training assignment. Too frequently, a pilot's home and even his family were under German occupation.

The other qualities most often demonstrated are flexibility and in-novativeness. Soviet air and ground crews found effective solutions for every problem they faced. For example, these pilots transitioned from aircraft with no radios to the P-39, which was equipped with two transmitters and three receivers. They came to regard the aircraft's ra-dios as one of its most important weapons. Pokryshkin and many of his pilots had their control sticks rewired so that all guns fired on a sin-gle trigger switch. Other such examples of innovation abound.

This book's descriptions of aerial combat and daily life in a tactical aviation unit on the Soviet–German front challenge our stereotypical view of the Soviet military machine during the Great Patriotic War. With the publication of *Attack of the Airacobras*, we can see more clearly now.

Frank Borman
Colonel, USAF (Retired)

PREFACE

I want to give special recognition to former navigator of the 100th Guards Fighter Regiment, Hero of the Russian Federation Colonel (retired) Mikhail Georgievich Petrov, for countless consultations on various technical aviation issues and examples of the tactical employment of the P-39 Airacobra in aerial combat with enemy fighters and bombers. His observations and contributions have made possible an all-encompassing discussion of many aspects of the daily life of air crews and ground support personnel and of the combat employment of the fighters of 9th Guards Fighter Division units.

I had the honor of attending the Frunze Military Academy in the same class with Colonel Aleksandr Pokryshkin after the war. Late in 1943, in accordance with a regulation promulgated in October of that year, Pokryshkin had been recommended for his third award of Hero of the Soviet Union for personally downing fifty enemy aircraft. His award recommendation packet, however, was rejected in Moscow with the stunning annotation, "It is not deemed possible to award this rank to Lieutenant Colonel Pokryshkin because, fighting in an American aircraft, he has raised the prestige of foreign equipment." Lieutenant Colonel Pokryshkin was finally awarded his third Gold Star Medal in August 1944. He was the first Three-Times Hero of the Soviet Union in the Soviet Army. In 550 combat sorties and, by May of 1944, 137 aerial engagements, he had personally shot down fifty-three enemy aircraft.

In one of our conversations at the Frunze Academy, when Pokryshkin learned that I had fought the enemy on an American Lend-Lease Sherman tank, he said, "The glory that we earned on the battlefield is ours. But we are silenced regarding the means by which we beat the fascists. We can barely talk about it!"* These bitter words, obviously, were a consequence of the unjust treatment accorded this courageous fighter pilot.

*The "glory" is a reference to Pokryshkin's and Loza's Hero of the Soviet Union Gold Stars; the "means" is a reference to the American equipment they employed. [Editor's note]

With the publication of this book, fifty-six years after the end of the Great Patriotic War and sixteen years after the death of Marshal of Aviation Aleksandr Pokryshkin, the story of the Soviet Airacobra pilots of the 216th (9th Guards) Fighter Division is finally being told in English.
—D.L.

This book is the product of a suggestion I made to retired Soviet Army Colonel Dmitriy Loza in 1995 to "find a Soviet P-39 pilot and get him to tell his story." At the time we were working together to produce his own memoir, *Commanding the Red Army's Sherman Tanks* (Lincoln: University of Nebraska Press, 1996). That volume was followed two years later by Colonel Loza's second, wider-ranging anthology, *Fighting for the Soviet Motherland* (Lincoln: University of Nebraska Press, 1998). In early 1998 Dmitriy Loza began interviewing Hero of the Russian Federation Mikhail Petrov, former P-39 pilot and veteran ace of the 9th Guards Fighter Division. Colonel (retired) Petrov flew 352 combat missions, participated in eighty aerial engagements, and was credited with fifteen individual and one shared kill. He flew the P-39 Airacobra while assigned to the 100th Guards Fighter Regiment of the 9th Guards Fighter Division. Their collaboration, plus countless hours of archival and secondary source research and writing by Colonel Loza, has resulted in this unprecedented account of the Bell P-39 Airacobra in combat on the Eastern Front.

This work is divided chronologically into three parts that reflect the training and combat activities of the 216th Guards Fighter Division: August 1942 to May 1943, August to December 1943, and May 1944 to May 1945. Into the two gaps between these three chronological sections I have inserted several chapters that describe combat support and service support issues: aircraft maintenance, aviation logistical support, command and control, and navigational practices in the first instance; and frequent relocation of aviation units, airfield construction and defense, and, briefly, fighter tactics in the second instance. The material in these inserted chapters is wide-ranging in time and not bound by the chronology of the chapters that precede and follow them.

The original text contained many explanatory and source notes provided by the author, and I have added several notes to passages that benefit from additional information. These inserted notes are identified with my initials in brackets [JG]. Finally, the reader may be puzzled by the seemingly odd numbers that appear in the text to reflect altitude and distance. In the original Russian text, these parameters were expressed in meters and kilometers and generally in round numbers. For the American audience I have converted meters to feet to express altitude, meters to yards to express aerial engagement ranges, and kilometers to miles to express ground distance. The results of these mathematical conversions are seldom round numbers.

Several people have contributed to the assembly of materials for this book. On this side of the ocean I owe a large debt to Truman A. Partridge, Sr., who mounted a letter-writing campaign on my behalf to seek information and photographs from former Bell employees and P-39 aficionados. I greatly appreciate his editorial contribution and the information and photographs he provided, directly and indirectly. Ed Furler, Jr., provided photographs and Bell factory publications and also combed the manuscript for technical errors. Thanks also to William E. Painter, of the Kalamazoo Aviation History Museum, for reading an early draft manuscript. Dr. William Atwater of the U.S. Army Ordnance Museum at Aberdeen Proving Ground, Maryland, provided me with information regarding the ammunition for the 37mm cannon. Finally, thanks to my wife Debbie, who endured months of solitude in one part of our home while I worked on this project in another.

—J.F.G.

Attack
of the
Airacobras

INTRODUCTION

Adolf Hitler's plan for the invasion of the Soviet Union, Operation Barbarossa, targeted the Soviet Air Force as its first victim. Launched in the predawn darkness of 22 June 1941, the Luftwaffe struck ten forward airfields of the Soviet Union. Flying in groups of three, German bombers—Heinkel He-111s, Junkers Ju-88s, Dornier Do-17s—dropped fragmentary bombs on hundreds of aircraft, lined up wing to wing, on these exposed and poorly defended airstrips. The main Luftwaffe assault, a flotilla of some 500 bombers, 270 dive bombers, and 480 fighters, followed at daybreak. The sudden preemptive air strike heralded a larger German invasion force of some 3,800,000 men and 1,500 tanks. The epic Russo–German war began with an awesome display of air power.

The Luftwaffe's quick mastery of the airspace over the frontier signaled a summer of reversals and humiliations for the Soviet Air Force (*Voyenno-vozdushnyye sily,* or VVS). German air dominance soon ranged over a vast front extending from the Baltic to the Black Sea—some 2,000 miles. The initial stages of the "Great Patriotic War," as the Russians would soon call the war against Nazi Germany, demonstrated the lethal superiority of the Luftwaffe in both aircraft and air combat tactics. One famed unit, J-52 or the "Green Hearts," scored sixty-five victories on that first day. General Franz Halder, in his diary for 22 June, recorded the destruction of 800 Soviet aircraft with a loss of 10 aircraft! His estimates, as it turned out, were on the conservative side. While records are inexact, Soviet losses that day may have exceeded 1,400 aircraft on the ground and another 300 or so in the air. The larger tallies for the German air juggernaut were equally impressive: another 4,000 Soviet aircraft destroyed by the end of that first week; perhaps as many as 10,000 aircraft, mostly on the ground, by the fall of 1941.

Operation Barbarossa has lingered in popular memory as a defining historical moment. The image of debris fields of burned out Soviet aircraft continues as a fixed and immutable perception of the Soviet Air Force in World War II. This widely held view in the West, if accurate for the opening months of the war, fails to take into account that the VVS eventually did rebound and ultimately win mastery over the

Luftwaffe, one of the more surprising achievements of Soviet arms in World War II. The air war in the east, as in a theatrical performance, must be viewed in terms of the last act, not just the opening scenes.

The VVS displayed a remarkable resilience and a capacity for recovery, which became apparent to German airmen as early as April and May of 1943. The arena for this rebirth, beginning with Soviet fighter aviation, came in the North Caucasus campaign. Here in the skies over the Kuban region at the eastern edge of the Black Sea, Soviet fighter units scored their first significant victory over the highly vaunted Luftwaffe. This VVS air victory came ironically when Luftwaffe air supremacy appeared irreversible. At this stage of the war the German forces had reached the outer limits of their advance into Soviet Russia.

Control of the air became a vital factor for both sides in the remaining two years of the war, allowing each side to concentrate air power along a vast front where sudden shifts in offensive and defensive operations were common. For the VVS, the Kuban signaled a decisive shift to the offensive; there would be no going back to the passive and defensive posture of the past after this exhilarating and redemptive air triumph. While the Kuban episode ranks as a benchmark in Soviet air fortunes, the story has been obscured by the fact that it was fought out in a peculiar trough of time in 1943—between two epic Soviet victories at Stalingrad and Kursk.

The sudden rebirth of Soviet fighter aviation placed enormous burdens on the Luftwaffe, coming at a critical juncture when German air planners could only deploy a finite number of air units to cover the vast occupied Russian landscape. From 1943 on, the thinly spread Luftwaffe did not receive any major reinforcements in aircraft and personnel; in fact, as the war progressed, many German air units were withdrawn from Russian service for Reich defense against the Allied strategic bombing campaign. By contrast, Soviet air power became more muscular and lethal, being augmented by Lend-Lease aircraft shipments and, more important, a massive stream of newly designed aircraft from Soviet aviation plants. The Kuban air victory then represented a benchmark for the Soviets in a brutal air war against a formidable enemy.

As the war progressed, the VVS became a vital component in what the Soviets called combined arms warfare. This evolving mode of warfare called for the close interaction of air, ground, and, if required, naval forces. The culminating moment for the VVS came in April and May of 1945, when Stalin deployed some 7,500 aircraft for the final assault on Berlin. The Soviet Union ended World War II with the largest tactical air arm in the world, one linked organically to the ground forces and fully capable of sustaining air operations for extended periods with huge reserves of aircraft and crews.

The Kuban air triumph, it should be noted, coincided with the arrival of the Lend-Lease Bell P-39 Airacobra on the Russian front. This surplus American fighter, considered obsolete by the British and the Americans, entered Russian service in the North Caucasus sector in late 1942. Durable and quite agile as an interceptor below 15,000 feet (typically the air combat zone on the Russian front), the P-39 became a timely and welcome addition to Soviet fighter units. Russian pilots, in particular renowned aces Aleksandr Pokryshkin and Grigoriy Rechkalov, found the P-39 to be an effective fighter against the Messerschmitt Bf-109, scoring forty-eight and fifty air victories, respectively. Dmitriy Loza describes in detail for the first time this extraordinary achievement through the saga of the 9th Guards Fighter Regiment in *Attack of the Airacobras*.

The Soviet triumph in the skies of the Kuban cannot be explained solely through shipments of Lend-Lease aircraft (contributing roughly 11 percent of the Soviet wartime inventory), or even the impressive bravery of pilots such as Pokryshkin and Rechkalov. The reasons are much deeper, to be understood in the complex and often violent development of Soviet aviation under Stalin's erratic leadership. There is no small amount of irony in the fact that Stalin, who set the stage for the Operation Barbarossa debacle in 1941 with his negligence and political purges, also paved the way for the wartime military recovery of Soviet air power.

Stalin himself displayed a keen interest in aviation in the turbulent 1930s, as mirrored in his grandiose "Five-Year Plans" for the rapid industrialization of the Soviet Union. Stalin approved huge outlays of financial support for his highly visible aviation sector. Soviet propaganda trumpeted the growing military might of the VVS. Long-distance aviators became national heroes, as in the case of Valeriy Chkalov and Mikhail Gromov, who made successful flights across the North Pole. The airplane symbolized modernity and a vehicle to unite the vast regions of the Soviet Union.

Called "Stalin's falcons," Soviet pilots also participated in the Span-ish Civil War and aerial skirmishes against the Japanese in the Far East in the late 1930s. However, the privileged Soviet aviation sector eventually fell victim to the purges: for example, famed aircraft de-signer Andrey Tupolev was arrested temporarily, and no fewer than two Soviet air commanders were executed. Despite all the vagaries of the time, Soviet aviation possessed in the late 1930s a substantial in-dustrial base and a talented coterie of aircraft designers.

Even as Stalin chastised his air force on the eve of World War II, he took special pains to set new priorities for his military. In 1940, as the purges subsided, he ordered a massive overhaul of the aviation estab-lishment. The Spanish Civil War, where Soviet and German aviators served as "volunteers," demonstrated the superiority of the Luftwaffe in most aspects of aviation technology, which appeared to negate an enormous effort by Stalin to build a world-class air force. Conse-quently, Stalin shifted aircraft design emphasis to a whole new gener-ation of fighters and ground-attack aircraft at the expense of bomber development. The first fighters to emerge—the MiG-3 and LaGG-3— possessed the streamlined silhouette of a modern fighter but fell short of a performance standard to match Western designs. More work was under way on the eve of the war.

For the West, Operation Barbarossa exposed the VVS as a sort of aerial "Potemkin village," more propaganda and bluster than an air force with modern equipment, tactics, and genuine striking power. The Soviet capacity to manufacture military aircraft in large numbers suggested a pattern of quantity over quality. Moreover, the Soviet stress on building a large fleet of bombers, a brief flirtation with "Douhetism," now appeared foolhardy, a waste of national treasure, and an illusory deterrent against Germany in any future war.

Stalin's order for modern fighter and ground-attack aircraft designs brought to the fore a whole new generation of aircraft designers with Aleksandr Yakovlev in the lead. Two excellent designs emerged out of this shift in approach: the Yakovlev series of fighters, and Sergey Ilyushin's Il-2 ground attack aircraft. Both types were in serial produc-tion on the eve of Operation Barbarossa. But these modern warplanes had not reached operational air units in any significant numbers when hostilities began. One related factor, if largely hidden at the time, was the fact that the German preemptive strike had indeed destroyed many aircraft, even thousands, but these losses were mostly older obsolete types. No less important, a substantial percentage of the trained cadre of military pilots actually survived the worst of Operation Barbarossa, having been evacuated to the rear to fight another day.

The Luftwaffe's assault in its initial waves failed to neutralize or destroy many of the Soviet aviation plants. Wisely, Stalin ordered the evacuation of these plants—equipment and workers—to the east, beyond the Urals and outside the range of Luftwaffe bombers. Herculean in scope, this massive shift of the industrial base, including the many aviation plants, would become a key to the ultimate Soviet victory over Nazi Germany. By 1943, despite all the chaos and disruption of the evacuation process, Soviet aircraft production had managed to resume a near normal level of productivity. The transplanted aviation industrial base only augmented its productive capacity in the remaining years of the war, rolling out over 100,000 modern aircraft by the war's end. Lend-Lease shipments of raw materials such as aluminum, machine tools, and 14,000 aircraft of various types only reinforced the Soviet Union's war-making potential.

In the wake of Operation Barbarossa, Stalin altered his approach to the war's management, embracing a new pragmatism in the selection of his generals and wartime subordinates. Where once political and ideological factors fueled the great purges, Stalin now displayed a keen interest in merit advancement. This war-induced sobriety dictated an end to mass purges in the context of the war emergency. For the leadership of the VVS, he appointed an obscure and relatively low-ranking air commander named Aleksandr Novikov, a talented and energetic officer who had displayed great gallantry in the Leningrad sector at the start of the war.

The Novikov appointment set the stage for a whole series of reforms of the air force. These reforms began in the spring of 1942, at a vulnerable moment in Soviet fortunes, and would be critical in reorganizing the VVS for its hard-won triumph over the Luftwaffe. Novikov imposed from the top down a relentless drive to adapt to the very best technology and methods—even if it meant a systematic copying of the enemy. There was a keen desire, at the outset, to reshape the organization of the Soviet Air Force, to make the air arm an effective part of the combined arms mode of warfare. Having taken this rational step, Novikov then refashioned the whole matrix of VVS operational art—a shift in approach that would cast a long shadow on the postwar Soviet Air Force.

Novikov, if not well known in the West, emerged between 1942 and 1945 as one of the more dynamic Allied air commanders. His wartime record reflected high energy and innovation. Success, however, did not necessarily bring rewards or career advancement: he was demoted in the immediate postwar context with other war heroes such as General Zhukov. This demotion, if arbitrary and unwarranted, did not result in imprisonment or execution for Novikov, the fate of two of his predecessors on the eve of the war. Novikov was a strong advocate of the centralization of air power. To achieve this end, he reorganized the fragmented Soviet air arm into "air armies." Each air army, consisting of fighters, bombers, and ground-attack aircraft, was attached to an active *front* rather than a military district or geographical region. This allowed for mobility, concentration of power, and flexible response. Novikov oversaw the organization of eighteen air armies during the war. Depending on the shifting wartime context, these air armies could expand to between 2,000 and 2,500 aircraft.

Air armies became a vital, often lethal, component in combined arms operations, when the Red Army launched massive offensive operations against the German army. The VVS, by design, served as a sort of "flying artillery" for the ground forces. Once committed to a major offensive, an air army, acting alone or in concert with other air armies, routinely and swiftly asserted air supremacy over an active *front* or breakthrough corridor. The Luftwaffe, now weakened by attrition and permanently on the defensive, offered only token resistance to the Soviet Air Force at this late phase of the war.

The timely arrival of the P-39s in the North Caucasus gave Novikov and his air army commanders not only an opportunity to experiment with an unfamiliar American fighter but a chance to develop techniques for radio communication. Lend-Lease shipments of modern radios provided the means for the VVS to perfect techniques for command and control. The newly organized air armies required effective air-to-ground and air-to-air communications, especially in sorties over the vast and diverse terrain of the North Caucasus. Prewar Soviet fighter aircraft, if rugged and agile, were legendary for their primitive instrumentation. When flying these austerely equipped aircraft, Soviet pilots typically used visual signals instead of radios, except on rare occasions when a squadron leader alone possessed a radio. From the Kuban period onward, the VVS would make excellent use of radios (and later radar) to develop the new offensive mode of fighter operations.

As Dmitriy Loza chronicles for us, fighter air combat tactics became a compelling concern for Soviet air planners once they passed through the crucible of Operation Barbarossa. Novikov encouraged innovation in the field, among all his division and regimental commanders, even the open copying of enemy technology and technique, if deemed essential to victory. Such a wartime call for adaptability, if officially encouraged, ran against certain conditioned reflexes within the air force, in particular the palpable fear in the officer corps that any criticism of established procedures might be perceived by the political commissars as disobedience, even treason. Nevertheless, Novikov left no aspect of VVS operational art outside his scrutiny. The winds of adaptation and innovation swept through the air force in 1942 and 1943; the near destruction of the VVS sanctioned the whole process of seeking out new methods. In time, Novikov's pragmatic spirit reached Konstantin Vershinin, air commander of the 4th Air Army posted to the North Caucasus. Vershinin, in many ways, reflected the mixed reflexes of a typical commander: he discerned the new atmosphere and felt emboldened to approve many tactical reforms in the field, but he proved to be very cautious and measured in his approach.

The wartime pressure for change also came from below, especially from frontline pilots who were restive with the older methods. No individual fighter pilot would be more important in articulating this mentality than Aleksandr Pokryshkin. As a combat pilot, he had narrowly escaped the onslaught of Operation Barbarossa, and he emerged from the disasters of the first months of the war with deeply felt resentment over the lack of Soviet preparedness in 1941.

Pokryshkin became a keen student of German air combat tactics, having observed at first hand the combat prowess of the Luftwaffe in the opening weeks of the war. He advocated prompt adaptation to the enemy's manifestly superior tactics, even as he explored the wider gamut of air warfare. Pokryshkin called for the adoption of a new set of tactics based on experience, not abstract theory. When seeking these changes, he and other pilots were repeating the same process undertaken by the RAF at the start of the war, when they, too, felt compelled to adopt the Luftwaffe's advanced techniques for air combat. The German tactic of an element leader and a wingman, operating in two- *(Rotte)* and four- *(Schwarm)* aircraft formations, allowed for maximum striking power, vertical maneuver, and defense. By contrast, the prewar Soviet manuals on air combat tactics called for the use of three-aircraft formations, which had proven stilted and ineffectual against the enemy.

At the core of air combat, in Pokryshkin's mind, was a simple formula: "altitude, speed, maneuver, and fire." Pokryshkin deemed all these factors essential, but he considered vertical advantage the key to success and personal survival. Attacking from altitude gave the fighter pilot a distinct edge in any combat scenario, allowing for freedom of maneuver, observation of the enemy, and the element of surprise. In the Kuban, Pokryshkin and his fellow pilots found a flexible context in which to forge these new tactics, which arrayed fighters in echelons by altitude and depth. Soviet pilots found the P-39 to be an effective fighter in this altered tactical setting to attack enemy bombers or to engage in air-to-air combat with the enemy.

Any advocate of reform ran the risk of personal peril on the ground, perhaps demotion or imprisonment. Pokryshkin's boss, Vershinin, as noted, welcomed innovation, but he feared getting too far out ahead of the reforms. Pokryshkin, in turn, faced some anxious moments in this charged atmosphere. Loza reveals that at one juncture Pokryshkin was asked to surrender his Party card (always a grim harbinger of arrest) and accept a temporary demotion in rank. Yet Pokryshkin persisted and prevailed. Ultimately he became a three-time winner of the "Hero of the Soviet Union" Gold Star, arguably one of the Soviet Union's most celebrated war heroes.

Loza's analysis of the Kuban air battle finds confirmation in the recollections of German airmen who flew in the North Caucasus campaign. When the National Air and Space Museum sponsored a special seminar on German air power in 1987, there was a unique opportunity to record the observations of German fighter pilots, including Guenther Rall, a veteran of the Kuban action and third-ranking ace of World War II, with 275 victories, most of which were tallied on the Eastern Front.

Rall observed that Soviet fighter aviation displayed a new aggressive posture in late 1942 and early 1943, to the surprise of German air units grown accustomed to a more passive and ineffectual foe. He confirmed that Soviet fighter units now approached them in pair and "finger four" formations, showing boldness and greater coordination. German air units, both bombers and fighters, now routinely encountered spirited fighter interception over Soviet territory. The Kuban, as he remembered it, offered the first real challenge to the Luftwaffe in the Russian campaign.

Like most German fighter pilots, Rall expressed a certain disdain for P-39 Airacobra, observing that he and his squadron mates often joked about the Airacobra's automobile-style doors. Yet, he affirmed, such an aircraft in capable hands was a formidable challenge to German fighter pilots flying F and G models of the Messerschmitt Bf-109. When the Soviets began to use radios, Rall indicated that his squadron mobilized a number of Russians to monitor the communications chatter between Soviet pilots, a ploy the Russians were very slow to realize. This constant monitoring of Soviet fighter units, according to Rall, allowed his air unit to become familiar with the names of certain Russian pilots, in particular, Aleksandr Pokryshkin. Another vivid memory for Rall concerned the slang and vulgarity punctuating Russian radio traffic—the Russian interpreter entertained his German hosts with descriptions of these earthy exchanges between the Soviet airmen. In time, he remembered, the systematic monitoring of radio communications became a high priority for German military intelligence. Knowing the whereabouts and intentions of the VVS became essential for the Luftwaffe after 1943, when German air units found themselves in permanent retreat.

The story of the P-39 in Russian service, as told by Loza, offers the reader an insightful account of squadron life, as well as of the careers and personalities of some of Russia's most renowned aviators in World War II. The combat path of the 9th Guards Fighter Division is welcome because this celebrated air unit is remembered as one of the most successful in the war. Pokryshkin, of course, is at center stage because of his critical role in reshaping air combat tactics. But there are others, such as Grigoriy Rechkalov, who shot down fifty German aircraft in the P-39 Airacobra. We also see the exploits of other celebrated pilots such as Georgiy Golubev, the Glinka brothers, and Nikolay Lavitskiy, to name just a few.

When Loza tells the story of the Kuban air battle, he also showcases in miniature the larger story of the rebirth of Soviet air power. Outside Russia this story has been largely untold, except episodically. Often, too, Western accounts of the VVS lack detail or historical accuracy. *Attack of the Airacobras* supplies a fresh reassessment of a critical chapter in the air war in the east in World War II.

Von Hardesty
National Air and Space Museum
Smithsonian Institution

PROLOGUE

During the Great Patriotic War, each branch of the Armed Forces of the Soviet Union had units and formations that were exceptional for some particular reason. A famous officer may have commanded them. Or they were distinguished by the exceptional mass heroism of their personnel, whose actions are recorded in the glorious annals of the struggle against the fascist invaders. There are several examples of such units: the 316th Panfilov (8th Guards) Rifle Division in the battle for Moscow, named for its commander, Ivan Vasilevich Panfilov; Chuikov's warriors (62d Combined Arms Army), commanded by Vasiliy Ivanovich Chuikov during the heroic defense of Stalingrad; and 150th Rifle Division, whose scouts—Sergeant Mikhail Yegorov and Junior Sergeant Meliton Kantariya—raised the Banner of Victory over the Reichstag in Berlin on 30 April 1945, earning them both the rank Hero of the Soviet Union.

In the Soviet Air Force, the 216th (subsequently 9th Guards) Fighter Division is clearly regarded as such a "right flank" formation.[1] This unit was unique in two ways: the division remained a component of the Reserve of the Supreme High Command (RVGK[2]) throughout an extended period of the war, and from the end of 1942 until the complete defeat of fascist Germany in 1945 its units were equipped with American P-39 Airacobra fighter aircraft that had been delivered to the Soviet Union under Lend-Lease.

Depending on the concept of the planned operation, this division was assigned to an air army of a particular *front*. After the conclusion of combat actions on a given axis, the division was withdrawn from the *front* and reassigned to the RVGK.

The 9th Guards Mariupol-Berlin Fighter Division was formed in May 1942 as the 216th Division.[3] It was assigned at various times to the 4th, 8th, 5th, and 2d Air Armies, and in cooperation with other fighter formations provided cover to the ground forces of Southern, Trans-Caucasus, North Caucasus, and 1st and 2d Ukrainian *front*s in defensive battles in the Donbass and on the Don, in the battle for the Caucasus, and in the Donbass and Melitopol, Lvov-Sandomir, Sandomir-Silesia, Lower Silesia, Upper Silesia, Berlin, and Prague offensive operations.[4] The division participated in the air campaign in the Kuban in 1943.[5]

For its combat achievements the division was redesignated as the 9th Guards Fighter Division in June 1943, awarded the honorary titles "Mariupol" (June 1943) and "Berlin" (June 1945), and awarded the orders of Lenin, Red Banner, and Bogdan Khmelnitskiy 2d Class.[6]

The division's units produced brave aerial warriors who became the pride of Soviet aviation. Forty-six of its pilots received the high rank of Hero of the Soviet Union; three of these (Grigoriy Rechkalov, Dmitriy Glinka, and Aleksandr Klubov) earned this highest award twice, and the renowned commander and ace Aleksandr Pokryshkin three times.

The fact that new Lavochkin and Yakovlev fighter aircraft received their first combat exposure with pilots of the Mariupol Division at the controls is testimony to the high fighting reputation of this division among similar Soviet Air Force formations. For example, air combat experience revealed that the armaments (one 20mm cannon and two heavy machine guns) mounted on the Yak-3 were sufficient for engaging enemy fighters but less than adequate for the rapid destruction of bombers. At a minimum, two or three cannons were required to ensure the destruction of the Ju-88, He-111, and the specially armored Henschel-129 in an initial pass. The division later successfully tested the La-7 equipped with two cannons.

From May 1943 until the conclusion of the war in the west, the basic units of the 9th Guards Fighter Division were the 16th, 100th, and 104th Guards Fighter Regiments. Each regiment comprised three squadrons with twelve aircraft in each.

Many of the P-39 Airacobras received in the Soviet Union through Lend-Lease arrived bearing American recognition markings (white star with red center on a blue disk). Our aviators painted the entire star red and the circle around it white so that the star would be highly visible in flight.[7]

TRANSLATOR'S COMMENTS

A number of factors led to the delivery of large numbers of the Bell P-39 Airacobra to the Soviet Union under the auspices of the Lend-Lease program in support of the Soviet war effort against Germany. Historical descriptions of the Lend-Lease program frequently begin with reference to President Franklin Roosevelt's "garden hose" analogy, used by the president at a White House press conference on 17 December 1940.[8] President Roosevelt was attempting to garner continued public support for providing war aid to Great Britain, as well as for the Lend-Lease legislation pending in Congress at the time. The Lend-Lease Act was later approved by a large congressional majority and signed by Roosevelt on 11 March 1941. At the time of the signing, the principal intended recipients of the aid were Great Britain and China.

That all changed when Hitler's forces invaded the Soviet Union on 22 June 1941. Despite years of mutual mistrust and suspicion between the governments of the United States and the Soviet Union, almost overnight our enemy's enemy became our friend. But many officials in our government were not especially eager to begin shipping military equipment and other forms of war aid to the Soviet Union. These officials questioned the Red Army's ability to withstand the Wehrmacht's offensive, which was rapidly overrunning large portions of the Soviet-occupied Baltic littoral and western Soviet Union. The Soviet government's first formal request for Lend-Lease aid was made to Under Secretary of State Sumner Wells in Washington on 30 June 1941.[9] In a more detailed request made just days later, the Soviet government asked for, among other military equipment items, 3,000 fighter planes.

In late July, Secretary of War Henry L. Stimson authorized the release to the Soviet Union of 150 fighters that had already been shipped to Great Britain and another 50 from a British order not yet shipped. These aircraft were export Model 14s, known in the United States as the P-400 and referred to by the British as the Airacobra I.[10] This version of the P-39 was powered by a 1,150-horsepower Allison V-1710-E4 engine and armed with a 20mm Hispano-Suiza cannon, two Browning .50 caliber machine guns, and four Browning .303 caliber machine guns. After testing the Airacobra against its own Spitfire and Hurricane, as well as a captured Messerschmitt Bf-109E, the Royal Air Force determined the Airacobra to be inferior and late in the fall of 1941 rejected it for subsequent British service.[11]

The first Airacobras were shipped in crates from Great Britain to Soviet northern ports in late December 1941 or January 1942.[12] Some of these aircraft were assembled near the unloading port and delivered directly to Northern Fleet or Karelian *Front* air force units, while the others from the initial shipment were moved by train (still crated) or flown to a test facility at Ivanovo, approximately 150 miles northeast of

Moscow, for a series of rigorous engineering and flight tests. The Aira-cobra I passed these tests and was issued to Soviet Air Force units in the spring of 1942. The shipment of large quantities of Airacobras from the United States was also apparently begun in the spring of 1942, in advance of the signing of the Washington Protocol by representatives of the Soviet and American governments in early June of that year.[13]

Mass delivery of the P-39 to the Soviet Union was accomplished pri-marily by two routes. The first was by ship to the Persian Gulf port of Abadan in present Iran. These aircraft were factory-crated, first in a single crate that was so large it could not fit in the hold of most ships, and later in three smaller crates.[14] After being unloaded at Abadan, the crates were moved to an adjacent airfield and unpacked, and the air-craft was assembled under the supervision of Bell factory technical representatives.[15] The aircraft were then test-flown by American and Soviet pilots, flown to Teheran for inspection and acceptance by Soviet technical representatives, and finally flown to air bases in the Soviet Union by Soviet ferry pilots.[16] Approximately 2,050 P-39s were deliv-ered to the Soviet Union via this route.

The second primary route was the Alaska–Siberia ferry route (ALSIB), by which aircraft were flown from the factory in Buffalo, New York, to Great Falls, Montana, and then north across Canada to Fair-banks, Alaska.[17] After Soviet government inspection and acceptance in Fairbanks, Soviet ferry pilots flew the aircraft across Siberia to the So-viet–German front, making refueling and rest stops at many interme-diate bases. Approximately 2,600 Airacobras were delivered by this route, beginning in August 1942.[18]

An additional 110 P-39s were delivered to the Soviet Union by ship over the Murmansk route, these being the Airacobra Model 14s trans-ferred from Great Britain in late 1941 and early 1942. Depending on the source, a total of from 4,423 to 4,750 P-39 aircraft were transferred to the Soviet Union during the war, approximately 50 percent of all Lend-Lease fighter aircraft received by the Soviet Union.[19]

While several variants of the P-39 were shipped to the Soviet Union, the majority of them were Q-models. Powered by the Allison V-1710-85 engine rated at 1,125 horsepower, this model of the P-39 per-formed at a level equal to any fighter aircraft the Soviet Air Force had in service at the time. It was armed with a 37mm cannon that fired through the propeller hub, two .50 caliber synchronized machine guns mounted in the upper nose, and two .50 caliber free-firing machine guns that were pylon-mounted under the wings. At the Soviet government's request, the wing-mounted machine guns were later deleted.

One of the enduring myths regarding the P-39 Airacobra in Soviet use is that because of its armaments, in particular the 37mm nose cannon, it excelled as a ground-attack aircraft, even a "tank buster." In translating and preparing this manuscript for publication, I have had the opportunity to peruse several Russian-language sources. Mentions of the employment of this aircraft in the ground-attack role are so rare in these sources as to be exceptional. None of these incidents involved German armored targets; most frequently the aircraft were strafing a train, column of trucks, or troops in the open.

What, then, could be the origin of this "tank buster" myth? It appears to be largely of postwar invention. Wartime reports that filtered back to the Bell Aircraft factory in Buffalo from newspaper correspondents and official American and Soviet government sources are laden with references to the Airacobra's employment in the air-to-air role.[20] The articles based on these reports stress the effectiveness of the P-39's armaments against German aircraft and rarely mention ground targets.

The "tank buster" myth has its roots in the misunderstanding of the general wartime role of the Red Air Force and in the imprecise translation of specific Russian-language terms that describe this role. Red Air Force fighter formations were subordinated to Red Army ground commanders at the *front* level (a *front* being the equivalent of an American or British army group). The numbered air army commander received his air mission orders from the ground *front* commander to whom the air army was subordinated.[21]

The specific Russian-language term most often used to describe the mission and role of Airacobra-equipped Red Air Force fighter units, in this manuscript and other Russian-language sources, is *prikrytiye sukhoputnykh voysk* [coverage of ground forces]. As this book makes exceedingly clear, this mission involved flying from the airfield to the coverage area, then patrolling to prevent German bombers from dropping their deadly cargo on the heads of Soviet ground troops. Pursuant to this mission, Soviet fighters frequently engaged German fighters escorting German bombers and apart from German bombers, over German-controlled territory and over Soviet-controlled territory. Notwithstanding the presence of German escort fighters, a portion of the Airacobra force was always designated to attack the German bombers. This tactical mission is never described in Russian-language sources with terms that could be translated "air superiority mission."

Frequent misunderstanding in this country as to the combat role of the P-39 in Soviet use is based in part on imprecise translation of the term *prikrytiye sukhoputnykh voysk* to "ground support." The latter term, as it is understood by many Western military historians and readers, suggests the attacking of ground targets in support of ground troops, also called "close air support." Thus, with a slip of the translator's pen, the role of the P-39 in Soviet use has been misconstrued from "coverage of ground forces" to "close air support."[22] Did a Soviet Airacobra pilot ever strafe a German tank? Undoubtedly. But this was never a primary mission or strong suit for this aircraft. By no stretch of the imagination could the Bell P-39 Airacobra ever be labeled a "tank buster." Dmitriy Loza's *Attack of the Airacobras: Soviet Aces, American P-39s, and the Air War against Germany* gives us our first accurate and detailed picture of how the Airacobra did contribute to the Soviet victory over Germany.

PART ONE

August 1942 to May 1943

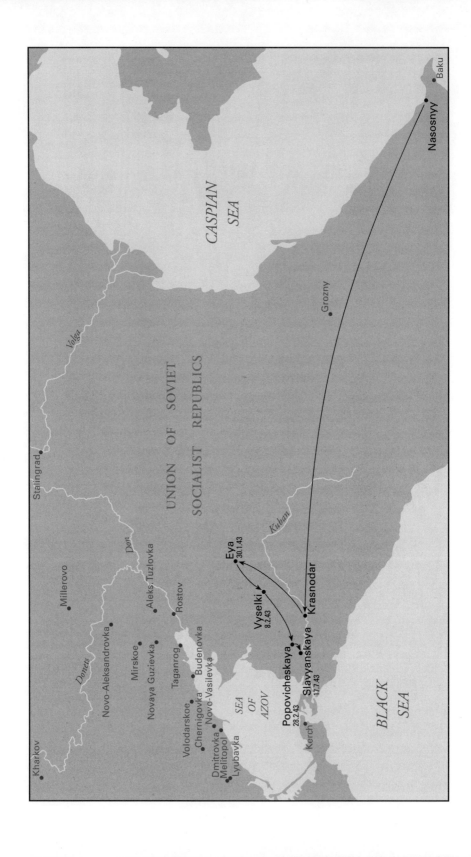

CASPIAN SEA

Baku

Nasosnyy

Grozny

UNION OF SOVIET

SOCIALIST REPUBLICS

Volga

Stalingrad

Millerovo

Don

Aleks.Tuzlovka

Novo-Aleksandrovka

Kharkov

Donets

Mirskoe

Novaya Guzievka

Taganrog

Rostov

Budenovka

Kuban

Krasnodar

Eya
30.1.43

Vyselki
8.2.43

Volodarskoe

Chernigovka

Novo-Vasilevka

Dmitrovka

Melitopol

Lyubavka

SEA
OF
AZOV

Popovicheskaya
28.2.43

Slavyanskaya
1.7.43

Kerch

BLACK
SEA

Transition Training

The summer of 1942 was characterized by heavy combat. The requirement of Stalin's Order No. 227 was categorical—"Not one step backward!"[1] In late August, 216th Fighter Division received a directive: 16th Guards Regiment units were to turn their Yak-1 aircraft over to the neighboring 45th Regiment, commanded by Major Ibragim Dzusov, and be prepared to depart for transition training to new equipment. At the time none of the air crews realized that a special day was approaching. Soviet combat aviators would cross an historic line to become foreign equipment operators. Until the final defeat of the hated enemy, they would fight in Allied—American—fighters called Airacobras.

A large group of pilots of 16th and 45th (it later also became part of the 216th Fighter Division) Fighter Regiments arrived in the Trans-Caucasus, at Nasosnyy station, several miles northwest of Baku on the Caspian Sea coast. These men were assigned to the 25th Reserve Regiment, where new, young pilots underwent flight training and experienced pilots received transition training to new types of aircraft.

Veteran pilots had an established routine. Whenever they arrived at a new base they attempted quickly to gather information regarding the new surroundings and then evaluated their situation. On this occasion their conclusions were worse than disappointing. The aviators' desire to receive the equipment quickly was an unrealizable dream. They wanted to return to the front as soon as possible but they had to be retrained. How long would it take them to master the equipment? One thing was clear, it would not happen soon. Several "wingless" units that had arrived here almost two months earlier were in the queue in front of them.

Living conditions in the reserve regiment were Spartan at best. Nasosnyy was a small town not equipped for such a large military contingent. Retired Colonel Yuriy Maltsev recalls, "We were short of everything—even beds in the barracks and chairs in the dining facility. Breakfast for the air crews began at 0430, dinner was served from 1600 to 1800, and supper from 2200 to 2300. We literally took the cafeteria by storm. They fed the pilots the standard rear-area ration[2]—primarily barley porridge, which we ate with pieces of dried bread because we had no forks or spoons!"[3]

Despite these difficult living conditions, the fighter pilots assiduously studied their new, for them unusual, "trans-oceanic" aircraft. Without exception they all understood that the sooner they mastered the Lend-Lease Airacobras, the quicker they would return to the front. The aircraft was equipped with many nonstandard tactical and mechanical features, beginning with its tricycle landing gear with nose wheel. The excellent forward visibility afforded by the tricycle gear simplified takeoffs, landings, and taxi of the aircraft, which was important for a pilot departing on or returning from a combat mission. The aircraft could take off and land even on relatively soft dirt strips without fear of nosing over.

The engine was located behind the pilot's cabin. This arrangement permitted the pilot to be positioned somewhat forward, ensuring him a good view during aerial combat. The engine's placement behind the pilot also permitted the nose portion of the fuselage to be more pointed in comparison to aircraft of standard configuration. This improved the airframe's overall aerodynamics.

The cockpit canopy was fixed. Doors, similar to those found on a car, were affixed to both sides of the cabin.[4] These doors were hinged at the front and opened at the rear. The right door was for the pilot's routine entry and exit from the cabin; the left door was a spare whose use was not recommended because engine control rods were positioned close to it. The glass windows of both doors could be lowered at all air speeds. In the event the pilot had to exit the aircraft in flight, the doors could not be opened normally but had to be jettisoned. Special handles were mounted internally and externally to provide this capability.

As later became clear, it was somewhat dangerous to exit this aircraft in flight, particularly in a left spin.[5] There was always the possibility of the pilot being struck by the tail assembly. Some pilots were killed in this manner and many others were injured.

Certain deficiencies in the construction of the cockpit must be noted. For example, the cockpit canopy contained a large number of glazing screws whose ends were covered with rubber caps. However, over time the rubber dried out and lost its elasticity, and these protective caps fell off. Spare rubber caps were not available. As a result, sharp threads were exposed in a number of cases. In a spin a pilot was severely thrown around in his seat and could easily strike his head on one of these screw ends. One also could catch their sharp points during entry or exit from the aircraft.

The fighter had powerful armaments, capable, with careful aiming, of defeating any enemy air target with the first pass. So that the P-39's center of gravity would not shift excessively during firing, the links of the heavy machine guns and expended cannon casings were collected in the lower portion of the front fuselage in special containers, which were emptied by maintenance personnel after the fighter landed.

Expended shell casings and loose links from the wing-mounted 7.62mm machine guns were discarded into the air through case and link ejection chutes. Heated air from the radiators was routed to these guns through flexible hoses to prevent them from freezing in flight.

A gun camera was mounted in the right wing in several variants of the Airacobra, and an identification radio was mounted behind the pilot's seat under the cockpit canopy. The aircraft had armor protection for the engine, oxygen bottles (Airacobra I), and pilot's cabin. The pilot was protected from the rear by the engine, behind which was positioned an armor plate. Directly behind the pilot's head was bullet-proof glass 2.5 inches thick. Another armor plate was positioned beneath the pilot. The pilot was protected from the front by bullet-proof glass approximately 1.4 inches thick, to which was affixed an overlaid armor plate. In addition, the propeller reduction gear was protected by five armor plates. These, in turn, protected the cabin from the front. Taken altogether, these various forms of armor plate gave the pilot a double layer of protection from both the front and rear hemispheres.

Our aviators welcomed one particular tactical-technical characteristic of the P-39 with special satisfaction—its navigational equipment, which permitted flight operations in inclement weather and at night. I will say, however, that in practice they rarely had the opportunity to use this equipment.

And so, the first familiarization with the Airacobra took place. In principle, the aircraft was well liked. Our pilots became acquainted with its other combat characteristics and technical aspects in the course of subsequent study of the mechanical parts and during use of the aircraft.

As I have already pointed out, pilots of various regiments were packed into the garrison at Nasosnyy station. It was a genuine aviation "anthill." Training was conducted at a high level of intensity, for all practical purposes interrupted only by sleeping and eating. Time was precious. Fierce battles were being fought on the banks of the Volga River in the fall of 1942 and early spring of 1943. To a man, all the aviators were consumed by a burning desire to rejoin the fight.

The personnel of 45th Regiment did not experience any particular difficulties in their transition to the new fighter. A major contributing factor to the ease of their transition was the fact that many of them had already flown the Curtiss P-40 Kittyhawk. Both the P-39 and P-40 were powered by the same basic Allison V-12 engine. Their navigational instruments and flight controls were similar. The primary difference between the two aircraft was the tricycle gear with nose wheel of the Airacobra versus the tail wheel of the Kittyhawk. In fact, the rear position of this third wheel made the Kittyhawk significantly more difficult to land. The preferred method of landing the Kittyhawk was to touch all three wheels down simultaneously, while the Airacobra was landed on the two main wheels. When the landing speed began to slow, the nose of the aircraft smoothly dropped and the front wheel made contact. After nose wheel contact, the pilot controlled the rollout with the brakes.

The pilots of 16th Air Regiment were the first to encounter the Lend-Lease fighters. Before this transition training they had engaged the enemy while flying Soviet-built fighters. They and their technical specialists had to undergo the full transition program, which they did with varying degrees of success.

All personnel who participated in the transition training initially experienced some difficulty in mastering the P-39's radio equipment. At this time Soviet fighters were not radio-equipped. The P-39, conversely, had a veritable arsenal of communications equipment: three receivers and two transmitters. They ensured reliable communications of the pilots among themselves in the air, as well as with command and control stations on the ground.

All the men had to work hard. They had to master the five "boxes" (as the pilots called the radio sets) with their countless switches and knobs. The primary task was to learn how to maintain crisp, precise, businesslike communications between crews in flight and with the ground vectoring station. This was not as simple as it sounds. A new term—"radio discipline"—appeared in the aviators' lexicon. It imposed great responsibility and rigid demands on the crews.

Frankly speaking, not everything went smoothly at first. The pilots were worried that this additional operational requirement would distract them from their basic mission—to find and destroy enemy aircraft. While they were dealing with this concern, they had to spend considerable time in acquiring correct radio transmission habits, such as speaking briefly, providing the most necessary commands at a given moment, and reporting the most critically required information. In short, they had to learn not to fill the air with useless chatter. Later, during heated aerial engagements with the Luftwaffe, our Airacobra pilots confirmed what they had learned in practice, that radio communication was also a weapon, and a considerably powerful one at that.

It later was demonstrated that crews of 16th Guards Fighter Regiment had learned their lessons well. Of the countless communications training exercises, they had to master one—learning the materiel aspect of the radio set and methods of manipulating it. They had already received almost complete preparation for the difficult task of exchanging radio messages during combat.

As early as September 1942, Guards Captain Aleksandr Pokryshkin, a squadron commander, had learned that our own aircraft plants were beginning to equip fighter aircraft with on-board radios. With advance warning of this innovation, the Airacobra pilots prepared to take advantage of it. They understood that there might not be adequate time at the front to master this new and sorely needed means of command and control.

Initially they familiarized themselves with the appropriate regulatory documentation pertaining to radio communications. Then they organized exercises for the careful study of the subject. Other units in the regiment began to emulate the innovations of the 1st Squadron commander. At the top of the list of training tasks was the procedure for in-flight radio conversations. The crews worked exceptionally hard to achieve brevity in their transmissions. All extraneous phrases were absolutely excluded in transmitting information or the commands of group leaders. Pokryshkin incessantly preached, "A radio conversation is like a shot from a machine gun or cannon. It is exceptionally brief, clear, and timely!" Every day he drilled into the fighter pilots the no-tion that each extraneous word represented precious flying time lost. "Seconds wasted in speech can make you lose the fight! Wasted time in a rapidly unfolding aerial engagement can mean death!"

The months of intense training in a half-starved condition and appalling living accommodations passed quickly. The pilots were beginning to know their new equipment, were learning how to fly it, and were undergoing the required gunnery training. Critically evaluating their preparation, they felt that on the whole they were prepared for combat in the Airacobra. But aircraft were unavailable not only for the 16th and 45th regiments but also for the units ahead of them in the queue.

Specially trained ferry pilots were bringing P-39s into the Trans-Caucasus from Iran. Whether their capabilities were limited, or there were problems in the assembly of the aircraft that were being brought to Teheran from America by sea, or for other reasons, the anticipated large quantities of aircraft did not arrive.

The transitioning pilots of 25th Reserve Air Regiment cultivated good contacts with the ferry pilots. A number of issues regarding the construction of the Airacobra and especially its employment were discussed and clarified. As time permitted, the ferry pilots carefully and unselfishly assisted the transitioning pilots.

The first crews to receive their own Airacobras were the fortunate pilots of 45th Fighter Regiment. Their commander was an Ossetian, Major Ibragim Dzusov. We have a saying: "At home even the corners help" [English equivalent, "There's no place like home!"].[6] Perhaps the fact that this training had been conducted in the Trans-Caucasus had given Dzusov an advantage.[7] He immediately led his unit back to the front, as if he had never left it. And in early March 1943, his Airacobra pilots began active combat in the skies of the Kuban.

Only in March 1943 did 16th Guards Fighter Regiment receive their new P-39s. They fought their first air combat in the new aircraft on 9 April over Taman Peninsula.

These two units comprised the "combat core" of 216th Fighter Division. Here began the glorious combat path of these Soviet pilots in American aircraft.

The Skies of the Kuban

The battle in the skies of the Kuban from April to August 1943 greatly influenced many issues of the combat employment of aviation in general and of fighter aviation in particular in the VVS (*Voyennyye Vozdushnyye Sily,* or air force) of the Red Army. Here old fighter tactics were finally abandoned, and new methods were established and tested in fierce engagements with the enemy. In a word, the Kuban skies became, as it were, a "field academy" that exposed a number of key problems in the tactics of employing fighter units and formations. The combat experience gained in the skies above the Taman Peninsula was subsequently passed along to other fronts of the Great Patriotic War.

The essence of the earlier existing methods of covering ground forces and the conduct of aerial combat with the enemy involved several elements. The mission statement specified the area of deployment of the fighter groups sent out for these tasks, their altitude, and their loitering speed. Arriving in the designated zone, the fighters formed into a large circle and flew over the protected unit or area at minimal speed, looking back over the tails of their own machines. As the pilots themselves expressed it, "We circled like a carousel." As a rule, approaching Messerschmitts dove into this combat formation from above, gaining incontestable superiority by their altitude and the swiftness of their attack.

The regiments of 216th Fighter Division were mainly equipped with the competent P-39, a fast, maneuverable, and powerfully armed (with both cannon and machine guns) fighter that was equal in speed to the enemy Bf-109 and FW-190 fighters in use at that time.

The first encounters with enemy fighters showed that the Airacobra could compete with its German opposition in vertical and horizontal maneuvers. Starting at the same altitude with enemy fighters and correctly using the P-39's speed, our pilot could quickly outclimb the Bf-109F and Bf-109G. When pulling out of a dive, the Airacobra, having significantly greater gross weight than the Messerschmitt, fell somewhat behind in gaining altitude, but it then quickly overtook the enemy. The Messerschmitt, losing speed, would be forced rapidly to transition to horizontal flight.

Combat practice showed that even though doing so conserved fuel, flying the Airacobra at low speed was a mistake from the tactical perspective. The slow-moving aircraft did not have sufficient energy and the enemy gained a quick advantage. The instructions and regulations in effect at that time required the maximum presence of fighters over the battlefield. This could be achieved by the minimum expenditure of fuel while flying at economic speeds. But it turned out that flying in this manner prevented the P-39 from using its good maneuver qualities rapidly to gain the best position relative to the enemy. At reduced speeds our aircraft were unable to execute a rapid turn or other maneuver. The division command drew the appropriate conclusions from this and ordered the aircraft to patrol at maximum cruise speed, at the expense of reduced station time (for the Airacobras, twenty to thirty minutes). This change in flight regime produced immediate results. Aerial engagements conducted at high speeds, even with an enemy superior in number, concluded with victories for our pilots.[1]

In horizontal maneuverability the P-39 was superior at all altitudes to the German fighters of the types that existed at the time. Not once in countless aerial battles did the Germans attempt to conduct an engagement in a turn. As soon as our pilot went after a Messerschmitt or Focke-Wulf from the rear, the German pilot would quickly attempt to disengage by diving. In a brief time the Airacobra also caught up to its target in a dive.[2]

The experience of countless aerial engagements showed that the significant quantity of armaments and skillful aerial maneuver of the Airacobra made this airplane a threat to the enemy. From interrogation transcripts of shot-down and captured German pilots in mid-April 1943, it became clear to our command that the Germans had rushed a group of twenty experienced aces to Taman Peninsula at the end of March. Their mission was to clear the airspace of Soviet Airacobras and Spitfires in active air operations. Success in this mission would ensure freedom of action for the Germans' own bombers against Soviet troop formations.[3]

The qualitative and quantitative superiority of the P-39's armaments enabled it to destroy targets with two or three short bursts. The strike of a single 37mm cannon shell from an Airacobra frequently destroyed a Messerschmitt or Focke-Wulf. A precision cannon shot into any part of a bomber disabled the enemy aircraft. Enemy air crews greatly feared encounters with the P-39.[4]

Deficiencies in the tactical employment of fighter units were noted in late March and early April 1943. They manifested themselves in the density of a fighter group's combat formation, its lack of echelonment in altitude and depth, underevaluation of the actions of pairs, attempts to conduct combat in turns and climbs in fast-moving aircraft, and giving first priority to enemy fighters rather than bombers, forgetting that the bombers were the primary target for destruction.[5]

An order from 4th Air Army (11 May 1943) summarized the lessons of the initial battles in the Kuban sky. In particular, this document noted that the principal deficiency in the combat actions of fighter aviation was the absence of functioning pairs of fighters. The consequence of this was imprecision and difficulty in maintaining the group's combat formation. The order further stated that fighter pairs were assigned by a division-level order and that two pilots who had been paired could not, under any pretense, be separated without permission of the division commander. Special flights were to be conducted by assigned pairs in the course of combat training. Commanders were to take note of any and all measures for strengthening pairs. When aircraft were shot down by the leader of a pair, the wingman in the pair recorded with specific indicators that he had participated in the destruction of the enemy in cooperation with his permanent pair partner. The pair leader and his wingman were to be recommended simultaneously for official awards. The award recommendation was to contain a special annotation that the wingman fought the air battle together with his commander and how many and what type of enemy aircraft were downed by the two pilots acting as a pair.[6]

Another directive (from the commander-in-chief of the Red Army VVS from 30 May 1943) provided a detailed study of the nature of German air activities and included an analysis of the deficiencies in the employment of our fighters. According to this directive, enemy bombers flew toward their targets in groups of from thirty to sixty aircraft and attacked the target from various directions (a "star" raid). They were escorted by a powerful fighter group that had been dispatched to the target area ahead of time. Small groups of Bf-109s and

FW-190s provided direct protection for the Ju-87s and Ju-88s. Upon encountering Soviet fighter aircraft sent out to intercept them, German fighter pilots were to attempt to engage them in battle, thus freeing the bombers to accomplish their mission. And they frequently achieved their goal.

The document went on to note the basic tactical deficiencies in the actions of 4th Air Army fighter units and formations. Becoming engaged in combat with enemy fighters distracted the Soviet fighters from their primary mission of destroying the bombers; patrolling groups were attacking the enemy not on the approaches to the target but directly over it; and some of the Soviet fighter groups were not listening to the ground vectoring station. Commands from the ground frequently were issued at the moment of the engagement, when the dueling pilots could never hear anything; pairs were not working together properly; echelonment by altitude and depth was not maintained in constructing the combat formation; and the "free hunting" method was not sufficiently used for employing fighters over enemy territory.

The directive demanded that during the organization of battle by our fighters against enemy aviation, the bulk of our own aircraft be designated for engaging the enemy on the approach to the front line and intercepting him on his return routes. Commanders were urged to make the aircraft pair the basic component of groups in the air as quickly as possible. A fighter combat formation had to be echeloned by altitude and depth; all pilots, and particularly flight leaders, were to be warned that failure to maintain communications with the vectoring radio station, and further, to ignore its commands, was failure to comply with a combat order; in turn, vectoring radio stations were to limit their transmissions to calls to alerted fighter groups over the battlefield. Signals and commands from the vectoring station were to be brief, precise, and clear; all air crews were to be reminded of the order of the supreme commander-in-chief [Stalin] concerning the most important mission of fighter forces—destroying enemy bombers.[7]

A 7 July 1943 directive from the commander-in-chief of the Red Army VVS emphasized that cooperation between pairs and groups of aircraft, as well as surprise and altitude superiority, had not become the basic principles for ensuring success in aerial combat. There was not the necessary broad implementation of force buildups in engagements for the purpose of creating the most favorable conditions for our pilots and preventing the enemy from having numerical superiority.

As before, the destruction of enemy bombers had not become Soviet fighters' most important mission. Too often Soviet fighters expended all of their efforts in combat with enemy fighters and in so doing enabled the enemy bombers to attack ground targets unhindered.

The document went on to direct commanders to evaluate the accomplishment of combat missions not by numbers of sorties and quantity of expended ammunition but by the achievement of operational-tactical results (how aviation enabled ground units and formations to accomplish their assigned missions to occupy a given objective, force a river, and so on, or prevented enemy air strikes against river crossings, and so on). It further ordered commanders to organize command and control of aviation on the ground and in the air primarily by radio; to gain air superiority before the start of ground force operations by means of massive air strikes during the day and systematic night actions against enemy airfields and by destruction of his aircraft in the air on the approaches to the front line by fighters specially designated for this purpose; to "free hunt" broadly with our fighters over enemy-occupied territory to destroy enemy aircraft and to intercept them on the approaches to the front line; to devote special attention in the training of fighter pilots to working out in the shortest time the final assignment of pairs and the cooperation of pairs in aerial combat; in order to improve the coordination of pairs and to achieve more precise interaction between fighters, to conduct constant bonding of pilots in pairs, to implement this by official order to the regiments and in the future to launch aircraft only with their designated pairs; and to assign to the wingman of the pair responsibility for supporting his leader's actions.

At the same time, the order continued, the leader of the pair was to be held responsible for the loss of his wingman; the fighter combat formation was to be echeloned by altitude and in depth at all times, always taking into account the enemy's use of altitude and his methods of action; to follow the practice of free hunt by ace pilots on those sectors of the front where aviation main forces were operating, and not to be tied down by any specific missions. Aces always and everywhere had only one mission—to destroy enemy aircraft in the air, using favorable conditions in the air situation whenever possible, and in all cases of air combat to create numerical superiority for our fighters over the enemy through the timely massing of forces by assembling separate patrols that were in the air and alerting on-call units from the nearest airfields.

The order reminded commanders that victory in the air would be gained by surprise, superiority in altitude, and numerical superiority.

The numerical ratio of fighters required for covering the flights of *shturmoviki* and bombers was determined based on our aviation units' combat experience over the Taman Peninsula.[8] It was recommended to send a group of twenty to thirty fighters to the zone of the assigned mission some five to seven minutes before the appearance of the Il-2s or Po-2s to clear the sky of enemy fighters. Each group of eighteen to twenty-four bombers was to be escorted by six to eighteen fighters, and four to six fighters for eight *shturmoviki*. If the air situation was favorable, then fighter cover could be lighter. Our forces could be quickly strengthened if the situation became more complicated.[9]

The very intense struggle with enemy aviation over the Taman Peninsula in April and May brought to light a number of deficiencies in our crews' flight and gunnery training. A special commission of 4th Air Army headquarters revealed a number of lapses in this area of our units' combat readiness. The results of inspections were laid out in an order of the army commander, "Concerning deficiencies in the work of flight and gunnery service,"[10] which noted numerous deficiencies: The commanders of all regiments lacked flight and gunnery training. Some pilots feared patrolling in pairs outside visual contact with the remaining aircraft of the group. Frequently, groups of aircraft became engaged in battle all at once, not holding back a portion of their strength for covering the zone of action. The result was unanticipated attacks by Messerschmitts and Focke-Wulfs that had approached undetected out of the sun or from behind clouds. Pilots sometimes failed to complete initiated attacks by totally destroying the enemy aircraft. Cases were noted when our fighters left enemy aircraft untouched, permitting them to return to their own airfield. This was allowed to occur even in the absence of superior enemy air forces. Our pilots often broke off from attacks on enemy aircraft in a straight line, without any kind of maneuver. Our fighter units suffered totally unjustified losses as a result of this lapse. Control was lacking for the quality of aerial battle. Flight leaders did not always see and take note of the mistakes of each individual pilot, and gun camera film was not used as a means of control in all units. Pilots were being insufficiently circumspect on the approach routes to their coverage zone, in the course of aerial engagement, and during their return from a combat mission. Instances were observed when a Bf-109 approached from the rear, attached itself to the tail of our fighters, and quietly shot them down sequentially.[11]

The army commander ordered implementation of several measures to correct these deficiencies. Responsibility for flight and gunnery training of the young air crews was placed on the squadron commanders. Regiment and squadron commanders were quickly to undergo flight and gunnery training. The deputy division commander for flight and gunnery service would train the former, and the deputy regiment commander for flight and gunnery service the latter. Under the general supervision of the division deputy commander for flight and gunnery service, a chart was maintained at the vectoring station showing the names of regiment commanders, their deputies for flight and gunnery service, and, when possible, the squadron commanders. For better control of the results of aerial combat and training of air crews, gun cameras were to be mounted and used in all fighter aviation units.[12]

The principal provisions regarding the assembly of combat formations of fighter units were developed over five months (March through July 1943) of continuous air combat with the enemy. They consisted of the following:

A combat formation was echeloned by altitude and depth in groups and between pairs. The formation consisted of two to three layers or tiers. The lower-tier group (from one-half to two-thirds of the available strength) normally patrolled at altitudes slightly above (325 to 650 feet) the altitude at which enemy bombers operated. Sometimes this group was at the same altitude as the enemy bombers.

The second-tier group (from one-half down to one-third of the available strength) was held at an altitude of from 1,650 to 6,550 feet above the lower group. The upper (third) group, normally a pair of Airacobras, operated at altitudes of from 16,400 to 23,000 feet and had the mission of free hunting in an assigned area, pinning down superior enemy forces should they appear, or destroying individual aircraft that were attempting to flee. Reliable radio communications and, when the weather permitted, visual contact were maintained between all three groups.

Mixed groups of aircraft by type (Yak-1, P-40 Kittyhawk, Airacobra) were frequently assembled in the division and regiments. In this case, the Yak-1 and P-40 worked at the lower altitudes and the Airacobras at the higher.

Experience showed that this structure for the combat formation was correct. But sometimes unnecessary losses resulted when fighters of the third (upper) group did not accomplish their covering missions and instead, when the situation did not require it, dropped down to assist their comrades flying below them who were engaged in aerial combat. At times the aerial combat itself was transformed into a disorganized, congested melee, which made maneuver and command and control difficult. By violating the established structure of the combat formation, pilots placed themselves in an unfavorable and at times dangerous position relative to the enemy.[13]

Several negative aspects were revealed in the combat actions of units of 216th Fighter Division in the first half of May 1943. The air crews had not studied the tactics of the actions of various branches of enemy aviation properly. For example, enemy fighters were used in small groups of from two to ten aircraft, echeloned in altitude and depth; because our fighters were loitering almost in the heavens, at 6,550 feet and higher, enemy bombers penetrated to their intended targets at low altitudes, all the way down to treetop level.

Enemy fighters attacked from above straight down, from above inclined laterally at an angle of thirty-five to forty degrees, and from below and behind. They fought primarily in horizontal and vertical maneuvers with broad use of the element of surprise. The air crews of our regiments opened fire at the enemy aircraft at extended ranges (700 to 1,400 yards), which most of the time got the enemy's attention but did not hit him.[14]

Here are the combat results of the 216th Fighter Division in the skies of the Kuban in early 1943: In April, 968 aircraft sorties were flown resulting in seventy-one air battles. Of these, forty-three were fierce aerial engagements with groups of from four to thirty-five Bf-109F and G models, and also the FW-190.

Whereas in March the enemy flew 4,820 aircraft sorties, in April the enemy carried out 16,690 sorties against the forces of North Caucasus *Front*. Approximately 13,000 of these were bomber and approximately 3,000 fighter; 890 bombing strikes were conducted. In April the Germans employed powerful massed bomber groups; on some days as many as 200 to 300 aircraft were operating simultaneously. This tactical method obviously was dictated by the insufficient quantity of fighter aviation for covering small groups and the sharply increasing opposition of our fighters.

In April, 216th Fighter Division lost twenty-nine aircraft (twenty-one Airacobras, three Spitfires, two Il-2s, one Yak-1, and two training aircraft) and twelve pilots.[15]

In May, when the division averaged a 73.7 percent daily readiness rate, division units flew 1,777 sorties and fought 156 air battles. Our losses were thirty-eight fighters to enemy fire and four in accidents, with the loss of twenty-six pilots.

The division flew 517 sorties in June, 280 of these to clear the sky and cover our ground forces. Our pilots fought thirty-two aerial engagements, losing four aircraft in combat and one in an accident. Two pilots were killed.

In July the division sortied 709 aircraft, 277 (39 percent) for air reconnaissance, 280 (36.5 percent) for clearing the sky and cover of ground forces. Six of the division's pilots were lost in thirty air battles.[16]

The struggle in the skies of the Kuban was an important stage in the actions of fighter aviation that played a positive role in the development of issues relating to the structure of combat formations, tactics of air combat, and a number of other problems associated with the employment of the Soviet VVS. This is confirmed by the sampling of documents cited in this chapter. These are but a small portion of the articles, brochures, and posters that appeared in the central and army press and that generalized the positive experience of these bitter and continuous battles.

On the Left Wing of
the Soviet–German Front

Some of the most important events of the Great Patriotic War occurred from the end of 1942 and into the middle of 1943 on the left (southern) wing of the Soviet–German front: the epic Stalingrad and Kursk battles, the great struggle in the Kuban, and the liberation of the Donbass and left-bank Ukraine.[1]

The situation of the German forces deteriorated considerably after their defeat at Stalingrad. Despite this, the German command unveiled new plans for an offensive in the Caucasus. In particular, a special role in the execution of these plans was given to the group of forces on the Taman Peninsula. Their mission was to hold securely to the bridgehead for a subsequent attack along the eastern littoral of the Black Sea and onward to Groznyy and Baku. At the same time, this offensive would attract as many forces of the Red Army as possible from other sectors of the front.

Army Group A, comprised of Seventeenth Field Army (sixteen divisions) and First Panzer Army, was deployed here, supported by Fourth Air Fleet. On the approaches to the Taman Peninsula the enemy created a heavily fortified defensive belt, the so-called Blue Line, which extended from the Sea of Azov to Novorossiysk. Along this line were deployed 440,000 German soldiers and officers.

Lacking sufficient forces to hold the Taman bridgehead, the Germans intended to disrupt the offensive preparations of the Soviet forces with air strikes. For this purpose, they concentrated 820 combat aircraft of Fourth Air Fleet on the airfields of the Crimea and Taman. An additional 200 bombers, based in the Donbass and southern Ukraine, were also dedicated to this sector.

Goering sent his best aviation units—Udet, Mulders, Green Heart, and other squadrons—to the Kuban. A special group of German aces who flew the newest models of the FW-190 (air-cooled radial engines, armed with four powerful cannons) also arrived on the Taman Peninsula.

The VVS of North-Caucasus *Front* had 250 aircraft in the 4th and 200 aircraft in the 5th Air Armies, 70 in the aviation group of Black Sea

Fleet, and 60 bombers of long-range aviation (ADD).[2] Altogether the *front* had some 600 aircraft at its disposal.

By 20 April, 2d Bomber and 2d Mixed Aviation Corps and 282d Fighter Division had been added to the *front*'s air assets from the Stavka reserve. The *front*'s ADD was also reinforced with the addition of 62d Bomber Division to the existing 50th Bomber Division. Now the *front* had at its disposal some 900 combat aircraft, of which 370 were fighters, 170 *shturmoviki,* 165 daylight bombers, and 195 night bombers.

The ground situation in the Kuban became critical beginning in March 1943. Fierce battles were waged one after another on three sectors of the left wing of the Soviet–German front: in the Myskhako area, for Krymskaya village, and along the Blue Line.

Regiments of 216th (9th Guards) Fighter Division, equipped with American Airacobra and Kittyhawk fighters, directly participated in these battles. An amphibious assault force was landed on the west shore of Tsemesskaya Bay on the night of 4 February 1943. The detachment, commanded by Major Tsesar Kunikov, captured a small beachhead in the area of Stanichka, which the forces of 18th Army managed to enlarge to 2.5 miles in width and 1.5 miles in depth. Subsequently this beachhead received the name "Malaya Zemlya" [small land]. A stubborn defense of this beachhead began on 16 February and lasted until 16 September.

The enemy undertook numerous attempts to eliminate this beachhead. The German command hurled 450 bombers and approximately 200 fighters against the forces of 18th Army and the amphibious troops. These German aircraft were opposed by 500 of our own aircraft, of which 100 were bombers. Countless intense aerial engagements were fought over these several months, and eventually the enemy was defeated.

Fighter aircraft of the 4th Air Army conducted 111 air battles in March alone, of which 51 (46 percent) were fought by 216th Fighter Division. The division at this time was comprised of the 735th Ground Attack, 42d Fighter, and 45th Fighter Regiments.[3] Pilots of the 216th Division were responsible for approximately 70 percent of the enemy aircraft claimed shot down and 50 percent of the claimed enemy aircraft damaged. Airacobra and Kittyhawk pilots lost thirteen of their own.

An operational pause ensued. On the morning of 29 April, forces of the North Caucasus *Front* began a breakthrough of the enemy defenses in the area of Krymskaya. Our fighters fought in forty-two group air battles on the first day of this offensive.

After the liberation of Krymskaya, formations of North Caucasus *Front* began preparations for a new offensive operation, the purpose of which was to break through the Blue Line, which extended along seventy miles of front with a depth of twelve to fifteen miles. This heavily fortified German position was breached in the course of the Novorossiysk-Taman operation (9–10 September 1943).

In the spring of 1943 the Soviet Air Force was growing markedly in both a qualitative and quantitative sense. This growth provided the first realistic opportunity to establish air superiority on a number of operational axes. Thus, the first air operation on the Kuban sector of the Soviet–German front was conducted between 20 and 29 April. The purpose of this operation was to weaken to the maximum extent possible the enemy air units based on airfields in the Crimea, Taman, and southern Ukraine, thus ensuring that the ground forces would accomplish their assigned missions during the upcoming offensive.

Four air armies (4th, 5th, 8th, and 17th), the air forces of the Black Sea Fleet, and some ADD formations participated in this operation. Soviet fighter and bomber pilots subjected eighteen enemy airfields to massed air strikes over the course of several days (primarily at night). *Front* and naval aviation operated mainly against the closest airfields, and long-range bombers against similar targets that were located to depths of 185 to 220 miles from the front line.[4] VVS efforts were concentrated against those airfields where air reconnaissance had detected the largest concentrations of hostile aircraft. The enemy suffered significant losses to our ADD formations.

In order to avoid further losses, the German command was forced to transfer a portion of its aviation from the frontal zone to rear-area airfields of the Donbass and southern Ukraine. This significantly helped the Soviet VVS gain air superiority in the skies of the Kuban.

It can boldly be asserted that the period from April to the beginning of June 1943 was one of great accomplishments for the Airacobra pilots of 9th Guards Fighter Division. Later (20 November 1945), the commander-in-chief of 4th Air Army, Colonel-General Konstantin Vershinin, in a letter addressed to the newly appointed commander of this formation, wrote:

This glorious division played a particularly significant role in the air battle for the Kuban in the spring of 1943. In these battles the division's pilots rightfully gained primary position among fighter formations. They were pioneers of vertical maneuver. Armed with the newest equipment—high-speed fighters—they quickly mastered methods of combat and successfully destroyed enemy aircraft.

For the most part, the pilots of 9th Fighter Division developed everything that was learned in the course of these air battles in the Kuban. Their combat experience was broadly publicized and copied in other fighter divisions.

In air battles for the Kuban the division demonstrated not only courage and bravery but also mastery in the handling of a proven threatening weapon.

In truth, the 9th Guards Division made a significant contribution to the operation by substantially weakening the enemy air grouping on the southern wing of the Soviet–German front. Three, and sometimes four sorties in a day, each one involving an air battle, became the norm for Airacobra pilots during this period. The pilots were able to sleep two or three hours a night, but sometimes not at all. In an overwhelming majority of cases, the Airacobras withstood this colossal load.

The air battles for the Kuban, in which Soviet aviation significantly degraded the enemy's aerial might, played a positive role in the overall struggle for air superiority in the subsequent stages of the Great Patriotic War. Soviet aviation conducted approximately 35,000 aircraft sorties from 17 April to 7 June, of which 77 percent were by *front* aviation, 9 percent by long-range aviation, and 14 percent by aircraft of Black Sea Fleet.[5]

In their scale and by the results achieved, the air battles in the Kuban went far beyond the parameters of the ground operation of North Caucasus *Front*. They were a school of combat mastery for Soviet VVS, that exerted a positive influence on their operational employment. Many issues in the tactics of all types of aviation, but especially fighter aviation, were developed and subsequently improved. The experience of combat operations in the Kuban showed that the struggle for air superiority could be successful if it was not limited to the assets of a single *front* but conducted by several air armies over a large territory. In this case, the enemy was deprived of the possibility of freely maneuvering his aviation forces.

First Air Battles

The arrival at the front of units of 216th Fighter Division, whose pilots had been transitioned to the P-39 in the 25th Reserve Regiment, occurred not simultaneously but sequentially: 45th Fighter Regiment landed on Krasnodar airfield on 9 March 1943 with seventeen Airacobras and two Kittyhawks.[1] This regiment was subordinated directly to the commander of 4th Air Army. By 18 March its subordinate units were filled out with combat equipment: eighteen Airacobras and eight Kittyhawks. Exactly one month later—on 9 April—the 16th Guards Fighter Regiment (thirty-two aircraft) arrived at the same landing fields where the 45th was located. The 104th Guards Regiment (thirty-one P-39s) was added to the division on 4 May. Because its air crews still needed careful training in several aspects for accomplishment of their air combat missions, 104th Fighter Regiment did not participate in combat operations until 26 August.

Pilots of the 45th Regiment were the first to climb into the skies of the Kuban in their newly issued Airacobras. The pilots were beginning to feel comfortable with their new aircraft in heated engagements with the enemy. The aircraft's positive and negative characteristics were being discovered in combat conditions. After several days of combat actions, the pilots were convinced by their own experiences that there was more to like than dislike about the P-39. This greatly pleased the aviators and presented them with a good opportunity to combat a powerful and crafty enemy with good results.

The German command quickly reacted to this characteristic of the Soviet aviation units that had so recently appeared in the Taman area. As has already been noted, the Germans had assembled a special group of experienced aces in the Kuban at the end of March. Their most important mission was the destruction of the fighters most dangerous to the Luftwaffe—first of all the P-39, and then the Kittyhawks. Is this not in itself a significant indicator of the good quality of the Lend-Lease Airacobra?

On 10 March, eight Airacobras of 45th Regiment departed on the first mission to the area of Abinskaya. They were piloted by Dmitriy Glinka, Gedaliy Mikityanskiy, Dmitriy Shuropov, Nikolay Lavitskiy,

Nikolay Kudrya, Dmitriy Koval, Pavel Berestnev, and Vasiliy Sapyan. The leader of this group was Senior Lieutenant Dmitriy Glinka.[2]

This was the "combat christening" of the Allied aircraft that had only recently been mastered. It was a confirmation of the pilots' knowledge and skill as well as the tactical and technical characteristics of the aircraft itself. It was trial-by-fire in the sky—severe, at times unequal, intense, and deadly. The pilots' fervent desire to defeat the hated fascists in the same way that their brave Soviet soldiers had at Stalingrad was a guarantee of the Airacobra's future successes. By this time the fortunes of war had turned in their favor. This was the long-awaited opportunity to drive the enemy westward to his complete and utter defeat. The Airacobra's powerful cannon and machine-gun armaments and fairly good flying characteristics were inspiring and raised the already high morale of the regiment's pilots. The air crews of the 45th Fighter Regiment were immeasurably thankful to their commander, Major Ibragim Dzusov, who had managed to cut short their sojourn in the rear. The front awaited them; they sought aerial combat with the cursed occupiers.

Much depended on the flight leader in aerial combat. Dmitriy Glinka was an experienced fighter pilot.[3] By this time he had more than 100 combat sorties, had participated in forty aerial battles, and had personally downed fifteen enemy aircraft. The award recommendation packet for bestowing on him the rank Hero of the Soviet Union had already been sent to Moscow.

Regiment commander Ibragim Dzusov understood that the results of the first battle in the new equipment would have no small psychological effect (positive or negative) on the entire regiment. Therefore he named experienced pilots to this first group to sortie. He had full confidence that these crews would be successful in this first engagement. The regiment commander said this to his subordinates when he assigned them to the mission. Dzusov concluded his preflight instructions with the admonition, "Try hard, try very hard! Practice makes perfect!"

The mission was clear: support the combat actions of our bombers. In addition, he advised them that a decisive combat success would provide a great morale boost for the other air crews.

All the pilots of the group assembled before the flight. The group was divided into two foursomes—a strike group and a covering group.

Glinka himself headed the first group and Lieutenant Gedaliy Mikityanskiy the second. Mikityanskiy trailed Glinka somewhat in combat experience. He had approximately 100 sorties, thirty-five aerial engagements, and five downed enemy aircraft.

Dmitriy Glinka gave each pilot a specific flying mission. He also passed on to each one the regiment commander's requirement: fight bravely and demonstrate to both Soviet and German air crews that daring aviators had arrived in the skies of the Kuban and they had a swift and powerfully armed fighter.

Dmitriy Glinka characterized their opponent's actions in recent battles: echelonment of fighters in altitude and active attacks to engage our patrols in combat and distract them, thus ensuring freedom of flight for the Ju-87 and Ju-88 bombers to their strike areas.

The group's combat formation was a right echelon, with the covering group 550 yards in front of and above the strike group. One pair of P-39s in each foursome was to engage the enemy fighters while the second pair went after the enemy bombers. Depending on the specific combat situation, the leader of each foursome had the latitude to change the role of the pairs in his group.

Glinka assigned to his own foursome the mission of attacking enemy bombers or another group of enemy fighters. The developing air situation would dictate their actions. Within each foursome the pairs were to cooperate with each other in their fires, maneuver, and constant readiness to come to their comrades' assistance. An interval of 550 to 660 yards between aircraft was specified.

"Vigilance, vigilance, and one more time—vigilance!" Glinka also ordered strict radio discipline. Everyone was to be listening to his receivers, one tuned to the ground vectoring station and the other to the subgroup leaders. Only with the initiation of aerial combat were the pilots to begin transmitting.

The signal for launch was given (by radio, backed up with a flare gun). The subgroup pairs took off one after another. One minute later, Glinka's eight-ship group was assembled in the specified combat formation. The flight departed for the appointed area to link up with their bombers. Twenty Pe-2s appeared from the northeast.[4] Dmitriy Glinka reported link-up to the vectoring station: "We have begun our combat mission!"

Fifteen minutes into the flight, the Petlyakovs began to restructure their formation for the bombing run. At this time a group of four Bf-109s attempted to attack them from above. Mikityanskiy's subgroup established a firing screen in their path, forcing the Messerschmitts to break off their attack and seek cover in the clouds. Mikityanskiy and his pilots did not chase them because they did not want to leave the bombers uncovered even for a brief period of time. Dmitriy Glinka's subgroup flew cover some 2,600 feet above the zone where the Petlyakovs were working.

The mission was accomplished. The bomber crews set off on their return course. The eight-ship flight of Airacobras covered them from above and from the direction of the sun, the directions from which enemy fighter attacks were most likely to occur.

Then a command was issued by the ground vectoring station: "DB, go to area 8 (three miles west of Abinskaya)! Group of bombers! Attack!"

Glinka acknowledged the instruction and then ordered Mikityanskiy forward to engage the covering German fighters. Success depended on a rapid attack on the fighters by one group and a simultaneous strike against the bombers by the other group. The Airacobras had about one-half of their fuel remaining.

Mikityanskiy's foursome quickly closed with the six Bf-109s, which, despite some superiority in numbers, avoided a fight and took cover in the clouds. It became clear a short time later that these German fighters had also spotted Glinka's foursome headed toward the formation of enemy dive bombers. Gedaliy Mikityanskiy quickly assembled his two pairs in the zone above Glinka's fighters, screening them against attack from above. When the enemy did appear, he was met with cannon and machine-gun fire. One Messerschmitt began to smoke and headed west, losing altitude as it disappeared. The remaining "bandits" darted into cloud cover. The pilots of the covering group warily searched the skies in all directions, prepared to defeat an enemy attack from any direction.

The culmination of this aerial engagement was the strike group attacking the bomber formation. The P-39s cut into the dense formation of bombers from above and in front. Dmitriy set fire to one Ju-88 in his first pass and immediately pulled up in order to gain a suitable position for a second attack. Nikolay Lavitskiy cut apart an He-111 with his guns; Vasiliy Sapyan chased a Ju-87 to the ground. The rapidity and energy of the Airacobra pilots' actions, resulting in the almost instant destruction of three bombers, stunned the enemy. The dive bombers' formation fell apart as each of the aircraft dumped its bombs aimlessly. All of this made our own fighters' task that much easier. Glinka downed a bomber in each of two successive attacks, and Nikolay Kudrya one.[5]

Five Ju-88s and an He-111 did not return to their base. Our losses were zero. Outstanding! The air battle had been won; the results of the combat mission were exceptional. But the score could have been much higher. Two negative factors were revealed in the work of Glinka's group. Mikityanskiy's covering Airacobras operated somewhat passively, in a defensive rather than offensive style. The commander of the eight-ship flight, Dmitriy Glinka, did not devote sufficient attention to the command and control of the group as a whole. Rather, he concentrated all of his efforts on his own foursome, somewhat ignoring Mikityanskiy's foursome.

In the situation that unfolded (enemy covering fighters failed to engage), one pair of Mikityanskiy's foursome could have reinforced Glinka's attack group. Without a doubt, the fight's outcome would have been much more in the Airacobras' favor.

Dmitriy Glinka openly discussed the methods of conducting the aerial combat, his actions, and the results at the postflight debriefing in the regiment. Negative experience is also instructive in war.

The intensity of combat increased with each day. If on 10 March the squadrons of 45th Regiment flew twenty-five combat sorties, then on the following day it was thirty-eight and on the 13th of March—forty. During this period, three Airacobras received battle damage in dogfights, all three executing belly landings upon return to their airfields. Fortunately, the pilots were not injured. The repairs to the aircraft were performed in a few days.[6]

The enemy began to operate with visible caution after the air battle with Dmitriy Glinka's group on 10 March. In a majority of cases he declined to engage in dogfighting. In all likelihood, he was studying the tactical methods of employment of the newly arrived Airacobras.

For this reason, the productivity of the combat sorties of the fighter squadrons was low for almost an entire week. For example, twelve P-39s were escorting bombers from 5th Air Army in the Temryuk area on 14 March. They encountered eight Bf-109s but were unable to engage them. Senior Lieutenant Mikhail Petrov was extremely fortunate to down a single Messerschmitt.[7] Two days later, fifteen Airacobras were escorting Pe-2s of 4th Air Army in the same zone. Senior Lieutenant Dmitriy Shurubov shot down a single Bf-109.[8]

On 18 March, the 45th Regiment (fifteen P-39s and eight Kittyhawks) relocated to Popovicheskaya airfield.[9] Three days after this move, enemy air activity began to increase in intensity. As a rule, the enemy flew in groups of four Bf-109s and FW-190s. They attacked suddenly and at high speed (out of the sun or from behind clouds), then disengaged from the fight with a sharp turn to the flank or upward.

Here is one example of this tactic. A group of six Airacobras, led by Boris Glinka, was flying in cover of our own ground forces at the front line on 20 March. Before it reached the front line, in the area of Staronizhe and Steblievskaya, it was suddenly attacked from behind by four Bf-109s. The enemy managed to shoot down the trail aircraft of Sergeant Vladimir Kanaev. Both the aircraft and pilot were lost in the ensuing fire.[10]

An aerial engagement occurred on 22 March that veterans of the regiment have remembered for the rest of their lives. It is likely that the enemy remembered it for some time as well. A group of eight Airacobras, led by Senior Lieutenant Mikhail Petrov, was patrolling in the area of Petrovskaya. The ground vectoring station transmitted the signal "33" ("You may return home!"). The P-39s began to depart for their airfield. At that moment four Messerschmitts appeared on the flank. The group launched a persistent pursuit of our fighters, clearly intending to attack them from the rear quadrant. Petrov gave the command to come around 180 degrees to fend off the Germans' attack. The P-39s assumed an echelon right combat formation of two foursomes. The group of Messerschmitts that had been chasing them veered off.

The voice of Pavel Berestnev broke in, "Bandits, left 550 [yards]!" Another group of eight Bf-109s was preparing to attack Petrov's group from above. The P-39s made a ninety-degree turn. They were all now in a single line, prepared to counterattack the enemy eight-ship formation on a converging course. Then in the earphones came a subsequent, alarming report from Ivan Babak, "Messerschmitt behind us!" Thus warned, the P-39 pilots observed yet another group of German fighters, just now diving on Petrov's wingman. All the Soviet pilots understood that the first foursome of Bf-109s that they had detected were the bait. Their purpose was to attract the attention of our patrolling aircraft and create conditions favorable for an attack by the other two powerful groups. The Soviet aircraft would be subjected to attack from various directions (the "pincer" method) that they could not repel.

It became clear to the Airacobra pilots that they could not avoid this unequal, difficult battle. Strength in numbers and superiority in altitude—the most important components of success—were on the enemy's side. Equally as alarming was the knowledge that this engagement would not be over quickly, and the P-39s' fuel cells were approaching empty. In summary, the situation of Petrov's flight of eight P-39s was almost hopeless. Every pilot understood this full well. But despite this most difficult situation, no one faltered. Every pilot maintained his position in the combat formation without any sign of panic. The flight of eight drew together as if in a fist, prepared for any maneuver. In his own turn, the enemy appeared to be 100 percent certain that he would obtain a victory, and no small one at that.

Petrov issued a quiet, terse command, "Let's engage!" First one, then another group of German vultures attacked our fighters.[11] Each pair of P-39s flew in close coordination between themselves and other pairs. The Airacobras maneuvered feverishly in both the vertical and horizontal planes, changing their direction of flight often. This significantly hindered enemy pilots aiming fire at them.

The ring of encirclement around Petrov's group pressed in ever tighter. The P-39s made successive sliding turns, sharply changing altitude. This enabled the Airacobras to avoid enemy cannon tracers. Thus far they had suffered no losses. The score was zero-zero. How long would this last? Brief instructions from the group leader flashed across the radio, interspersed with warnings voiced by wingmen and commands from pair leaders. Strict radio discipline is top priority in such a complex situation.

Six Messerschmitts made a renewed attempt to attack from the flank and rear. Our pilots vigilantly monitored the enemy's maneuvers. The group faced this new threat with a rapid turn. Petrov constantly strove to engage the enemy on closing courses. This combat position of the Airacobras permitted their pilots to use the combined power of their machine guns and cannons to maximum effect.

At this moment one of the Bf-109s, positioned above, went into a steep dive and raced toward its selected victim. Its cannons erupted in long bursts. The Messerschmitt passed through the formation of P-39s like a meteor, its cannon shells having found a target. The aircraft of Aleksandr Poddubskiy shuddered, then turned over on its back and began to lose altitude in a flat spin.

In the literal sense of the word, the battle was raging. Tracers of our own and enemy aircraft guns were carving up the sky. The radio frequency was filled with shouted commands to Aleksandr: "Sasha, jump!" "Sasha, abandon ship!" Cutting through all of this traffic came the stern instruction of Petrov: "Poddubskiy, I order you to bail out!"

The efforts of Poddubskiy's comrades to help him were in vain. He could not hear them. Aleksandr Poddubskiy and his Airacobra plunged into the embrace of the Kuban steppe.

Encouraged by their first success, the enemy persisted in pressing from all sides on Petrov's group of seven fighters. The German fighters tried to break up the Soviets' combat formation so that they could chase them down singly. It is far easier to engage individual aircraft or small groups. The tracer fire at times reached such a high density that it would seem to eliminate any free space in which to maneuver. In this vortex of death our air crews did not lose their heads, they did not abandon their courage or resolve. Skillfully employing the maneuverability of their P-39s, just in time they careened out of the danger zone that just a few seconds later was filled with merciless lead projectiles.

Studying the archival documents and recollections of the veterans of this battle, one cannot but be amazed. How did Senior Lieutenant Petrov manage to maintain an unbroken combat formation, not to give up, to continue firmly to guide his subordinates? Without a doubt, his considerable front-line experience (Mikhail Petrov had been fighting since the first days of the war) played an enormous role here. It should also be stated that the group he was leading was composed of several veteran pilots: Boris Glinka, Ivan Babak, Nikolay Kudrya, and Dmitriy Koval. These pilots were pair leaders. After a brief time, the group leader and all of these men would be officially recognized as aces of the 45th Regiment.[12]

The battle continued in unbelievable gyrations of the aircraft of both sides. The air was torn by the churning of powerful motors, the continuous rattling of machine guns, and the basso voice of cannons. The first Bf-109 dropped to the earth like a stone. Soon a second Messerschmitt was set on fire. Apparently, a burst from an Airacobra had penetrated its fuel cell. The pilot put his aircraft into a dive, thinking in vain that he might in this manner extinguish the flames. He was finished!

Suddenly the alarming words of Glinka sounded across the radio: "I am wounded, disengaging!" An enemy round had struck the cockpit of his aircraft. The lieutenant guided his P-39 into a descent in an effort to break away from the fight more quickly. Four Bf-109s were already rushing down behind him to finish off his damaged Airacobra. Young pilot Sergeant Nikolay Kudryashov—Boris's wingman—skillfully fended off the first, second, and third attacks of the enemy ships. The German pilots understood that they would not penetrate to their selected target and instead turned all of their firepower against Kudryashov's Airacobra.

After several passes the enemy managed to set it on fire. Nikolay reported by radio: "BB [*Boris Borisovich Glinka*], I am on fire, cannot cover you any longer!" He placed the aircraft up on its wing and began to pull away, perhaps hoping to distract the attacking Messerschmitts to himself. They did not go after him, considering him already defeated.

The sergeant began to gain altitude as if in preparation for a parachute jump from his burning aircraft. At that same time, the Messerschmitt closed in on Boris Glinka's Airacobra. His life now hung by a thread.

In a flash, in view of all the group's pilots, Kudryashov's aircraft turned and bore down like a burning comet on the Bf-109 that was closing in on his commander's P-39. In just a few seconds Glinka's ship would be cut by deadly cannon fire. The bright flash that accompanied the collision of Kudryashov's Airacobra with the Bf-109 lit up the heavens. Pieces from both fighters flew off in all directions.

We had an expression in our wartime military forces: "Give your life, save a comrade!"[13] This expression found its practical application in this critical moment. By the death of the enemy and his own sacrifice, the sergeant saved the life of a courageous officer, in the process displaying the highest degree of front-line comradeship.

Like a scene in a kaleidoscope, the situation in a fast-moving aerial battle changes instantly and often drastically. Just moments after Kudryashov's ramming incident, the circumstance was almost repeated. This time the Airacobra of Senior Lieutenant Ivan Shmatko had caught fire. The enemy managed to separate his wingman—

Sergeant Nikolay Kudrya—from the main group. The sergeant was in mortal danger of falling to the next enemy burst.

Wasting no time, the senior lieutenant prepared to ram the German fighter to protect his wingman. He could have parachuted from his already burning aircraft—his unwounded condition made that a viable alternative. However, the officer chose another alternative—deliberate suicide for the sake of saving the life of another.

These two fiery ramming incidents had a decisive influence on the subsequent course of this lopsided battle. The unbelievable actions of the Soviet pilots demoralized the German aviators. Their own actions revealed a lack of confidence. Their attacks weakened and then were broken off entirely. Despite clear numerical superiority, the Germans hastily retreated from the battlefield.[14]

One might reasonably ask why, when his group got into such a difficult situation, Petrov did not request reinforcement from the ground vectoring station. On 22 March, eleven Airacobras and seven Kittyhawks were combat ready in the squadrons. Petrov did not make such a request because he knew that at that moment every aircraft in the regiment was committed. A small remnant of fighters was covering the Popovicheskaya airfield and conducting reconnaissance of the enemy.[15]

Five P-39s returned to the airfield. Only three of them were undamaged; the remaining two had many holes in their wings and fuselages. Pilots Mikhail Petrov and Ivan Babak were not wounded.

Of this group of pilots, by war's end Ivan Babak would shoot down thirty-three enemy aircraft (awarded Hero of the Soviet Union on 1 November 1943), Boris Glinka thirty-one (awarded Hero of the Soviet Union on 24 May 1943), and Nikolay Kudrya ten (awarded Hero of the Soviet Union on 24 May 1943 and killed on 26 May 1943).

The New Methods Win Out

The old withers away and is replaced by the new, both in nature and in the lives of people. This is an immutable law that no person or thing has the power to change. So it is in the military sphere, too, in the tactics of ground or air operations.

In the first months and difficult battles of the Great Patriotic War it became clear that the Red Army could not successfully fight its powerful enemy using old methods. This was especially felt by fighter pilots (but not only fighter pilots), who were fending off powerful strikes of the German air armada. These men searched for, found, and employed new methods of conducting air battles with the enemy. Modernized aviation equipment that was introduced into the force helped to accelerate this process.

The great innovator in the fundamental issues of fighter aviation tactics was a pilot from the ranks, Captain Aleksandr Pokryshkin. He spoke out boldly against the outdated provisions of the regulations and instructions. His bitter personal combat experience and that of many of his comrades gave him the right to follow this path. For this he was punished with particular severity and at several levels. A recommendation to award him the rank Hero of the Soviet Union was withdrawn; he was dismissed from his unit and assigned to a reserve regiment, which also meant curtailment of his combat flights; and he had his Party membership card taken away. It would not be an exaggeration to say that a person of that time who had been subjected to all these sanctions had much to fear. His wife, Maria Pokryshkina, later wrote, "In the struggle for his new tactical methods, Pokryshkin could easily have been shot for unlawful conduct."[1]

A great deal has been written about Pokryshkin's new tactical methods of air combat for fighters. He began to develop his theories in 1942. By mid-1943 his tactical methods had been fully adopted by Soviet aviators of all the fighting fronts of the Great Patriotic War. There was scarcely a more brilliant triumph in the military sphere.

I think it worthwhile to explain succinctly the essence of Pokryshkin's tactical method, in order to help the American reader assimilate this account about the combat actions of the Airacobra pilots,

which were always complicated, arduous, and exceptionally dangerous. For fighter pilots, it could not be any other way.

Pokryshkin espoused a "formula for victory" that some authors regard as a classic distillation of the essence of air combat: "Altitude,
speed, maneuver, fire!" Pokryshkin himself later found it necessary to
call this a "formula of terror," that in form was significantly more modest, but on the other hand by its literal meaning was much more precise. These four firmly interrelated components, inseparably welded
together, were the foundation stones of success in air combat. They
worked even when faced with superior enemy forces.

Altitude. It is not by accident that the highly decorated ace placed
this principle at the top of his list. It is the first principle among
equals. Pokryshkin taught that a pilot should at all times strive to be
above his enemy.

Having launched into the heavens, a pilot should have the power to
attack the target at high tactical or, more accurately, combat speed.
Without speed one cannot execute precision maneuvers, carry out an
annihilating attack, or reach the range of effective cannon and machine-gun fire in an extremely compressed time.

Altitude gave speed, which was gained not only by the power of the
engine. A direct consequence of this amalgam of altitude and speed
was the prospect of rapid movement of the combat formation of a pair
of fighters or a patrol group to any required sector of the sky. This
opened a broad expanse of sky for successful engagements in the vertical plane, the more so in that the P-39 could keep pace with the Bf-
109 in horizontal and vertical maneuvers.

Everything that he had conceived of and thoughtfully considered,
all that he had drawn from his own successes in aerial combat,
Pokryshkin submitted to the judgment of his fellow pilots during their
transition training in 25th Reserve Regiment. "The new collectively
discovered tactical methods were adopted for use by all the fighter regiments," Pokryshkin acknowledged with unconcealed pride.[2] The fates
were kind. There were enough like-minded thinkers and, in the fore-
seeable future, actual practitioners of the newly developed ideas. The
new method and its promise for success were not only attractive but
brought the spirit of each fighter pilot renewed hope, of defeating the
enemy decisively and fighting with greatly reduced losses. The pilots
now had the controls of a very capable fighter that, when combined

with the unusual tactical methods of engaging the enemy, would bring the required success in combat and the most rapid achievement of final victory.

Pokryshkin's new tactical method brought changes to the old way, which rigidly outlined the parameters of the mission of providing close air support for ground forces in a specific area during the mission. No deviations in flight were allowed! The aircraft arrived at the specified zone in a tight formation and began to orbit the area at a low speed. The pilots called this "riding the carousel," basically chasing their own tails in the sky. They flew in this pattern, which yielded the initiative to the enemy, on a regular basis. The enemy did not interfere and took advantage of the superiority it offered him: using altitude and the speed it provided, he swiftly attacked these Soviet formations and, as a rule, inflicted heavy losses.

To replace the "carousel," Pokryshkin suggested another combat formation upon a patrol's arrival in the zone of probable encounter with the enemy. This new formation was a "bookshelf" of pairs of fighters deployed toward the sun, one pair above the other (in two to four tiers). The altitude spacing between them was 1,000 to 1,650 feet en route to the engagement area, and up to 6,550 feet in the engagement area. With this dispersion, the formation occupied from 6,560 to 19,680 feet of vertical airspace. Pokryshkin recommended that this "bookshelf" formation become the basic combat formation for Soviet fighter aircraft.

Pokryshkin also advocated a different approach to the area of combat actions. The patrol should climb to an altitude somewhat above the specified mission altitude, increase speed, and enter the zone of coverage at high speed and slightly decreasing altitude. If there were no enemy aircraft in the vicinity, the aircraft had sufficient momentum to climb back up to altitude. This maneuver was to be repeated over and over until an enemy target appeared. The Airacobras traced an arc in the sky like an immense pendulum, its convex arc oriented toward the ground. Using this unique method of coverage, the patrolling aircraft were always capable of making a lightning "eagle strike" on enemy aircraft.

Pokryshkin recommended that approaching enemy bombers (a fighter's primary target) be attacked over German-controlled territory, not over Soviet-controlled territory. There were several reasons for this. Frequently they had not yet joined with their Bf-109 or FW-190 fighter coverage. The enemy did not anticipate an attack over his own territory and therefore could more easily be surprised, with greater losses as a result. When attacked in this manner, German bombers dropped their bombs aimlessly in order to get away. Better that these bombs be dropped on German than Soviet troops. Unfortunately, senior Soviet air commanders were not quick to adopt this method.

Pokryshkin employed yet another important tactic in the course of his aerial battles and persistently trained his subordinates to do likewise: break up formations of Ju-87s and Ju-88s into separate small groups and individual aircraft. It was essential to attack and destroy the first—normally lead—dive bomber in each approaching echelon. When this goal was achieved, enemy pilots normally lost their confidence and departed toward their own airfield, dropping their ordnance haphazardly in the process.

To our great fortune, two important circumstances came together in the skies of the Kuban in the spring of 1943. The Supreme High Command made the decision here to conduct the first operation to seize air superiority. And the great innovator in the sphere of fighter aviation tactics, Guards Captain Aleksandr Pokryshkin, happened to be on this sector of the Soviet–German front. The Kuban skies became his laboratory, his test range, where new methods of fighter operations suggested by this intrepid ace were introduced, modified when necessary, and honed in frequent fierce aerial battles. From the Kuban these new tactical methods triumphantly spread to all the fronts of the Great Patriotic War. The Kuban was the birthplace of Pokryshkin's "formula of terror."

Here are some specific examples that show the combat actions of pilots who were operating by Pokryshkin's rules.

On 8 April 1943, having finally received their Airacobras, 16th Guards Fighter Regiment arrived at Krasnodar airfield and joined 216th Fighter Division. Guards Captain Aleksandr Pokryshkin commanded the 1st Squadron. At this time the air and ground situation was quite intense. The ground forces were fighting fierce battles in the areas of Krymskaya and Myskhako. The Airacobra pilots had to launch aircraft just two days after their arrival. They flew twenty-eight combat sorties on 10 April, thirty-two on 11 April, twelve on 12 April, and thirty-nine on 15 April. Enemy (and friendly) losses, respectively, were: four (two), four (one), seven (zero), and nine (two).[3]

Unfortunately, they did not have the two to three days' time for the standard preparation of air crews for the upcoming battles. The pilots had to gain familiarity with the area of intended operations simultaneously with their accomplishment of assigned missions. There was no other way; the situation dictated the rules of the game. Fortunately, the majority of the regiment's pilots had been on active duty for some time, which enabled them to cope with the difficulties that arose in these unusual circumstances. They were fond of saying, "We have a full measure of courage and experience. To destroy the enemy—that's a matter of personal honor!"[4]

The Airacobra pilots fought an air battle on 10 April. This was the first test of the new, carefully thought out, and oft-discussed methods of fighter operations. The squadron commander (Aleksandr Pokryshkin) ordered one group of six Airacobras to cover the ground forces in the immediate vicinity of Krymskaya. This was a main stronghold of the enemy's defenses in the Blue Line. The large railroad and road intersection here that led to Novorossiysk, Taman, and Temryuk was an important operational target. The main effort of the formations of North Caucasus *Front* was directed toward this locale. Fierce aerial battles would be fought in the sky above this village for several consecutive days.

The patrol under the command of Aleksandr Pokryshkin was flown by pilots who were fully supportive of his tactical theories: Grigoriy Rechkalov, Georgiy Golubev, Vladimir Berezhnoy, Mikhail Sutyrin, and Boris Kozlov. Before the flight, the group leader [Pokryshkin] gave instructions regarding the combat formation during the approach to the objective and upon initiation of air combat. His subordinates understood clearly that they would employ the new "bookshelf" formation. They had talked about the advantages of this formation, explained it, outlined it on paper, and drawn diagrams in the sand.

The Airacobras approached the forward edge of the battle area. The squadron commander communicated with the ground vectoring station by radio. He reported their arrival in the mission area and requested an update on the enemy air situation. The ground vectoring station responded with a report of "no enemy in zone" and instructed the patrol to remain in sector 7 (Krymskaya) and await further instructions.

Both the regimental commander during his assignment of the mission and the command post required Pokryshkin's group to patrol by the old method: fly in a large circle over the objective. Once again, orbit in an obsolete manner, flying the deadly and dangerous carousel.

Completely on his own initiative, Pokryshkin did something else. He led his group to the south, toward the Black Sea, simultaneously gaining altitude. Altitude was the first principle of the all-powerful "formula of terror." Pokryshkin formed his six-ship flight into a "bookshelf" inclined to the left, toward the sun.

At the endpoint of this route, over Novorossiysk, the six aircraft circled to the right and flew rapidly back toward Krymskaya. The pairs quickly repositioned themselves to the right of their squadron commander, deployed in tiers and again toward the sun, always the dangerous sector. As the Airacobras flew toward the objective, the pilots slowly traded altitude for increased speed. This maneuver enabled them to acquire a sorely needed advantage. The aircraft gathered maximum speed—the principal enabler of maneuver. This facilitated their sudden appearance over Krymskaya and, should they encounter the enemy there, the rapidity of their "eagle strike" against him. The reserve of speed that was gained through altitude loss also permitted them to regain altitude relatively easily after the first attack. They would not have to force their P-39s' motors. For a brief time the aircraft traced a path of movement through space similar to a pendulum (gain altitude—lose altitude—gain altitude). This was the beginning of the practical implementation of the new patrolling method.

Krymskaya appeared under their wings. LaGG-3s were circling above the village, covering the target by the ineffective means mandated in the current regulations. Pokryshkin was disheartened by the picture unfolding before him. If even two Bf-109s had appeared on the scene, as had Pokryshkin's own group, the Messerschmitts would have had no difficulty in disposing of the two Lavochkins.[5]

As before, there were no enemy aircraft in the zone of responsibility of Pokryshkin's six-ship flight. Rigidly maintaining their established formation, the Airacobras climbed slowly upward. Before reaching the Kuban River they turned to the west and flew back toward the village, once again gaining speed as they lost altitude. As they had before, the pilots held their "bookshelf" formation in a stable manner on the flank of the lead pair, inclined away from the pair and upward. This fanlike formation enabled them to search for the enemy over a broad area and simultaneously made it more difficult for the enemy to detect the patrolling P-39s as they cut through the sky.

Reliable radio communications between aircraft guaranteed firm command and control by the group and pair leaders and permitted them to issue timely warning to the air crews regarding a threat that might appear from any direction. Radio communication was the glue that held the combat formation together and made it possible to concentrate the patrol's efforts at the required point along the march route or in the zone of coverage. Communications became an equivalent element of the combat characteristics of the P-39, a serious weapon for achieving success in aerial engagements.

The group was once again over Krymskaya. The scenario that Aleksandr Pokryshkin had played out in his mind just ten minutes ago was unfolding before their eyes. Eight Bf-109s were attacking four Lavochkins that had formed a defensive circle. The Airacobra pilots did not detect any other enemy aircraft in the vicinity. Pokryshkin's pilots had no difficulty in analyzing the enemy's tactical plan: this was a fighter force sent out to clear our fighters from the target area. This meant that bombers should soon appear to deliver their bomb loads. Pokryshkin's group had some advantages: altitude, speed, and surprise. They would soon make good use of all these superiorities. He who anticipates usually wins!

The squadron commander issued a brief radio command: "Eleven o'clock, down thirty degrees, bandits. Attacking! Cover me!" The clock method and degrees from the transmitting aircraft's course were used to call out directions. This simple but effective method had been developed in the 1st Squadron for rapid orientation of crews in the air regarding the location of the target.

Seconds later, Pokryshkin dropped like a stone on the leader of the enemy fighters. It was a precision "eagle strike" against which there was no possible defense. A cannon burst passed through the Bf-109 at close range (the ace's favorite method). The Messerschmitt burst into flames with a brilliant flash. Only by chance did Pokryshkin avoid collision with it as he pulled up sharply.

At the same time, a pair of the uppermost tier of the "bookshelf" engaged another Bf-109 during an attempt by the enemy group to avoid the Airacobras' attack by seeking altitude. Grigoriy Rechkalov found a decelerating Messerschmitt in his crosshairs.

The enemy lost three fighters in the first lightning attack of our patrol. He lost his numerical superiority in an instant. This stunned him. The remaining five intact fighters flew away to the west, their motors smoking at full throttle. Pokryshkin's group did not pursue them. In anticipation of the approach of enemy bombers, they had to conserve both fuel and ammunition. For a good hour the Airacobra pilots passed like a swinging pendulum over the forward edge. But the bombers never made an appearance—a direct consequence of the six P-39s' high-speed attack on the fighter screen. The enemy's planned bombing strike on our ground units had been disrupted.

Guards Captain Pokryshkin led his group into combat three times that day. Only in the last flight did the aviators encounter six Bf-109s, which were being flown extremely cautiously. The German pilots showed the tactical acumen of experienced aviators sent out to ascertain the air situation. Our command had learned through interrogation of a captured German pilot that a select group of enemy aces had arrived in the Kuban especially to combat the Airacobras. It is possible that these were the vanguard of this group.

A brief but fierce dogfight ensued, in the course of which Boris Kozlov's P-39 was damaged. The Guards senior lieutenant held it out of a spin with difficulty, and when he felt that he could no longer control the aircraft, he gave it full throttle and rammed the Messerschmitt that was setting up to attack Mikhail Sutyrin. Both aircraft plunged toward the earth. Though seriously wounded, Boris managed to abandon his crippled Airacobra and parachuted to safety. He ended up in a hospital and never did return to the regiment.[6]

Kozlov's decisive actions changed the outcome of the battle literally in seconds. The enemy hurriedly raced toward his own lines. Combat ramming was not an uncommon tactic of Soviet aviators during the war.

The ferocity of the air battles grew with each passing day. The second and third weeks of April, one could say, were "star-studded" for the fighter pilots of 216th Fighter Division. In continuous and intense daily battles, they added to the count of enemy losses from the night raids of our bombers on his airfields. Three and sometimes four combat mission sorties, each one with an engagement, became the norm for the Airacobra pilots in the skies of the Kuban. Senior Lieutenant Dmitriy Glinka, a pilot of the 45th Fighter Regiment, flew nine combat sorties on 12 April. Even for one so healthy as he, such a physical and psychological load was not borne without consequences. After sleeping for thirty-six hours, he was grounded for a week with a diagnosis of "excessive exhaustion." But he did not serve his full sentence. Having rested somewhat, he took active part in air battles on 15 April. This courageous pilot could not sit on the sidelines when so much was happening in the skies over the Kuban.

In this period the pilots were able to sleep for only two or three hours a night, and sometimes not at all. In the overwhelming majority of cases, the Airacobras withstood this unbelievable flying load. This was due to the efforts of the technical personnel of the regiments and division. There were, however, isolated cases when the equipment failed.

On 12 April 1943, a patrol group of 45th Regiment was covering ground troops in the Abinskaya area. They got into a dogfight with fifteen enemy fighters at an altitude of 6,550 feet. The enemy strength was more than twice that of the Soviet formation. Our aviators had a difficult time in this, their second battle of the day. Despite the difficult situation, they achieved a superior result: five to zero. Senior Lieutenant Mikhail Petrov and Sergeant Nikolay Kudrya each shot down one Bf-109; Sergeant Vasiliy Sapyan set two enemy fighters on fire; and Lieutenant Boris Glinka downed a Ju-88.

Vasiliy Sapyan had to come out of his second successful attack with a steep dive and left turn. His Airacobra reached a speed approaching 420 mph in this dive. The sergeant heard a sharp knock in the tail assembly and the aircraft began to respond badly to the flight controls. He reported the damage to his lead and received permission to withdraw from the battle. He made it to the airfield and landed with great difficulty. The squadron engineer and mechanics quickly discovered that excessive overloading had caused a deformation of the aircraft's vertical stabilizer from the first to the fourth ribs.

Similar battle damage occurred on 13 April on an Airacobra piloted by Senior Lieutenant Arkadiy Fedorov. Quickly, after a careful technical investigation and establishment of the cause of the disfigurement of the vertical stabilizer, all pilots were ordered not to execute a right or left turn in a dive and to limit their dive speed to 400 mph.[7]

News of the first good combat results of the newly arrived Airacobra pilots reached their brother 45th Regiment. Welcome guests from this unit dropped in on Pokryshkin's squadron with questions regarding the successes of their colleagues. The division commander, General Aleksandr Borman, decided to put a stop to this spontaneous activity and ordered the regiments quickly to conduct an organized exchange of experience. In addition, the general himself conducted a session with the units' command and staff personnel at which the lessons of the combat over the previous three weeks (late March and early April) were analyzed in detail.[8]

The division's crews, especially the Airacobra pilots of the 16th Regiment, greeted this important measure with satisfaction. The entire "winged collective," not just one squadron, should be defeating the enemy with skill. We had a saying at the front, "Without hesitation, reveal to others the secret of how victories were gained over the enemy!"

Nor did the command and staff of 4th Air Army overlook this issue. Over the course of April 1943, all aviation units were issued instructions regarding the most productive tactical methods and combat formations for fighters, the improvement of cooperation between patrolling pairs, the preservation of superiority in altitude, maximum utilization of vertical maneuver in air battles, and the necessity to be constantly searching the sky for the enemy and to engage him in combat.[9] This was the result of a discussion of the tactics of fighter aviation with the army staff, who had invited in several Airacobra aces: Pavel Kryukov, Dmitriy Glinka, Vladimir Semenishin, and Aleksandr Pokryshkin.

A conference of commanders and air crews was convened at Krasnodar. General Konstantin Vershinin, commander of 4th Air Army, invited the attendees to discuss how better to defeat the enemy in the air. He gave the aviators a general overview of the ground and air situation, dwelling on the most important problems of the combat employment of bomber, ground-attack, and fighter aviation. Then he touched upon the main issue that was the reason for assembling the air army's officer corps. "The most urgent problem that our aviators have to resolve is gaining overwhelming air superiority here in the Kuban. We must become the complete and total masters of the sky. In the past the enemy imposed his will upon us, but now he is becoming subject to our will. Our task is to take the total initiative into our own hands."[10]

Many attendees at the conference gave presentations, among them Aleksandr Pokryshkin. He touched upon two hotly discussed issues: He openly expressed his disagreement with the order that strictly specified the speed of fighters patrolling over coverage zones. He considered it unacceptably low. Pilots in high-speed aircraft were "bound hand and foot," deprived of the possibility of rapid vertical maneuver at the start of a battle with the enemy. Pokryshkin also drew attendees' attention to the issue of not crediting pilots for enemy aircraft shot down over territory occupied by the enemy. He carefully sketched out the obvious contradiction: The assigned mission was to intercept and destroy enemy aircraft on the approaches to the front line, but the results of these battles were not counted. This counting system to some degree justified the actions of pilots who tried not to penetrate enemy-held territory but instead patrolled and engaged enemy aircraft only over their own forces.

In concluding his presentation, the celebrated ace made some critical observations regarding another standing order—the requirement for confirmation of downed enemy aircraft by ground forces. If a fighter was working over enemy-held territory and destroying hostile bombers and transports, who would confirm these kills?

All of Pokryshkin's observations not only met with the approval of the fighter pilots present but also resonated with the commanders. After a brief intervening period, reports of pilots and other crew members who witnessed the destruction of enemy aircraft were accepted for official confirmation of kills in the 4th Air Army, and soon in the entire VVS of the Soviet Army.[11]

The pilots who attended this conference left completely satisfied that from that moment forward the combat experience of the Red Air Force's top air warriors would be valued. The command was finally reevaluating a number of orders that were inappropriate for the circumstances that had developed at the front.

The combat actions of the mid-April period required immediate resolution of one important problem. The enemy had begun to approach the front line at high altitudes (above 13,000 feet). For example, on 15 April three encounters with enemy aircraft and the ensuing engagement occurred at altitudes of 9,850 to 13,000 feet, and in the last engagement of the day (the seventh), the pilots were forced to fly at an altitude of 16,400 feet.[12] The pilots had not flown above 9,850 feet in earlier engagements. The Airacobra pilots had difficulty conducting the battle because they were flying without oxygen masks. At these significant altitudes they were experiencing oxygen deprivation, which led to rapid fatigue. Most unfortunate in this story was the fact that the Airacobras had the necessary equipment for high-altitude flight but the oxygen tanks were empty. "Nobody told us to fill them," was the excuse from the support units.

Aleksandr Pokryshkin categorically ordered his regimental armaments officer, Guards Captain Yakov Zhmud, to quickly organize the filling of oxygen tanks. The airfield-engineer service never failed to accomplish this task again.[13]

As of 15 April, the division's units had the following available strength in combat-ready aircraft: 45th Regiment, ten Airacobras and five Kittyhawks; 16th Guards Regiment, twenty-two Airacobras; 766th Ground Attack Regiment, ten Il-2 Shturmoviks; and 42d Regiment, ten Yak-1s.

In this situation, the crews of 45th Regiment were primarily used for covering the Popovicheskaya airfield and landing fields of the 4th Air Army's bombers and *shturmoviki* from 17 to 26 April. Instructions arrived in this regiment on 27 April to transfer the remaining pilots and aircraft: six Airacobras to 16th Guards Regiment and two to 298th Fighter Regiment.[14] By the middle of May, 45th Regiment units were not participating in combat operations. They were receiving new aircraft and preparing arriving pilots for upcoming battles.

The principal burden of covering ground formations in this intervening time lay on the shoulders of the pilots of 16th Guards Regiment. Combat on 15 April was exceptionally intense. The regiment's pilots scrambled to meet enemy fighters and bombers seven times before noon. Almost all of the battles were conducted at altitudes of from 9,850 to 16,400 feet.

Two morning encounters of patrolling groups with the enemy concluded without result. In the first, Guards Major Pavel Kryukov led four Airacobras against ten Ju-88s and two Bf-109s, and in the second Guards Captain Aleksandr Pokryshkin led four P-39s against thirty Ju-88s and Ju-87s. In fact, the enemy aircraft dropped their bombs on troop targets along the immediate forward edge. The Airacobra pilots attempted to attack the dive bombers but every time were blocked by dense enemy anti-aircraft fire. The Germans had brought 88mm anti-aircraft guns closer to the forward edge, which permitted them to establish a line of barrier fire at a range of up to 6,550 feet above our positions.

This new twist in the organization of the defending forces' air defense drew the attention of our ground force commanders. Anti-aircraft cannons, in addition to their primary role, could also be employed as antitank weapons. Thus, the enemy, while establishing a fire curtain in the air against attacking Airacobras, revealed one of his measures for strengthening his defenses in the area of Krymskaya. This was taken into consideration during the planning for the employment of artillery in the course of suppressing enemy targets. The necessary adjustments were also made in the axis of attack of our tank units.

The third combat sortie on 15 April (four P-39s led by Guards Junior Lieutenant Viktor Naumenko) lasted ninety minutes. The patrol was flying over the Krymskaya area at 13,100 feet. As the mission was about to end, the ground vectoring station reported the approach of a group of approximately twenty enemy bombers escorted by four fighters. They quickly crossed the forward edge and began to penetrate to our positions. In this situation, the fire of enemy anti-aircraft cannons would not interfere with an attack by the Airacobras. Naumenko instructed the pair of Guards Lieutenant Vladimir Berezhnoy to engage the Messerschmitts while he led his own pair into the formation of Ju-87s and Ju-88s. Their P-39s firing with both cannon and machine guns, Viktor Naumenko and Nikolay Iskrin cut through the formation at an altitude of 9,850 feet, downing one bomber each.

At the same time, Berezhnoy's pair dropped like stones onto the covering fighters. Vladimir, attacking from close range, set one Bf-109 on fire. The remaining Messerschmitts began to pull away toward their own front line, in an effort to draw the P-39s of Berezhnoy and Guards Lieutenant Mikhail Sutyrin into range of the anti-aircraft cannons. Berezhnoy ordered Boris to follow him as they disengaged from the battle and sought altitude. They joined the Airacobras of Naumenko. The group drew together into a compressed formation in anticipation of further action, which quickly began. The ground vectoring station informed Naumenko that enemy escort fighters were entering his patrol zone. The foursome of Guards Major Pavel Kryukov had taken off at 1015 and was hurrying to assist them. Naumenko was given permission to return to his airfield in fifteen minutes.

Kryukov and his group climbed to an altitude of 13,100 feet and took a position behind some clouds. Their goal was to get above the enemy bombers and approaching Messerschmitts. The latter, without question, would immediately turn on Naumenko's Airacobras. Kryukov warned Naumenko of this by radio and at the same time asked him to engage the Messerschmitts hurtling toward him. He then would attack the enemy from above. By all appearances the Germans had not detected Kryukov's foursome. This is just one clear example of cooperation in the air that was dictated by the conditions of the developing situation.

The general situation in the patrol area of Guards Junior Lieutenant Naumenko would soon become greatly complicated. Therefore, the ground vectoring station "Tiger" called out yet another group, this time to reinforce Kryukov. Aleksandr Pokryshkin took off with four P-39s at 1020.

In all probability the Germans were also continuously monitoring the air over our positions. As soon as the two additional flights of Airacobras (Kryukov and Pokryshkin) set a course toward the battle area, the bombers dropped their bombs aimlessly. Turning around, they disappeared at top speed, covered by the four Bf-109F and G models.

"Tiger" issued new instructions: "Group of fighters coming from southwest. Be alert!"

And so, as Naumenko led his patrol back to their airfield, the eight Airacobras of Kryukov and Pokryshkin were left to face no fewer than fifteen Messerschmitts (four escorting the bombers and up to two additional flights approaching).

Pavel Kryukov's assumptions were justified. Four Messerschmitts, not having detected his group, chased after Naumenko's P-39s, which had formed a defensive circle. The enemy's first attempt to attack them head on was unsuccessful. The Bf-109s shot upward as their pilots sought altitude and a good position for a second attack from above. However, this maneuver made them exceptionally good targets for Kryukov's group waiting above.

Every moment is precious in a high-speed aerial fight. Here, as in no other circumstances, one cannot afford to waste time. Kryukov ordered his two pairs of fighters to attack. Four lightning-quick "arrows," deployed abreast, raced downward from out of the clouds. Their "eagle strike" converged toward the "fowl" as they closed the range to the targets. As the Airacobras' machine guns and cannons fired, a stream of cannon tracers cut through the Bf-109 that was attacking Naumenko. Andrey Trud, Arkadiy Fedorov, and Pavel Gorokhov each downed an enemy aircraft in the first pass. Three enemy fighters disappeared in one instant.[15]

At 1100 on 15 April, a twenty-minute dogfight ensued between eight P-39s (Pokryshkin and Kryukov) and sixteen enemy fighters. The enemy had an absolute superiority of two to one. In these circumstances, our pilots had every right to avoid combat, but they were confident of their new tactics and stayed to fight.

How much strength and energy did an aerial engagement require from each of its participants? What kind of enormous psychological and physical stress did an Airacobra pilot experience in each high-speed maneuver? Even I, who have experienced ground combat, find this difficult to imagine. Yes, we "ground pounders" also had to face the enemy in deadly combat, sometimes for many days running. However, the time we spent under this kind of pressure was measured by somewhat different parameters than in the boundless sky. There, events were compressed into a series of high-stress, high-speed maneuvers, the purpose of which was to gain a favorable position for a subsequent rapid attack on the enemy. The aircraft, both ours and the enemy's, were moving at top speed. The firing conditions were infinitely more complex: a pilot had to place his aiming sight on a rapidly moving target. A fighter pilot had to possess exceptionally good vision in order to estimate accurately the range to the target and fire a precision cannon or machine-gun burst. Veteran fighter pilots all acknowledge that after a dogfight, and the more so a fierce one, their head was spinning and their ears ringing. Aerial combat was stressful, indeed.

Eight Airacobras versus sixteen Messerschmitts. What could serve to counter the enemy in such a difficult situation? Courage and will, a burning hatred for the enemy, and an enormous desire to overcome him no matter what it cost. All of these things were only an undergirding of the most important factor—the skillful actions of each individual pilot, pair, and group. And the majority of 1st Squadron pilots possessed these most important qualities in ample quantities.

The most experienced pilots were in the air at that moment: Aleksandr Pokryshkin, Grigoriy Rechkalov, Pavel Kryukov, and Arkadiy Fedorov. Together they comprised one-half of the patrol force. Would that every combat sortie had contained a core group such as this! The multitiered combat formation of pairs of Airacobras occupied a broad expanse of sky. This meant that the German pilots were pinned down both vertically and horizontally in the engagement zone.

The leaders of the two groups (Kryukov and Pokryshkin), understanding without question that the unfolding dogfight would be fierce and exceptionally dynamic, reminded their crews of the necessity to observe strict radio discipline. It would be difficult, and at times impossible, to command and control the battle without radio communications.

The strength of their numbers gave the Germans courage. Dividing their force into two groups of eight aircraft, they attempted to climb above the covering P-39s, but this tactic failed. The pair of Guards Lieutenant Andrey Trud (his wingman was Pavel Gorokhov) rushed to engage the right-flank enemy foursome. Trud downed a Bf-109 with an attack into its belly, and Gorokhov set another Messerschmitt on fire with a cannon burst into its fuselage. Both damaged fighters limped away to the southwest, losing altitude. It was a pity that the Soviet pilots had not managed to destroy them. This was a result of commencing fire from the Airacobras at too great a range. It would have been more dangerous for the attacking aircraft to move in closer. Regardless, two P-39s versus four Messerschmitts resulted in two enemy fighters lost in the first moments of the battle. This rapid success gave the Soviet pilots great encouragement.

The two Airacobra group leaders coordinated their actions by radio. Kryukov's Airacobras were to engage the enemy fighters, no matter how difficult. If they could fulfill the role of element cover for the entire formation of eight fighters, even just for a brief time, Pokryshkin's foursome would have complete freedom of action.

While Kryukov's fighters began to accomplish the first part of the plan, Pokryshkin led his subordinates in an almost-vertical dive from an altitude of 13,100 feet. The four Airacobras came together as if in a fist and attacked the Messerschmitts that Kryukov's pilots were distracting.

This eaglelike, dagger thrust by Pokryshkin's flight came as such a surprise to the enemy that he simply could not defend against it. Immediately two Bf-109s were sent tumbling end over end and crashed into the ground west of Nikolaevskaya. Pokryshkin's flight executed a high-speed climb, turned 180 degrees, and launched another attack from above.

For several seconds before the diving Airacobras commenced firing, the five Messerschmitts raced about aimlessly, literally like beheaded chickens. The enemy had no other means of escaping the cannon and machine-gun tracers. Pokryshkin, Trud, and Rechkalov plummeted toward the earth like meteors. Only Paskaev managed to catch a fleeing enemy aircraft in his sights, but its pilot was saved by seeking cover in a small storm cloud. The enemy pilots considered it prudent to avoid a continuation of this dogfight. They all fled to the southwest, some by seeking altitude, and others by diving steeply. Thanks to the decisiveness and persistence of the Soviet pilots, this twenty-minute engagement ended with a remarkable score of five to zero in their favor.[16]

The creator of this new tactical method for fighter aviation had every reason to be happy. The methods he had proposed for destroying the enemy had been displayed in the best possible light. The executors of these methods—the Airacobra pilots—deserved the highest praise.

The pilots of the neighboring 45th Regiment also fought bravely against German bombers and fighters. This regiment's squadrons flew thirty aircraft sorties in the areas of Gladkovskiye, Alegro, and Krymskaya on 15 April, and fought three engagements, each time against superior enemy forces. They downed seven Ju-88s and seven Bf-109s, while losing four of their own aircraft.[17]

What was the secret of such positive results? They attacked boldly, taking advantage of the rapid acceleration and speed of the P-39. At the same time, the enemy was denied the time he needed to collect himself and to undertake effective countermeasures. The Airacobras' powerful cannon and machine-gun armaments cut through the enemy aircraft. All the Soviet pilot had to do was hit the target.

Of no less significance was the participation in these engagements of battle-tested pilots who had been "cured" in the smoke of combat experience: Mikhail Petrov, Boris Glinka, Nikolay Kudrya, Pavel Berestnev, Gedaliy Mikityanskiy, and Dmitriy Koval. In the first half of April alone, each of these pilots added to their official personal scores respectively (aerial engagements/downed enemy aircraft): five/three; six/five; ten/five; seven/four; eleven/three; and four/four.[18] All of them were recommended for the high rank of Hero of the Soviet Union in May 1943.

The first battle for pilots of the 45th Regiment on 15 April commenced at 0850 and lasted until 1015. Eight Airacobras were divided into two equal groups, led by Senior Lieutenants Mikhail Petrov and Boris Glinka. They were patrolling in the area of Krymskaya and Sheptalskaya at an altitude of 13,100 feet. Ground vectoring station "Tiger" alerted the Airacobra pilots to the approach of no fewer than fifteen Ju-88s, accompanied by a modest group of fighters. By the enemy's past actions this was an indication that they intended to drop their bombs along the immediate front line and were relying on their own ground anti-aircraft fires to supplement the fighter cover.

The Soviet group leaders began to exchange detailed plans for their four-ship groups by radio. The remaining crews listened attentively to the radio traffic without interrupting. Petrov suggested to Glinka that the Soviet fighters should engage the bombers over enemy territory by simultaneous attacks from above and below. This would place the battle somewhat to the rear of the enemy anti-aircraft fires and thus provide some degree of protection to the Soviet crews. Glinka concurred, indicating that Petrov should come in under the bombers and he would take his group to altitude to engage the fighter cover. If that tactic was successful, Glinka could then attack from above, out of the sun.

Upon their approach to the front line, the groups executed a maneuver to avoid anti-aircraft fires (change of course, speed, and altitude to reduce the probability of flak damage). They safely passed over the front line at an altitude of more than 16,400 feet and then dropped down. After transitioning to their "bookshelf" formation of stepped pairs, the P-39 pilots had dominance over a broad expanse of the sky. They detected below them a formation of fifteen to sixteen Ju-88s, four He-111s, and four Bf-109Fs.

In accordance with the agreed-upon plan, Mikhail Petrov's group, using the cover of scattered clouds, initiated a sliding descent. Boris Glinka led his group upward in an almost vertical climb. If the enemy had detected our fighters, he might have interpreted their departure from the engagement area in various directions as a refusal to fight. His subsequent actions confirmed this conclusion. Neither his fighters nor his bombers changed formation, continuing to track to the north-east toward their intended target.

Seconds later, both groups of Soviet fighters were in position and initiated the attack. The simultaneous strike from above and below produced a good harvest. Glinka fired a single burst into a Ju-88, which exploded and fell to the earth in pieces. Berestnev also set a Ju-88 on fire. Petrov caught in his sights a Bf-109 that had cut across his path. Three enemy aircraft were downed in the first pass—not a bad result!

The Airacobras hurtled toward a predesignated rally point. Their first effective high-speed swoop had seriously disheartened the enemy. While the bomber crews began to drop their loads, the German fighters circled around the combat formation, prepared to intercept any Airacobras that made a second approach toward the bombers.

After a brief radio conversation, Petrov and Glinka agreed not to make a second attack on the formation. Their first attack had accomplished the primary mission, to disrupt the air strike on our ground troops. The dense bomber formation had dissipated, opening a large window through which the German anti-aircraft gunners could fire at the Airacobras without fear of hitting their own aircraft. It would have been dangerous to continue to operate by the initial plan. They had to disengage. As if to confirm the correctness of their decision, a German flak round damaged the P-39 of Sergeant Vasiliy Sapyan. He headed toward his airfield, smoking and losing altitude.

Despite the pilot's best efforts, he was unable to reach Popovicheskaya airfield. Wounded, barely able to control his aircraft, Sapyan had to put it down in a forest. The P-39 was totally destroyed. Vasiliy received several bruises and two light wounds that required two weeks of recuperation in an infirmary.

Dmitriy Glinka was leading six aircraft in the second battle of 15 April (1120 to 1230). Their mission was to provide cover to ground forces in the area of Neberdzhievskaya, Semiskhodovskiy, and Krymskaya. Their orbiting altitude was 13,100 to 14,750 feet. They conducted the engagement at an altitude of 11,500 feet. Half of the group were veteran combat pilots: Dmitriy Glinka, Nikolay Kudrya, Pavel Berestnev, Gedaliy Mikityanskiy, and Ivan Babak. In two weeks of April this cohort had a combined combat score of twenty-one aircraft destroyed (six, six, five, three, and one, respectively).

They arrived in the appointed patrol zone at the designated time. The ground vectoring station reported to the group leader that the air situation was quiet. The ground vectoring station came back on the air several minutes later and reported two small fighter elements and ten bombers approaching from the southwest. The group leaders fully anticipated an enemy attempt to penetrate their coverage zone with fighters in order to ensure the successful work of the bombers. It would be a pitched battle. They would have to fight force with force. We had a saying at the front: "Avoid actions that establish a pattern and you will have fewer losses!"

Glinka issued an order: "Babak's pair, provide cover. The rest of you follow me! We will hit them like a fist from above and below, then from below and above." This plan envisioned striking the German formation primarily in the vertical plane. The Airacobras were somewhat superior to the Bf-109F and G models in maneuverability in that mode. Dmitriy Glinka had decided to use this particular characteristic of his fighters to full advantage.

The enemy was already near. His formation included four Ju-88s and twelve Bf-109F and G models. The primary goal of the Soviet fighter strike was to destroy the German fighter cover.

Four of Glinka's Airacobras were above the approaching enemy formation, with a covering pair higher still. On command, the entire patrol withdrew in the direction of the sun, making detection of their approach more difficult for the enemy pilots. While the Germans had a twofold numerical advantage, the Airacobra pilots had altitude in their favor, could execute their first attack out of the sun, were equipped with more powerful cannon armaments, had a large proportion of experienced pilots, and had the highest morale. In every battle before this, and in this battle as well, they did not spare their blood or even life itself in order to destroy the enemy. Scorning death, the Soviet aviators fought and would continue to fight with the German invaders, without consideration for their numbers. The Soviet pilots were bold in their plans and brave in executing them. The liberation of their Motherland was more important than anything else.

When the moment of truth arrived Glinka issued the command to attack. Four Airacobras, deployed in a line, dove almost vertically into the formation of Messerschmitts. Launching their strike from altitude at maximum speed and conducting a vertical maneuver, they were implementing all of the ingredients of the "formula of terror." When the P-39s closed to effective firing range, their silent weapons began to spit fire, sending forth a hail of lead. The P-39s turned the enemy aircraft into chunks of metal. The Soviet pilots did not spare their shells and cartridges in the first pass (it was always decisive), nor did they waste them. Kudrya, Berestnev, and Mikityanskiy quickly destroyed three Messerschmitts. As the "fiery sword" passed through the enemy combat formation, German aircraft veered off in various directions. Glinka managed to catch up to one "bandit" and set him on fire with a short burst. In this situation, the crews of the bombers had no alternative but to flee the battlefield. They dove toward the ground and, taking cover in the terrain, took a reverse course.

At the same time, the attacking Airacobras turned 180 degrees and climbed back up to altitude in order to pursue the enemy fighters. The airspace was alive with aircraft of both sides—climbing, turning, diving, waging an air battle in which it was hard to tell friend from foe. Revving motors, tracer streams, smoke trails from falling fighter aircraft. Whose? It was difficult to say with any certainty. A pilot caught the enemy in his sight, fired a burst, then threw his machine into a turn or climb to avoid the tracer of the enemy aircraft on his tail. In spite of all the confusion, Nikolay Kudrya "bagged" yet another Bf-109G. Sergeant Konstantin Panov kept pace with his leader and shot down his own Messerschmitt. But at that moment he fell under enemy fire. His Airacobra went over on its left wing and quickly began to lose altitude. Kudrya raced toward his wingman, covering him against a follow-on enemy attack. He escorted his wingman to a safe distance from the engagement zone and then returned to resume battle with the enemy. The wounded Panov managed to coax his machine to a neighboring airfield at Novovelichevskaya and landed it with great difficulty. The Airacobra required at least two days of repair, and the pilot almost a month in hospitalization.[19]

In any air battle the commander in charge should determine in a timely manner that moment when he must decide whether to continue to fight with the enemy or quickly to cease fighting and depart the engagement area. Three factors are working simultaneously or consecutively: one's own losses; the amount of fuel remaining in one's tanks; and the availability of ammunition. In this specific example, the two latter factors dictated the leader's decision to break off the engagement. Glinka gave his subordinates the command, "Everyone—33 (return to base)!" He ordered Babak to cover the disengagement action.

During the time interval between the second and, on this day, third and last battle (1655 to 1800), the pilots had an opportunity to discuss their experiences in these battles. This was a good, constant tradition that was violated only with rare exception. The impressive successes of the 45th Regiment pilots in the first half of the day were the result of persistent and rapid attacks by pairs and groups. Despite the enemy's numerical superiority, the Airacobra pilots had been able immediately to impose their will on him and to maintain that advantage until the completion of the engagement.

There were additional important factors that contributed to the Soviet success. The Airacobras attacked, as a rule, in sectors that were "dead space" or areas of limited visibility for the enemy pilots. This was combined with the high speed of the P-39s' approach to the target selected for destruction. Finally, the groups and pairs coordinated closely among themselves and exercised strict radio discipline.

This combination of factors was to be employed countless times in subsequent aerial battles. All the participants of the postflight briefings came to this same conclusion in their discussions. One of the aviators let slip an unusual remark: "These Germans are a greedy lot! Today we put it to them. Without question, the fascists have their own sense of accomplishment. Their pilots will make every effort to make us pay for their losses. We must keep our guard up!" This was a valid point. At this time the Germans still had a considerable number of aircraft in the skies. For this reason, in several days the first campaign of the Great Patriotic War for air superiority in the skies of the Kuban would begin.

The complement of the patrol (four Airacobras and three Kittyhawks) for the next sortie on 15 April included several experienced and bold pilots: Mikhail Petrov (leader), Dmitriy Glinka, Pavel Berestnev, Dmitriy Koval, and Nikolay Lavitskiy. Senior Lieutenant Lavitskiy had fought in six aerial engagements and destroyed three enemy aircraft in the first half of April.

The group approached their patrol area over Krymskaya and began to execute their assigned mission. Thirty minutes later they received an alert from the vectoring station regarding the approach of enemy bombers. In the designated sector the pilots spotted twelve Ju-88s escorted by six Bf-109Gs, flying at an altitude of 13,100 feet. The flight of Airacobras and Kittyhawks was flying approximately 2,600 to 3,000 feet higher than the German formation.

The differing technical and tactical characteristics of the P-39 and P-40 aircraft that made up the patrol made it necessary to fight the battle at two levels, the Kittyhawks at the lower level and the Airacobras above them. Petrov directed his Kittyhawks to go after the bombers and the Airacobras to engage the Messerschmitts. It would have been better, of course, had the Soviet patrol been comprised entirely of the P-39, which performed better at altitude than the P-40. In the current situation, the group leader always had to monitor the location of the P-40s and be prepared to render assistance to them. This was further required in that two of the three P-40s were being flown by young inexperienced pilots.

In going after the Messerschmitts the Airacobra pilots took the brunt of the engagement upon themselves. They attempted to hold their engagement area in proximity to the bomber formation. This would help them to achieve several positive outcomes. Once they had engaged the "bandits" in proximity to the bombers, the Soviet pilots could at any moment in the fight penetrate into the bomber formation and fire on an enemy aircraft. This would keep them close to the Kittyhawks, and the Bf-109s would be forced to fly in and around the Ju-88s they were escorting, considerably reducing their free maneuver space. This close proximity of the engagement area to the bomber formation brought with it additional danger: the Soviet aircraft could fall under the dense fires of the bombers' gunners.

Dmitriy Glinka downed an enemy fighter in the first head-on pass. It plummeted to the earth in a burning heap. Lavitskiy's tracer stream cut through a fleeing bomber. Dmitriy Koval flew with exceptional skill and bravery. He penetrated to the bomber formation and downed two of them with short successive attacks. At this same time, Berestnev fired an accurate cannon burst into the tail of a bomber and sent it to the ground in an uncontrolled spiraling dive. The first Soviet casualty then occurred when Sergeant Anatoliy Bezbabnov's Kittyhawk was set on fire.

Despite his already significant losses, the enemy continued to resist fiercely, launching several frenzied counterattacks. This was a clear indication that an overwhelming majority, if not all, of the enemy pilots were combat veterans. Two Messerschmitts set upon Petrov's P-39, damaging it. The Airacobra became difficult to control. Senior Lieutenant Petrov ordered Dmitriy Glinka to assume control of the group and, covered by his wingman Nikolay Kudrov, withdrew from the fight. After a brief interval of time he was forced to abandon the aircraft for his parachute.[20]

The newly appointed group leader quickly came under attack by four "bandits" coming from four directions. Dmitriy Glinka circled like a spinning top, seeking to avoid the wavy streams of cannon and machine-gun tracers. Unfortunately, he could not escape from the ring of enemy fire and his aircraft received a number of serious hits. His comrades helped him disengage from the battle and he made a forced landing.

The results of this aerial engagement were felt by both sides. Five enemy aircraft and three friendlies (almost half of the patrol) had been shot down.[21]

The Sky Was Ablaze

The air forces of the opposing sides collided in fierce battles in the skies of the Kuban in the second half of April and early May. The sky was ablaze. Myskhako, also known as *Malaya zemlya* ["small land"], was the key piece of terrain on the captured western shore of Tsemesskaya Bay. The victory here of the amphibious landing force personnel who had fought against superior enemy forces for 225 days and nights was a great accomplishment. They had overcome a thousand and one deaths every minute. By the end of the battle the rocky surface of the bridgehead was completely covered with a layer of shrapnel from aircraft bombs and artillery and mortar shells, as well as a liberal portion of rifled projectiles. The ground burned under the troops' feet. The fighting men did not waiver, they stood erect. Twenty-one men were later awarded the rank Hero of the Soviet Union for their actions in this beachhead.

Myskhako joined the ranks of the greatest, most heroic defensive battles of the Great Patriotic War: Brest fortress; the struggle of twenty-eight *Panfilovtsy* with scores of German tanks at Dubosekovo siding; and Dom Pavlova [the "Pavlov house"] during the Stalingrad battle.

The pilots of 216th Fighter Division were contributors to the successful holding of *Malaya zemlya*. Soviet aviators destroyed 152 enemy aircraft around Novorossiysk in the period from 17 to 24 April, with another 30 falling to anti-aircraft fire. Our own losses were approximately one-half of the enemy's.[1]

On 17 April the Germans undertook another of their countless attacks, attempting to push the landing force on *Malaya zemlya* back into the water. The Germans launched simultaneous offensives on other sectors of the front around Novorossiysk, hoping to push back formations of the 18th Army that had established a semicircular position around the city and port.

Both sides were introducing large air formations into the action. Scores of red-starred and "crossed" fighters, ground attack aircraft, and bombers darkened the sun. At times the sky became too crowded. But the Airacobra pilots sought and found airspace in which to defeat the enemy. Here are several examples of some of the lesser and greater engagements around Novorossiysk and Myskhako.

The pilots of 16th Guards Fighter Regiment sortied to this area for combat missions twice on the first day of renewed active enemy air operations. Eight Airacobras (four-ship flights led by Aleksandr Pokryshkin and Dmitriy Glinka) took off early in the morning to escort bombers that were delivering a strike on concentrations of enemy infantry and tanks in a dried river bed near Myskhako.

Tsemesskaya Bay came into view. Four Messerschmitts bore down on our aircraft. Glinka's flight immediately turned to engage them. The enemy pilots evaded the fires of the P-39s with hurried maneuvers. "DB" [Dmitriy Borisovich Glinka] set off in pursuit of them. Pokryshkin attempted to reason with him by radio and advised him to break off the chase. They could not hastily leave the Pe-2s without reliable cover. A special group of Airacobras had been designated to sweep the sky of enemy fighters.

But Glinka remained deaf to Pokryshkin's entreaties. The heady aroma of battle took priority over reason. He had only to catch the Messerschmitts with his cannon fire, then continue precisely to accomplish the assigned mission. This experienced pilot, it appeared, had completely forgotten the enemy's fighter tactics: he sent out four to six aircraft as "bait" to attract our escorts, then used a more significant force of Bf-109s to break through to our Petlyakovs flying their mission.

This particular circumstance once again emphasized the correctness of 1st Squadron commander Pokryshkin's advice in regimental and divisional meetings regarding the logic of forming groups for combat actions in various units. "DB" was also a squadron commander, from 45th Fighter Regiment. It was fortunate that Glinka quickly came to his senses and corrected his gross error. He rejoined his group to Pokryshkin's Airacobras.

One after another the Pe-2s went into their dives. Pokryshkin withdrew his four-ship flight somewhat to the south, toward the sea, and gained altitude. Dmitriy did the same but toward the north. This two-sided coverage of their bomber formation permitted them to intercept enemy aircraft approaching from any direction: Glinka from the land and Pokryshkin from the water. Pokryshkin took upon himself the primary responsibility for covering the Petlyakovs after they had completed their drops. They would disengage from the target, turn out over the water, and assemble for their subsequent return to base. This was one of the most critical moments of their actions. The bomber formation inevitably would be strung out, and some of them might inadvertently even be left behind. This was the best time for the enemy "hunters" to attack.

Pokryshkin intently searched the airspace and periodically reminded his subordinates to do the same: "Everyone be observant!" Glinka responded, "Roger, we are looking." By this short response, "DB" acknowledged that now he would carry out all instructions of the 16th Regiment squadron commander [Pokryshkin], who was the leader of the combined eight-ship flight. In the air (as on the ground) there should not be "separate princes." Be the group of Airacobras large or small, it could have only one leader, the more so when that leader was an experienced ace such as Aleksandr Pokryshkin. There could be only one commander.

The situation began to get complicated. The Airacobra escorts' "quiet" combat actions, one might say, had come to an end. Pokryshkin noticed streaks of dust on Anapa airfield, which meant enemy fighters were launching. He quickly passed this information to his subordinates. Almost at the same time the Airacobra pilots observed the approach of several groups of bombers on an intersecting course and at the same altitude as themselves. They were carrying a multi-ton deadly cargo to Myskhako, escorted by no fewer than ten Messerschmitts and Focke-Wulfs.

Pokryshkin ordered Dmitriy Glinka to engage the "bandits" coming up from Anapa airfield while he took his own group of four to intercept the bombers and their escort. In a situation like this, when the enemy held numerical superiority, only the boldness of one's actions, combined with the suddenness of the attack and a storm of cannon and machine-gun fire, could permit them to gain the upper hand. To some degree, the size of their force was relegated to lesser importance.

Pokryshkin's foursome (Vadim Fadeev, Grigoriy Rechkalov, and Mikhail Sutyrin) cut into the formation of Ju-87s with such high velocity that the enemy pilots (both fighter and bomber) could hardly track them. The Airacobras' dense fires wreaked havoc among the targets. Vadim Fadeev was especially effective. He shot down a Ju-87 in his first pass and several minutes later downed a Bf-109. Rechkalov shot down a Focke-Wulf in a head-on pass. Pokryshkin cut into the fuselage of a Ju-88 with cannon and machine-gun fire, causing the enemy aircraft to break into two large pieces as it fell. One of Pokryshkin's innovations had helped in dealing with the enemy formation.

After an air battle in early April, Pokryshkin had returned to his airfield with a considerable amount of unfired ammunition. By design, the cannon and machine guns were wired with separate firing triggers that were squeezed separately (cannon with thumb button on top of the stick, machine guns with index finger on the front of the stick). The machine-gun trigger was significantly easier to manipulate. And in a rapidly unfolding engagement with the enemy, it was not an easy matter to manipulate one's fingers. Guards Captain Pokryshkin gave the matter some thought, and then consulted with the regimental engineer, Guards Captain Yakov Zhmud. At Pokryshkin's request, Zhmud agreed quietly to wire the cannon switch into the machine-gun switch on Aleksandr's control stick. Pokryshkin doubted that the regiment commander, Nikolay Isaev, would approve of this modification.

On his next mission sortie, the 1st Squadron commander managed to conduct a one-time test of his innovation. The massed fires of his 37mm cannon and two .50 caliber machine guns blew up a bomber in the air. The eyewitnesses to this stunning display of the fire effectiveness of "13" (Pokryshkin's call sign and also his tail number) informed their colleagues.[2] The Guards captain was beset with questions: "What was your firing range? What did you use for an aimpoint?" If the day before he had a secret, then after this mission he passed it along to all of his friends. He explained to them the modification that had been made to the control stick of his Airacobra.

To a man, the squadron's pilots "bombarded" Yakov Zhmud simultaneously. They requested that he reconfigure their own triggers as soon as possible. Several days later, unbeknownst to the regimental commander (unfortunately, the capriciousness of some front-line commanders forced their subordinates to resort to such secretive activities), the work was completed. The firing effect of a single trigger squeeze by each P-39 had increased substantially.

Returning to the aerial combat over Myskhako, the Airacobra pilots closed with the formation of bombers to destroy their selected targets. When the formation began to break up, the P-39s went inside it for the kill. Pokryshkin and his subordinates employed this superior tactical method later, in a majority of their air battles. The primary advantages: fearful of shooting down their own aircraft, in a majority of cases enemy escort pilots could not conduct concentrated fires at the attacking P-39s; and our pilots expended minimal time in unnecessary maneuvers, an extremely important factor in a rapidly flowing battle.

The decisiveness of the Airacobra strike on the numerically superior enemy and the excellent results thereby achieved had a salutary effect on the Pe-2 crews. Having closed on the bombers, they opened fire with their nose machine guns. An unfathomable scene unfolded in the sky above Myskhako. Scores of aircraft (our own and the enemy's) were hurtling on various courses; tracers of cannon and machine-gun bursts were etched across the sky. Everything was scrambled together.

Dropping their bomb loads wherever they fell, the enemy bombers were turning and fleeing to the west. The Pe-2s ceased firing, tightened up their formation, and set a course in the opposite direction.

The four-ship flight of Dmitriy Glinka executed the mission assigned to it by Pokryshkin. Not only did they prevent the enemy fighters from approaching the engagement area, they shot down two Bf-109Fs.

Pokryshkin ordered all fighters to return to base, Glinka's group at 13,100 feet, his own group at 9,850 feet, keeping the Petlyakovs in sight at all times.

It turned out that all that had just occurred was only "small potatoes," with the real test yet to come. Ten Focke-Wulfs suddenly appeared, the second enemy reinforcements. Their pilots showed great resolve. They planned first to engage Glinka's Airacobras, flying above, and then from this favorable position launch a subsequent attack on the Petlyakovs, or P-39s. The three remaining aircraft of Glinka's flight (Aleksandr Molchanov's aircraft had been damaged and he had left the scene) disrupted the enemy's plan by diving into the overcast, hoping to break out near Pokryshkin's aircraft.

On their return leg two Petlyakovs fell out of formation, presenting a good target for enemy fighters. Not losing any time, Pokryshkin drew his own flight in closer. It was not too late to attempt to assist the pair of Petlyakovs. Two Focke-Wulfs, diving from the concealment of one cloud to another, were already closing on the two slow-moving aircraft. Pokryshkin executed a turn and then in a dive came up on the tail of an FW-190. His wingman, Mikhail Sutyrin, took the second FW-190 in his sight. Focused on their pursuit of the Pe-2s, the enemy pilots forgot to look in their rearview mirror. They did not notice the approaching danger and paid dearly for it. Aleksandr increased the speed of his Airacobra and closed to the effective firing range. A "tripled" tracer stream (from the simultaneously firing cannon and two heavy machine guns) emptied into the Focke-Wulf. It suddenly fell off course and several seconds later disappeared into the sea, along with its pilot. Mikhail managed only to catch the second FW-190 with a burst as it broke off its attack. It flew off in the direction of Anapa, losing altitude and trailing smoke.

Pokryshkin's four-ship flight caught up to the Petlyakovs. They had to be watched carefully. Nearby, Glinka and the other two remaining pilots of his group were chasing, and being chased by, enemy fighters. Pokryshkin wanted to go to their assistance but could not leave the Petlyakovs on their own yet. So he radioed to Glinka to hold on until his group could enter the fight.

Pokryshkin accomplished two things with these brief radio transmissions: he informed both Glinka and the enemy of his intended future actions. His radio call sign ("13") was well known to the German pilots, who already were beginning to respect his fighting reputation. When Pokryshkin joined his four aircraft to Glinka's three, highly experienced pilots (Pokryshkin, Fadeev, Glinka, and Rechkalov) sat in the cockpits of four of the seven Airacobras.

In its own way, Pokryshkin's radio transmission was also a form of psychological warfare against the enemy, and it worked. At this time the enemy had a total of eighteen Bf-109s and FW-190s in the engagement zone, a 2.5-to-1 superiority over the Soviet combined group. The subsequent nature of the enemy's actions revealed that approximately ten of his pilots were somewhat timid in their flying, indicating some degree of inexperience. They flew around on the periphery of the engagement box, acting as cover for the core group of eight fighters.

Pokryshkin quickly evaluated this situation and issued instructions to his entire group by radio. As before, continuing to hold the reins of control in his hands, he instructed his pilots not to allow the Germans to get an altitude advantage (one of his axioms was "Be above, not below, the enemy!"), to prevent the enemy groups from coming together (it would be easier to defeat them piecemeal), to employ, whenever possible, a firing screen and attract the enemy into it, to prevent the enemy Messerschmitts and Focke-Wulfs from penetrating to the Petlyakovs, and to come quickly to the assistance of any pilot who called for it. Radio communications were a powerful weapon in a rapidly changing situation.

Pokryshkin's plan was well conceived. The Airacobras continued to accomplish their mission of escorting the bombers; to tie themselves down in direct battle with enemy fighters would open the way for enemy fighters to chase after the Pe-2s. The defensive tactics employed by the P-39 pilots somewhat encouraged the enemy. His eight "active" fighters attempted more than once to come within effective firing range of Pokryshkin's group, but they were driven back by intense fire, losing one FW-190 in the process.

Like flashes of lightning, brief exchanges broke out first in one and then in another sector of the engagement zone. The Bf-109s and FW-190s were also flown by seasoned pilots, who bided their time. They came at the Airacobras from various directions and at high speed. The excellent maneuverability of the P-39s saved them from deadly enemy tracer streams. Unfortunately, not every pilot was able to maneuver his aircraft in a timely manner. The P-39 flown by Senior Sergeant Petr Tabachenko received serious damage to its tail section. He barely made it back to Krasnodar airfield.

Finally, the arrival of Soviet reinforcements in the form of twelve Yak-1s changed the tide of the battle. They struck at the enemy and immediately downed two Messerschmitts. The Germans abandoned their efforts to reach the Pe-2s and began to conduct a defensive battle, gradually withdrawing to their own lines.[3]

On all the remaining days through April 27, the units of 16th Guards and 45th Fighter Regiments carried out, for the most part, missions for escorting bombers that were conducting strikes on German troops around Novorossiysk. Groups from various squadrons of these two regiments were designated for this purpose. While not the most effective, this method of forming combat groups resulted from a general shortage of combat-capable aircraft. On 21 April, for example, combat-ready fighter strength in the 16th Guards was ten Airacobras and in the 45th Regiment only four. These numbers were eleven and six, correspondingly, on 25 April.[4]

Several unusual events occurred during the combat actions over

Myskhako and Fedorovka. On 23 April, a group of six P-39s from 16th Guards Fighter Regiment fought two engagements, the second with ten Bf-109s and two FW-190s at altitudes of 6,550–9,850 feet. The fight was brief and exceptionally intense. Maneuvering in a sharp turn for a follow-on attack on a Bf-109, pair leader Guards Junior Lieutenant Vasiliy Mochalov caught the tail of his own aircraft in the propeller of his wingman, Guards Sergeant Yuriy Sapunov. His controls not responding, Mochalov abandoned the aircraft as it spun and parachuted to safety near Gelendzhika.[5]

On this same day, Lieutenant Andrey Trud of 16th Guards Fighter Regiment was attacked by a Yak-1 fighter while returning from a combat mission. The Yak pilot, ignorant of the fact that American-manufactured fighters were operating along this particular sector of the front, had mistaken the Airacobra for a German aircraft. The aircraft was damaged to the extent that Trud had to make a forced belly landing at Starosteblinskaya airfield.[6]

Similar incidents took place at other times and places. For example, four Yak-1s attacked the fighters of Aleksandr Pokryshkin and Petr Tabachenko over Soviet-occupied territory on 28 April. Despite the transmission of signals by radio and the maneuvers of the aircraft, the Yak pilots did not stop firing. As a result of their actions, Pokryshkin's Airacobra received serious skin damage and a destroyed landing light. It took almost eight hours to repair the aircraft.[7]

There were three incidences of firing on Airacobras, Kittyhawks, and Spitfires by Yak-1s on 29 April, and two additional cases on the next day.[8] The headquarters of 4th Air Army undertook urgent measures to issue the tactical-technical and appearance characteristics of Lend-Lease P-39s to the flying crews of units equipped with indigenous aircraft. This significantly reduced the frequency of such friendly fire incidents.

The intensity of combat for gaining of air superiority grew not by the day but by the hour beginning on 20 April. Units of 16th Guards Fighter Regiment fought three aerial engagements on 21 April, four on 24 April, and six on 29 April. All these actions occurred over Myskhako and Krymskaya.[9]

One of the most productive air battles in the skies over the Kuban occurred on 25 April. In the morning the commander of 16th Guards Regiment assigned the following combat mission: the first patrol group of eight Airacobras was led by Vadim Fadeev; the second group, led by Aleksandr Pokryshkin (six aircraft) would sortie forty minutes later. The mission was to provide coverage over Krymskaya village.

The experienced pilots understood that such a long time interval before the launch of Pokryshkin's group might detract from the accomplishment of the overall mission. Therefore they agreed among themselves that if necessary, the 1st Squadron commander [Pokryshkin] would launch his aircraft prior to the time designated by the regimental commander. This would occur upon a code-word command spoken by Fadeev over the radio. The mission of the first group was to engage the enemy fighters that were normally dispatched to clear the sky over the objective prior to the bombers' attack. The mission of the second group was to intercept the bombers. For this reason, the forces were distributed by time and target.

As Fadeev's Airacobras launched, Pokryshkin's crews sat in the cockpits of their P-39s at readiness level no. 1.[10] They turned on their radios and listened attentively to the traffic on the air. This allowed all pilots simultaneously to receive information regarding the air situation in the area where Fadeev and his subordinates were working. Approximately twenty minutes passed. Then Fadeev's shrill voice broke the silence: "This is '*Boroda*' ['the beard' (Fadeev wore a beard)]. I see eight Messerschmitts. Prepare for battle!" The last phrase was the agreed-upon command to sortie Pokryshkin's group. While Pokryshkin's fighters were reaching the objective area, the enemy bombers would also be approaching.

Off to the right of Krymskaya, Fadeev's patrol was engaging the Messerschmitts. Vadim refused suggestions of assistance, stating that his group had already downed three "bandits" and could handle their mission. Fadeev and Pokryshkin confirmed their plan in a brief and calm radio exchange.

Ahead, to the left and below toward the front line, three groups of nine Ju-87 dive bombers were approaching, escorted by four fighters. Pokryshkin ordered Grigoriy Rechkalov and his wingman to provide cover while he attacked the bombers with the remaining four aircraft.

The Airacobras dived rapidly on the first flight of nine enemy bombers. Pokryshkin tore a Ju-87 to shreds. Vladimir Berezhnoy set a second one on fire. The remaining bombers dropped their bombs and scattered in all directions, diving toward the ground and the safety of their own lines.

Without wasting valuable time, Pokryshkin's group waded into the second group of nine. Pokryshkin downed his second bomber. Over the next several minutes, the enemy aircraft dropped their ordnance and turned back in panic. The third group of nine did not wait to suffer the fate of those who had gone before them and dropped their bombs on the heads of their own troops before they rushed to the rear. Pokryshkin caught up to the fleeing Germans and shot down a third Ju-87 with a well-aimed burst.

At this time, having shot down one Bf-109, the pair of fighters led by Grigoriy Rechkalov was fighting off three other Messerschmitts. Pokryshkin's group did not press their pursuit of the departing bombers and turned back to help Rechkalov. The enemy pilots broke off and headed for home.

Pokryshkin quickly assembled his six-ship flight and went to the aid of Vadim Fadeev. Detecting the approach of reinforcements, the German fighters, diving steeply, disengaged. The surrounding skies were now clean of enemy aircraft. Replaced by Pokryshkin's three pairs, Vadim Fadeev's flight could return to the airfield.

In this battle two groups of Airacobras shot down a total of eleven enemy aircraft without any losses of their own. This outcome demonstrated the effectiveness of timely reinforcement and skillful coordination between and within units, as well as the employment of the new tactical methods.

Division staff personnel initially did not believe the report concerning the results of the battle. They decided to reconfirm the numbers. They could not imagine that it was possible to destroy so many enemy aircraft and return to the airfield with just bullet and shrapnel holes in our own aircraft. They contacted the ground forces' command post where, fortunately, the deputy commander of the North Caucasus *Front*, Lieutenant General Ivan Maslennikov, was located. He informed the staff that he personally had witnessed the aerial battle from the forward edge and saw the burning enemy aircraft fall to the earth.[11]

On the morning of 28 April, a flight of eight P-39s under the command of Aleksandr Pokryshkin departed for Kerch Strait. The 1st Squadron commander had long held the desire to engage the enemy over his own positions. Utilizing the rapid pendulum method of patrolling, the Airacobra pilots anxiously awaited the approach of enemy bombers. With full fuel cells, the Airacobras could remain in the air approximately two hours.

The aviators were absolutely confident that the enemy would appear from the direction of the Crimea. They were not mistaken. Soon the reflections of the sun's rays off of the upper surfaces of aircraft signaled their approach. They were on an easterly course. Pokryshkin gave a terse command to his group: "West, large group bombers! We will close. Fedorov—distract escort fighters! The rest of us will attack the bombers!"

Having the advantage of altitude, the eight P-39s rushed toward their targets. Near Kerch Strait the pilots saw three echelons of Ju-87s, each echelon containing three nine-ship bomber groups in a compact formation. The echelons were spaced just under two miles apart. This echelonment of the enemy formations in depth was to the Soviets' advantage, as it would allow them to engage the enemy groups sequentially. The high density of each nine-ship flight was a guarantor of effective cannon and machine-gun fires against them.

The pilots of Arkadiy Fedorov's flight flew particularly skillfully. Despite enemy numerical superiority (nine Bf-109s), they engaged them in battle. The bombers now were left without escort. The two pairs led by Pokryshkin took advantage of the developing situation, attacking the bombers with an "eagle strike."

The bombers' rear-facing gunners unleashed a storm of machine-gun fire that was of such density as to make penetration to the flight leader seem impossible. Three seconds, not more, were required to close to the range of effective aiming and firing. In this brief fragment of time the P-39 pilot had to pass through the dense streams of machine-gun tracer. The high speed of the approach to the selected target and the constantly changing profile of the diving fighter created large lead angles for the enemy gunners that prevented aimed fire at the attacking fighters. This maneuver was an almost 100 percent guarantee of success in the attack.

Having broken through the machine-gun barrier fire, Pokryshkin shot the lead bombers at point-blank range and then zoomed upward. The downed aircraft was probably the enemy group commander. As a rule, his loss led to a disruption of command and control and had a bad psychological effect on the enemy pilots.

Pokryshkin made a follow-on attack on another aircraft in the same group, leading to the dispersal of the entire formation. The other pilots of Pokryshkin's group did not fail to take advantage of this opportunity and shot down three bombers. Having dropped their bombs where they fell, the enemy fled in disarray and confusion. Now they could be destroyed one at a time. However, Pokryshkin immediately ordered an attack on the second group of nine. As only a portion of the enemy bomber formation had been disrupted, this decision was completely correct. The action that had been initiated had to be carried to its logical conclusion.

The strike on the next twenty-seven bombers was also lightning-quick and bold. This time Pokryshkin's group dove through the fire screen like a meteor. Pokryshkin immediately cut down the leader of the center group of nine Ju-87s, then set a second bomber on fire with a rapid follow-on attack. The other Airacobra pilots flew their aircraft in an equally daring and decisive manner. Each of them shot down a single bomber. The rapidity and precision of the attack disrupted the enemy's plan. The Germans had no choice but to drop their deadly cargo and hurriedly return to the west.

There remained the following third echelon of enemy dive bombers. The 1st Squadron group reassembled to attack this force. The enemy, struck dumb by the high number of German aircraft in the formations flying in front of them downed by the Airacobras, did not tempt their fate. They hastily dropped their bombs and reversed course. The mission was accomplished completely—the bombing of our troops did not occur. Now it was possible to pursue the fleeing Ju-87s.

At exactly that moment a terse order came over the radio: Aleksandr Pokryshkin's group was to proceed immediately to the area of Krymskaya, where a formation of Messerschmitts had appeared. The Airacobras quickly reformed into a combat formation and hurried to the designated zone. They left twelve burning and smoking bombers in the sector of Kerch Strait and Verkhne-Bakanskaya. Not bad work for the Airacobra pilots.

Pokryshkin's group of eight fighters caught up to a group of Bf-109s over Krymskaya. These were apparently the fighters that Fedorov's group of P-39s had engaged before the arrival of their bombers. The enemy was unable to reach his assigned target. Our pilots had outsmarted him. While they were waiting here for the arrival of the Airacobras, the latter were inflicting heavy damage on the bomber formation as it approached the front line. The patterned actions of the German aviators had cost them dearly. Our patrol had achieved impressive results. Meanwhile, Pokryshkin's group was not yet free to depart for home. Their work period was not yet over. Although they had fuel, ammunition was in short supply. It was not the best of situations.

Fate chose this moment to present the Airacobra pilots with another stern challenge. The Airacobras were orbiting at maximum speed. The vectoring station alerted "13" [Pokryshkin] to the fact that enemy bombers with fighter escort were approaching from the direction of the Black Sea. Pokryshkin's eight-ship group turned to meet the approaching armada—approximately fifty aircraft. This demonstrated the enemy's intent to conduct a massive air strike on Soviet ground units.

Battle, probably of great intensity, could not be avoided. Such a powerful enemy could only be overcome in a most fierce struggle. But Pokryshkin's pilots had almost nothing left in their ammunition trays to shoot at them. What to do? Pokryshkin made, at first glance, a reckless decision: "Everyone close in tightly on me! We will make a psychological attack!" A psychological attack—in the air? This was not unusual in the ground war, but had there been similar examples in aviation units on other fronts of the Great Patriotic War? I cannot cite an analogous example.

Arkadiy Fedorov engaged the enemy escort fighters. Pokryshkin's group, compressed into an aerial fist, flew directly at the front of the Junkers formation, demonstrating an intent to ram. The German pilots, already familiar with such actions by "crazy" Russian pilots, lost their nerve. The bombers, their precision columns broken, turned toward the sea. Low on fuel and practically out of ammunition, Pokryshkin's pilots did not pursue them. They had driven the enemy back with his own fear, and that was sufficient.

A replacement group of fighters finally arrived on the scene. Satisfied with their battle results, the Airacobra pilots of 16th Guards Fighter Regiment returned to their airfield at full strength.[12]

Operational command and control of the aircraft in the air by the ground vectoring station had yielded appreciable results. Well-coordinated actions such as this became necessary. Thus, for example, on 29 April the commander of 216th Fighter Division Major General Aleksandr Borman, located at a command post near the front line, received a report of the approach of twelve enemy fighters. Aleksandr Pokryshkin's squadron happened to be providing the fighter cover at that moment. Having received a report of the air situation from the ground vectoring station and carrying out its commands, the Airacobra pilots flew to a suitable position and a short time later attacked the enemy. They destroyed eight Bf-109s in a brief engagement. It turned out that eight Ju-87 bombers were following behind this cover. With the assistance of the same ground vectoring station, P-39s from 45th Fighter Regiment were sent out under the command of Captain Dmitriy Glinka. All the enemy aircraft were destroyed.[13]

At the time of these air battles in the Kuban, command and control of aircraft going out on missions was accomplished from the divisional command post through the main vectoring radio station. This radio station was deployed near the command (observation) post of the senior ground force commander.

In the first ten days of the air campaign the basic efforts of fighter aviation were normally concentrated on the destruction of enemy fighters, not the bombers. To the credit of aviation commanders and their pilots, it should be noted that they quickly realized their error and did not repeat it in the future.

Here, in the Kuban, the enemy's air power was broken to a significant degree. This played a positive role in the overall struggle for air superiority on the Soviet–German front. In the period from 17 April to 17 June 1943, the 4th Air Army, aircraft of the Black Sea Fleet, and long-range aviation flew 12,000 aircraft sorties, of which 50 percent were attacks on enemy personnel and equipment on the battlefield. Some 285 aerial engagements were fought.[14]

During this period the pilots of 216th Fighter Division flew 2,711 combat sorties and conducted 118 aerial engagements. The division lost twenty-nine aircraft over the course of the month: eleven Airacobras shot down, eight that did not return from combat missions, and two to other causes; three Spitfires that did not return from combat missions; two Il-2s and one Yak-1 shot down, and two lost to other causes. Personnel losses were thirteen pilots lost in air combat, seven that did not return from combat missions, four that died in accidents, and two who were lost to other causes, a total of twenty-six aviators.[15]

The combat actions in the skies of the Kuban had a positive influence on the operational employment of the Red Army VVS. The tactics of all branches of aviation, but particularly of fighters, received development and subsequent improvement. The basic maneuver in aerial combat became vertical. To a large degree, this was made possible by the equipping of our units with high-speed, well-armed fighters and by their skillful employment by crews dispersed by frontage and altitude in combat formations comprised primarily of pairs of fighters.

The successful actions of aviation units depended also on the timely reconstitution of aviation units with new combat equipment. The Airacobras continued to arrive through Iran for the 216th Division and other units. The fighters were delivered across the Caucasus Mountains by special ferry pilots and turned over to representatives of line units at staging bases.

The division received such a delivery of P-39s on 25 April. Many pilots received new aircraft, including Guards Captain Pokryshkin. The aircraft crew chief Grigoriy Chuvashkin painted the number "100" on its fuselage in large numerals, so that the commander would be highly visible in the air. The famous ace kept this tail number until the end of the war.

The Kuban brought glory to the division's regiments. In its complement brave aerial warriors were raised up who became the pride of Soviet aviation. Twenty of these pilots became Heroes of the Soviet Union and Aleksandr Pokryshkin and Dmitriy Glinka received this honor a second time for their participation in battles in this area.

Wild Vadim

The galaxy of legendary pilots of 16th Guards Fighter Regiment, along with Aleksandr Pokryshkin and the brothers Boris and Dmitriy Glinka, Grigoriy Rechkalov, and Nikolay Kudrya, has also been joined by Vadim Fadeev. He was an exceptional, in many respects colorful aviator who deserves individual consideration. He made his first flights in a training aircraft of the Kuybyshev flying club and completed the Chkalov Military Aviation School in 1940.[1] Fadeev made his first combat flight in August 1941 as a senior sergeant in the 446th Aviation Regiment at Rostov-on-Don. He had no equal in daring. He flew at minimum altitude during ground attacks of enemy targets, strafing enemy infantry and cavalry at almost point-blank range.

November 27 of this first difficult year of beating off the enemy invasion was a special day in Fadeev's military biography. An eight-ship formation of I-16s, led by the senior sergeant, was attacking enemy troops and artillery positions in the area of Five Brothers' Hill (Bolshiye Saly settlement, northwest of Rostov).[2] Fadeev's flight was supporting our infantry from the air. The infantry unit had already attacked this key enemy position several times without success. Intensive fires were now suppressing them. The Polikarpov pilots could well see the enemy defensive positions and the German artillery battery that was pounding the Soviet infantry with shells every minute. Vadim led his fighters over the battery position. As it turned out, though, it had good anti-aircraft coverage. A fragment of an enemy anti-aircraft shell penetrated an oil tank of Fadeev's aircraft, allowing its contents to spray into the air stream.

This created a real possibility of disabling the motor by causing it to overheat and then seize. In such extraordinary circumstances there is only one way out—seek altitude in order to reach one's own positions by gliding. The motor stopped turning with a scraping metallic noise. Now the only audible sound was the wind whistling past the falling I-16. It dropped quickly, through 160 feet, 80 feet, 50 feet, 30 feet, until Vadim belly-landed the fighter near the forward edge of our infantry positions. He had just managed to overfly the enemy positions into our own lines. Dust enveloped the aircraft. The pilot flew out of the cockpit like a bullet and immediately ran away because the aircraft might explode. Fortunately, it did not. Several soldiers hurried toward him to take him back to their trenches.

Vadim vaulted into a deep communications trench and immediately asked a soldier to lead him to the nearest commander. A few minutes later he was rendering his aerial reconnaissance report at the rifle regiment command post. Fadeev suggested that mortar and artillery fires be directed at the enemy targets before they had an opportunity to reposition. The regiment commander passed the reconnaissance report up to division headquarters. A storm of artillery and mortar fire rained down upon the Germans. Soviet infantry squads surged forward. Vadim could not remain a casual observer. He pulled his pistol from its holster and joined the attacking infantrymen as they captured Five Brothers' Hill.

Senior Sergeant Vadim Fadeev received the Order of the Red Banner (second in rank only to the Order of Lenin) for his initiative, composure, courage, and heroism. Few personnel received this high award in the most difficult days of fiery 1941. Subsequently his wartime path led Fadeev to the 16th Guards Fighter Regiment. He flew both the Airacobra and the Kittyhawk during his transition training in the 25th Reserve Regiment. While he fell in love with the P-39, he also had fond memories of the P-40 and named his pet stray dog "Kitty."

The dog was an ordinary but unusually clever mutt. He understood his master well, following him everywhere step for step. In the mornings he sat near the entrance to the house where the pilots were quartered and anxiously awaited Vadim's appearance. As soon as his favorite pilot took a seat in the back of the crew truck, Kitty leapt up onto the fender, then the hood, and finally onto the roof of the truck's cab. Sprawled out on the roof, the dog extended its snout toward the back of the truck and did not take its devoted eyes off Fadeev. Vadim always had something tasty in his pocket for his pal and treated him with it. After this the dog raised his paw for a "handshake" and Vadim patted him on the head. Day after day the pair showed up at the airfield together. The Guards senior lieutenant headed to the command post for instructions and Kitty trotted off to the revetment where "his" fighter was parked.

Before he taxied the aircraft, aircraft maintenance supervisor Lieutenant Grigoriy Dolud usually placed Kitty on the wing. The mutt crawled to the forward edge of the wing and lay there quietly, legs outstretched. When the motor started, he jumped down onto the tarmac and raced back to the revetment of Fadeev's Airacobra, where he always awaited Vadim's return from a combat mission.

The multifaceted talent of this twenty-five-year-old fighter pilot was revealed to the 16th Guards Fighter Regiment during a brief period of the intense Kuban air campaign. He was a master of poetry, a remarkable public reader, and a tactful man who possessed a wonderful sense of humor. Veterans recall how he literally made up different stories as he went along and deftly connected them to a given situation or the conversation of the moment. He was particularly adept at recounting the details of a just-completed battle. Minutes after landing he would assemble alongside his P-39 the maintenance personnel who were not involved in servicing other aircraft. Climbing out of the cockpit, Vadim would step out onto the wing, straighten himself up to his full height, and laconically recount the course of the engagement. He was normally silent or modest about himself and his own role. He mostly talked about his comrades who had accompanied him in the mission.

Maria Pokryshkina recalled one conversation with Fadeev shortly after she had married Aleksandr Pokryshkin. Vadim and Aleksandr, both squadron commanders, were great friends. Maria, glancing at the powerful figure of this "second Ivanovich" [his patronymic was the same as Aleksandr Pokryshkin's], asked how such a tall person as he managed to stuff himself into the cockpit of a P-39. He smiled and replied, "Maria, have you ever seen a folding meter stick?[3] In the cockpit of the aircraft I bend around the floor, and then I can get my full length inside."

This extemporaneous response expressed all that was Fadeev: humor, improvisation, and never a lack for words. Thirty years later, Georgiy Golubev wrote the following about Fadeev. "The image of this remarkable pilot, of the great spirit of this man with the thick bushy beard on a handsome, tough face, often arises in my conscious vision. All of his external characteristics not only made him attractive but also created an atmosphere of confidence around him. He was the favorite of the entire squadron and those who had the privilege of meeting him quickly came to respect him. He was well known throughout the entire division."[4]

This is how Vadim Fadeev was regarded among his fellow aviators. In the air he was transformed. He became frenzied and craved combat. In every battle he fought with all of his might for a victorious conclusion. He was always querying the ground vectoring station, "Where is the enemy?" The strength of the enemy force did not concern him. At times the Guards senior lieutenant permitted himself to go "outside the envelope" in a combat sortie—he would pull a prank now and then. One time it nearly cost him his life.

On 16 April Vadim executed an unusual stunt. His group was returning from a patrol on which he had shot down two Bf-109s. All of his subordinates had made their landings. Vadim made a low-level, high-speed pass over the airfield, barely clearing the surrounding tree tops. Vadim executed a vertical climb and then began a series of complicated aerobatic maneuvers. He showed great skill in handling his aircraft. Everyone present on the ground marveled at his mastery in completing the maneuvers. But just at that moment the unimaginable happened: out from behind some clouds appeared a flight of Bf-109s. The Germans made straight for the tail of Guards Senior Lieutenant Fadeev's aircraft. Arkadiy Fedorov raced for his own Airacobra and managed to shout into the radio, "*Boroda* [Beard], Messerschmitts on your tail!"[5]

Fadeev avoided the enemy cannon tracers with a rapidly executed turn. Not pressing their luck, the Messerschmitts hurriedly disappeared into the overcast. The reckless and thoughtless conduct of his friend angered Pokryshkin to the depth of his spirit. He was literally boiling with rage. After Fadeev landed, Pokryshkin went up to him and, not restraining himself, launched into a tirade.

"What are you doing, Vadim? Are you trying to kill yourself with stupidity? You are a commander, but you have set a foolish example for your subordinates. A few more seconds and you would have been dead."

"Aleksandr, don't swear at me! I saw the Messerschmitts in time. I was just trying to provide a little entertainment."

"You are behaving like a strutting rooster; you are demonstrating to everyone unnecessary, wild recklessness. And not only today. On missions you turn off your transmitter and sing arias from operas. At times you thoughtlessly chase after individual 'bandits,' throwing the fate of the rest of your patrol group to the winds. Who needs your clowning around?"

"You're right. I give you my word as a friend, I will not do this any more!"

Promises are easier to make than keep. Unfortunately, Fadeev could not totally remake himself, although after this incident he did try with all his might to avoid rash, indiscreet mistakes.

The growing intensity of combat demanded renewed effort from each aviator and even more so from commanders of all categories. Vadim flew many missions and gave devoted attention to his subordinate pilots in the squadron. He carefully prepared them for the flight and briefed them in detail regarding the missions just flown. The results of his combat actions are evident in the following statistics: He downed a Bf-109 in the first mission of the day on 11 April 1943; on 13 April another Bf-109; and on 16 and 29 April he "doubled." Fadeev had his most productive day as a pilot on 17 April over Myskhako. He personally destroyed a Ju-87 and a Bf-109, and another Bf-109 in group combat. On 20, 21, and 24 April he downed a total of three "bandits." In eight sorties "Boroda" was credited with twelve enemy aircraft. Vadim increased his score by an additional two in early May.[6]

Battle followed battle. Each of them was differentiated not only by the area of the engagement or the strength of each side. The primary difference was in the actions of the Airacobra pilots: their daring, composure, spirit, and unflagging stubbornness and enormous desire to destroy as many Germans as possible. Duels in the sky demanded prudence, economy of effort, and no small measure of fervor from the pilots.

It was 17 April, the middle of the day. Pilots were flying their second sortie in the Myskhako area. The Airacobra pilots knew that the brave troops of the amphibious landing force were anxiously awaiting their arrival over the beachhead. The fighter crews had a moral obligation to prevent enemy bombers from reaching the ground troops' positions. Vadim Fadeev was in a strike group along with Aleksandr Pokryshkin. On this occasion the 1st Squadron commander led his eight-ship formation by a difficult but safe route over the foothills of the Caucasus Range, and then out over the Black Sea. Near the foothills they had to fly through thick overcast. Finally, off to their right, they saw Novorossiysk below, enshrouded in smoke. The Myskhako Peninsula could be identified by the frequent flashes of exploding artillery shells.

By all appearances, the situation would lead to an air battle in just several minutes. Off the coast from Anapa, coming out of the sun, were several waves of Ju-87 dive bombers loaded with fragmentation bombs for Novorossiysk and escorted by fighters. In addition, Messerschmitts and Focke-Wulfs were taking off from Anapa airfield on the left, trailing yellowish streaks of dust.

A dozen Ju-87s approached first to the Myskhako area, accompanied by nine Bf-109s. Just as in the past, so also in this engagement the Airacobras deployed to face the enemy across a broad front. This tactic brought all of his forces into the battle, leaving no portion of his formation free. At the same time it reduced everyone's ability to maneuver and marshal forces at the required time in a dangerous sector.

Appropriately in this situation, Pokryshkin commanded: "Berezhnoy, go after the 'bandits,' we will take the bombers!" And he rushed into the attack. Pokryshkin struck at the lead aircraft of the first echelon. Fadeev dove into the middle of the formation, forcing it to disperse. This was a vital success because it permitted the piecemeal destruction of the enemy force, one aircraft at a time. Having begun the attack, the fearless ace did not have to look to the sides or rear. He was covered by his wingman, Andrey Trud. Vadim attempted to expend the minimum time in any engagement. "Rapidity of actions is the first cousin of success!" was the rule that constantly guided Vadim Fadeev.

On this occasion he broke through the enemy fire screen in an almost vertical high-speed dive. It would have been practically impossible for the bombers' gunners to get a sight picture on such a target. Their only alternative was to put up a screen of barrier fire.

Seconds remained. The wings of a Ju-87 filled the rings in the gun sight and Fadeev squeezed the trigger. A red-white dagger of combined cannon and machine-gun tracers arced into the upper portion of the bomber's fuselage. The bomber faltered, dropped at the nose, and after flying forward another fifty yards fell out of the sky. Fadeev's Airacobra was already seeking altitude. He turned almost 180 degrees and made a second "eagle strike," this time on a Bf-109, which fell into the sea. By the end of this air battle, he and Aleksandr Pokryshkin had dispatched another "bandit" who was attempting to attack a Pe-2 that had fallen out of formation.[7]

Fadeev's last battle was on 5 May 1943. His front-line path in an Airacobra turned out to be painfully short. Forces of the North Caucasus *Front* had captured Krymskaya village and were continuing their offensive toward the west. The weather was unsuitable for flight operations in the morning, clearing off somewhat only in the early afternoon. Aleksandr Pokryshkin led a patrol flight that included Vadim Fadeev and his wingman, Andrey Trud. The six-ship flight headed for Amanat village in order to clear the area west of Krymskaya—the most likely route of enemy bombers.

They quickly reached the front line. For unexplained reasons, Fadeev's pair, flying to the left of Pokryshkin, began to drift farther and farther to the left. Pokryshkin was concerned. He queried Vadim by radio: "'Boroda,' this is '100,' close it up. Why are you breaking contact?"

"We're turning in!"

The rapidly changing situation prevented Fadeev from accomplishing the required maneuver to close with the patrol's main body. At this very moment several unescorted Heinkel-111s appeared from out of the overcast, and then a group of Ju-87s. They began to reform for their target run. Pokryshkin's flight dove into the column of dive bombers. In turn, several Bf-109s attacked Pokryshkin's group. The two forces circled around. The relatively low altitude of the encounter and the cloud layers prevented the Airacobra pilots from employing their normal vertical maneuver. Just the same, Pokryshkin's Airacobras managed to drive the Messerschmitts into the clouds and Grigoriy Rechkalov's pair pursued and shot down two fleeing bombers.

During this time another tragedy was unfolding farther to the east: A superior force of enemy fighters had engaged Fadeev's pair. The only witness to the dramatic event was his wingman, Andrey Trud, who gave the following account to his comrades. They had encountered and engaged eight Bf-109s around Krymskaya. The enemy managed to separate and isolate the two Airacobras from each other. Several Messerschmitts pushed Andrey away and he had no opportunity to cover his leader. Vadim was alone in a circle of enemy fighters. Both men were in a most dangerous situation. In one moment of the battle Trud heard a transmission from his squadron commander: "This is Fadeev. I am heading home!"

By the sound of the voice, Trud felt that *Boroda* was wounded. He was alarmed at Fadeev's prospects. Without hesitation, taking a left half-turn and then a dive, Andrey aligned his P-39 on one of the Messerschmitts. The enemy pilot veered off to the flank. Trud used full throttle and raced like a beam of light through a hole in the enemy formation. He took cover in the nearest overcast and then steered his Airacobra in the direction that Fadeev had taken. Trud saw an aircraft impact on the ground but could not identify it. He hurriedly searched for his pair leader, without success. Then he rejoined the flight of Guards Major Pokryshkin.[8]

Georgiy Golubev writes in his book that the Germans planned to lure the Soviet ace into a trap. They had long hunted "Boroda." They managed to catch him with a specially developed plan on 5 May. Here is Golubev's version.

Upon Fadeev's approach to the front line, the enemy sent out eight Bf-109s to meet him. A pair of Messerschmitts slipped past the nose of Fadeev's fighter at high speed. A second pair was drawn away, and the four remaining ships hung over our two aircraft.

Seeing the enemy in front of him, Fadeev went into the attack. But it took some time to close on an enemy who was moving at high speed. Having noted that Fadeev had been distracted by the bait, the four high-flying Messerschmitts launched their own attack. They fired on the Soviet fighter from a dive. Fadeev was wounded in his side by fragments of an exploding cannon shell.

The fighter's motor began to miss. He had to land. But where? All around was marsh. And the pilot was wounded.

The damaged fighter continued to lose altitude, closer and closer to the dense growths of reeds. Apparently Fadeev struck his head on the instrument panel upon landing and lost consciousness.[9]

There is no simple answer to the questions regarding the death of Vadim and his final resting place. Aleksandr Pokryshkin was inclined to believe that the waters of the Kuban marshes received Vadim into their cold embrace. Perhaps this is how, and why. Had the pilot fallen on solid ground, his family would have been able to confirm his identity by any one of a number of documents, his identification tag, his officer's identification booklet, his serial-numbered medals (Fadeev was wearing the Order of Lenin and two Red Banners on his fatigues), and his Party card, which he carried in his inside breast pocket.[10] Finally, the Airacobra held factory and tail markings. Something from this multitude of indicators would have been preserved. Local inhabitants would have found them and reported their finds to responsible authorities. But this information was never forthcoming. The regiment and division command made several vain attempts to investigate Fadeev's fate.

The men of his squadron waited a long time for Vadim's return. It became clear that he had perished. The assertion that Fadeev is buried in the central park of the settlement Kievskoye of Krymskiy Rayon, Krasnodar Kray, is no more than wishful thinking.[11] Yes, there is a grave marker at that location, but in it rest the remains of someone else, not Vadim Fadeev. Perhaps someday his descendants will find the remains of the intrepid hero and his last aircraft.

I must present the words of the one person who knew Fadeev better than anyone else, his friend Aleksandr Pokryshkin. Here is what he wrote regarding the causes of the untimely death of the commander, 2d Squadron.

It cannot be considered simply a random incident. Vadim was an experienced pilot, a mature aerial warrior. Sometimes he displayed excessive self-confidence and did not give due respect to the enemy. I pointed out these deficiencies to him, but in his youth he did not always listen to my advice. At times he was ruled by spontaneous impulses. Thus it was on his last flight.

Did he, as a squadron commander, decide that he had the right to complete independence in the air? I do not know. But what happened happened. Vadim fought like a hero in his last battle. Even here, though, it seems to me that he underrated the enemy when he accepted engagement with twelve Messerschmitts. He did not even report to us by radio that he had run into trouble. I do not have the slightest desire to throw any shadow over the bright image of Vadim Fadeev. But courage in battle should always be combined with sober calculation and discipline.[12]

The personnel of 16th Guards and the division's other regiments were shaken by the death of this courageous ace, carefree fellow loved by all, one of the most productive and fearless Airacobra pilots. He made a significant contribution to the final victory.

The Motherland highly valued the feat of one of her sons. On 24 May 1943, by order of the Presidium of the USSR Supreme Soviet, Guards Captain Vadim Ivanovich Fadeev was awarded the rank Hero of the Soviet Union posthumously for exemplary execution of combat missions of the command and for bravery and heroism displayed at the front.

His comrades remember him. A number of memoirs contain references to him. His family name, along with those of other Heroes of the Soviet Union, is inscribed in gold letters in the Hall of Heroes of the Kiev memorial complex of the Ukraine National Museum of the History of the Great Patriotic War and on the tablets of the Moscow memorial to victory in the Great Patriotic War.[13]

Pass the Experience Along

"Study your own and the enemy's combat experience and incorporate it into your daily practice!" This golden rule was faithfully observed in the 216th Fighter Division and 4th Air Army. Without a reasoned approach to the issue at the front, it would have been impossible to count on success in one-on-one combat with a powerful enemy. "Not only know the methods of combat that have been found to be effective yourself but also teach them to your comrades!"[1] This was a common practice that was accomplished to improve everyone's capabilities. It also guaranteed final victory with fewer losses.

Lieutenant Colonel Ibragim Dzusov conducted an expansive conference with the air crew and maintenance personnel of 16th Guards and 45th Fighter Regiments at the division headquarters on 17 April 1943.[2] Aviators who had been in aerial engagements and had personal experience in the destruction of enemy fighters and bombers gave presentations at this conference. They discussed the successful employment of new tactical methods used by pairs and groups.

Dmitriy Glinka gave a presentation:

Against a multitiered formation of enemy aircraft we have countered with a combat formation that is even more echeloned by altitude. This has permitted us to be masters of the sky on practically every mission sortie. Sudden, rapid strikes by Airacobras against Bf-109s and Ju-87s from above have always yielded excellent results.

On 10 March alone, groups from 45th Regiment (led by Senior Lieutenants Mikhail Petrov and Aleksey Poddubskiy) shot down eight enemy fighters in three fierce aerial battles. Petrov shot down two bombers. It is possible to "cut up" a bomber with cannon and machine-gun fire from behind and below. This is one of their dead spaces. After you build up speed in a dive, close with the target selected for destruction and fill your sight with its belly. The Airacobra pilots of 16th Regiment—Ivan Olefirenko, Nikolay Starchikov, Arkadiy Fedorov, and Pavel Eremin—have often used this effective method.

Aleksandr Pokryshkin also presented at this conference.

We have the means to beat the enemy. We have received aircraft with powerful armaments. We have thought much and worked hard regarding fighter tactics: the structure of our combat formation (the "bookshelf"); a new method of patrolling over the front line ("pendulum" passing through space); and the sudden rapid attack from above ("eagle strike"). These methods have not come about by chance. We suffered unjustified losses fighting by the old method. A feat requires a combination of daring and thought, mastery and search. The first combat test of our new ideas in aerial combat are giving us hope. In a recent battle our group (two pairs of Airacobras) skillfully engaged nine Messerschmitts. We shot down the enemy leader in the initial "eagle strike." The upper pair sent a second Bf-109 to the ground. Yet another aircraft downed by Grigoriy Rechkalov considerably demoralized the remaining six enemy pilots. Diving steeply, the Germans flew away to the west.

Chief Marshal of Aviation Konstantin Vershinin, the former commander of 4th Air Army, recalls in his memoirs, "These meetings (at divisions and in the army) were not conducted without heated arguments. Sometimes one or another method had been subjected to confirmation in the air. In the end, we worked out a common opinion regarding this, and many other, issues. We adopted many positive recommendations that after generalization were issued as orders, and we were guided by these orders in all aviation formations."[3]

I must also mention one good and stable tradition. Pilots and leadership personnel from fighter units based nearby were reciprocally invited to these conferences to exchange experience. This practice helped improve the combat effectiveness of the commanders and air crews of neighboring units. The new methods of fighter tactics developed in separate units became available to many other units in a short period of time. This played a significant role in the battle for air supremacy over the Kuban.

Another effective form of transferring experience to pilots arriving at the front was to send a group of pilots from 216th Fighter Division, along with their equipment and support, to host airfields for brief periods of time. The instructors in this group organized exercises with the local unit in the tactics of our own and enemy fighters, relying heavily on the experience of recently fought air battles. Then they conducted training air battles in the area of the base. Our experienced pilots led patrols during sorties to accomplish assigned missions.

For example, the 3d Fighter Corps arrived in the Kuban in early April 1943. On instructions of the commander of 4th Air Army, the 216th Fighter Division sent a group of experienced pilots to this formation. These pilots spent five days familiarizing the new air crews with the peculiarities of fighter operations on the Taman Peninsula. During this time they participated in several combat sorties as flight leaders. Among these "instructor" pilots were ace brothers Boris and Dmitriy Glinka from 45th Fighter Regiment, who had thirty destroyed enemy aircraft between them by this time.[4]

The command and staff of 4th Air Army undertook an enormous effort in March and April to generalize and convey combat experience to the air crews. During this period of time all aviation units were issued detailed orders regarding the most promising tactical methods and combat formations for fighters, the improvement of cooperation within pairs, the preservation of altitude superiority, maximum employment of vertical maneuver in aerial combat, and the necessity of constantly searching for the enemy and skillfully engaging him in combat.

Visits were organized for the division and regiment commanders to the main ground vectoring station. Here they had a full opportunity to observe their subordinate pilots in combat with the enemy and to take note of the positive and negative aspects of their actions.

Along with this, great attention was devoted to publicizing the heroic feats of pilots of all branches of aviation through army and division newspapers. The army newspaper *Krylya Rodiny* [Wings of the motherland] actively spread word of Aleksandr Pokryshkin's air combat tactics, especially during the period of the Kuban battles. Pokryshkin himself appeared in the pages of these newspapers. The celebrated ace wrote more about his comrades and less about himself, but he had a lot to write about: 1st Squadron commander had shot down twenty-five enemy aircraft in the Kuban.

A large-scale aerial battle between the two sides for air superiority was unleashed over the Taman Peninsula in the second half of April. During this time the central army newspaper *Krasnaya Zvezda* [Red star] began the publication of excerpts about air battles with enemy fighters on the southern wing of the Soviet–German front.

The distribution of aviators' positive experience was not limited to the forms described above. The 16th Fighter Regiment began to print brochures, leaflets, and posters about the masters of air battles. The pilots attentively studied the habits of the best "winged knights" of the actively engaged formations and took them to heart.

The low-level press—combat leaflets—played a large role in imparting the experience of recent combat to air crews. These leaflets, with titles like "Soldier's Truth" and "Forward Area Leaflet," were handed out on flight lines, in command posts, and in the dugouts for air crews and maintenance personnel, usually once or twice a day.[5] Each of these leaflets succinctly described a feat of this or that pilot, mechanic, or other specialists in the service units. The "secret" of how the success was achieved was revealed: in the work of a maintenance specialist on the ground or a pilot in the air; how the pilot attacked and shot down an enemy, from what range, using what angle of attack, and where the rounds were aimed. The leaflets passed these "golden nuggets" of victories gained along to young pilots and taught them the tactics for destroying the enemy.

There was one more method of sharing experience during this period—the postflight discussion of the actions by the group and pairs, during which a detailed analysis was made of the positive and negative aspects of the flight just completed. Pilots critiqued their own and their comrades' actions. Available pilots who did not participate in the sortie were required to attend these discussions. This permitted all the pilots to learn constantly from the experience of others.

Combat Successes and Losses

On 29 April forces of the North Caucasus *Front* began breaking through the enemy defenses in the area of Krymskaya. The enemy resisted fiercely, hanging on to each defensible hill and position. He realized he was quickly losing ground. Soviet units and formations were turning the war around. After Stalingrad they had begun to drive and were continuing, albeit slowly, to push the enemy to the west. And the Germans had ceased to be the masters in the sky. They were exerting desperate efforts in order to maintain superiority over the territory of the battles that were now breaking out in the Kuban.

The intensity of air combat remained quite high before 10 May. Having received new aircraft, the 45th Fighter Regiment was undergoing extensive training in preparation for upcoming actions. The 16th Guards Regiment, as before, was fulfilling the basic mission for covering the attacking Soviet ground forces. It was a difficult task, both for the ground units and for the pilots. The spring weather was problematic. Rain quickly submerged the dirt airstrips in mud, and the wet and overused roads complicated the transport of everything that was required to support combat fighter operations.[1]

Over the course of May the division's regiments displaced to three airfields: 16th Guards and 45th Regiments to Popovicheskaya; 42d Regiment to Krasnoarmeyskaya, and 57th Regiment to Slavyanskaya. The 16th Guards and 57th Regiments had 30 days of flying weather, 45th Regiment 14.5 days, and 42d Regiment 20 days. The average daily number of operational aircraft in these regiments was eighteen P-39s, twelve Spitfires, seventeen P-39s, and twenty-six Yak-1s, respectively. The average flight hours for the month per operational aircraft was 29.5 in the 16th Guards, 21.1 in the 42d Regiment, 14.5 in the 45th Regiment, and 36.1 in the 57th Regiment. This low indicator was explained by the reduced combat readiness of air crews (wounding of pilots, a spring malaria outbreak, and other illnesses).[2]

At the end of April and for the entire month of May, the Airacobra pilots of 16th Regiment covered the combat formations of 56th and 37th Combined Arms Armies in the areas of Abinskaya, Krymskaya, Lower Grachevskaya, Upper Adegam, and Krasnaya Pobeda villages. Accomplishing their assigned missions, the division's units flew 1,777 aircraft sorties in May and participated in 156 aerial battles, of which 30 were with large groups of fighters and bombers.

Our losses in the division, shot down in aerial engagements, were twenty-seven aircraft; an additional nine did not return from combat missions; and one was lost to other causes, a total of thirty-seven aircraft. Personnel losses in 16th Guards were six pilots shot down in aerial battles and one not returned from a combat mission; in 45th Regiment, two and one, respectively. Each of these regiments also lost a pilot in an aircraft crash.[3]

During their time at the front (45th Regiment—three months, 16th Guards—two months), the time of peak losses of aircraft and personnel, especially experienced pilots, was May. There were a number of objective and subjective factors for this.

The fierce daytime clashes of fighters and night attacks of our bombers on enemy airfields had inflicted significant losses. As we now know, the German command at this time was secretly preparing an operation in the Kursk and Orel region, the goal of which was to take revenge for the defeat of their forces at Stalingrad. The enemy's Taman grouping, in addition to earlier assigned missions, in the operational plan was to provide reliable cover of the flank and rear of attacking forces during the Kursk battle.

After the liberation of Krymskaya on 5 May, our forces were in heavy fighting for the heights west of the city for another week. The capture of this area and subsequent advance into the enemy's dispositions brought the advancing formations into the rear of his defenses and opened a direct route to Novorossiysk. The enemy fought with the stubbornness of the doomed, and this indeed was now his tragic fate. The hour of reckoning had come! The enemy hurled significant reserves to this sector of the front and concentrated a large aviation grouping here. The aerial engagements were fierce. Our fighter pilots selflessly flew into battle with a numerically superior enemy. They attempted, at any cost, to prevent enemy bombing of our ground forces. Squadron commander Vadim Fadeev and flight commanders Dmitriy Koval and Mikhail Sutyrin ultimately died brave deaths in these air battles. Both Fadeev and Koval were awarded the rank Hero of the Soviet Union posthumously.

Battle after battle, their intensity did not subside. The missions assigned to the aviators were significant and the means to accomplish them were limited. The division had thirty-four serviceable Airacobras at the beginning of May.[4]

Early in the morning, 8 May. A flight of four aircraft from 1st Squadron of 16th Guards Fighter Regiment sortied on a mission. The leader of this flight was Aleksandr Pokryshkin. Their mission was to provide air cover over the area southwest of Krymskaya village. The "ground pounders" were advancing step by step there in heavy fighting, with the enemy's resistance increasing each hour. The enemy committed fresh reserves to battle. "Enemy number two"—the weather—was merciless to our infantry and tanks. Forces could not maneuver or deploy along muddy, broken-down dirt roads and rain-soaked fields. Soldiers and officers sank up to their hips and tanks up to their turrets in mud.

The steppe is predominately flat, with almost a total lack of terrain relief in which to seek camouflage. Ju-87s escorted by considerable numbers of Messerschmitts at times came down out of the low-hanging clouds to drop their high-explosive bombs and at other times dove from higher altitude. Right behind them poured Major Aleksandr Pokryshkin's group of Airacobras.

At this early hour the sky was not yet blue, the early morning sun creating a variety of hues in the overcast. In connection with this meteorological condition, the enemy came in at a significant altitude. The P-39s had to do the same. It was inevitable that the clash between the two forces would be at the upper limits of the Airacobras' flight envelope.

The patrol reached Krymskaya. Dense clouds covered a broad expanse of sky. To go around these clouds would entail a great expenditure of time (by aviators' standards) and would take the fighters too distant from their assigned coverage zone. Pokryshkin made the decision to fly through the cloud cover. His wingman, Guards Junior Lieutenant Vladimir Stepanov, lacked experience flying in such difficult weather conditions. He became separated from the group and subsequently got lost in the boundless sky. Searching for him would have been like looking for a needle in a haystack. The squadron commander [Pokryshkin] ordered Stepanov to return to base, while he remained without the direct coverage that a wingman provided. This was a dangerous predicament for the flight leader. Only the most experienced pilot, who was confident of his own strength and experience and knew his flying machine well, could have made this decision. Pokryshkin later regretted that he had taken such a young pilot as his wingman on so dangerous a mission. Three aircraft now remained.

Ground vectoring station "Pelican" reported the approach of bombers toward the front line in a sector to the west of Pokryshkin's small patrol, closing rapidly. There was insufficient time to gain altitude for an "eagle strike." The dense layer of clouds at altitude would further complicate such a maneuver. In this situation the highest level of vigilance was required from each individual pilot and the group as a whole. In the cabins of these three Airacobras sat the battle-tested pilots Aleksandr Pokryshkin, Dmitriy Koval, and Mikhail Sutyrin.

It must be acknowledged that the enemy enjoyed the advantage over the handful of Airacobra pilots in several respects: he had superiority in strength; on this particular morning the enemy maintained control of a broad expanse of sky; to give them their due, the enemy pilots were fighting stubbornly and skillfully, reflecting the experience of their recent combat. It must also be recognized that special aviation units had been brought to the Kuban to destroy our Airacobras, Kittyhawks, and Spitfires.

The developing situation demanded one thing—rapid and decisive action before the enemy bombers crossed the front line. At the moment, the enemy fighter escort was nowhere in sight. Pokryshkin understood all these factors well. To win the next several minutes from the enemy was no small gift. The group leader led his subordinates on a direct closing course with the enemy formation. He knew that the enemy would seek to avoid a frontal attack. The three Airacobras burst into a formation of Ju-88s. The 1st Squadron commander shot down the lead aircraft with a long burst of cannon and machine-gun fire. This was his normal practice and he taught it to his subordinates. The Airacobras rocketed through the dense column of enemy bombers at maximum speed.

The sudden attack of the Airacobras and the downing of the lead enemy aircraft yielded immediate results. The German bomber crews opened their bomb doors and began to drop their high explosive cargo. The formation of bombers dispersed. Chaos reigned in the air as the bombers turned back toward the west in a disorganized manner, with the three P-39s following in hot pursuit. Pokryshkin and Sutyrin each shot down another Ju-88. The Airacobras climbed for altitude and cloud cover but instead ran into another formation of bombers, also unescorted. The enemy was flying over its own positions, and his fighters, in all probability, were circling around somewhere closer to the front line, awaiting the bombers' arrival.

Koval fell like a stone on the enemy aircraft on the formation's right flank, and Pokryshkin attacked the left machine. Two burning "flares" disappeared into the dense, low overcast. Dmitriy Koval shot up the tail of a bomber at close range from above and behind. The aircraft immediately dropped one wing and continued its flight for several seconds. Then, breaking up into pieces, it rapidly fell out of sight. While pulling away from this attack, Dmitriy's Airacobra fell under the combined fires of two bombers. His motor began to misfire.

In just a few moments the situation in the engagement zone had gone from complicated to almost impossible. Six Messerschmitts suddenly appeared and pounced on Koval's "wounded" P-39. They fired into it at point-blank range. His comrades could give him no cover. The remaining pair of P-39s had to disengage quickly if they wanted to survive. The ratio of forces was unequal and they were running low on both fuel and ammunition. Pokryshkin issued the command to break contact and the two Airacobras immediately sought cover in the thick clouds. They took a compass heading back to their airfield.

As one who knows about combat from personal experience, even now I admire the rapidity of the aviators' reaction to this extremely difficult situation. The high speed—at times super high speed—of aerial engagements demands literally lightning-fast, precise reactions to a situation by a fighter pilot. The aircraft's velocity alone necessitates at the very least that a pilot think at twice normal speed. There is no place for slow thinkers in aviation, the less so in fighter aviation.

Pokryshkin and Sutyrin arrived safely at Popovicheskaya airfield. Vladimir Stepanov had landed here, undamaged, considerably earlier. And so, during the first week of May the 1st Squadron lost two of its most experienced air warriors, Vadim Fadeev and Dmitriy Koval (130 combat sorties, 29 air battles, 11 personal and 3 shared victories), both Heroes of the Soviet Union. This was a terrible, irreplaceable loss.

After 10 May the offensive of formations of the North Caucasus *Front* was halted. Relative calm ruled in the air. Following established tradition, the air crews studied the lessons of their most recent battles. The regiment commander, Lieutenant Colonel Nikolay Isaev, spoke at a meeting of pilots. He cited the basic numbers: how many sorties and hours were flown; the number of aerial engagements and enemy aircraft shot down; and our own losses. He did not conduct an in-depth analysis of the changing situation in the skies of the Kuban, but it had changed considerably: our successful application of new tactical methods; an enemy that operated in large fighter groups that attacked in a frenzy, aiming their primary strike at the high-speed, well-armed Airacobras; and the continuous attempts to use the advantage of altitude. Every day it was becoming more difficult to shoot down Messerschmitts.

Aleksandr Pokryshkin gave a presentation. His words were a reflection of his comrades' deeply felt pain: "The cause of our pilot losses in April and early May battles was patrolling in small groups (four, at best six aircraft). We were opposed by large groups of enemy bombers with heavy Messerschmitt escort."

Pokryshkin's statement was no revelation. More than once in the recent past the 1st Squadron commander had attempted to convince the regiment commander that they could no longer fight in this manner. The stock response was, "Obey your orders!" Of course, they were obeyed, but at what cost? A man who had not participated in aerial combat, who had not even flown an airplane for a long time, was giving orders that affected men's lives. He was shortly thereafter relieved of command of this celebrated fighter regiment. For the good of everyone, it should have happened much sooner.

"Despite the enemy superiority in numbers, the Airacobra pilots have selflessly thrown themselves into the attack. We have attempted, frequently sacrificing ourselves, to disrupt the bombing of our 'ground pounders.' This is the true reason for our great losses!" Pokryshkin continued boldly. "The only remedy is to go out on missions in two or three six-ship or eight-ship groups."

"We have to take the availability of aircraft into consideration," noted Isaev.

"The sortie load on air crews can be increased. The men are prepared for this. Losses in fights with the enemy cannot be totally avoided. But I am convinced that by using more powerful groups we can reduce these losses."

Several accidents occurred during the period when 45th Fighter Regiment was reconstituting its equipment and training new personnel for upcoming combat activity. Airacobras were destroyed and pilots killed.

P-39s with type-83 and -85 Allison engines were arriving to equip the squadrons of this regiment.[5] The majority of them did not run smoothly during the transition from high rpms to low rpms. The aircraft were difficult to recover from a spin. According to the conclusion of a division technical commission, these two deficiencies were the principal cause of a number of accidents.

On 11 May at 1320, Junior Lieutenant Dmitriy Korovin was executing an aerobatic maneuver in the training zone at an altitude of 16,400 feet. His aircraft went into a flat spin from a deep left turn and spun all the way to ground impact. The command post, which had the pilot under visual observation, gave the command to bail out several times. The aircraft's initial altitude made this entirely possible. However, Dmitriy did not abandon the Airacobra's cabin. In all probability he was trying to save the aircraft. By this time he had flown 112 combat sorties and fought in four aerial engagements, in which he had shot down three enemy aircraft. He was a successful combat pilot. The Airacobra fell not far from the airfield. The aircraft was destroyed and Korovin was killed.[6]

There was another accident and aircraft lost on 12 May. Junior Lieutenant Nikolay Kudrya was conducting a training flight in the local area. During the accomplishment of a sequential maneuver a gauge indicated that the engine was overheated to 120°C. The pilot brought his aircraft in for a landing. During his approach he committed an annoying and unforgivable mistake—he lowered his landing gear too late and flared the aircraft too early, losing speed. All these factors taken together led to a situation wherein the Airacobra fell to three points of contact from a height of ten feet and then flipped over. The impact turned the aircraft into a pile of scrap metal. The pilot was extracted from the aircraft with several moderate injuries. He was at fault in the accident.

A careful analysis was conducted with the air crews after this incident, and then an inventory was made of the equipment. It was determined that the guilty party should pay for the destroyed or damaged aircraft. A special commission established the magnitude of the inflicted losses and the sum of money required for compensation. Legal proceedings were opened in other cases. Nikolay Kudrya did not have to pay for his blunders. He had fifty-five combat sorties, had participated in twenty-six aerial engagements, had destroyed nine enemy aircraft, and had 1 shared victory. This pilot perished in a subsequent dogfight with the enemy on 26 May.

There was another unfortunate incident involving an Airacobra on 26 May. This time it was the young pilot Junior Lieutenant Nikolay Ostrovskiy and the cause was lack of discipline. Here is what happened. Ostrovskiy developed too much speed while taxiing his aircraft from the weapons boresighting stand to its parking spot. He did not react in a timely manner to the mechanic's signal, who was warning the pilot of danger. The P-39 burrowed into the earthen wall of the revetment. The aircraft received serious damage to the propeller blades, along with the main gear and the nose wheel strut.

In accordance with wartime laws, Ostrovskiy could have been subject to severe punishment for disabling a piece of combat equipment, but fate managed to reschedule his final reckoning. Ostrovskiy had arrived in 16th Guards Fighter Regiment in the fall of 1942 after completion of pilot training school. His flight training, as a check ride demonstrated, was not exceptional. Additional training was begun for the inexperienced pilot. He was giving his full effort to the task.

The merciless war dealt a terrible blow to the young officer. Pokryshkin came upon Ostrovskiy with a letter in his hands, tears streaming down his face. When questioned by the squadron commander, Ostrovskiy, not hiding his tears, handed Pokryshkin the correspondence. It informed him that Ostrovskiy's entire family—father, mother, brothers, and sister, who had remained in occupied territory— had been shot by the Germans for contacts with partisans.

The great tragedy that had befallen his subordinate and comrade touched Pokryshkin. "Fascist beasts! The hour will come when we will settle all accounts with them!"

On 15 April Ostrovskiy sortied on a mission as a wingman. The engagement that followed took a wrong turn. He found himself alone against a pair of experienced German "hunters." They shot him down in a difficult, lopsided battle. Fortunately, he landed successfully. He was ordered to take three days of rest, but he was restless and wanted to get back into the fighting. He persistently requested permission to be put back on the schedule.

On 17 April Pokryshkin took Ostrovskiy on patrol as wingman in his own pair. They had to provide cover over the Myskhako area. On the way to the mission area the engine of Ostrovskiy's Airacobra began to knock, then smoke. It could start on fire at any moment, and, in fact, it already had. Only after a second stern order from his pair leader did the pilot turn back to the airfield. On the way he was ambushed by "hunters."

The details of his death became known on the following day, from local inhabitants who witnessed the unfolding drama. Two Bf-109s ambushed Ostrovskiy over Kubanskaya, attacking him and setting his aircraft on fire. Nikolay abandoned the burning Airacobra and deployed his parachute. The Germans shot him under canopy.

The news stunned the pilots of 1st Squadron. The commander—Pokryshkin—took it especially hard. His inexperienced subordinate had died tragically before he had had the opportunity to avenge the deaths of his parents and siblings. Pokryshkin made a promise to himself: henceforth he would always shoot enemy pilots under parachutes. Those beasts should not expect any mercy!

On 4 May the 104th Guards Fighter Regiment was assigned to the 216th Fighter Division. From this day until the end of the Great Patriotic War the division consisted of three base units: 16th, 100th, and 104th Guards Fighter Regiments.

The 104th Guards Fighter Regiment had been at a rear-area airfield for two months and had not participated in combat actions. Its air crews were undergoing intense training. Some twenty-five pilots were trained for combat in the Airacobra during this time, and sixteen of them were transferred to the 16th Guards Fighter Regiment.

On 6 July the 104th Guards Fighter Regiment had nine pilots who were fully qualified in the Airacobra and sixteen who were undergoing training in the UTI-4 and preparing for subsequent instruction in the P-39.[7] The process of preparing aviators for flying fighters with which they were unfamiliar was prolonged and required considerable effort by the trainees and expenditure of equipment.

In mid-May the forces of the North Caucasus *Front* began preparation for breaking through the Blue Line.[8] The intensity of combat actions in the air weakened. Air raids by both sides became episodic. As a rule, sorties were flown by small groups, and fighters engaged in dogfights on a sporadic basis. One of these engagements deserves mention as an example of the failure to observe established regulations and thoroughly developed practices of cooperation in combat. It was an example of the grandstanding efforts by some pilots to increase their personal score of downed enemy aircraft. In doing this, they forgot to accomplish their functional obligations and placed their comrades' lives in jeopardy.

It was 22 May. Pokryshkin had been instructed to report immediately to the regimental command post. Lieutenant Colonel Isaev assigned a mission to sortie immediately in a six-ship formation to Krymskaya.

"Rechkalov will lead the second pair of your group, and Lukyanov the third," he said.

Pokryshkin responded, "Comrade commander, this is a combined team of officers who are equal in duty position. Permit us to sortie in a coordinated group! It will be easier to accomplish this mission!"[9]

"There is a heavy cloud cover over Krymskaya. 'Tiger' [the ground vectoring station] ordered us immediately to send out the most experienced pilots. Don't argue with me. Take off as soon as possible!" Isaev had difficulty understanding the argument of his 1st Squadron commander, his misgivings regarding the success of the combat mission. Pokryshkin argued unsuccessfully with the nonflying commander and then followed orders.

The group was on the approaches to Kievskaya village. Two Bf-109s darted out of the overcast from the right. Without informing the leader [Pokryshkin], Rechkalov took off after them, attracting Lukyanov's pair in the process. Lukyanov and his wingman occupied the upper covering tier of the "bookshelf" combat formation. The "bookshelf" instantly fell apart. Someone's desire to increase his personal score of shot-down enemy aircraft had taken the upper hand, at the expense of the common cause. Pokryshkin had been correct in his doubts. Now he was flying into the enemy's rear accompanied only by his wingman Petr Tabachenko. They would face incredible danger.

Aleksandr Pokryshkin spotted nine Messerschmitts flying above them and warned his wingman. Moments later two of these Bf-109s suddenly attached themselves to Pokryshkin's tail. Pokryshkin and

Tabachenko turned 180 degrees and rushed into a head-on attack. The Germans turned in the opposite direction. The wingman "bandit" was slow in his maneuver and presented his belly to the 1st Squadron commander's sight. A short and furious burst sent the Messerschmitt to the ground trailing smoke and flames.

Pokryshkin and his wingman chased after the remaining Bf-109, but he was lucky. Tabachenko spotted four supporting enemy fighters to the right and above his pair. He voiced an alarm over the radio. The pair executed a combat turn to face the enemy in another frontal attack. The enemy flashed by, gaining altitude. Possessing numerical superiority, he did not shy away from this somewhat risky type of maneuver. In all probability, the enemy pilots hoped moments later to press the Airacobras into their favorite "pincers."

Pokryshkin's pair beat off the attacks of enemy groups coming at them from various directions for not less than ten minutes. The Airacobra pilots were twisting and turning like squirrels in a cage. Rechkalov's four aircraft had not made an appearance, and now they were needed badly.

The fact that the Luftwaffe pilots were acting somewhat timidly saved the Russian pilots. In all probability, the decisive attack and downing of one of their Bf-109s had had a psychological effect on them, but this circumstance did not prevail for long. A pair of Focke-Wulf 190s suddenly appeared. Now it was ten against two, an unbelievable and unsustainable force ratio. The Focke-Wulfs opened fire from a range of approximately 2,200 yards, evidently as a warning. The wingman of the German pair dived under Pokryshkin's Airacobra. Pokryshkin ordered his own wingman, Tabachenko, to hold his position.

But Tabachenko was wounded and needed to disengage in order to return to his airfield. One could not imagine a worse predicament. Pokryshkin considered several options. It would be dangerous to escort Petr—the entire flock of "buzzards" would rush in pursuit of them. There would be no cover from their destructive fires. Pokryshkin made an extremely courageous decision, to engage the enemy and tie him down in battle. In this way he could best ensure the safe return of his wingman to base.

Pokryshkin ordered Tabachenko to head for an airfield at Krasnodar while he provided cover. Never in battle, before or after this occasion, did Pokryshkin have to execute so many simple and complex maneuvers, to fly with such great skill as he dodged countless tracer streams. The 1st Squadron commander, continuing to fight off enemy attacks, vigilantly tracked the enemy group, prepared at any moment to engage those who attempted to pursue Petr Tabachenko.

Only when he received by radio the news that his wingman was approaching Krasnodar did Pokryshkin make a sharp turn and, diving toward the earth, disengage from the battle. He left the Germans looking like fools. An easy prey that was in their hands, so to speak, had suddenly disappeared. Pokryshkin had defeated them not with force but with ability.

After landing, Pokryshkin had a stern and objective conversation with Rechkalov. The squadron commander did not accept any excuses for his reckless behavior in the recent flight. Pokryshkin had a similar conversation with Lukyanov, the other pair leader, later in the day.

On 28 May, eight Airacobras of 45th Regiment fought another battle with ten Messerschmitts and two Focke-Wulfs that was quite instructive in many respects. The Airacobras' combat mission was to provide cover to ground units in the area of Plavnevskaya, Kievskaya, and Tambulovskaya villages. The mission altitude was 13,125 feet in partly cloudy skies.

The group consisted of Major Fedor Telegin (65 missions, 13 engagements, 3 victories), Captains Dmitriy Glinka (167, 53, 23) and Oleg Raskidnoy (2, 1, 0); Senior Lieutenant Ivan Svinarenko (95, 17, 1); Junior Lieutenants Konstantin Panov (10, 4, 1), Nikolay Kudrya (53, 27, 10), Aleksandr Molchanov (25, 1, 0); and Lieutenant Nikolay Lavitskiy (189, 69, 17). It was of some note that more than half of the patrol consisted of experienced air warriors (Glinka, Telegin, Svinarenko, Lavitskiy, Kudrya), two of whom were already Heroes of the Soviet Union (Glinka and Kudrya). The group leader was Dmitriy Glinka.

Glinka spent a day carefully preparing the group that had been designated for the next mission sortie. This was necessitated by the fact that these crews had not flown a combat sortie for some time while the regiment was reconstituting in personnel and aircraft. Serious attention was devoted to the selection of pairs: Telegin–Svinarenko, Glinka–Raskidnoy, Kudrya–Molchanov, and Lavitskiy–Panov. The leader in each pair was the pilot who had a requisite number of combat sorties, experienced aerial engagements, and destroyed enemy aircraft. Major Fedor Telegin had the least kills among the pair leaders at three. The three wingmen on the whole were young pilots who had recently arrived at the front after completing aviation academies and schools.

Glinka constructed the combat formation in accordance with all the parameters of the "formula of terror"—echeloned by altitude ("book-shelf"). The covering pair of Telegin and Svinarenko was at the upper tier (13,100 feet). Below them at 8,200 and 6,550 feet were Glinka–Raskidnoy and Kudrya–Molchanov, respectively. The two lower pairs of P-39s were the primary flight of the combat formation, its active strike segment. The remaining two pilots were focused on the same objective. He who maintained the altitude advantage and attacked the enemy energetically could count on success.

The pair of Lavitskiy and Panov was the reserve force. Maneuvering both horizontally and vertically, this pair could, when necessary, rapidly increase the strength on the threatened axis or sector (on command from Dmitriy Glinka or by decision of Nikolay Lavitskiy).

Uninterrupted radio communications permitted all elements of the combat formation to join together whenever the situation required. The radio was an important weapon of victory over the enemy. Glinka demanded the strictest observance of radio discipline in the air from his subordinate pilots.

The variable southern spring weather was bringing in frequent dense or broken clouds, creating favorable conditions for the concealment of the aircraft of both sides. Consequently, a sudden attack from behind clouds was quite likely, followed by rapid departure to cloud cover after the strike. All this demanded the highest level of continuous vigilance from each participant in the air battle.

The methods of the combat action were worked out in detail. Upon observation of the enemy, the primary reaction was to immediately impose our will on him—combat in the vertical plane. The Germans avoided this whenever possible. Irrespective of the size of the enemy group, the Soviet pilots would attack it without any hesitation. Pilots had to launch frontal attacks skillfully, taking into consideration the enemy's actions. The powerful cannon and machine-gun fire of the Airacobra was dangerous to any type of German aircraft.

Mutual assistance in an aerial engagement is the key to overall success, maximum preservation of participants' lives, and protection of the aircraft. Careful preliminary preparation for the execution of an upcoming mission was repaid with interest. This does not mean that, based on the specifically developing situation in the zone of confrontation with the enemy, necessary changes were not introduced in the construction of the combat formation or the tactics of the group as a whole and of each pair individually.

The patrolling Airacobras encountered the enemy above Plavnevskaya village. The multitiered construction of Glinka's group forced the Germans to disperse their own aircraft by altitude. The first, very important component of the intended plan had been executed. The enemy had submitted to our will by altering his combat formation from a tight group into a vertically dispersed group. The pairs of Telegin, Glinka, and Kudrya immediately sprang into action. Lavitskiy and his wingman orbited off to the flank, intently following the course of the battle by the group's main forces, prepared to come to the aid of their comrades at the required moment.

Major Telegin's pair attacked two Bf-109s on a converging course at an altitude of 13,125 feet. The enemy fighters broke off, attempting to climb away from our fighters. Telegin and Svinarenko hurriedly zoomed upward. After a left turn they closed with and fired in salvo at the same enemy pair. Telegin's burst was the more precise. A Messerschmitt, oscillating back and forth from wing to wing, turned over on its back and disappeared into a lower cloud layer, smoking heavily. The second "bandit" rushed to the flank and departed to the west in a dive.

At this time Glinka and Raskidnoy, concealed in clouds at 8,200 feet, with a bump in altitude and a left turn launched a frontal attack on a pair of Messerschmitts that had suddenly appeared out of a dense white cloud. Glinka set the wingman on fire and then led his own pair yet higher. They noted that two Bf-109s were diving on Kudrya's pair from above and behind. A rapid left turn and downward rush brought them into firing range of the enemy, and they covered their comrades with a solid barrage of cannon and machine-gun fire. The two "bandits" dove down and to the right, where they fell into the sights of Lavitskiy and Panov. Another two burning flares lit up the sky.

Kudrya and Molchanov, alerted to the approaching danger in time, quickly gathered altitude and, using the overcast, attacked a pair of FW-190s from above and behind. Molchanov shot down one of them and the engagement continued. Now there were eight Airacobras against seven German fighters.

Significant success had been achieved with a few simple maneuvers, and the ratio of forces had been brought to even. Despite their large losses, the enemy pilots did not attempt to disengage. The Germans continued to focus on Kudrya's Airacobra. Fifteen minutes after the engagement had begun, this was now the center of the battle, four Bf-109s against the pair of Nikolay Kudrya. Nikolay and his wingman circled and turned at an altitude of 5,600 to 6,200 feet. Glinka and his wingman were working their own fight about 3,300 feet still higher.

Kudrya shot up the lead "bandit" in a frontal attack. At this instant two Messerschmitts jumped him from behind clouds. They struck Nikolay's P-39 from close range and a favorable higher position. Nikolay's wingman, attempting to evade an FW-190 attacking him from behind, was not in a position to help his commander. Molchanov only caught a glimpse of a bright fiery splash and the falling ball of flame that was Kudrya's Airacobra.

This intense and fiercely fought battle had lasted for twenty to twenty-five minutes and ended with a highly favorable score of six to one in favor of the Soviet pilots. This result was achieved because of the correct arrangement of the combat formation of Glinka's group and the skillful use of clouds for concealment. Regarding coordination between the patrol's pairs, it was accomplished well at the beginning of the battle. Closer to the end of the battle coordination was disrupted somewhat. This lapse in fact led to the death of Hero of the Soviet Union Nikolay Kudrya.

The pilots came to full agreement at the postflight discussion of this highly successful battle: the success achieved in the first minutes of the fight (five enemy fighters shot down in a brief period) somewhat enervated the Airacobra crews. The enemy was sufficiently resolute in a psychological sense. Dmitriy Glinka committed an error in the supervision of his subordinates. With the peaking of the battle at the altitude of Kudrya's pair, he should have immediately strengthened this dangerous sector with Lavitskiy's pair. While this maneuver was indeed accomplished, unfortunately it came too late. This was the primary cause of the loss of one pilot.[10]

At the end of May several noncombat losses of pilots were added to the month's combat losses. An accident occurred in 16th Guards

Fighter Regiment on 25 May. An Airacobra was being ground-tested after repairs had been completed, in the presence of senior flight and squadron maintenance personnel and the pilot. All of the fighter's systems and instruments were functioning normally. The pilot, Vladimir Stepanov, received permission to make a test flight.

Over the course of a seventeen-minute flight the pilot checked the aircraft at all engine speeds, made several aerobatic maneuvers, and fired the cannon and machine guns. He took the aircraft up to its maximum speed and then closed the throttle and began to glide, making a landing approach. In his final turn, at an altitude of thirty-five to fifty feet, the pilot lost the required landing speed and stalled the aircraft. It plummeted to the ground. The Airacobra was damaged beyond repair, but the engine was intact and could be used as a spare. Stepanov received several serious injuries and died several hours later.[11]

On 30 May a similar accident occurred in the 45th Fighter Regiment. Junior Lieutenant Yuriy Malinin stalled his Airacobra at an altitude of 165 to 200 feet. The aircraft fell on its left wing and then somersaulted. The pilot was sent to the hospital in serious condition, with a fractured skull, facial injuries, left eye destroyed, and an open fracture of his left shin.

The cause of this accident was overexhaustion. The pilot had flown a large number of sorties (as many as four per day) in the period leading up to the accident. He had already flown two combat missions on 30 May for a combined flight time of more than two hours. Yuriy Malinin was executing his third sortie without sufficient rest. A contributing factor was the failure of his propeller governor. The propeller departed from its normal working parameters and developed a speed of more than 3000 rpm. Coming in for a landing on his fourth go-around, Malinin made an error in his flight control.[12]

On order of the division commander, over the course of the next four days the experienced pilots of each regiment gave instruction to their young pilots on how to recover an Airacobra from a spin, using the UTI-4. Check rides were then conducted with all pilots.

These measures led to a reduction in aircraft accidents, but incidents could not be completely avoided. The design peculiarities of the Airacobra conditioned its frequent habit of spinning. Only great experience in flying the P-39 safeguarded against such accidents.

First Priority — the Aircraft

Aviation engineering support is the special support of combat actions and training activities of aviation units and formations. It includes organizing the technical exploitation of aviation equipment, making timely and appropriate repairs of aircraft, maneuvering repair units and technical assets for the exploitation and repair of aviation equipment, and doing the engineering calculations necessary to providing this support. Aviation engineering support also encompasses measures undertaken by commanders to ensure full utilization of aviation units' maintenance and combat capabilities, the conduct of chemical defense of personnel, aviation equipment, and repair units, and the continuous improvement of forms and methods of organizing the technical exploitation and repair of aviation equipment. During the war, aviation engineering support was executed by the aviation engineering service.[1]

A number of duty positions were associated with providing this support. An aviation division included a deputy commander for aviation engineering service and engineers for field repair, armaments, and special equipment. Fighter regiments had a senior engineer (the deputy commander for equipment utilization), engineers for field repair and armaments, and a deputy senior engineer for special services. An aviation squadron had an engineer (senior technician, also the deputy commander for equipment utilization) and a deputy senior technician for special services. There were regimental specialists for armaments, aviation instruments, special equipment, and radios in the squadron. A flight had a senior aircraft mechanic and a radio mechanic. Each aircraft had a crew chief, to whom were subordinated a mechanic and a special equipment technician.

Special services was a group of specialists who maintained electrical and radio equipment, instruments, and oxygen systems. When required, specialists from the regiment for armaments, instruments, radio, and oxygen equipment assisted in readying aircraft for combat missions.[2]

The primary tasks of aviation engineering service were preparing aircraft for accomplishment of their combat mission and conducting rapid and appropriate repair of damaged equipment. The first mission included preliminary preparation of aviation equipment, preflight preparation, and preflight inspection.

Preliminary preparation of the fighters for their next flying mission included a postflight inspection and correction of deficiencies noted during the flight and uncovered during inspection; refueling the aircraft with fuel, oil, and special fluids; replenishing the ammunition for cannon and guns; and checking the condition and readiness of the calibrated devices and test equipment.

Preflight preparation was conducted in accordance with a flight planning table and consisted of the following: preflight inspection; check of fuel, oil, special fluid, and oxygen levels and ammunition supply; mounting of removable equipment (for example, drop tanks, and cameras); a running check of the engine; and function checks of the armaments and other components, mechanisms, and instruments. The crew chief and his subordinates, assisted by specialists from the service group, carried out this preparation. The pilot checked the functioning of the engine and the mounting and functioning of the radio and avionics equipment before he flew the aircraft.

The service group consisted of several technical specialists who prepared the aircraft in accordance with their specialty. As a rule, there were four service groups: aircraft and engines, armaments, controls and avionics, and communications.

The preflight inspection was an inspection and function check of the aircraft, conducted with the goal of determining its actual readiness for flight in accordance with the assigned mission. It was done by technical personnel of the aviation unit to which the aircraft was assigned.

Each Airacobra had a flight journal or log that was maintained by the crew chief. In this journal he recorded all deficiencies revealed during flight or during the inspection, and also the work accomplished to correct them. In addition, a control list of aircraft readiness for launch was filled out. This was a special form used to manage the volume of work of the service group, the results of preflight inspection, the checking of systems, and the fuel and ammunition status of the P-39s. It was maintained with the goal of increasing the accountability of the air crews and technicians for the condition of the aircraft and the quality of their preparation for combat missions.

Repairing damaged aircraft was a rather difficult enterprise in field conditions. Forms of repair included capital repair (at factories and bases) after the exploitation of a prescribed resource (e.g., engine hours) or damage to basic component elements (e.g., airframe), preventive repair carried out after a specific number of flight hours or specific period of use, and routine repair performed to correct deficiencies in individual subsystems and components that were observed during use of the Airacobras. These repairs were accomplished by exchanging, cleaning, lubricating, and adjusting worn or damaged parts and subsystems.

Preventive and routine repairs were conducted in stationary troop-level repair shops and in mobile aviation repair shops (PARMs).[3] The PARM was responsible for routine and, in isolated cases, preventive repair of the P-39 in field conditions, repair of instruments and aircraft ground service equipment, and also repair of the equipment of troop-level maintenance units. A PARM's equipment and tools enabled it to conduct mechanical, sheet metal, riveting, coppering, welding, heat treating, joinery (many Soviet-manufactured aircraft had structural components made of wood), control surface fabric repair and painting, and other types of repair.

Years have passed, yet every pilot with whom I have spoken about this subject recalls his aircraft's mechanic with love, warmth, and enormous gratitude. This toiler seemed to know neither sleep nor rest. He always gave himself to his aircraft, preparing it for new aerial engagements. He monitored his assigned aircraft to the point of take-off and waited on the ground nervously for the return of his pilot and machine. Let it be holed or battle-damaged, so long as it returned. He would "treat" the wounds of his P-39 in short order and the Airacobra would once again depart on a mission to pound the hated enemy. Pilots, technicians, mechanics, armorers—together they all formed a strongly bonded combat family.

Konstantin Sukhov, commander of 1st Squadron, 16th Guards Regiment, wrote about this after the war: "Was I satisfied with my crew? They were outstanding! My flight technician Grigoriy Klimenko and aircraft mechanic Ivan Yakovenko, a diligent, painstaking man in his thirties, worked with precision and harmony. Yakovenko was an outstanding specialist who loved his profession and treated the combat equipment with respect. His fellow young mechanics learned a great deal from him."[4]

General Grigoriy Dolnikov writes in his memoir: "Senior Sergeant Ivan Petrov was the mechanic of my aircraft. When I landed and informed him of a victory in aerial combat, he was unspeakably proud, as happy as a child. 'Today my commander shot down another Focke-Wulf.' Then he set to work on my aircraft."[5]

In aviation, as in no other branch of the armed forces, there were many women. Thus, in October 1943 there were eighty female Komsomol members in various duty positions in 216th Fighter Division.[6] Among the aviation specialists, a large group of the fairer sex serviced the combat aircraft of 100th Aviation Regiment. Delicate and shy, yesterday's schoolgirls showed up in aviation units in soldiers' uniforms. And what a burden they carried almost daily, dealing with front-line soldiers without a word of complaint! These young women refueled aircraft with fuel and oil, cleaned and reloaded machine guns and cannons, packed parachutes, and even assisted the technical specialists in repair of the Airacobras. While the pilots slept, these women washed their sweaty, sometimes bloody uniforms and stitched white collar liners into their tunics.

Maria Panchenko mastered her specialty of packing parachutes. The regiment's pilots knew that if the situation required them to abandon their aircraft in flight, the parachute packed by the hands of this "black-eyed beauty" would not let them down. She was also the regimental letter carrier. Combat comradeship and years of friendship in the difficult wartime period led many men and women to fall in love with each other. Maria Panchenko became the wife of Vasiliy Sapyan; combat armorer Zina Zotova changed her family name to Sanyut; and happy Grunya Yakubova gave her heart to the brave pilot Pavel Berestnev. Vera Bezverkhnyaya took one of the Proninykh brothers for her husband.

The year 1943 was a turning point for 216th Fighter Division. It was a so-called "first course" of training for the pilots, when they had to fight the enemy in the new and unusual Airacobras, test it in combat. The technical specialists had to study and learn, literally on the march, the construction of many subassemblies and components and to repair and replace any that did not function properly. The technical personnel passed this difficult test with honor, supporting the combat labor first of the 45th and later the 16th Guards Fighter Regiments in the heated battles over the Kuban.

Here are some statistical measures of the work that was accomplished during this period. During March 1943, P-39 and P-40 Kittyhawk aircraft (45th Fighter Regiment had nine of the former and six of the latter) were experiencing leaks in the fuel, oil, and cooling systems after twenty-five to thirty hours of use. A careful inspection of these systems was conducted, all clamps were tightened, filters and seals were examined, and landing gear systems were inspected. All observed deficiencies were fully corrected. During the course of this work the technical personnel gained skill in accessing the subsystems and along with this increased their professional knowledge.[7] By April, the technical specialists of the regiments, the PARM-3, and PARM-1, had mastered, on the whole, the repair of the P-39.

After two to three weeks of flights, the spark plugs began to fail on some Airacobras. There were no spares. Soviet-manufactured plugs were substituted, with favorable results. A standing order was promulgated that limited their use to fifty hours, followed by mandatory replacement. Practice showed that even one failed spark plug caused the P-39 to vibrate heavily.

There were nine observed cases of failed generators—the armature windings burned up. This was a consequence of poor factory assembly and mounting. The armature was loose in its bearings and wobbled to one side or another, rubbing the insulation from the windings. This created a short circuit. These generators were replaced by Soviet-produced items and voltage regulators. The division PARM-3 prepared 130 adapters for mounting this generator on the Allison motor, eliminating the problem entirely.[8]

Soviet-made altimeters and air temperature gauges were mounted on many Airacobras. The most frequent failures were of the coolant temperature gauge, caused by the sensor burning out.[9]

In view of the absence of oxygen masks (they were still en route), in less than one day the PARM-1 prepared adapters for using Soviet-produced masks and supplied them to all crews. These were replaced after receipt of the American masks.

There was an unusual breakdown of two Airacobras: a deformation of the vertical stabilizer occurred from the first to the fourth rib and the upper portion at the mounting point of the radio antenna was deformed. Analysis of the defect indicated that this damage resulted from dive pullouts with a left turn at speeds of 400 to 420 mph. The tail section was not built to withstand the resulting forces (it consisted of one main reinforced stringer and six lightened ribs of 0.8mm duraluminum). A second weakness of the vertical stabilizer was the large spacing between ribs (twenty centimeters between the first and second ribs, twenty-one centimeters between the second and third ribs, and twenty-five centimeters between the third and fourth ribs). The tail section experienced significant loading when the aircraft was pulled out of a dive. Its ribs did not withstand this loading and began to distort. The skin of the tail section was stretched from the inside and the tail fin cracked. Air passing across the crack that formed in the upper portion of the tail enlarged the crack.

To prevent the further occurrence of this damage, pilots were limited to a speed of 400 mph during a dive and were instructed not to combine the pullout with a turn, but rather to transition to level or upward flight. At a dive speed approaching 470 mph, the entire tail section could break away from the aircraft.[10] Aircraft that had this type of damage to the tail section were sent to army repair facilities and never were returned to the regiments.

The aircraft of Grigoriy Dolnikov received serious damage in air combat on 20 April 1943. The tail section and right wing root were riddled with bullet holes and the landing gear was damaged. Despite the extent of the damage, Sergeant Yuriy Gladko, the flight technician, repaired the Airacobra in one day.[11]

April was a busy month for the repair shops. The technicians of PARM-1 and units together repaired eleven Airacobras and three Kittyhawks of 45th Fighter Regiment, four Airacobras of 16th Guards Fighter Regiment, and five Spitfires of 57th Guards Fighter Regiment. Some of these aircraft required upwards of twenty man-hours of labor.

May brought a whole new host of problems. In the first week, 45th Fighter Regiment received twenty-nine Airacobras from an aviation base in Ivanova. These aircraft were fitted with the Allison type-83 and -85 engines. It soon became clear that during the transition from high revolutions per minute (rpm) to low rpm the majority of these engines experienced misfires. Overcooling was a major concern. The engine picked up rpm poorly at high altitudes, where the ambient air temperature could be as low as −80°C [−112°F].

Pilots made an effort to test the new aircraft thoroughly in every flight mode. This testing revealed the following parameters. The type-83 and -85 engines produced 1,200 horsepower. This model P-39 was heavier on the controls at an altitude of 12,000 feet than the model received previously. Its vertical and horizontal speed was greater, particularly at altitude. The fighter accelerated more quickly, was steadier in a dive, and was difficult to recover from a spin.[12]

There were three incidents of landing gear failing to lower after 100 flight hours. The cause was a clutch facing worn smooth. On two aircraft this led to a partial retraction of landing gear in flight. The clutch was completely burned out on one P-39.[13]

The engineering and technical personnel of the regiments and airfield service battalion (BAO) put forth maximum effort to ensure that the assigned missions could be accomplished.[14] The engines of the newly received fighters were their greatest concern. The Allison's oil filter was supposed to be changed after each ten hours of engine time. The supervisory maintenance personnel in 9th Guards Fighter Division made the decision to change the filters after each flight. Division mechanics checked the spark plug gap every twenty engine hours, and unit mechanics made the same inspection at the intervening ten-hour interval. Carburetors were cleaned frequently and all chassis components were inspected carefully after each landing.

In essence, maintenance personnel were working overtime. Before engines had even cooled down from a flight, mechanics were swarming over them checking and replacing items and burning their hands. Specialists literally covered the Airacobras. They topped off the fuel and oil tanks, loaded the ammunition trays, replaced rivets, straightened metal, and patched bullet holes. They hurried. The first large-scale campaign for air superiority was being waged in the skies over the Kuban.

May was also a month of intense combat activity, in which the division flew 1,777 combat sorties and conducted 156 aerial engagements, 30 of them fierce battles with large groups of enemy fighters and bombers.[15] In six weeks of employment of the Airacobra, the PARMs, technicians, mechanics, electricians, and radio repairmen mastered their repair.[16]

In August, units of 9th Guards Fighter Division participated in the liberation of the Donbass. The intensity of the air battle was moderate. The aviation engineering service was faced with the task of improving the units' combat readiness rate. The average percentages in the regiments were 50 percent in 16th Guards Fighter Regiment, 80 percent in 100th Guards Fighter Regiment, and 88 percent in 104th Guards Fighter Regiment. The overall division readiness rate was 72 percent.[17] The sharp reduction of readiness of the P-39 for accomplishment of its assigned missions, especially in 16th Guards Fighter Regiment, was caused by problems with the Allison engines. Nine of these engines removed from aircraft were found to have failed connecting rod bearings and broken connecting rod cap bolts.

Another cause of engine failure was inappropriate use of the aircraft. The 16th Guards Fighter Regiment showed disregard in the forming of groups of fighters for missions. Some fighters in a group had supercharged engines (P-39) and some had unsupercharged engines (P-40).[18] Those who scheduled aircraft did not pay much attention to these details. When patrolling and engaging the enemy, pilots of unsupercharged aircraft were forced against their wishes to overload their engines while executing various maneuvers.[19] The consequences of these stresses were quickly manifested in failed connecting rod bearings and end cap bolts. The engine of Guards Junior Lieutenant Yakov Shanin seized from overheating. Another engine showed metal filings in the oil filter.[20] It took an aircraft mechanic four man-hours to change out the connecting rod bearings.

The removal and installation of an Allison power plant was a difficult operation requiring considerable time, skill, and effort. One or two mechanics could not perform this task. Senior division engineer Lieutenant Colonel Dmitriy Emelyanov made the decision to create emergency repair teams. The crew chief and mechanics of the disabled aircraft and other available mechanics, along with specialists from PARM-1, were assigned to these teams. These well-qualified groups could replace a failed Allison engine in about thirty-six hours.[21]

The P-39 with type-83 and -85 engines had Aeroproducts propellers. Previously delivered Airacobras were equipped with Curtiss Electric propellers. Few of the Curtiss-equipped aircraft remained in the 9th Guards Fighter Division by late August 1943. Disassembly and inspection of these aircraft after 100, 130, and 150 hours showed that all internal components of the propeller, both electrical and mechanical, were in excellent condition. Thus it was decided to establish the teardown time for the Curtiss propeller at 150 hours in lieu of the recommended 100 hours.[22]

At the end of August the Aeroproducts-equipped aircraft delivered a little "gift" to the mechanics: the seals in their hydraulic systems began to leak. Hydraulic fluid began to leak onto the propeller blades, which caused a vibration in the engine. Senior Sergeant Viktor Korotkov, an aircraft mechanic in 16th Guards Fighter Regiment, made a thorough investigation of the problem and developed a repair procedure. He was ordered to train other P-39 mechanics and technicians. Korotkov demonstrated the sequence of disassembly of the Aeroproducts propeller, washed the internal spaces of the blades, replaced the seal, assembled the propeller, and reinstalled it. At the same time he did a function check of the propeller at various engine speeds.

Volodarsk airfield (16 September 1943). Airacobras arriving in the units demonstrated an "annoyance." The starter gear tended to lock up during startup of the engine. At the suggestion of Guards Sergeant Nikolay Lazarenko, an electrical equipment expert, a supplementary spring was installed that pushed the engagement lever of the starter gear to the rear (disengaging the starter from the flywheel). This completely solved the problem of premature engagement.[23]

A new oxygen apparatus had been installed on Airacobras that arrived in the division in the fall. Its distinguishing characteristic was that the oxygen mask also served as a protective mask. This was an excellent concept, but this innovation turned out to be cumbersome. It had a long and quite thick accordion hose that was uncomfortable for high-altitude flights. The PARM quickly developed an adapter, and units conducted a mass replacement of the new masks with the old masks.[24]

The booster coils on the engines began to fail more frequently with the onset of cold weather. When the temperature fell below freezing, or even close to it, it was impossible to start these engines. Coils of Soviet production were installed on all of these engines in place of the originals. An additional ten coils were stocked in each regiment as spares.

Throughout 1944, 9th Guards Fighter Division units were based primarily on dirt airfields. This was less than desirable for several reasons, both for the personnel and the equipment, and led to frequent breakage of Airacobra undercarriages and tire blowouts. For example, three aircraft in 16th Guards Fighter Regiment suffered rupture of the front tire or inner tube during the month of May. This occurred on average once in twenty landings. The cause was poor quality materials from the factory.[25]

Many aircraft suffered deformation of the shock absorber mount of the nose wheel during the May–June period of massive aerial combat over Jassy, Romania. This defect showed up after forty to forty-five landings.[26] The nose gear was not manufactured with sufficient strength. The technical staff of the squadrons and regiments corrected this deficiency with minimal expenditure of time. They were delayed, however, by a shortage of spare parts. The solution was found in removing parts from Airacobras that had been shot up or crashed. Each regiment had a special team of mechanics (three to four men) for this purpose.

As before, the weakness of the connecting rod bearings in the Allison engine was again revealed. They tended to fail at approximately the fifty-hour mark. When spare parts were available, regimental specialists and repair teams from the PARM-3 (division) replaced the bearings in an operation that took four to five hours.

Another problem with the Allison engine showed up in Moldavia. Beginning in May 1944 and with each subsequent month, ten to twelve aircraft in the division showed cracks in the high-voltage current leads of the distributor.[27] On average this occurred at seventy hours of engine life. It was a direct consequence of poor quality of the base material of the leads. Some aircraft did not sortie for several days because of a shortage of these parts. In May, the technical personnel of the units repaired eight Airacobras and the PARM-1 another two.[28]

New defects emerged in the P-39 aircraft in June 1944: cracks in the instrument panel mounts (five cases); upon starting the engines of two aircraft, there was a rupture of hose fittings on the line from the recovery pump to the bypass valve; and many fuel cells failed. Aircraft repairs accomplished in June in 100th Guards Fighter Regiment included thirty-two routine and eighty-seven minor jobs by the regiment mechanics and ten routine and fifty-three minor jobs by the PARM-1.[29] Unit mechanics of 16th Guards Fighter Regiment carried out routine repair of eight aircraft and minor repair of an additional forty. The PARM-1 made routine repair of nine Airacobras and minor repair of another fifty-five. Seven engines were replaced.[30]

A technical conference was held in 16th Guards Fighter Regiment on 7 September 1944. The conference's purpose was to discuss the lessons of the aviation-engineering support of the Lvov–Sandomir offensive operation. The experience of this and previous combat operations permitted maintenance supervisors to draw a number of practical conclusions. These conclusions would assist in the subsequent work of fighter unit maintenance personnel to accomplish all their normal support functions and to carry out timely and appropriate repairs.

Past practice had confirmed that it was expedient to leave aircraft that could be repaired in five days on their airfields. P-39s that required from five to ten days for repair were to be evacuated to the nearest repair base. Airacobras were sent to railroad-mounted repair shops for capital repairs or extensive preventive maintenance.[31] It should be noted that such a railroad-mounted repair facility followed the 216th (9th Guards) Fighter Division in all of its operations.

In order to prevent disruptions in the repair of aircraft in the regiments due to a shortage of spare parts, the PARM-1s carried supplies of expendable materials sufficient to support fighter operations for five to seven days. The special sections of the PARM-1 (special equipment, armaments, and so on) carried a twelve- to fifteen-day supply.[32]

The speakers at this conference addressed their experience regarding a number of issues.[33] In 3d Squadron, two blades of a four-bladed propeller were shot through (wet ammunition caused delayed firing of the machine guns). There were no spare propeller blades. Squadron and regimental technical personnel replaced the reduction gear of the Aeroproducts propeller with a Curtiss reduction gear and then installed a three-bladed Curtiss Electric propeller. In June, conversely, maintenance personnel removed the three-bladed Curtiss Electric propellers from three P-39s and installed the four-bladed Aeroproducts propeller.

The 37mm cannon was replaced on one aircraft in 2d Squadron. Due to a production defect, the extractor was not extracting fired cases. Airacobras damaged in aerial combat were being returned to flying status in one to two days. Altimeter failures occurred seven times in the May–June period. Two new altimeters were installed, and the shafts were replaced on the remainder. These shafts broke for the simple reason that they were frequently subjected to heavy vibration in their instrument panel mounting during engine testing on the ground.

Flight indicators were being damaged if they were not caged during landing of the aircraft. The pilots were not giving sufficient attention to this sensitive instrument. There was a single case in which a P-39 made a hard landing off the airfield with gear down. The shock jarred the altimeter loose from its mounting and it fell to the floor. Rapid repair of the fighters was ensured after the reinforcement of the division with a PARM-3 and of each regiment with a PARM-1.

During the preparation of the Berlin offensive operation, the aviation-engineering leadership of the 2d Air Army and divisions gave serious attention to the creation of a supply of spare engines for Airacobras (engine failures for various reasons had been a frequent occurrence in past battles). Calculations were made of the possible requirement for P-39 power plants based on the anticipated Allison engine life of 150 hours. Of the 1,089 fighter aircraft participating in this operation, 354 were Airacobras.[34] Planners anticipated a total of 18,000 aircraft sorties for the duration of the operation, an average of 16.6 sorties per aircraft. The Allison engines' share of the sortie total was 5,870 (354 × 16.6). If each sortie lasted one hour, this operation would consume thirty-nine Allison engines (5870 ÷ 150). The air army also created a ten-day supply of high-demand spares and expendable materials at its airfields.

Unit maintenance personnel supported four sorties per aircraft per day during the Berlin operation. The 9th Guards Fighter Division aircraft flew 2,070 total aircraft sorties in the month of April (16th Guards Fighter Regiment 783, 100th Guards Fighter Regiment 784, 104th Guards Fighter Regiment 497). Division losses in combat were four in 16th Guards, two in 100th Guards, and one in 104th Guards. Two aircraft were destroyed by accidents in 100th Guards and one in 104th Guards. One pilot was killed when his aircraft was downed by anti-aircraft artillery, one pilot died on the ground, and two pilots were missing in action.[35]

Logistical Support

Combat employment of aviation formations and units is impossible without timely and full-scale logistical support. Air armies were formed in *front*s in 1942. Beginning with this period, aviation logistical support became an independent system that included command and control organs, along with subordinate support and repair units. The logistical support of an air army included a logistical headquarters, departments of technical supply, airfield construction, wheeled transportation and mechanized assets, fuel supply, conventional troop supply, and medical service. The *front* VVS logistical system that was created during this period existed with minor variations until the end of the war.

In accordance with a directive from the chief of the VVS Main Directorate, a rear logistical area was established for aviation forces that extended rearward in two zones. The first zone was from 30 to 90 miles and the second 90 to 250 miles from the front-line trace.[1] Active *front* aviation formations and units were based in the first zone, while reserve units were based in the second zone. Stocks of all types of supplies were established in each zone in accordance with the type of aviation units based there.

The quantity of aircraft in the Red Air Force began to grow markedly beginning in 1942. Naturally, this led to an increase in the volume of work for logistical units in support of flight operations. A department to manage wheeled transportation and mechanized logistical assets was organized in each *front* in July. At this time there was a shortage of heavy cargo trucks that would have provided mobile platforms for refueling long-range bombers. Special vehicles of *front* aviation were used to carry this fuel, but this stopgap measure did not fully address the problem. It took five or six trips, each twenty to twenty-five minutes long, to refuel one aircraft of this type. Another solution was found: expendable fuel dumps were created near long-range aviation refueling locations. This reduced by one-third the time required to top off these aircraft.

The experience of combat operations in the first two years of the war made clear the need for subsequent improvement in the logistical support of the Soviet Armed Forces. An "Instruction concerning the chief of VVS logistical services and the chief of air army logistical services" was implemented in August 1943. In accordance with this document, all supply services and their depots, as well as some of the technical units responsible for utilization and repair of airfield technical support assets, were incorporated into the logistical arm of the VVS.[2] In this same year, the department of employment of wheeled transportation and mechanized assets of VVS logistical support was reformed into a directorate.

In all the *fronts*, great attention continued to be devoted to *maskirovka* measures to hide primary airfields from enemy reconnaissance and to conduct imitation activities in order to portray false airfields.[3] With these purposes in mind, existing *maskirovka* assets were reorganized into forward *maskirovka* teams. The duty position of *maskirovka* service chief was established in air armies.

The size of the air force continued to grow as new types of aircraft were added to the fleet. The tempo of the combat actions of Soviet ground and air forces continued to accelerate. Taken together, all this led to an increased demand for materiel assets and required subsequent improvement of aviation logistic support.

The definitive form of aviation fuel supply service for the VVS was developed in 1944 and 1945, when the fuel supply department was reorganized into a directorate. A fuel supply department was simultaneously created in the air army and a fuel depot was added to its logistical structure in 1944. A department of fuel, lubricants, and aviation oil (GSM) regeneration [recycling] was set up in the airfield basing district (RAB),[4] specifically in the forward aviation supply depot.

Medical support issues did not go unnoticed. The medical department in the headquarters of the commander-in-chief of the Soviet Army VVS was reformed into the Directorate of Medical Service. A 200-bed army aviation hospital was established in the table of organization and equipment of the air army medical service in June 1944, followed a short time later by a mobile sanitary-epidemiological laboratory.

This "in-house" medical establishment ensured the successful resolution of two critical problems: carrying out qualified treatment of wounded and sick aviators, and returning them to their units after recovery. This was important from the standpoint of maintaining unit manning levels of flight-qualified and technical personnel and increasing the combat capability of aviation units.

In 1942, the sanitary-epidemiological condition of the Red Army was clearly worsening, first of all in typhus and typhoid fever, and also in tularemia. The increase in infectious diseases was a consequence of the poor epidemiological state of the combat zone due to the broad spread of infectious diseases among the local population who had lived in occupied territory and of Soviet war prisoners who had been liberated from imprisonment. The fact that the air army had its own epidemiological laboratory permitted the medical service operationally to conduct field sanitation protection of the zone of actions of subordinate units.

The system of materiel-technical support for the air division and its subordinate units was implemented by forces and means of the RAB and its assigned units. The RAB was the primary logistical support organization. It not only supplied aviation units with everything required to perform their combat mission but also developed the airfield network and acquired and stockpiled materiel assets.

The RAB consisted of a headquarters, separate communications company, wheeled transportation battalion, forward aviation and field military supply depots, engineer-sapper service, and anti-aircraft defense service. In addition, the RAB had an airfield clearing detachment and mobile aviation repair shops (PARMs).

As a rule, the RAB supported an aviation corps or two to four aviation divisions. An aviation division did not have any organic logistic support. Issues of their logistic support were resolved by the RAB and airfield service battalions (BAO). An RAB exercised control over four to eight BAOs. A single BAO serviced two single-engined aviation regiments or one twin-engined regiment. In mid-February 1942, the Red Army had 275 BAOs that supported the combat efforts of 356 single-engined regiments and 91 twin-engined regiments.[5]

A BAO was a self-contained logistical unit. It consisted of a headquarters, airfield service company, wheeled transportation company, communications company, mine-sapper, *maskirovka*, chemical, and medical services, services for the supply of provisions, ammunition, fuel, aviation and common parts, mobile aviation repair shops (PARM-1), and oxygen-generating station. Airfield-technical companies from the RAB were attached to these battalions in the winter in order to maintain airfields in usable condition.

Provisional airfield groups were created for timely preparation of the airfield network during operations. Each group consisted of three or four airfield-engineer battalions, several excavation teams (two to three from each BAO), a mine-clearing detachment from the mine-clearing service of the RAB or BAO, and medical personnel. Each provisional group was assigned three to four Po-2 aircraft, one radio set, and five to six trucks.[6] Control of these provisional groups was centralized at the air army level or they operated in accordance with the RAB chief's plans. They were headed up by representatives of the leadership component of airfield construction departments (air army and RAB airfield-engineer battalions).

In the course of an offensive, the provisional airfield groups advanced directly behind the first echelon of the attacking ground units and formations. With the permission of the ground forces *front* commander, forces and means from ground forces and the local population were assigned to airfield construction (rehabilitation) tasks. The majority of airfields prepared during the war were constructed of local materials (primarily dirt). On average, the construction of such an airfield required two or three days. In 1944 and 1945 this time was reduced to twenty-four hours. For example, in the Vistula–Oder operation (12 January to 3 February 1945), eight airfield-engineer battalions constructed fifty-five and rehabilitated twenty-five airfields for 16th Air Army. On average, twenty to twenty-five hours were spent in the construction of a single airfield, thirty-six hours if one takes into account the displacement of the BAO to the new construction site.[7]

Airfields captured from the enemy in the course of an offensive operation were widely employed for basing our aviation. Thus, in March 1945, during a maneuver to bypass Vesprem, Hungary, my 1st Battalion of 46th Guards Tank Brigade was assigned the mission of capturing an airfield north of this town. We seized the indicated facility, as they say, "still warm." Twelve Bf-109 and FW-190 fighters in full working order were parked on its ramp. In order not to expend scarce main gun rounds and machine-gun ammunition for their destruction, we drove over their tails with our Sherman tanks.

According to the experience of many aviation formations, the capture of enemy airfields permitted our forces to satisfy approximately 30 percent of our total requirement for aviation basing sites. As a rule, the Germans completely destroyed their airfields during their retreat. They dug up the dirt runways during the warm months or mined them and demolished hard-surface strips using powerful explosives or large aviation bombs. In cases of demolition, craters with a diameter of twenty yards and a depth of six yards were left in the strips. Airfield-engineer battalions from the RABs carried out the rehabilitation work on such airfields. Frequently the troops from a BAO, along with the local populace, were assigned to this effort. The mine-sapper service cleared mines from the areas adjacent to the runways.

One of the important tasks of the commanders and staffs of the formations was the *maskirovka* of their subordinate units at their bases. The BAO *maskirovka* service carried out engineer measures for concealing active airfields and imitating housekeeping activity at false airfields. The continuous implementation of a set of *maskirovka* measures ensured the preservation of a significant quantity of aircraft, personnel, materiel supplies, and airfield-technical support assets. An April 1944 directive of the chief of staff of the Red Army VVS required that aerial photographic reconnaissance of active airfields be conducted every two days to inspect the effectiveness of *maskirovka* measures.[8] When shown by this photography to be necessary, additional or corrective work was accomplished in support of airfield *maskirovka*. The study of documents regarding this issue indicates that during the period 1 May 1942 through 1 May 1945, of 2,246 observed cases of enemy aircraft flights against aircraft basing facilities of all types, two-thirds were conducted against dummy airfields.[9]

Maintaining airfields in a condition to support flight operations during the fall and winter rainy periods was particularly difficult. During these seasons, more basic landing strips were constructed using gravel, crushed rock, and on rare occasion wood. Local construction materials were widely used for this purpose.[10]

During the war considerable experience was obtained in the use of metallic landing mats. They were first installed on three airfields in Ukraine (Poltava, Mirgorod, and Piryatin) for receiving American long-range bombers that were taking part in shuttle operations. Sets of these landing mats were delivered from the United States.[11] The assembly-disassembly features of these mats substantially accelerated the construction of new aircraft-basing facilities and greatly improved their usability. The unquestionable achievement of this innovation was the practicability of its multiple use. For example, the steel mats were removed from one airfield, transported 110 miles, and laid down on another airfield in ten days in support of 3d Air Army in the Vistula–Oder operation in March 1945.

A final remarkable adaptation occurred late in the war—the use of autobahns for runways. In the spring of 1945, a section of the Berlin–Breslau autobahn 75 feet wide by 4,920 feet long was prepared for landing aircraft in two days. Some 313 cubic yards of sand, 654 cubic yards of crushed rock, and 150 concrete slabs were used in its construction; 688 sorties were flown from this strip in eighteen days.[12]

Another important aspect of logistic support of aviation formations and units was the provisioning of weapons, ordnance (bombs and bullets), and mechanical supplies. These materials arrived in air divisions and regiments through a centralized VVS logistic system. But GSM (petroleum, oil, and lubricants), foodstuffs, clothing, and other similar types of supplies came from *front* and army warehouses and bases. Railroad and wheeled-vehicle transport, and in some cases air and animal-drawn transport, were used to deliver these supplies to airfields. Wheeled transportation was normally centrally controlled.

A directive of the chief of the general staff of the Red Army (from 10 October 1941) established the following procedure for stockpiling materiel at airfield basing sites. Airfields were to maintain ammunition in sufficient quantity to support the requirements of two to three days of combat operations by the formations and units located at the airfield. If necessary, BAO transportation assets would lift and move this materiel to new airfield locations. Basic reserve supplies were to be stored in forward, primarily *front,* aviation depots.

Front aviation depots with primary supplies were to be echeloned to the rear, 125 to 185 miles from the forward edge. As has been noted, later this depth was subdivided into two zones, the first 30 to 90 miles and the second 90 to 250 miles from the forward edge. Forward aviation depots were to maintain a ten-day working supply of ammunition for their supported units.[13]

In those cases when the RAB commander did not know which aviation units he was responsible to supply, it was recommended that he base his calculations on the premise that 50 percent of his requisitions would come from fighter and ground-attack air regiments, and 50 percent would come from bomber regiments.

Forward aviation depots were to maintain not more than thirty-five to forty railroad car loads of technical supplies and other types of property and ammunition, not counting their own assigned equipment.[14]

In 1943, in accordance with an order of the USSR People's Commissar of Defense, departments of common troop supplies and field military supplies were created in the RAB. Not less than a twenty-day supply of foodstuffs was to be concentrated in depots under the control of the field military supply department, with a continuous effort being made to add to this supply. This same department was responsible for maintaining stores of common supplies.[15]

Aviation units located on the territory of a given RAB became eligible to receive all forms of provisions. The creation of these organs permitted the emergence of a unified system of supporting aviation formations and units with everything that was required for the daily existence of the flight crews and support of the technical component, and hence the accomplishment of the assigned missions.

An analysis of the operations conducted (duration of preparation, conditions of cargo movement, transportation capabilities) shows that the on-hand quantity of supplies at the beginning and in the course of combat operations varied in significant degrees: at airfields, from a one- to five-day supply; and at forward aviation depots, up to a three- or four-day norm for all aviation units serviced by a given RAB.

Materiel was delivered to the basing area of an air army (to army, RAB forward aviation depots, individual airfields) by railroad transportation. The enemy undertook considerable efforts to slow down or interrupt the flow of cargo by this means. The active interference of his aviation against railroad facilities, the slow rehabilitation of track and roadbed, and the shortage of rolling stock led to a substantial reduction of the proportion moved by rail. Wheeled transportation became the primary means of moving cargo, particularly from major supply facilities to airfields.

The air army chief of logistic services frequently used trucks belonging to the BAO, RAB, and army in a centralized manner for this purpose. They were formed into convoys. In many cases, all the tanker transport was used in the same fashion for the rapid and complete supply of aviation units with fuel.

During operations of 216th Fighter Division in the Kuban (until mid-1943), there were no interruptions in the supplying of its regiments with the required materiel assets. With the movement of ground forces to the west and frequent relocation of aviation units to airfields in the Donbass, difficulties sometimes arose with supply. In September and particularly in October 1943, in connection with the great distance back to army depots and the absence of railroad lines of communication in the basing region, 460th and 785th BAO of 32d RAB were forced to move required cargoes up to 185 miles with their own transportation assets. From 16 September to 23 October, fuel was hauled some 185 to 215 miles from Bataysk, Shakta, and Volnovakha to the Volodarsk airfield network, where 16th Guards and 45th Air Regiments were located.

The late delivery of special fuel and ammunition for the Airacobra frequently imposed strict limits on the combat sortie rate of units equipped with this aircraft.[16] By the end of October, the foodstuff supply base of 4th Air Army was still located in Rostov-on-Don and Volnovakha. This affected the quality of food served to the divisions' airmen, forcing the BAO rations departments to rely on local food supplies. The assortment of foodstuffs available in these newly liberated regions was not great, and quality was somewhat low.[17]

In November 1943, the chokepoint of logistic supply for the division was the shortage of spare parts for the P-39. By this time, many Allison engines had been run up to their maximum recommended hours and needed repair and rebuilding. The supply of new engines was inadequate. Maintenance units also lacked oxygen supplies or generation equipment to recharge the on-board oxygen cylinders. This circumstance significantly affected the outcome of aerial combat and the quality of combat actions of patrolling groups. Enemy bombers frequently arrived at areas covered by our fighters at altitudes on the order of 20,000 to 21,000 feet. Flying without oxygen masks, Airacobra pilots were unable to conduct successful intercepts at this altitude. The enemy frequently bombed their selected targets without interference.[18]

In battles in May and June 1944 at the Prut River (northeast of Jassy in Romania), the division was based at Stefaneshti airfield. The division had displaced to this airfield on 11 May. The 495th BAO provided the division with all forms of supply. Accommodations were prepared for the troops but not equipped with all the basic necessities. The pilots slept without any bedding for ten days. Only at the insistence of the division command was the situation finally corrected.

This basing district was experiencing an acute shortage of

wheeled transportation. One relatively old truck, which was frequently out of service, was set aside to provide services for the fighters. This 1.5-ton truck was used not only to accomplish work on the airfield (its primary mission) but also to haul food to the troops. It also frequently was needed to deliver pilots to their aircraft just at the time when it had departed on some other errand. Meals were frequently delivered late. It was not unusual for eight hours to pass between breakfast and lunch.

The regiments were in poor shape regarding their stockage of spare parts. Requisitions for parts often went unfilled. Unit maintenance personnel sometimes got by using modest supplies of components they had removed from P-39s damaged in combat or in accidents.

In July and August 1944, the soldiers of 9th Guards Fighter Division played an active role in the Lvov–Sandomir operation of First Ukrainian *Front* (13 July to 30 August 1944). On 8 July, before the operation began, the division's regiments were concentrated at Kuzmin airfield, which was serviced by 718th BAO. The fighters worked from this airfield all of two days, then displaced to the Mikhaluvka region. Here, 379th BAO supported the fighters' accomplishment of their combat missions. On 20 July the division moved again, this time to Neznanuv airfield, serviced by 694th BAO. On 24 July the division displaced to Guycha airfield, where 432d BAO provided for all the needs of the Airacobra pilots. On 27 July the division's fighters moved to Smolintse airfield, supported by 388th BAO.

The division's soldiers were well received at every airfield with the exception of Neznanuv. At this location, sleeping quarters had not been prepared and the troops slept without bedding for four days. The technical department of 694th BAO functioned satisfactorily.[19]

At all the other sites listed above, services were organized at a high level. Only two times (at Guycha) were sorties interrupted because of a shortage of engine oil. Insufficient quantities of fuel were delivered on three days (8, 9, and 10 August) at Smolintse airfield, resulting in the grounding of twelve Airacobras of 16th Guards Fighter Regiment with empty fuel cells.[20]

On 18 August the division flew to the airfield at Stale, where the 694th BAO provided support. The foodstuffs department of this BAO fulfilled its obligations in an exceptional manner, but the same cannot be said for its technical department. Unserviceable aircraft were not repaired for five to ten days because of a lack of spare parts. On 30 August 1944, contaminated oil was delivered for topping off the Airacobras' oil tanks.[21] Even the wheeled vehicles experienced a shortage of fuel. The duty truck was supplied with sufficient fuel for only two round trips. As a result, after accomplishing their combat mission, the air crews had to walk from the aircraft to the 16th Guards Fighter Regiment command post. This delayed the receipt and compilation of their mission reports and the dispatch of the information to division headquarters.

The division was located at Mikshishuv airfield in Poland from 18 August 1944 to 6 January 1945. First the 379th, and later the 388th BAO supported 16th Guards Fighter Regiment; 299th BAO supported 100th and 104th Guards Fighter Regiments. There were several instances of delivery of fuel for Airacobras to the Mikshishuv airfield without an inventory sheet, and the fuel truck's tank had not been filled.[22] This led to delays in fighter sorties on combat missions.[23]

Living conditions at Mikshishuv airfield were not the best. The soldiers of 16th Guards Fighter Regiment were housed 1.2 to 1.8 miles from the airfield in Mikshishuv village. The regiment's technical personnel and young mechanics from the support units lived on the airfield itself, under the aircraft and in makeshift lean-tos. The aviators joked, "Heaven is having a Bell and a tent!" (This is a paraphrase of a Russian saying, "Heaven is having a young lady and a tent!") Some of the officer and senior technical staff were housed in private apartments in the village of Stale, 220 to 330 yards from the airfield.

The construction of troop shelters proceeded very slowly. Ten weeks after the troops' arrival at Stale airfield, three of these temporary facilities had been built for the technical staff and young specialists of 16th Guards Fighter Regiment. It took almost three months for a shelter to be constructed in which the air crews could rest, though by this time they were no longer conducting active combat operations.

Preparation of the equipment for winter use was not carried out in an organized fashion. Warming covers and heating equipment for the P-39s were not delivered on time. In November the division requisitioned 120 covers but were issued only 44 for their Airacobras. The delivery of compressed air was delayed, preventing the timely purging and recharging of one squadron's aircraft with winter hydraulic fluid.[24]

Interruptions in fuel deliveries had a negative impact on the combat readiness of the regiment's fighter units. For example, thirty-two aircraft were not refueled on the night of 21 to 22 April 1945. Two days later, eighteen P-39s in 16th Guards Fighter Regiment sat for a night with empty fuel cells at Burau airfield. This was at the height of the Berlin operation (16 April to 8 May 1945), the final strategic offensive in the Great Patriotic War.

During the entire examined period of combat operations of 216th (9th Guards) Fighter Division (March 1943 to May 1945), there were a number of significant difficulties in the division's logistical support. At times these difficulties sharply reduced the combat capabilities of the division's units. These difficulties can be divided into four categories.

The first—exceptional difficulty—was the chronic shortage of spare parts. This delayed, at times for long periods, the repair and return to use of aircraft damaged in combat or in accidents.

The second—great difficulty—was the untimely delivery of fuel and the delivery of engine oil of insufficient quality. Combat-capable aircraft could not sortie without fuel and serviceable oil.

The third—simple difficulty—was the persistent shortage of wheeled transportation assets in the BAOs. This lack of transportation was the root of many other problems: delays in refilling GSM stocks, constant difficulties with displacing ground elements to new airfields, and interruptions in the combat activities of the fighters. The absence of sufficient numbers of common and specialized trucks, too, often disrupted flight operations for one reason or another.

The fourth—ordinary difficulty—was frequent incidences of unsatisfactorily organized movement of aviation unit personnel and their prepared rations.

Despite all of this, the air crews and engineer-technical specialists coped with their assigned missions. It was very difficult, but each aviator and support soldier performed the task assigned and frequently did more than was required. These were ordinary Soviet young people, highly motivated in their deeds and attitude, who were driving the enemy from our territory, which he had occupied, forcing the fascist beast back into his own lair.

Before the war we used to sing a song that contained the words, "Don't bother us and we won't bother you. If you grab us, we won't let go of you!" The Germans were not convinced of the truthfulness of this warning and paid the price. They paid a steep price.

Command and Control of Fighters

Unlike other types of aviation, the combat actions of fighters are exceptionally intense and fast-moving. They are limited in time by the fuel supply in the aircraft tanks. Fighter aircraft streak out into the sky like arrows fired from a bow. The pilot seeks out a target, attacks it with a burst of cannon or machine-gun fire, then finds another target, and a third, constantly monitoring the expenditure of fuel. When the amount of fuel remaining is slightly more than is required for the flight home, the pilot returns to his airfield. The simultaneous conduct of all these activities requires the highest degree of command and control of fighter units and formations, from the moment of their takeoff through their return to the airfield and landing.

Putting high-speed aircraft of domestic manufacture and also from Lend-Lease deliveries into service in the Red Army VVS required the utmost firmness, resourcefulness, single-mindedness, and rationality from commanders at all levels in the supervision of their subordinates. Senior commanders' efforts in these matters had to be supplemented by a broad demonstration of reasoned initiative and independence in the lower echelons of command.

The point of departure for this analysis will be April 1943, when 216th Fighter Division began to execute assigned missions as a full-strength combat unit (45th, 16th, and 42d Fighter Regiments) equipped with Airacobra aircraft. Command and control of fighter aircraft in the air was regulated by the provisions of the "Instructions for command and control, early warning, and vectoring of aircraft with radio" approved by the commander-in-chief of the Red Army VVS.[1] The vectoring network included radio transmitters located at the command posts of the air army, aviation divisions, and regiments, and also radio stations positioned along the front line at 1.2 to 3.6 miles from the forward edge and 5 to 6 miles apart. The radio transmitter network operated both command and information nets (frequencies). In addition to transmitting information concerning the air situation in a particular zone, the transmitters vectored fighters to enemy aircraft and were used to control any air battle that developed. The radios were also used for directing *shturmoviki* against ground targets.

Moving from the general to the specific, here is how this system was used in the case of 216th (9th Guards) Fighter Division in the daily combat actions of its subordinate units. In the course of intense aerial engagements in the skies over the Kuban, division commander Major General Aleksandr Borman was continuously located at the main radio station for vectoring and controlling the air battle. This station was deployed two to three miles from the front line, not far from the command post of the ground forces commander for whom the fighter coverage was being supplied. The air division headquarters maintained reliable wire communications with General Borman using an ST-35 apparatus.[2] This contact kept the division staff constantly aware of the ground and air situation. All of General Borman's positive and negative observations were quickly relayed to the flying crews located at the airfield.

The division commander's presence at the vectoring radio station had an exceptionally positive influence on the outcome of an air battle. Knowing that their actions were under vigilant control from the ground, pilots made every effort to accomplish all instructions passed to them quickly and precisely. Pilots also knew that in the event of a radical change in the air situation, the required information would be quickly passed to them. They always would receive assistance and warning regarding danger. If circumstances required it, the division commander could intervene without delay in the actions of a group of fighters that had been sent out and could influence the outcome of the air battle with his recommendations or orders. The regiments' air crews highly valued the work of the vectoring transmitter and the significance of the radio in its command and control role.[3]

One time, after the close of the Great Patriotic War, some soldiers asked Twice Hero of the Soviet Union Grigoriy Rechkalov (415 combat missions, 112 aerial engagements, 49 personal and 6 shared kills), "Which was more valuable to you in the aircraft that you flew so successfully against the enemy—speed, the powerful cannon–machine-gun weaponry, the view from the cockpit, or the reliability of the engine?" The experienced fighter ace replied, "All the listed characteristics of the aircraft were very important. In aggregate they laid the foundation for success in an intense and rapidly unfolding aerial engagement. But more important than any of these was the radio."

In the April and May 1943 combat in the Kuban the principal deficiency of radio communications that made normal command and control of a group more difficult was the simultaneous use of a large number of aircraft transmitters in a limited sector of the front on a single frequency. When a patrolling group had entered an aerial engagement using the radio to the fullest, a newly arriving group or groups would begin to establish contact with the command post transmitter at the front line. The result of this was congestion on the frequency, which interfered with the vectoring station's attempts to establish contact with the approaching fighter units.[4]

The division commander at the vectoring station literally had to force his way through the scores of voices on the frequency, briefly indicating to what quadrant the aircraft were to fly. When the aircraft arrived in a particular sector, the local ground controller assumed responsibility for them.

For example, during the battles for Krymskaya and Kievskaya in May 1943, two division representatives were stationed at the command post of 38th Combined Arms Army. Their duty was to report the air and ground situation to their pilots and vector them to enemy aircraft. These same officers periodically (immediately if required) informed the division headquarters regarding all events that transpired in the patrol area and in front of the ground units. These reports permitted timely decisions to be made to reinforce an operating group or to dispatch a larger body of fighters to destroy enemy bombers.[5]

Broad employment of the radio in the air permitted our aviation units in the Kuban to fly in echeloned pairs by altitude, creating the so-called bookshelf formation. This formation was used during flight toward the front line and when searching for the enemy. To form the "bookshelf," each pair positioned itself some 2,000 to 2,600 feet above the pair below and inclined toward the sun. This made their detection by the enemy more difficult and in addition created favorable conditions for attack against enemy aircraft.

Skillfully organized command and control by radio from the ground and in the air sharply increased the effectiveness of fighter aviation. Air crews began to operate in a more organized fashion, maintaining close interaction among themselves and quickly concentrating their forces in the required direction at the critical moment of the air battle.

The massive equipping of our fighter aircraft with radios, and later the introduction to the forces of ground radar stations, made it possible, for the most part, to provide fighter cover to ground formations from alert status on the airfield. In connection with this, the patrolling method of coverage lost its earlier tactical dominance.

At this time the air armies, corps, and divisions received new operating instructions, contained in the "Instructions of the commander-in-chief of the Red Army VVS for command and control of fighter aviation in the air" of 8 May 1943. This regulation contained the following provisions:

1. The observation post of the [air] division or corps commander should be located in the vicinity of the ground army commander in whose interests the aviation unit is operating. At this observation post, maintain a radio transmitter-receiver by which the aviation commander supervises his subordinates who are in the battle area and directs them toward enemy aircraft, indicating to them by radio favorable headings and altitudes.

The lead aircraft of a group receives the unit commander's instructions by radio, confirms their receipt from the vectoring station, and in turn relays the commands to the air crews of the remaining aircraft.

With this method of command and control the pilots understand that their unit commander is observing their actions from the ground, that he is helping them to become better oriented regarding the air situation, and that he is sending patrols toward enemy aircraft for attack and simultaneously warning them of danger that the pilots cannot always detect themselves. This enables the pilots to work confidently and to achieve the greatest success in their actions.

This method of command and control from the ground also gives unit commanders the ability to acquire experience in directing the tactics of the aerial engagement and to teach their subordinates with specific examples.

2. At airfields, subordinate supervisory personnel, the deputy commanders of large units, and their chiefs of staffs who are supervising takeoffs and landings are preparing for the dispatch of the next group. Maintaining direct communications with their commander by radio or telephone, they receive supplementary instructions from him.

Command and control that is built around these principles is most effective during combat engagements.[6]

Giving enormous significance to the radio as the most important means of commanding and controlling aviation units and formations, the People's Commissar of Defense issued Order No. 363 of 10 August

1943, "Concerning giving incentives and awards to personnel of the Red Army VVS for increased qualifications in radio communications:"

1. Pilots who qualify at the appropriate class in radio communications are to be paid a one-time bonus at the following levels: 3d class qualification—25 percent of base pay; 2d class qualification—50 percent of base pay; 1st class qualification—75 percent of base pay; master qualification—100 percent of base pay. Pilots who receive the qualification "Master of aerial radio communications" will be recommended for an official award.

2. For each downed enemy aircraft that is detected with the assistance of vectoring by radio, the following monetary awards are announced:

A pilot who is qualified in radio communications and who detects an enemy aircraft and downs it based on instructions from a vectoring radio station receives 500 rubles above the sum indicated in NKO [People's Commissariat of Defense] Order No. 489 of 17 June 1942.

A ground controller who directs a fighter pilot to an enemy aircraft by radio, who organizes their contact and assists in the aerial engagement by radio, as a result of which the aircraft is shot down, receives 300 rubles.

3. The chiefs of communications of fighter and *shturmovik* aviation regiments who organize radio communications in an outstanding manner (air-to-ground vectoring station, air-to-air between aircraft crews, and air-to-landing field for the return of fighters and *shturmoviki*) are to be recommended for official awards if no fewer than 20 percent of pilots in their regiment have 1st class qualification, 30 percent have 2d class qualification, and 50 percent have 3d class qualification.

4. The commander, chief-of-staff, and chief of communications of reserve fighter and *shturmovik* aviation regiments are to receive monetary awards in the amount of one month's pay after the graduation of 120 pilots who are fully qualified in the conduct of two-way radio communications in flight.[7]

Radio communications issues received continuous attention from the higher Red Army VVS leadership. A follow-on order from the commander-in-chief of Soviet aviation was published on 23 August 1943, "Concerning deficiencies in the work of the radio vectoring network." This order laid out in a detailed manner some of the shortcomings in this area and listed measures to correct them:

Experience has shown that the system of alerting fighter aviation, vectoring it to a target, and controlling it in the air through a ground radio vectoring network is a necessary means of ensuring success in aerial combat.

The use by aircraft and ground radio stations of a single frequency in the vectoring network requires particularly careful organization of radio use and the strictest observation of radio discipline on the air. Meanwhile, the effectiveness of the work of vectoring networks has been reduced, and in a number of cases in air armies has been made almost impossible for the following reasons:

1. Ground radio stations of the vectoring network are being used for the exchange of documents between headquarters, paralyzing the work of aircraft radios. Command radio sets intended for this purpose are sitting idle.

2. Aircraft radios, when airborne, are loaded up by aircrews with unnecessary chatter (radio checks, conversation that has no bearing on command and control); crews are forgetting to turn off their transmitter after using it and the entire flight is conducted with the transmitter keyed.

3. In a number of units, the technical personnel tune aircraft radios without confirmation using control signals; they perform their duties in a hurried manner. Sometimes they tune with engines running rather than using batteries, which leads to imprecision in tuning.

4. All aircraft and ground radios are not being carefully tuned to one frequency of the vectoring network before flights. The control signals provided for this purpose by army RAT stations are not being used at airfields.[8]

5. Before departure on combat missions, flight crews are not instructed by the regiment communications chiefs, but are supplied with notes containing coded call signs, which pilots take with them in flight. Sometimes they write this information on instrument panels or shields, and this classified radio data can be accessed by the enemy in the event the aircraft does not return from the mission. I order:

When aircraft are in the air, limit the work of ground vectoring radio stations only to the delivery of necessary commands and alerting units to launch aircraft.

Transmit all remaining queries and reports by command radio sets on other frequencies.

That all air crew personnel observe radio discipline in the air; unnecessary chatter that not only blocks the air waves but also informs the enemy regarding our intentions is prohibited.

Transmit controlled frequencies for tuning receivers only through the RAT radio from VVS headquarters. Engineer-technical personnel with special equipment and regiment chiefs of communications are to become involved in issues of tuning aircraft and airfield radios using signals from army radio stations and in monitoring radio discipline in the air.[9]

By September 1943, the German forces on the left [southern] wing of the Soviet–German front had been pushed far to the west. The en-

emy had managed to delay for some time the advance of our formations in the sector south of Melitopol and along the Molochnaya River.
The first half of October was characterized by stubborn battles to
break through the enemy defense along this line and rapid forward
movement by the attack groupings whose task was to pursue the retreating enemy forces in the second half of October. Enemy aviation
was not particularly active in front of the formations of Fourth Ukrainian *Front* in this period. This inactivity was probably associated with
relocation to airfields in the area of Kiev and Kriviy Rog.

A new, more effective means—radar—was introduced into the command and control of aviation in the last quarter of 1943. In particular,
9th Guards Fighter Division received one RUS-2 radar set in October.
This new equipment immediately permitted a large portion of the regiments' forces to be held at airfields, in readiness for immediate takeoff
upon alert by this radar set. As a rule, two groups of fighters were maintained on call, one group of twenty to thirty fighters and a second group
of twelve to twenty.[10]

The first weeks of use of the RUS-2 demonstrated its capabilities. It
could detect targets at a range of fifty to sixty miles, and sometimes at
eighty to ninety miles if the enemy aircraft were flying at an altitude
of 9,800 to 13,000 feet in a formation of no fewer than six to ten aircraft. When the ceiling was 5,000 to 6,500 feet and enemy bombers
went out on a mission following the lower edge of the cloud base, the
radar could detect the formation at a distance of twenty-five to thirty-
five miles from the front line. Coincidentally, this is approximately the
same distance from the front line that the RUS-2 radar was located, in
the opposite direction.

Calculations showed that in this situation the enemy bombers
would reach the front line in four to five minutes, and our fighters,
based some fifteen to eighteen miles from the front line, would require one to three minutes to take off after being alerted and five to six
minutes to reach the area of coverage, a total of eight to ten minutes.
In this time the enemy would be able to accomplish his bombing mission. In order to prevent this outcome, the RUS-2 was repositioned at
six to three miles from the forward edge.

9th Guards Fighter Division began to operate in the interests of formations of 51st Army in the Crimean bridgehead on 19 November 1943
using information provided by the RUS-2. The presence of the radar set

Fighter Command and Control   147

constantly monitoring the airspace permitted the command to maintain modest forces for coverage—a group of from two to ten aircraft, depending on the situation. To provide equivalent coverage without use
of the radar set would require one pair of fighters at a rate of ten hours
per day, or approximately 215 aircraft sorties.

Using information received from the RUS-2, on-call groups took off to
intercept the enemy and successfully conducted aerial engagements.
Experience showed that the presence of the radar apparatus in the division yielded an economy of 50 percent in fuel and engine hours.[11]

Combat employment of the RUS-2 led to the conclusion that a daily
struggle had to be waged to reduce the takeoff time of on-call fighters
upon alert. These fighters should depart on a mission not later than 1
to 1.5 minutes after receiving the alert signal in any airfield conditions
or time of year. This required the elimination of all causes that might
delay a rapid takeoff. It was necessary to have engines prewarmed, taxi
the Airacobras to the takeoff position, maintain observation for visual
signals from the airfield command post, achieve simultaneous takeoff
of four aircraft,and prevent any kind of circling over the airfield.[12]

Of course, a complete and clear picture of the actions of enemy
aviation over his territory could not be obtained based on information
from the RUS-2. The apparatus detected the flight of enemy transport
aircraft in the depth of enemy dispositions, the rebasing of aviation
units to new airfields, the departure of fighters on reconnaissance and
cover flights, and the approach of bombers to the front line (to a heading accuracy of seven degrees). Practice showed that with the help of
the radar apparatus, the nearest active enemy airfield could be located
with an accuracy of 1.8 miles.[13]

The correct locating of the air target and its composition were
made significantly more difficult when the enemy transitioned to actions by small groups of aircraft. In this case, errors with the dispatch
of patrolling groups increased markedly.

Thus, the radar determined a target's course, speed, and approxi-
mate number (a single aircraft, flight, group, large group). With consis-
tent detections came the possibility of determining locations of
bomber airfields, their flight routes to the objective, and the areas
where they joined up with their fighter coverage. Having established
their basic flight route using the radar apparatus, the Soviet vectoring
network systematically monitored the progress of the enemy aircraft.

This greatly facilitated the planning of their interception. Small groups of "hunter" fighters were sent out to destroy the enemy bombers or to disperse them before they joined up with their fighter coverage. More powerful groups of fighters were sent up to destroy Ju-87s and Ju-88s well before they crossed the front line.

By observing daily for the flights of enemy aircraft it was possible to draw conclusions regarding several tactical methods the enemy used in the employment of his aviation. A new manner of bomber use was established: during flight over our territory toward their intended target, the aircraft flew along a route that contained several legs with sharp deviations in heading. Their intent was to confuse our air observation and reporting posts.

Occasionally the enemy used the following tactic. While approaching the front line and, obviously, having received information that a significant Soviet fighter force had been vectored toward them, the German bombers would begin to circle some twelve to fifteen miles from the front line. They remained in this "safe" zone until our patrols had departed from the target area, then continued with their bombing mission.[14]

An example of close cooperation between the radar station and patrolling groups occurred on 8 November 1943. Ten Airacobras were sortied based on a report from the radar station. They were not only able to prevent the enemy from reaching the target—a river crossing—but also to inflict heavy losses on the attacking air formation. The enemy lost four of nine Ju-87 bombers and one of four Bf-109 fighters. All P-39s returned safely to their airfield.[15]

A precise methodology was developed in the combat actions of the fighter regiments during the second half of 1943. The airspace above the area designated for coverage was divided into several zones. These zones were numbered and marked on our pilots' maps for target designation.

A group of fighters on alert took off upon a flare signal from the airfield command post, where a target plotting board for the RUS-2 was located. Experience showed that it was most practical to give the flare signal for takeoff of the alert group after the second detection of a group of enemy aircraft, which occurred one to two minutes after its initial detection. This permitted the radar operators to determine the area toward which the enemy aircraft were flying.

When the alert fighter group was in the air, the lead pilot received a command by radio to fly to a specific zone already marked on his map. After a number of radar sightings of the enemy formation, more precise vectoring of the fighters toward the enemy formation was also passed by radio.

To save time, the scrambled P-39s assembled as they were gaining altitude and assumed a combat formation while en route to the intercept. Approaching the designated coverage zone, the group made contact with the radar vectoring station and, vigilantly monitoring the airspace around them, executed the vectoring commands from the radar station. For its part, the vectoring radio station monitored this message traffic and remained informed of the time the alert fighter group took off and which zone the airfield command post directed the fighter group to based on information gained by the RUS-2.

The 9th Guards Fighter Division always employed an RUS-2 radar station in the offensive operations of 1944. If the regiments were based no more than nineteen to twenty-five miles from the front line, the radar station was positioned near an airfield and wire communications were established with it. Fighter groups scrambled to counter enemy bomber attacks based on alerts provided by the radar.

On 26 July 1944 at 1955, the RUS-2 detected a group of fifty enemy aircraft some thirty miles southwest of Yaroslav (Lvov–Sandomir operation). The enemy formation was flying on a course toward the river crossing at Rodimno. After a second detection that established the route of this aerial target, the command was given to scramble an alert group (six Airacobras) of 100th Guards Fighter Regiment. The fighters lifted off one minute later. At 2001 the radar station intercepted a second group of up to eighteen enemy aircraft flying to join the first group. In all likelihood, these were the escort fighters. A second group of six Airacobras from the same regiment was scrambled at 2003 to reinforce the six already aloft, and a third group of six was dispatched at 2023.

In a short time our patrols were reliably covering the river crossing, circling above it at altitudes of from 3,300 to 9,800 feet. According to information received from the RUS-2, shortly after the initial radar detections the enemy bombers and fighters had joined together in one common combat formation and headed toward the river crossing. When this formation was 7.5 to 11 miles from its intended target, it turned and departed to the west. Clearly it had been warned by its controllers positioned along the front line concerning the strength of Soviet fighter coverage over the intended target.

Anticipating a second attempt to bomb the bridge, at 2045 the division command sent out a fourth group of six Airacobras from 100th Guards Fighter Regiment to loiter over the crossing site. This preventive action was warranted. At 2052, the RUS-2 station reported that it had detected approximately twelve bombers 19 miles west of Yaroslav that were heading toward the river crossing. When they approached to within 7.5 to 9 miles of the front line, the enemy aircraft made several circles and then departed back to the west.[16]

The RUS-2 station that was assigned to the division on 20 July provided 1,151 indications of enemy aircraft overflights in a ten-day period. Eight scrambles were conducted based on these reports, with one resulting in an intercept. This engagement ended in the destruction of two Bf-109s. This radar station was not particularly effective because of its considerable distance (from thirty-seven to eighty miles) from the covered area.

In the beginning of March 1945, battles were being fought on the west bank of the Oder River. More than once the enemy attempted to push back the formations of 41st Army, which was holding a front about fifty miles wide. The most intense days of combat were 3 and 7 March. Despite unfavorable weather conditions, the fighter regiments of 9th Guards Fighter Division engaged in intense flight operations.

To maintain close cooperation with the covered ground formations, the fighter division commander organized an observation post collocated with the commander of 52d Army on the outskirts of Buntslau, eleven miles from the front line. The fighter division commander had at his disposal an RUS-2 radar station, a radio station for commanding and controlling his aircraft in the air, and direct telephone communications with his division headquarters. Positioning the radar apparatus in this way enabled the fighter division to accomplish several missions: cover the combat formations of the ground units; intercept enemy reconnaissance and "hunter" aircraft; based on radar data, provide longer-range vectoring of our own reconnaissance and "hunter" aircraft against enemy air targets; and provide information concerning the air situation to headquarters and patrolling aircraft. Taken together, all these mutually supporting command and control measures permitted the fighter units to provide timely and reliable protection to the defending ground formations.

Having successfully defeated countless enemy attacks, the forces of First Ukrainian *Front* went over to the offensive on 15 March. This marked the beginning of the Upper Silesia operation (15 to 31 March 1945).

As has already been noted, on-alert groups were launched after the second detection by the radar station of the hostile aircraft's position and direction of flight. After the Soviet fighters had taken to the air, the radar station determined the positions of both groups of aircraft, ours and the enemy's. It was possible to distinguish the two groups from each other only because the flight leaders' Airacobras were equipped with SCh-3 (*svoy-chuzhoy,* friend-foe) devices of Soviet production. In the entire division, fifteen P-39s were equipped with this device: five each in the 16th and 100th Regiments, four in the 104th Regiment, and one in the division headquarters.

Responses provided by this instrument made it possible to recognize an aircraft as friendly or not using the radar apparatus, vector our own aircraft equipped with the SCh-3 to enemy aircraft, monitor the flight path of our own air crews and assist them in the event they became lost, guide covering fighters into link-up with their bombers or *shturmoviki* for their subsequent joint flight to the target, provide information to groups of loitering fighters concerning the approach of enemy aircraft toward the covered zone, and send a coded signal to the radar station.

Vectoring from a ground station remained the basic method of command and control of Red Army VVS fighters in aerial combat throughout the Great Patriotic War. If in the first period of the war the air unit commander observed with binoculars and communicated by radio to a single aircraft—the flight leader—by late 1943 the air unit commander was aided by radar and the ability to talk to all airborne aircraft. Much of this improvement in command and control of fighter aircraft was a result of the excellent communications equipment installed on each P-39 Airacobra.

Navigational Support

During the Great Patriotic War the navigational service was a special service in military aviation whose function was to support the piloting of various types of aircraft. Navigational support was a combination of measures that ensured the greatest precision, reliability, and safety of aircraft flights, their timely arrival at assigned targets, and accurate destruction of the target. As it related to aviation units and large formations, navigational support was a form of combat support and included the following: preparation of reference data and navigational calculations; timely supply of topographical maps of the area of operations to the air crews; organization of employment of ground-based radio and radar assets (this included the use of the RUS-2 radar set and a radio-homing station to assist pilots who had lost orientation in bad weather); development of suggestions to the commander regarding navigational support; and resolution of navigational tasks during combat missions.

Navigators, together with appropriate staff and engineer-technical service personnel, performed these missions in aviation units. A unit navigator was a designated person who had special training, ensured the precise and safe piloting of aircraft, and was responsible for supervision of the navigational service at all levels of command. Table of organization positions existed for division and regiment navigators and a deputy squadron commander who doubled as the squadron navigator. The regimental navigator was considered one of the assigned pilots and took an active role in combat operations in a fighter aircraft. Matters pertaining to navigational service in a flight were handled by the flight commander.

The scope and contents of the navigational support measures depended on the navigational situation, combat conditions, nature of the assigned missions, technical characteristics of the unit's aircraft, navigational and gun sight equipment and armaments of the aircraft, pilots' level of training, and the assessment of the appropriate staff regarding all of these factors.

The division navigator provided overall supervision of this service, determining each component of the training mission and their sequence and duration. He provided the required data for close coordination with the navigational service at the air corps and air army and frequently with the ground forces *front* staff.

The busiest and most important time in navigational preparation was the period immediately before a combat operation. The navigator of a fighter regiment had significant responsibilities in this period and during the assigned combat missions. Practically all of the issues related to navigational support were resolved at this level. The quality of this preparatory work laid a foundation for the fighter pilots' successes in the upcoming air battles.

Navigators were especially busy when replacement pilots arrived in a unit. Their first task was to determine the new pilots' proficiency level in using the Airacobra's navigational instruments. Unit navigators ascertained the pilots' ability to read a topographic map, their knowledge of the theoretical fundamentals of orientation in the air, the procedure for maintaining communications with the vectoring radio station, and when necessary with the RUS-2 and radio-beaconing stations.

If any deficiencies or gaps in the pilots' knowledge were revealed during these examinations, immediate corrective measures were taken, including the organizing of exercises and classroom training. With the mounting on Airacobras of the SCh-3 device, much attention was given to training and habituating pilots in its use.[1] Along with this, a procedure was worked out for establishing contact with the *front* ground radio direction finder or division (air corps or air army) homing station in the event of loss of orientation.

At the conclusion of all of this training, each new pilot had to take an examination on these subjects. This concluded the theoretical phase of the evaluation and training of pilots' navigational skills. The pilots then transitioned to the next level of training—the acquisition and reinforcement of practical skills and habits. Training flights were conducted for this purpose. An airspace was designated over terrain with easily recognizable features, where pilots could practice their navigational and flying skills. This airspace was always in the immediate vicinity of the airfield basing district. Flights with the regiment or squadron navigator were initially conducted in a dual-control aircraft, after which a pilot flew solo in his assigned combat aircraft.[2]

Equally important and significant was the task of familiarizing air crews with the area of anticipated combat actions (over Soviet-held territory and enemy dispositions). Regiment and squadron navigators, together with the staff, developed an air route for this familiarization flight. This flight route normally was identical to the anticipated combat flight route. Selected in advance of the training, the route was a path that the units' aircraft could fly that would ensure reliable orientation, flight safety, and accurate arrival in the target area or assigned patrol zone. Several items were annotated on the flight map during the preparation of this route: the route line or path, checkpoints, distances and times of flight between checkpoints, bearing changes, and time calculations for reaching the target or designated point. In addition, noteworthy spot elevations of the area and the magnetic deviation were noted on the map. If the flight was planned for a significant distance (during rebasing, for example), the route was marked off in sectors of thirty to sixty miles for ease in calculating the distance traveled and remaining.

The document that resulted from this process became the basis of the instruction (oral or written) for navigational support of the division. The division document also specified the flight route for the regiments, flight altitude, and time of flight to the target area and return to the airfield. If the flight was to a new airfield network, this time of flight was the arrival time at the endpoint landing field.

The course that was announced for the flight followed the route indicated on the flight map. The initial heading or bearing of this course took into consideration the wind direction and speed measured at the departure airfield. Subsequent headings were adjusted for the wind encountered during the flight.

When a unit was relocating to another airfield network, frequently a transport aircraft (Li-2) flown by a pilot who was familiar with the route was designated as lead ship. Personnel aboard this aircraft made wind measurements en route. The data thus obtained were passed to the staff of the following air unit or formation by radio. Each pilot carefully studied and marked on his own flight maps the route that had been compiled on a topographic map and approved by the regimental commander for familiarization with the region of anticipated combat actions.

Navigators had additional responsibilities during combat operations. Most frequently the regiments received a mission for the entire day. Navigators determined the nature of the mission (reconnaissance, close air support, cover for a river crossing, escort bombers or *shturmoviki,* and so on) and time of flight. At the same time they re-ceived information regarding the nature of changes in the enemy's tactics (if any had been recently noted), along with supplementary in-formation for communications and radio beaconing.

Before taking off on the mission, the regiment (squadron) navigator was supposed to issue instructions. These instructions, which varied widely in accordance with conditions, contained elements pertaining to weather, reference points, and locations of ground units (any changes in the front-line trace); possible actions for individual crews that become separated from the group; and necessary amplifications regarding the procedure for establishing contact with the radio-beaconing station of the *front* (air army) and homing radio stations. Other instructions might include supplemental measures for ensuring normal landing at the air-field in the event of bad weather or delay in return to base due to night-fall (what color of rocket would be fired or pattern of ground lights or fires used).

Mikhail Petrov (at the time a squadron commander) recalls, "In March 1943, when 45th Fighter Regiment was based at Krasnodar air-field, despite the intensity of its units' combat efforts, there was not a single case of loss of orientation. The pilots used the Krasnodar wide-band transmitter as a homing station to guide them accurately into the airfield."

In the course of combat operations the division suffered a signifi-cant number of noncombat losses when young pilots became lost. For example, during the eight days of combat around Jassy, Romania (May to June 1944), there were six incidences of loss of orientation, four of which concluded with accidents (aircraft damaged during land-ing). This was the result of inadequate navigational training.[3]

In this same period, a number of pilots contacted the beaconing station immediately upon becoming lost. For example, Guards Junior Lieutenant Ivan Vakhnenko, who became lost in bad weather, re-quested a heading by radio. He carefully followed the course given to him and arrived safely at his airfield. The ground station continued to maintain communications with him and periodically confirmed the course his P-39 was following.[4]

In a critique of the combat actions in the Jassy operation, the com-mander of 9th Guards Fighter Division, Guards Lieutenant Colonel

Aleksandr Pokryshkin ordered, "I no longer want to see a single pilot depart on a combat mission without the course laid out on his map. Regiment navigators are responsible for this."[5]

During the division's participation in the Lvov–Sandomir operation (July 1944) in western Ukraine, its units encountered two major difficulties: difficult orientation due to the forested terrain and frequent unfavorable weather conditions. In this month alone seven pilots became lost, four of these from 104th Guards Fighter Regiment. Two Airacobras were destroyed and three more were damaged as a result of these incidents. The basic causes of loss of orientation were the weak training of the young pilots for their missions (routes not always marked on flight maps and calculations for flight not accomplished), failure to study adequately the region of combat activities, and failure to specify before launch the actions of individual crews who became separated from their groups. The majority of losses of orientation occurred when young pilots lost track of their group. Those who did become lost often had failed to request a radio bearing.[6]

A particularly great number of losses of orientation occurred in the first four days of the division's active combat operations (13 to 16 July 1944). Commanders at all levels took immediate measures to correct this situation. An order was distributed throughout the division to conduct a second confirmation of the pilots' knowledge of the region of combat actions. Educational work was stepped up and the pilots' attention was focused on the strict observation of discipline in the air. The elements of discipline stressed were radio communications procedures, maintaining proper position in formations, preserving the highest level of vigilance, preventing separation of individual aircraft from patrol formations, unauthorized departure of aircraft from the zone of an aerial engagement, and precise execution of commands from the ground vectoring and beaconing stations.

Preflight training and preparation were markedly improved, including those aspects that pertained to navigation. Postflight critiques of combat operations were intensified. The necessary conclusions were drawn that permitted the pilots to wage air combat with the enemy more successfully in subsequent battles. All these measures, when taken together, led to a sharp reduction in the incidences of pilots becoming lost. There was not a single such incident in August. Among the assets of ground aids to navigation, radio directional beaconing was widely employed. Requests were received from and bearings given back to sixty aircraft during the month of August.[7]

Veterans of the 9th Guards Fighter Division recall with unspoken gratitude the work of crews of the *front* radio homing station "Dunay" [Danube] during ground forces' offensive operations in Poland and Germany. It was mid-April 1945 and battles were being waged on the near approaches to the enemy's lair—Berlin. The 9th Guards Fighter Division was supporting the offensive of formations of 4th Guards Tank Army. Its fighter units had to function in exceptionally difficult weather conditions: dense smoke from fires in the forests and along the forward edge filled the sky. A dark gray shroud rose to an altitude of 4,920 feet, covering the airfield at Aslau, which was located near the front line at the beginning of the offensive.[8]

On 15 April, a group of eight Airacobras of 100th Guards Fighter Regiment was returning to its landing field after executing a combat mission. The patrol leader was Guards Lieutenant Grigoriy Dolnikov. The tight formation of fighters flew into a thick smoky overcast. Fearing midair collisions, the pilots broke from their combat formation. Almost immediately several tense radio calls went out to the powerful *front* beaconing station: "Dunay: Course to base!" The pilots were calling out to the distant radio beaconing station without observing the elementary rules of radio procedure. Everyone was requesting assistance at the same time. The operators at Dunay, of course, with such a din on the voice frequency, could not determine with any precision who was where and, naturally, were unable to give each pilot the necessary bearing for his flight home.

Dolnikov decided just as quickly to stop this "radio bazaar," but he was unable to do so. The female operator of the homing station beat him to the punch, bursting onto the frequency with a string of curses, followed by: "Boys! This is your mother speaking! I will guide you all home! Now be quiet! Make your request in turn. This is Dunay!" This scolding had the desired effect. The pilots stopped talking all at once. The first who dared to come back on the air was given the required bearing, followed by the remaining pilots. The entire group of P-39s safely completed their flight and landed at Aslau airfield.[9]

Loss of orientation, confusion, and the resulting accidents caused damage to expensive aircraft and the loss of priceless pilots. What was the cause? Some incidents were doubtlessly caused by pilots' inability to recognize terrain features on the ground. This frequently was the case with young and inexperienced pilots. However, there were a number of other, no less weighty circumstances that led aviators, both young and not so young, to such grievous consequences.

One must keep in mind that aerial combat of any sort is an intense activity that puts an enormous psychological strain on the pilot. He may face mortal danger several times in the course of an engagement. His life depends on his tactical skill and mastery of the controls of his aircraft. The question of "who will win out" in the duel with the enemy pilot is placed in sharpest relief. Close, but not entirely equivalent, is the confrontation on the ground between an antitank gunner and an enemy tank. In the latter case, nearby is a lifesaving trench or foxhole, or in the worst case a small mound of earth to serve as cover. But in the sky there is only the skin of the fuselage and the armor plating that may surround the pilot. The remainder of the airplane is vulnerable to machine-gun and cannon fire.

For the duration of the aerial engagement, which may last for twenty or more minutes, the pilot is executing countless simple and complex maneuvers. His body is repeatedly subjected to gravity forces several times his own weight. Veterans have recounted how they lost consciousness during some of these maneuvers. When the Airacobras were first employed early in 1943, they were not equipped with oxygen systems. Pilots had a difficult time flying at high altitudes. Mikhail Petrov recalls how after an intense dogfight he remained dizzy for some time, during which he was unable to say his own name without hesitation.

It is no surprise that on occasion, after participating in a life and death struggle with an enemy aircraft, a pilot could become lost. The paramount task was to accomplish the assigned mission, no matter how difficult, and return to one's airfield whole and undamaged, so as to be able to go out and fight the enemy again tomorrow.

Finally, some dogfights with enemy aircraft began in one zone and ended in another zone, sometimes many miles distant. It is no wonder in cases like this that pilots occasionally became lost or confused regarding their location.

Orders and instructions, no matter how strict, could not change these objective causes for pilots' loss of orientation or reduce the constant heavy pressure on pilots to accomplish their combat mission.

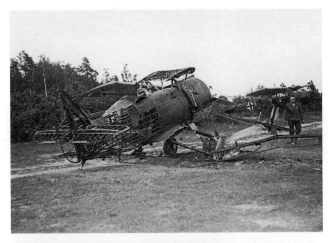

A German aviator has landed his Fieseler Storch to inspect damage to a parked I-15 biplane. (National Air and Space Museum, Smithsonian Institution)

A pair of I-15s destroyed in the Barbarossa attacks on the Red Air Force. (National Air and Space Museum, Smithsonian Institution)

A Polikarpov I-16 destroyed in the first days of the war. (National Air and Space Museum, Smithsonian Institution)

An Airacobra I built under contract for the Royal Air Force. (Partridge)

P-39Q-25s at Buffalo awaiting ferry flight to the Soviet Union. (Partridge)

P-39s on the assembly line in Buffalo. Items to note: 37mm cannon barrel protruding from the nose, pieces of armor plate already installed around the gearbox, and the three female workers installing wiring. (Partridge)

P-39Q-30s nearing completion on the Buffalo assembly line. The business end (1 × 37mm and 2 × 50 cal.) of a P-39Q is clearly shown on the rightmost aircraft. (Partridge)

53112

Approximately 2,050 P-39s were flown to the USSR through Alaska. This 1943 photograph of Ladd Field in Fairbanks shows P-39s in the foreground and A-20s in the background. (National Air and Space Museum, Smithsonian Institution)

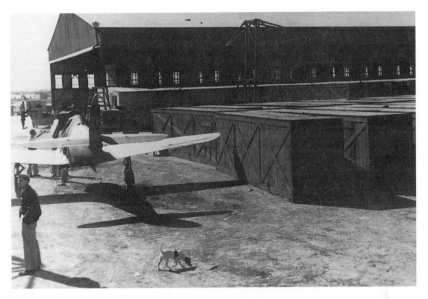

An assembled Airacobra stands parked beside several others still in shipping containers in Iran. (Furler)

Dual-control P-39 (UTI-4) in Soviet markings. (Petrov)

Above and facing page: Soviet
maintenance personnel at
work. (Petrov)

Crew rest. (Petrov)

Vadim "the Beard" Fadeev, killed in action on 5 May 1943. (Petrov)

From l. to r., Aleksandr Klubov, Grigoriy Rechkalov, Andrey Trud, and Boris Glinka. This photograph was taken between April and July 1944. (Petrov)

Grigoriy Rechkalov, with fifty-six personal and six shared kills, was the Soviet Union's number-four ace of the war. His fifty kills in the P-39 Airacobra make him the highest-scoring ace in that aircraft. (Petrov)

The right side nose of this P-39N is inscribed *Za Petyu Guchka* (for Petr
Guchek) and the left side of the same aircraft is inscribed *Za Vanyu Babak*
(for Ivan Babak). Guchek was Babak's wingman in the 100th Guards
Fighter Regiment. Shot down on 22 April 1945, while commanding the
celebrated 16th Guards Fighter Regiment, Babak was liberated from
German captivity by advancing American forces. Guchek remained in
the 100th GFR and was shot down and killed in action on 18 April 1945.
Grigoriy Dolnikov dedicated this aircraft to his two former squadron
mates after both had been shot down. (Petrov)

Driving an American Jeep, Aleksandr Pokryshkin surveys a downed
FW-189 "Rama." (Petrov)

Unidentified Guards lieutenant poses on the wing of his P-39. (Petrov)

From l. to r., Aleksandr Pokryshkin and Ivan Kozhedub, number-two and number-one Soviet aces, respectively, in an early postwar photograph. (Petrov)

Marshal of Aviation Aleksandr Pokryshkin, promoted to that rank in December 1972. (Petrov)

Soviet aviation personnel kneel on the flight line in front of their P-39s.
(Petrov)

PART TWO

August to December 1943

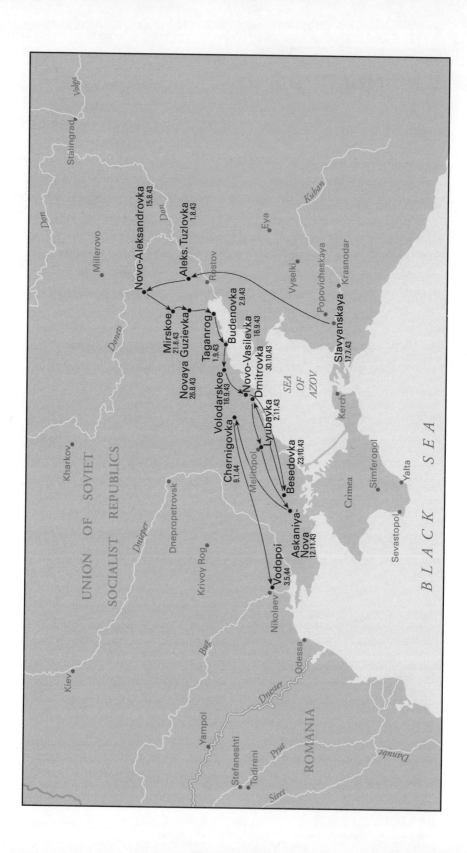

Stalingrad

Volga

Don

Millerovo

Don

Donets

Novo-Aleksandrovka
15.8.43

Aleks. Tuzlovka
1.8.43

Rostov

Mirskoe
21.8.43

Novaya Guzievka
26.8.43

Taganrog
1.9.43

Budenovka
2.9.43

Novo-Vasilevka
16.9.43

Volodarskoe
16.9.43

Dmitrovka
30.10.43

Lyubavka
2.11.43

Chernigovka
9.1.44

Besedovka
23.10.43

Melitopol

Askaniya-
Nova
12.11.43

Vodopoi
3.5.44

Nikolaev

Bug

Krivoy Rog

Dnepropetrovsk

Dnieper

Kharkov

Kiev

UNION OF SOVIET

SOCIALIST REPUBLICS

Kuban

Eya

Vyselki

Popovicheskaya

Krasnodar

Slavyanskaya
17.7.43

SEA
OF
AZOV

Kerch

Simferopol

Yalta

Crimea

Sevastopol

B L A C K   S E A

Dnester

Odessa

Yampol

Stefaneshti

Todireni

Prut

ROMANIA

Siret

Danube

A Wingman's Feat

The offensive of the forces of Southern *Front* for the liberation of the Donbass from the German occupiers continued in August 1943. The 16th Guards Fighter Regiment received the mission to cover the combat formations of General Nikolay Kirichenko's 4th Guards Cavalry Corps, which was operating jointly with General T. I. Tanaschishin's 4th Guards Mechanized Corps. Despite their sizable losses in the air, the German command continued to inject significant forces of bombers, covered by fighters, into the battle.

At 0530 on 23 August, a six-ship flight of P-39s led by Aleksandr Pokryshkin sortied from Mirskoe airfield. Pokryshkin kept another pair of fighters with his pair for the main force and assigned the third pair (Andrey Trud and Aleksandr Klubov) to a covering position some 985 to 1,300 feet above the attack group.

The weather was calm in a clear sky. The sun was just beginning to appear above the horizon. The ground was enshrouded in a light haze. The Airacobras' flight altitude was 13,125 feet. Soon the pilots could make out the front line beneath them—it was engulfed in smoke and fire. The ground forces were assaulting the strong points of the Muis front, which the enemy had erected over the course of two years.

Pokryshkin attempted to communicate with the ground vectoring station "Tiger," but it did not respond. In all probability, it had not yet managed to come back on line after a night relocation. In such situations the patrol transitioned to independent search for the enemy. This was not the best option, but there was no alternative.

The leader of the second pair, Viktor Zherdev, at this time reported to Pokryshkin the sighting of a group of aircraft at 120 degrees on the horizon. Pokryshkin acknowledged the transmission and ordered a left turn. Trading altitude for increased speed, the Airacobras closed with the targets, which were maintaining a course toward the front line. Pokryshkin was sure of himself. They would intercept the enemy on the approaches to the front line, disperse his combat formation with a sudden attack, and disrupt his bombing of our own forces.

Their speed grew with each second. They could now make out the silhouettes of the enemy bombers—nine Ju-88s covered by six Messerschmitts. A similar group flew behind the first at a distance of approximately 2,200 yards. The fighter cover for this second group was not in sight. Having detected the Airacobras, the enemy began to deploy from a column into a line abreast formation. This would ensure the best conditions for conducting massed aimed fires from their flexible machine guns.

Pokryshkin ordered Trud's pair to provide cover while he led the remaining crews in an attack. The six fighters escorting the bombers, in turn, began pursuit of the Pokryshkin-led subgroup. But Andrey Trud and Aleksandr Klubov blocked their path. The Messerschmitts zoomed upward, withdrew to the flank, and began to anticipate the position of the P-39s as they came away from their first pass. Trud and Pokryshkin turned into the Messerschmitts to conduct a frontal attack, but the Germans refused combat and dived below.

At this time Pokryshkin and his three comrades were rapidly executing a small maneuver to come into the tail of the bombers. The rear-facing cabin gunners of the German aircraft put up a fusillade of fire in an attempt to disrupt the P-39s' attack. But the Airacobras' attack angle was too great and the enemy tracer streams passed off to the side. This was a situation oft-described by Aleksandr Pokryshkin when training his young pilots in the fine art of aerial combat. "Speed and only speed will permit you to penetrate through this fire barrier, reach the enemy, and defeat him."

One of the bombers was trailing flames. Bombs spilled out of its belly as the crew unloaded the dangerous cargo in an attempt to take their damaged aircraft back to its airfield. It was an empty hope. A moment later the aircraft exploded.

Despite all of Pokryshkin's twisting and turning maneuvers, Golubev did not fail in his obligation as wingman to hang onto the tail of his commander. Georgiy noticed something flash past his Airacobra on the left side. He immediately rocked his aircraft and saw a thick black trail of smoke—a Bf-109 was racing toward his leader's P-39. Golubev broke into a sweat. Perhaps the German had already brought the crosshairs of his sight onto "100" and was waiting to reach the appropriate range. Pokryshkin was distracted by his own attack on another German bomber and did not notice the approaching danger. In many prior aerial engagements he had been reliably covered from the rear quadrant. At this precise moment in this battle "Three G" (Georgiy Gordeevich Golubev) had experienced a lapse of vigilance. The Messerschmitt had managed to penetrate into the space between his own "55" and Pokryshkin's "100." Since the days of the Kuban the Germans well knew who flew the aircraft with the number "100" painted on the side. They dreamed of the lucky moment when this aircraft might be in the gun sight of a Bf-109 or FW-190. That moment of great danger to Aleksandr Pokryshkin would arrive in mere seconds.

Fate had literally thrust a challenge into the face of Guards Junior Lieutenant Golubev. This was a test of the limits of his capabilities. He would accomplish an unusual feat or be a helpless witness to the death of his commander. By front-line standards, this was Georgiy's "moment of fame." Everything depended on his actions. Either he would punish himself for the rest of his life for not preventing a tragedy, or his comrades would proudly say about him, "He saved Pokryshkin in combat!"

Here is what Hero of the Soviet Union Georgiy Golubev wrote about this day some thirty years later.

I decided that even it if cost me my own life, I should save the commander. And I threw my fighter at the enemy. The enormous force of gravity swept over me and I momentarily lost my vision. Then suddenly I felt a sharp blow. The control stick was wrenched from my hand, the aircraft shuddered and began to turn over on its back rapidly toward the left. I found the stick and with difficulty brought the aircraft back to level flight. There was a hole in the center wing section and yellow-red flames were licking at the cabin. Gray streams of smoke trailed behind my aircraft.

I was not thinking of myself at that moment. The thought drilled through my brain, "The commander is in danger!" I recovered in time. My aircraft rose up in front of the Messerschmitt and at that instant a burst of fire intended for "100" passed through my fighter. My aircraft was on fire but I was alive. I recalled the time was 0610.[1]

While in the air Pokryshkin knew nothing about what was happening with his permanent wingman. Only later at the airfield did Konstantin Sukhov and Viktor Zherdev tell him about Golubev's unexampled feat. Pokryshkin was overcome by concern: Had Georgiy managed to make it to our own territory or, having bailed out, did he fall into the lap of the Germans?

After the moment of crisis had passed, Golubev was forced to gather all his strength and energy. Thanks to his combat comrades—Sukhov and Zherdev—the two Bf-109s did not get to him in the zone of the aerial engagement. Now his only hope rested in himself. By his calculations, Georgiy was not less than twelve miles from the front line. He had to stretch out his glide path. He tried with all his strength to hold the Airacobra at altitude. If the engine died he might be able to glide the aircraft for some distance. In normal circumstances he would bail out over Soviet-held territory. In order to reach that point he would stay in the burning aircraft until the last minute. When he abandoned the P-39, fire would singe his hands or burn his face.

There was no smoke or fire in the cabin yet. Golubev took off his oxygen mask and looked around. He saw two Messerschmitts making a left turn behind him to come in on his tail. There was no doubt as to their intentions. Now everything depended on the calculations of the Airacobra pilot and how his disabled machine responded to the controls. It responded badly. However, in such extreme conditions his life was worth fighting for and he did not give an inch to the more powerful enemy.

Georgiy continuously monitored the actions of the "bandits" as they closed with his Airacobra. The pilot mentally determined the range that would be most favorable for effective fire. When he thought the German aircraft had reached that line, he maneuvered his P-39 sharply to the right. At that exact moment the tracers of a cannon burst hurtled by and burst in bright flashes in front of his aircraft. He had survived the first pass.

After the attack the enemy aircraft climbed above for a possible second pass. Golubev took the same position as before, monitoring the airspace behind him as best he could. The situation was deteriorating with each passing moment. The smell of fire was penetrating into the cockpit, followed quickly by pungent smoke. Golubev was gripped by fear. His fighter could explode at any moment. There would be no time to bail out. He believed that the front line was still far distant. He had only one choice: as long as the Airacobra's engine did not die and the aircraft still responded to the control stick, though poorly, he would push for home.

Slowly losing altitude, the P-39 flew a straight course at high speed. The pilot noted dangerous tongues of flame licking at the back of the instrument panel. His right leg began to feel the heat. Georgiy had to remove it from the rudder pedal and draw it back toward his seat. Now he held the fighter on course with only the left rudder pedal and control stick. But soon the flame reached his left leg.

The cabin filled up with acrid smoke. Golubev became hot and began to have difficulty in breathing. He began to cough violently as copious tears streamed from his eyes. He could not see the Messerschmitts now. Perhaps the enemy aviators had decided that the Airacobra had taken enough lead and would go down without further action on their part.

Golubev wiped the tears from his eyes and looked below, trying to determine whose terrain he was overflying. A new problem arose—his clothing began to smolder. The front line should be behind him now. It would be dangerous to remain in the aircraft any longer. Georgiy jettisoned the side door with the emergency handle and covered his face with his hands to protect against the flames. He jumped.

To the joy of his comrades and of Georgiy himself, his ordeal had a happy ending. He landed in the neutral zone between the two sides. Initially he was taken to be an enemy pilot and was forced by two soldiers to throw his pistol on the ground. They led their "prisoner" to their regiment positions, where they checked his documents, then sent him to the rear.

Two days later, a *gazik* [small GAZ truck] delivered Golubev to his home airfield.[2] His "aviation family" was ecstatic. Their combat comrade had accomplished such an unusual feat and stood before them complete and unharmed.

Especially happy for the return of Golubev to duty was his pair leader, Aleksandr Pokryshkin. He gave his wingman a firm embrace and spoke a single, heartfelt *"Spasibo!"* [thank you].

Golubev was issued a new aircraft and rejoined the flight schedule the next day.

You Won't Get Away!

It was the end of August 1943. Battles were still raging in the Donbass. Having suffered a terrible defeat at Kursk and Orel, the enemy was hurriedly concentrating tank and infantry divisions for another push toward Kharkov.

The 16th Guards Fighter Regiment was escorting Pe-2 bombers that were conducting strikes against accumulations of enemy forces at the railroad junctions Ilovaysk, Khartsyzsk, and Gorlovka. These actions continued over the course of four days. Simultaneously the Airacobras actively conducted strafing attacks against enemy trains on the sidings, inflicting significant losses.

Then the regiment was diverted to provide cover for formations of the first echelon of the 44th Combined Arms Army. The 100th Fighter Regiment had been operating successfully in this role since the middle of August. Its pilots had shot down six enemy aircraft at the loss of one of their own.[1] Their aerial engagements and battles were of an episodic nature, the Germans not being particularly active.

The squadrons of 16th Guards Fighter Regiment were operating from Novaya Tuzovka airfield. In this relatively quiet situation, the 2d Squadron commander, Grigoriy Rechkalov, sent off Guards Junior Lieutenant Vyacheslav Berezkin in the first combat sortie on 24 August. He was designated as wingman to the flight commander, Guards Senior Lieutenant Viniamin Tsvetkov. The pair's mission was to reconnoiter the area east of Gorlovka. Having successfully accomplished their combat mission, on their return leg the P-39s were approaching the front line at an altitude of 13,125 feet. They made contact with the ground vectoring station.

"Attention '21'—below, altitude 4,900 feet, Focke-Wulf 189. Attack it!" air controller Nikolay Dvornikov passed along the division commander's order.[2] Tsvetkov looked down. He spotted a "Rama," escorted by four Bf-109s on a parallel course.[3] Viniamin took upon himself the difficult task of attacking the escort fighters and ordered Vyacheslav to attack the reconnaissance aircraft.

The FW-189 was well known to the Airacobra pilots. It was a slow-moving but quite maneuverable and armored aircraft of modest size.

All this taken together made it a difficult target to destroy. Experienced pilots always attempted to take out the "greenhouse" first, because that was where the crew was located.

Guards Senior Lieutenant Tsvetkov fell on the four "bandits" with an "eagle strike" and engaged them in battle. This was not the first time he had contended with a superior enemy force. It was his eighty-fifth combat sortie and forty-third air battle. The attack caught the enemy by surprise. One Messerschmitt had already vanished. The remaining three flew off in all directions. The flight leader did not attempt to pursue them but instead flew in circles, covering his wingman. He was ready at any moment to attack the enemy escort fighters.

At this time Berezkin was chasing the "Rama," coming up from its bottom rear. The FW-189 increased in size in the gun sight with each second. The young pilot was nervous and opened fire too early. The "Rama" quickly maneuvered out of the tracer stream. In the heat of battle he forgot Pokryshkin's simple advice: "When the wings of the attacking aircraft fill your sight, fire!"

The vibration of the Airacobra, moving at maximum speed, may also have contributed to the inaccuracy of the fire. Strange as it might seem, the enemy reconnaissance and spotting aircraft continued to fly deeper into Soviet-held territory, holding to a precise course and altitude. Clearly it was conducting aerial photography. This flight mode permitted the "Rama's" rear gunner to conduct more precise fire at the P-39. Berezkin avoided this fire and scrubbed off some speed to stop the shaking that was disturbing his aim.

At this moment the pilot's entire body felt a hail of bullets strike his aircraft. The P-39 shook. All of the pilot's attention was focused on the instrument panel, which showed normal readings. Seconds passed. Vyacheslav still did not see blood or feel pain. He was trying with all his might to bring the Airacobra closer to the target in order to get a sure kill. A person can continue to function in this manner until he sees his wound. Suddenly Berezkin turned over his left arm and saw that it was covered in blood. It also had ceased to respond to his commands. His left leg had also been hit. Now it was becoming difficult to control his aircraft. The burst that struck his aircraft moments earlier could hardly have done greater damage without killing him. The Airacobra pilot well understood his predicament.

The FW-189 continued to fly straight and level. It was as if its crew were throwing a challenge to the hapless fighter pilot. The rear gunner was probably waiting for the attacking Airacobra to approach closer.

In such situations a front-line pilot, particularly when wounded, became even more intense. All his remaining strength was marshaled for a final, unwavering move. For Berezkin this day's battle was his combat christening. He had been given the order "Destroy the 'Rama'!" He had to carry out this order at any cost. They say that one's last battle is his most difficult. I tend to believe that the first battle for someone who had just arrived at the front could be twice or three times as difficult.

Berezkin was seized by a singleness of purpose. He had expended enormous effort and energy in becoming a fighter pilot. Now an easy prey, an unharmed enemy aircraft, was flying forward into our zone. Berezkin was wounded and his Airacobra was damaged. He took comfort in one thing—his aircraft was still controllable.

"You won't get away!" Vyacheslav almost shouted, and gave his number "7" the throttle as he flew toward the hated "Rama." In such a critical moment the pilot and the aircraft become as one, as if the aircraft's engine and the pilot's heart were beating in unison.

The Airacobra pilot chopped off a tail boom of the FW-189 with the wing of this P-39. The enemy aircraft fell in a twisted heap toward the earth. His P-39 was also damaged. Falling over on its side, it began rapidly losing altitude. Berezkin jettisoned the right cabin door and, gathering his strength, jumped through the opening. The slipstream catapulted him away from the falling Airacobra. With his uninjured hand he groped for and found the parachute deployment ring and pulled it hard. He felt a strong jerk as his canopy opened.

Now he had another cause for alarm. On whose territory would he land? From above he could clearly see the zigzag trace of the front line and off to his right flank he could make out an enormous patch of woods. Smoke hid any additional features from his view in that direction. Vyacheslav glanced back and could barely make out the features of Amvrosievka in the far distance.

Finally his legs struck the ground. Berezkin fell down, then with difficulty collapsed his canopy and unstrapped himself from the harness. He did not have enough strength to get up. A troubling thought entered his mind: "Which side has this shot-up contested soil?" Hearing cautious steps, he removed his pistol from its holster and cocked it. They would not take him without a fight. Preferring death to captivity, he would save his last bullet for himself.

A head popped up from behind some bushes, wearing a *pilotka* [flat-sided military cap] with red star. Enormous joy filled Berezkin's spirit: *"Svoy!"* [I'm yours].

A rifle battalion medic worked Vyacheslav's wounds, then gave him the required inoculations and bandaged him. The troops fed him and then delivered him to the regiment aid station. That evening an ambulance was transporting the wounded, including Berezkin, to the rear. He inquired as to the route it would follow. Fortunately, the road passed not far from his home airfield. He convinced the medic to deliver him to Novaya Tuzovka.

The Ukrainian road had been broken up by tanks and trucks, pounded by artillery shells and aircraft bombs. It would have been a rough ride for a healthy person, but to the wounded it was torture. Although the ambulance driver proceeded carefully, it was not an easy journey for his passengers.

The pilot listened to the sounds of the surrounding terrain. Then he heard the familiar roar of an Allison engine. The ambulance stopped. One of the airfield maintenance personnel opened the back door and spotted Berezkin. Word quickly spread across the airfield that their missing pilot was alive and present. In just a few minutes a joyful crowd of pilots, mechanics, and service personnel had gathered around the ambulance.

An aviator firmly declared to the infantry medic, "Berezkin will not be traveling farther with you. We have our own aviation hospital where he will recover." They carefully removed Vyacheslav from the ambulance. As a sign of gratitude for the delivery of their brother to his home, they gave the medic and his driver anything that they had at hand: cigarettes, chocolate, even vodka.

The good news reached the regiment commander, Guards Major Aleksandr Pokryshkin. He quickly appeared among the scores of his subordinates. Berezkin, still lying on a stretcher, reported to the regiment commander his actions for the destruction of the "Rama." Listening to Berezkin, Pokryshkin caught himself wondering if this seriously wounded pilot would ever fly again.

After three months of hospitalization and one surgical operation, followed by intensive physical therapy for his left arm and leg, Vyacheslav Berezkin returned to duty. His wounded left extremities had almost completely recovered their strength and mobility. He returned to his Airacobra and fought bravely against the enemy until the end of the war.

Over the Molochnaya River

The advancing Soviet ground forces reached the Molochnaya River on 20 September 1943. The enemy had hurriedly prepared a new line of defenses on its western bank. The primary nexus of the enemy's resistance was Melitopol. The Germans managed for a brief time to delay the Soviet formations' advance. Fierce air battles were fought above this water obstacle for a week.

On 21 September a four-ship flight led by Pokryshkin conducted an engagement with an armada of enemy bombers in the area of Bolshoy Tokmak. No two air battles are exactly the same; each has its own peculiarities and outstanding features. So it was on this day.

The pairs were Aleksandr Pokryshkin–Georgiy Golubev and Viktor Zherdev–Konstantin Sukhov. It was a well-coordinated combat flight. The Airacobras crossed the front line at high altitude and headed toward Nikopol and beyond it Bolshoy Tokmak. Having reached that location, the group, on command of its leader, turned to the left ninety degrees. Sukhov spotted the enemy bombers first and reported it over the radio. There were many of them, column after column, at the same altitude as the P-39s. Their silhouettes were clearly outlined on the bright background of the sky.

Pokryshkin gave the order to conduct a frontal attack. Before such an attack could be carried out the four aircraft in the flight had to regroup into a more compact formation. A tight formation made their firepower more effective.

The Ju-87s were fast approaching, with no fighter escort in sight. The pilots searched the sky in all directions. No "bandits." Perhaps they had gone forward to meet the Airacobras on the approaches to the front line. They had passed without detecting our patrol, which by a circuitous route had found itself in the enemy rear area.

Pokryshkin's sharp voice suddenly broke radio silence: "Don't fire—Petlyakovs [Pe-2s]!" This command came only seconds before the entire flight would have commenced mass fire. It would have been a great embarrassment to have fired on their own aircraft.

The group rushed past the column of oncoming bombers. The group leader and the other pilots could not believe their eyes: black and white crosses on flat surfaces; yellow color on the wheel strut fairings. What kind of Pe-2s were these? They were genuine fascists!

Pokryshkin acknowledged his error. Later he candidly explained that at the last second it suddenly seemed to him that these were not Ju-87s but our own Petlyakovs. He had been momentarily blinded by the sun and made a mistake. He had to correct himself on the fly.

Distressed at the loss of surprise, Pokryshkin ordered a 180-degree turn. Now his flight of P-39s would have to attack from the rear, into the dense fires of the enemy gunners. They would pay for his mistake. The Soviet fighter group turned around. Zherdev's pair was already in the heart of the enemy formation. Pokryshkin and Golubev quickly joined them in a fight that had already begun. The P-39s moved through the lead column of Ju-87s. Pokryshkin fired at the lead aircraft from close range. A few seconds later a large blinding flash filled the windscreen of his Airacobra. The explosion enveloped the bombers. Pokryshkin's aircraft could not avoid the fireball. A large piece of the bomber's fuselage flashed past the Airacobra. The commander's P-39 flew into the flames on inertia; it shuddered once or twice as something struck it hard. An instant later the P-39 emerged from the fiery cloud. Another Ju-87 was burning nearby. This damage could have been the result of a sympathetic detonation from its neighbor.

The Guards major immediately turned toward the enemy bomber on the extreme right of the formation. A burst of fire passed into the bomber's right side, causing the aircraft to emit a stream of smoke. Turning his aircraft sharply, the German pilot threw it into a dive and jettisoned his bomb in an attempt to go back to the west. Pokryshkin went after the Ju-87 and caught it with a second burst of cannon and machine-gun fire. He pulled back sharply on his control stick to gain altitude. As the group leader, he needed to locate his subordinates.

He saw a bomber falling off to the right, the work of Zherdev's pair. Several parachutes hung in the air, all German bomber crewmen. Pokryshkin's memory resurrected the image of Nikolay Ostrovskiy. He also had been descending by parachute when the Germans showed him no mercy. They ruthlessly shot him in the air. Unable to contain his anger, Pokryshkin pressed on the trigger switch.

Zherdev and Sukhov were pursuing a fleeing bomber and drove it into the ground. The rear seat gunner fought back furiously, putting several holes in the pair leader's fighter. The bomber maneuvered wildly, hoping that in diving it could shake off the attacking P-39s by flying low. But the German miscalculated and attempted too late to transition his aircraft to horizontal flight. It settled, then struck the ground, and instantly exploded into pieces.

The battle continued. There were many targets yet to be serviced in the sky, but all the Airacobras were running low on fuel. It was time to go home! The brief but intense battle had ended with five bombers littering the fields around Bolshoy Tokmak. Pokryshkin's full-strength group assembled on the airfield. Zherdev's Airacobra had seven holes; "100" had two deep dents and soot and large oil spots all over its fuselage.

Another engagement was fought on 26 September. The ratio of enemy to friendly forces at the beginning of the battle was 14.5 to 1. Aleksandr Klubov led seven other Airacobras, flown by Konstantin Sukhov, Pavel Eremin, Nikolay Chistov, Aleksandr Ivashko, Viniamin Tsvetkov, Nikolay Trofimov, and Andrey Trud. They took off on an alert sortie and immediately headed for the west bank of the Molochnaya River to the area of Kuybyshevo and Burchak (southwest of Melitopol).

The voice of division commander Ibragim Dzusov sounded clearly in the pilots' headsets. He was at the ground vectoring station, urging his aviators into battle. He announced the enemy bomber formation's altitude at 13,125 to 16,400 feet. Dzusov ordered another eight Airacobras to sortie under the command of Sergey Lukyanov. With this group's entry into the battle the ratio of forces became seven to one in the Germans' favor.

Klubov and his pairs passed along the northern shore of Lake Molochnoe. Akimovka was visible below them. The enemy bombers were flying eastward from the direction of Kuybyshevo, their silhouettes barely visible. They were in tight formations, but the formations themselves were scattered about the sky. How many? It was difficult to say, but it was clear that there were a large number.

"Tiger" [the ground vectoring station] issued a warning: More than a hundred Heinkels and Junkers, escorted by twenty or more fighters, were approaching Burchak from the southwest. "Tiger" ordered all the Airacobras to go to Burchak. Klubov acknowledged the order.

He and his comrades would be the first to clash with this aerial armada. The correlation of forces was unbelievable. The courage of the

Airacobra pilots was not in question, but in this situation bravery alone was not enough. Until Lukyanov's group arrived, Klubov and his pairs had to defeat the enemy with skill despite their clear inferiority in numbers of aircraft. They had to conduct a rapid strike with high-speed maneuver and prevent the enemy from confining the Airacobras to one sector of the engagement zone. The battle would start with a lightning attack and a storm of cannon and machine-gun fire to defeat the target, then a maneuver to rapidly depart and reach a new position.

By radio Klubov assembled his eight Airacobras into a tight "fist" for a frontal attack. He ordered his formation to fly under the enemy bombers and execute the follow-on attack from below. This was a proven effective tactic in these conditions. Each pilot knew from his own experience that a sudden frontal attack against a superior enemy force stunned him with its daring and frequently, if even for a brief time, paralyzed enemy aviators. The primary objective in this attack was to shoot down several bombers from the lead nine-ship formation, in particular that formation's leader. This act had proven in many instances sufficient to cause confusion and uncertainty in the enemy ranks, and sometimes panic. Taking advantage of the developing situation, the Soviet aircraft would rapidly shift their attack to other elements of the enemy combat formation. Having fired up the enemy column more than once, the Airacobras would disengage below the enemy bombers and not above.

Although he was a firm believer in Aleksandr Pokryshkin's fighter tactics, in this particular situation Aleksandr Klubov was forced to depart from his rule: "Be above, and not below, the enemy." Altitude was dangerous because that was where the significant force of escort Messerschmitts was orbiting. Lukyanov's group, when it arrived, would engage them. After a series of frontal attacks on the He-111s, it would be better for Klubov's group to take cover below them and launch follow-on attacks coming back upward. The He-111s would themselves provide some shelter to the Airacobras against the fires of the Messerschmitts from the upper hemisphere.

The seconds ticked by as the two forces closed at high speed, eight "arrows" aimed at an armada of enemy aircraft. The targets increased in size with each second, little by little filling the sight rings. Finally, tracers of cannon and machine-gun fire began to write their death sentences.

Eremin and Sukhov were to the right of the commander, and Trud and Trofimov—the primary attack subelement—were on the left. These six aircraft were headed toward the lead Heinkels. After the first cannon and machine-gun burst the leader of the first enemy formation of nine bombers, having lost his left wing and motor, spun to the ground. A second Heinkel shared his fate. Racing forward, the pair of Chistov and Tsvetkov had already set upon another He-111. The burning pieces of this aircraft came apart as they fell. The first attack was highly successful, knocking down three bombers. A minute later all eight Airacobras had reassembled under the bellies of the lead column for another attack. Two more German bombers fell in flames.

Klubov issued a command to the third and fourth pairs to attack the second nine-ship formation from below. Chistov, Tsvetkov, Trofimov, and Trud shifted their attention to the next formation. Klubov's intent was to broaden the frontage of his attack on the enemy, to force the enemy to disperse his dense formation and drop his bombs before reaching their intended targets. Up above, Lukyanov's P-39s had arrived and were mixing it up with the escort Bf-109s.

Chistov and Trofimov did not miss their opportunity.[1] Sukhov and Eremin each shot up a Heinkel,[2] both of which fled westward trailing smoke. The Airacobras continued to engage the columns. Trud poured a stream of lead into the belly of an He-111 from fifty yards. The shock wave from the ensuing explosion shook Andrey's Airacobra. These close kills were not without danger for the attacker.

Klubov's eight-ship formation engaged German bombers until the Airacobras were low on fuel and ammunition. Klubov requested a "33" [return to base]. The ground vectoring station gave permission to break off the attack and return to base. Klubov's group had shot down eight enemy bombers and damaged another two. The Airacobras of Ivashko and Chistov were moderately damaged, but the Airacobra pilots reached their base and managed to land safely.[3] Trud's P-39 was covered with a thick dirty yellow liquid film from the propeller spinner almost to the vertical tail section—aviation oil from the exploding Heinkel.

Something else happened in the fall of 1943, an incident that was not settled for several months. On 30 September 1943, during a routine combat mission, Guards Junior Lieutenant Grigoriy Dolnikov was shot down and fell wounded into enemy hands. After almost three months of agonizing captivity, he managed to escape in late December. He ran with a partisan group until the middle of March 1944. Only on 20 April did the pilot arrive back at his own 45th (now 100th Guards) Fighter Regiment.

By the strict regulations that applied to former prisoners of war, Dolnikov should have been sent to a special camp for careful investigation of his behavior while in captivity. However, the commander of 9th Guards Fighter Division, Guards Colonel Ibragim Dzusov, would not consent to sending Dolnikov to the rear. This brave pilot was needed at the front. All the pilots called the division commander "Batya" [a Russian colloquial word for "father," its use here is equivalent to the expression "old man" in our own military services]. Colonel Dzusov told the SMERSH personnel, "Investigate him here. You can learn a lot by examining his skin and hands. And be quick about it!"[4]

One must give the appropriate organs their due. They did their business quickly. In a brief period of time they garnered information that cleared Grigoriy Dolnikov. The regiment commander, Guards Major Sergey Lukyanov, invited the recovering and resting pilot to his office in early May 1944. "We have not forgotten about you, Dolnikov. You have returned to your combat family, it is true. But you did not come here from leave or the hospital, but from German captivity. Your documents are in good order and you preserved your Party candidate membership card (he had hidden it in his boot, under the insole, which had destroyed it). Understand, we had to check out the entire period of your captivity. Today we received an outstanding report that confirms your devotion and dedication. We never doubted that for a moment. This is why the command appeared to have forgotten about you for a brief period. Now I am sending you to your 1st Squadron. You are back in the ranks!"

Grigoriy Dolnikov participated in several aerial engagements with the enemy around Jassy, Romania, as a flight leader. By 6 June 1944, the Guards junior lieutenant had completed twenty-nine combat missions in an Airacobra and conducted eleven aerial engagements in the Romanian sky, where he shot down five enemy aircraft. By the beginning of August, *Boroda* [bearded one] (the pilot had come out of captivity with a thick black beard and had kept it) already had ten destroyed enemy aircraft to his personal credit. By an unwritten law he was considered to have joined the ranks of the aces. In recognition of his experience and skill demonstrated in many aerial engagements, the division commander appointed Dolnikov commander of 2d Squadron.[5]

Covering an Amphibious Landing

Mariupol was captured in September fighting. The 9th Guards Fighter Division received the honorific title "Mariupol" for its support to the offensive. The advancing ground forces continued to move westward, toward Berdyansk. The enemy managed for a brief time to stabilize the front line on the near approaches to this town. The command of Southern *Front* decided to take Berdyansk with a combined attack of ground forces and an amphibious landing force of the Azov Flotilla. This amphibious force was to interdict the retreating enemy's path along the coastline between Mariupol and Berdyansk.

During the last week of September, formations of the 44th Combined Arms Army were being prepared for a breakthrough of the enemy defenses on the sector Gendelberg–Prishib. They renewed the offensive on 26 September and over the course of four days managed to defeat the enemy in this area and began to develop success into the depth of his dispositions.[1]

On 20 September, the 9th Guards Fighter Division received the mission to provide cover for the movement of the amphibious landing force by sea and its actions ashore in the landing area. Its units were not released from their previous mission to support the offensive of Lieutenant General Nikolay Kirichenko's 4th Guards Cavalry Corps along the Sea of Azov. The fighters were based at Volodarskoe airfield. On the second day representatives of the Azov Flotilla, led by their chief of staff, arrived at the division headquarters. Together the two groups set about to organize the joint actions. They prepared an imposing sand table at a camouflaged location. On this sand table the flotilla topographic specialists and aviators shaped a strip of terrain from the embarkation port to the landing area. The model showed the route of the amphibious force, the formation of transports and escort vessels during the crossing by sea, and the sequence of the landing of the sailors and the anticipated nature of their offensive on shore. In addition, outlined on a separate diagram was the time schedule for the periods of the amphibious force's actions (in the embarkation port, en route, in the landing area). All this aided the fighter division staff to understand fully the course of the operation and to comprehend visually its phases (by time and place).

Training exercises were conducted on this sand table over the course of two days with the division staff officers and pilots of the squadrons designated to support the landing. The efforts of the fighter squadrons in all periods of the amphibious operation were worked out in great detail. Each pilot had a complete appreciation of the march order of the escort vessels and transports in the crossing by sea and in the landing area. The crews received excerpts from the time schedule on which all the coordination signals had been written. This careful preparation was later repaid with interest.

In the first two days of the offensive of the first echelon of 44th Army, the staffs of the fighter division and Azov Flotilla attentively followed the course of the battle at the front line. These two command and control organs maintained continuous radio communications between themselves. The squadrons of the fighter regiments were in constant readiness to sortie in support of the amphibious force.

The enemy's defenses were broken early on the morning of 26 September. The tempo of the advance of our ground formations and units increased by the hour. The command was given to launch the amphibious force.

Eight Airacobras led by Guards Major Pokryshkin were the first to take off. He already had considerable experience in over-water flight, acquired during periods of "free hunting." Pokryshkin dispersed his combat formation of pairs in an extended "bookshelf." This gave coverage to a much broader expanse of sky over the embarkation port and the route to be followed by the transports and escort vessels. At the same time it supported reconnaissance of the approaches to the patrol area. Special attention was given to the western and northern directions—the most probable approaches of enemy aircraft from Crimean and southern Ukrainian airfields. It was foreseen that, if necessary, a portion of the pairs, on command of the group leader, would quickly respond to reinforce their comrades in a more dangerous zone. Dispersed in altitude and frontage, the formation could be closed up completely or partially in the shortest time in the specified, threatened sector.

Patrolling over the convoy of ships, the Airacobra pilots vigilantly searched the sky. The pair of Guards Lieutenant Andrey Trud and

Viniamin Tsvetkov flew south of Berdyansk, two experienced pilots in the most important sector. It would not be so easy for the enemy to penetrate from this direction. In fact, a short time later four Messerschmitts appeared in this area. Trud and his wingman attacked them, shooting down one and causing the remaining three to flee.

Senior Lieutenant Aleksandr Klubov and Lieutenant Viktor Priymachenko were patrolling northeast of Osipenko at an altitude of 11,500 feet. It was late in the morning. This was already the third shift of Airacobras that had sortied to cover the amphibious landing force, which was now approaching the coast. The air situation was quiet in this particular sector. Klubov and his wingman listened to radio traffic from an air battle over Berdyansk and farther south.

Viktor Priymachenko suddenly broke radio silence. His aircraft was smoking and he was losing altitude. It was a mystery to both Priymachenko and Klubov. Did an anti-aircraft round reach the Airacobra or did it come from an unseen Messerschmitt? Both pilots later confirmed that they had not spotted any "bandits." Could they have overlooked one? It was possible. During the lieutenant's time in the regiment (six months already), this was his third time to be shot down. Fortunately, he was not hurt. Not everyone was so lucky.

Priymachenko tried with all his strength and skill to reach our own territory but did not succeed. During the landing in enemy-occupied territory, the fighter touched down on uneven terrain near a deep ravine, bounced, flew another fifty yards, and came back down on the far side. The pilot was lucky. He could have ended up at the bottom of the ravine, with serious consequences for both the pilot and the aircraft.

The Guards lieutenant climbed out of the cabin and stood on the wing, looking around. He saw no one and jumped to the ground. Then he spotted someone running toward the aircraft. An old man ran up to him, breathing heavily. He was bent over with age. The old man urged him to flee the aircraft, pointing to the other side of the ravine and shouting "Tiger." Priymachenko did not immediately grasp what the old man was trying to say. He glanced in the direction the old man was pointing and there stood a heavy German tank. The pilot surmised that the Germans had taken him for one of theirs and had sent the "runner" to get him.

Viktor responded to the old man in Russian. Upon hearing Russian speech, the "runner" jumped back in realization of who stood before him. He glanced at the aircraft and saw the red stars. The lieutenant did not loiter. He jumped down and raced toward the ravine. At the same time that he jumped into the ravine he heard the explosion of a round where his fighter had stood. Viktor looked back from behind cover. His Airacobra was standing up on its right wing and was engulfed in flames. He understood that from the moment of his landing the P-39 had been in the tank's crosshairs. As soon as the Germans realized that their "runner" was fleeing, they fired at the P-39 with their main gun. The enemy was convinced that the pilot died in his aircraft. Thus it would have been, had not Viktor hidden in the ravine. The bursting radius of an 88mm high-explosive shell was large. The Tiger turned around and departed to the north.

Priymachenko hid for a while in the ravine and then later crawled into a tree farm, from which he made his way eastward. Bypassing villages and traveling only at night, on the following day he appeared at his home airfield. Viktor Priymachenko continued to fight the enemy until the end of the war.[2]

By the evening of 26 September the amphibious landing force had enlarged their beachhead. After two days of intense fighting, finally they cut the road that led to the west along the coast. The enemy's unhindered path of retreat was closed.

There was also fierce and continuous fighting in the sky above Berdyansk and the amphibious force's defense. The enemy, lacking sufficient infantry and tank forces, had decided to counterattack the sailors with his air force, to drive them into the sea with massed air strikes. In this way the Germans hoped to clear that same road for the withdrawal of their ground forces.

The sky was red in the east. The amphibious landing force had faced death for four days. They dug themselves deep into the narrow sector that they occupied. It would be no simple task to drive them into the sea. The Airacobras of 9th Guards Fighter Division gave them reliable air cover from morning to night. Mikhail Petrov led a flight from 100th Guards Fighter Regiment (Vyacheslav Antonev, Ivan Babak, Aleksey Trufanov). Their mission was to prevent the breakthrough of enemy bombers to the beachhead and simultaneously conduct reconnaissance of the western approaches to the beachhead. Flying at high altitude or at treetop level, the enemy was constantly trying to penetrate to the amphibious force's defensive positions.

Guards Captain Petrov observed an FW-189 "Rama" escorted by four Messerschmitts one kilometer north of his own location, at an altitude of 8,200 feet. The reconnaissance aircraft was holding on a course to the south, perhaps to observe and photograph the positions on the scrap of our liberated land.

Petrov issued a brief order to Ivan Babak's pair to destroy the reconnaissance aircraft. With his own wingman he went after the fighter escort. Babak and his wingman shot up the FW-189 in an initial attack from below, then after gaining altitude went to the aid of Petrov. Reliably covering his comrades, Mikhail Petrov also shot down one "bandit" on his third pass. The remaining three Bf-109s disengaged from the battle by diving away. None of the Airacobra pilots pursued them.

In this situation the group leader acted correctly and rationally by simultaneously attacking the "Rama" and the fighter escorts, depriving the enemy of the opportunity to maneuver. Two Airacobra pilots took the brunt of the aerial battle on themselves in attacking the four Messerschmitts. In turn the rapidity of the single precision attack by Babak's pair on the reconnaissance-artillery spotter aircraft brought rapid success. This pair immediately brought their P-39s to the assistance of their comrades. The final tally was two to zero. The FW-189 trophy was particularly important.[3]

Here are two examples of daylight engagements with the enemy.

On 29 September 1943, from 0830 to 1010, eight P-39s of the 104th Guards Fighter Regiment sortied under the command of Captain Konstantin Vishnevetskiy. His wingman was Aleksandr Zakharov. The remaining pairs were Lieutenant Vladimir Stepanov and Junior Lieutenant Genadiy Voroshilov, Junior Lieutenants Nikolay Novikov and Leonid Yazov, and Aleksandr Samykin and Georgiy Alekseev. Their mission was to provide coverage of ground forces in the area of Gendelberg and Prishib.

At an altitude of 14,750 feet, the group engaged nine He-111s headed for Bolshoy Tokmak. Four Airacobras attacked the nine bombers head on. The pairs of Samykin and Novikov covered their actions from above. One bomber, the lead aircraft, was shot down immediately. The column of Heinkels began to make a 180-degree turn to flee the engagement area, dropping their ordnance hurriedly. The explosions of these bombs raised countless fountains of earth in the Sadovaya area. Stepanov came up under one of the fleeing bombers and shot it in the belly, then escaped the fire of the rear gunner with a diving left turn. The Airacobras did not risk further pursuit of the bombers.

The pairs of Samykin and Novikov engaged four Bf-109s that had just appeared. Minutes later, they detected the approach of another nine bombers. Like the first formation, this group was also headed for Bolshoy Tokmak.

Captain Vishnevetskiy turned his entire flight around and led it into an attack on the new echelon of bombers. Having been alerted by the first echelon, the gunners in this group of bombers were prepared and forced the Airacobras to dive under their formation. Alekseev's P-39 received serious damage and was disabled; he made a forced landing on Soviet-held territory.

Genadiy Voroshilov reported to his pair leader the sighting of two groups of Ju-87s off to the right flank, in the area of Trudolyubovka. The situation was becoming more and more complicated. The commander reported this sighting to the ground vectoring station and requested assistance. He led his group in a follow-on attack on the nearest column. In order not to lose valuable time, they struck from below. Aleksandr Zakharov set an He-111 on fire. His pair leader, Konstantin Vishnevetskiy, came under heavy fire from enemy gunners and was seriously wounded. Losing and gaining altitude, his P-39 drifted off to the northeast. Aleksandr chased after it, covering his comrade against attacks by Messerschmitts. Konstantin reached the front line and with great difficulty landed the aircraft on its belly.

Six P-39s remained without a leader. As later became clear, Vishnevetskiy's radio had been damaged, preventing him from transferring command of the group to his earlier appointed deputy, Samykin. The latter, as luck would have it, had a malfunctioning transmitter. He could hear everyone but remained silent himself. He could not issue any orders or instructions.

Unfortunately, not one of the pilots displayed the initiative to take up the heavy reins of control of the battle. The flight, flying in pairs but separated from each other at great intervals, continued to fight the battle for some time. Leonid Yazov shot down a Ju-88 and Stepanov and Novikov each damaged another.

Despite what had happened, the pairs' uncoordinated attacks forced both approaching waves of bombers to drop their ordnance west of Trudolyubovka. The enemy did not succeed in delivering the high explosives to the target. This was no small feat. The heat of the battle dissipated with each minute and then faded. The fighters broke off for the airfield in small elements. What had begun as an organized group battle had ended in chaos.

This particular battle prompted the regiment command to address two issues. Subsequent large patrol groups went out with not one but two designated deputy leaders; and intense political work was done in the regiment's subordinate units. A number of conversations were conducted on the theme of displaying initiative in battle. Combat examples of appropriate actions by officers of the Red Army as a whole and from the regiment and division experience were discussed. The dominant theme through all of these examples was the requirement that when a commander was disabled, any officer should without hesitation replace him and continue the battle.

The standard practice in the Red Air Force was for all pilots to attend the briefing at which the mission was assigned to their group leader. They were thus fully acquainted with their commander's intent and decision. At a critical moment in the battle, should he have to replace the commander, any pilot could without difficulty continue to execute the previous plan or, if required, make necessary corrections.

On 30 September, from 1450 to 1530, a group of eight Airacobras sortied from 104th Fighter Regiment. Their leader was Guards Captain Grigoriy Shaposhnikov. Their mission was to protect ground forces in the area of Neydorf and Prishib. The assigned patrol altitude was 11,500 feet; the sky was partly cloudy with excellent visibility. The group leader reported their arrival in the patrol area to the ground vectoring station, "Tiger."

In response, "Tiger" informed him of an enemy bomber formation just two miles west of the patrol zone. Without delay Shaposhnikov led his group to close with the Heinkel 111s, to forestall their approach to the coverage area. This decisive action was doubly advantageous. It saved time and consequently fuel, and the enemy encountered our fighters over his territory. Hastily jettisoned bombs would cause losses among his own troops.

Shaposhnikov's pilots spotted the enemy formation (six He-111s and four Bf-109s) visually. The ratio of fighter forces was not in the enemy's favor. When the bombers detected the approaching Airacobras, their formation began to make a gentle left turn. The bombers began aimlessly to release their high-explosive bombs and then, dropping down to seek cover against the backdrop of the terrain, fled back to the west. Pursuing the enemy formation, Viktor Parshev and Nikolay Novikov each shot down one He-111.

The ground vectoring station came back on the air with another report. Two groups of Ju-87s, ten to fifteen aircraft in each group, were approaching the Oktyabrfeld area from the south. The normal reaction to this report would have been to conduct a rapid simultaneous attack: spread out the fighter force; engage the enemy in battle to encumber his ability to maneuver; impose our own tactical will on the enemy from the very beginning of the battle; and, finally, not waste time and precious fuel awaiting the approach of the enemy aircraft.

It was notable that Shaposhnikov had a sizable force under his control. He made the decision to divide his eight Airacobras into two equal groups. This permitted him to intercept two bomber groups at once. He issued the appropriate commands to his formation to keep Parshev's pair with himself and send the other two pairs under the command of Mikhalin to attack the second bomber group.

The P-39s closed with the approaching enemy bombers, gaining altitude to arrive at the target some 2,600 feet above the enemy aircraft. Six Bf-109s circled above the formation of bombers. Either they did not see our fighters or they feared leaving the column of dive bombers without immediate escort. In either case, they did not interfere. This circumstance emphasized once more the necessity of rapid attack, which is what the Airacobra pilots set about to accomplish.

Two four-ship groups, deployed across a frontage, almost at one and the same moment executed an "eagle strike" from above and in front against both waves of Ju-87s. Two smoking enemy aircraft fell out of the approaching columns. The bomber formations were broken up and the dive bombers split off in all directions, freeing themselves of their unwanted and dangerous cargo. They were trying as rapidly as possible to escape the engagement zone and head for home.[4]

The practice of battles in the second half of September showed that the leader of a significantly large group of fighters should position himself in the covering subgroup. This subgroup, supporting the actions of the strike group, had greater independence in selecting the form and time of its maneuver. The commander of the patrol would thus be freer in the engagement zone than the other pilots who were conducting the battle. He could oversee the entire battle or any portion of it, make the appropriate decision, and thus influence the course and outcome of the fight.[5] If the senior pilot of the group were located at the epicenter of the air battle, he would not have this opportunity.

The amphibious landing force continued stubbornly to hold on to its beachhead on the northern shore of the Sea of Azov. The enemy was denied a suitable axis for withdrawal of his forces and maneuver of his reserves and firing assets. Thanks to the active opposition of our fighters, German aviation did not succeed in accomplishing its mission to conduct massed strikes on the defended area.

Aleksandr Pokryshkin recalls: "We were not limited only to covering the amphibious landing. The sailors were satisfied with our ground attack activities against retreating enemy columns that attempted to break through the amphibious force's barrier."[6]

On the afternoon of 30 September, six P-39s led by the celebrated ace were returning to their airfield from the coverage zone over the amphibious force. Suddenly they spotted an enemy column of covered trucks with six towed guns. No less than a battalion of infantry was rushing toward the beachhead. Pokryshkin decided to disrupt the enemy's plan. Each fighter still had the minimal supply of ammunition, which had been saved in the event of an encounter on the way home.

The commander ordered his flight to attack the enemy at low altitude—ground strafing—and led his subordinates into the attack. In two passes they set all the infantry trucks on fire and damaged the guns. All that remained of the infantry battalion were soldiers and officers fleeing across the field. The artillery had been totally disabled. This was yet another essential service provided by the Airacobra pilots to the courageous sailors fighting on land.[7]

A Costly Mistake

"A battle does not pass without mistakes, even among experienced pilots!" A mistake frequently was paid for with blood, and sometimes a life. Mistakes were common. They were made by high, middle, and low levels of command, by soldiers, sergeants, and officers. In any situation they led to unjustified losses. One thing, to some degree, was comforting. "The misfortune of one person was the beginning of martial achievement by another."

It was 29 August. Six Airacobras from 104th Fighter Regiment were patrolling in the area of Marevka and Latonovo, east of Melitopol. The leader of the group, Major Vladimir Semenishin, was the squadron commander. They climbed to 16,000 feet upon arrival in the patrol zone, where they assembled and subsequently conducted an air battle. Spotting seventeen bombers off to their left, Semenishin led all of his fighters into the attack on the enemy. This was his first mistake. He did not designate a pair of P-39s for coverage of his combat formation from above. This was a failure of elementary precaution on the part of the leader and of every pilot in the group.

Such a significant force of Ju-87s could not have sortied with fewer than six Bf-109s for escort. Semenishin's group, while launching its attack on the dive bombers, did not take into account their fighter cover. This was a costly omission. Six Messerschmitts attacked the Airacobras from above at the moment of their closure with the bombers. They were between two "fires"—the large-caliber machine guns of the bombers and the cannons and machine guns of the Messerschmitts, with no possibility of maneuvering. The P-39s' fire on the Ju-87s was ineffective. Semenishin was himself shot down. Deprived of its leader, the Airacobra group dispersed in pairs and was forced to flee from the attacking enemy fighters.

At this time an additional fifty to sixty Ju-87s and He-111s accompanied by fourteen Bf-109s entered the engagement zone. The sky was full of enemy aircraft. The eight escort fighters of the second column of bombers rushed in to assist their six predecessors. The ratio of forces was now fourteen to five in favor of the enemy, almost triple the Soviet fighter force.

Another two P-39s (Aleksandr Vilyamson and Mikhail Likhovid) became targets for the German pilots. Vasiliy Drygin, Aleksandr Rumm, and Yuriy Maltsev managed with great difficulty to disengage from the battle and escape the horde of pursuing fighters. They brought their Airacobras back to the airfield with many holes in them.

Fifty percent of the patrol from 104th Fighter Regiment had been destroyed. This was the epitome of an unorganized battle: a thoughtless attack and disdain of the simplest tactical requirements of organization and conduct of an air battle (failure to reconnoiter the engagement zone before launching the attack, absence of a cover subgroup). Vilyamson and Rumm returned to their unit after a brief period, and Semenishin, having recovered in a hospital, came back to the regiment a short time later.

But he did not fight the enemy much longer. At the end of September Seminishin, leading a small patrol group, was involved in a lopsided battle with the enemy. Guards Lieutenant Colonel Semenishin shot down three enemy aircraft, but he was also set on fire and seriously wounded. He found the strength to abandon the Airacobra but died after he was unable to deploy his parachute.[1]

To some degree, these mistakes by young aviators who had just arrived at the front were excusable. The majority of the pilots in the group had sufficient combat experience. By this time, Semenishin had shot down ten enemy aircraft, Drygin seventeen, Rumm seven personal and one shared, Vilyamson eight, Likhovid five, and Maltsev four.[2] It is even difficult to say what prevailed over the common sense of both the leader and the led: the heat of battle, confidence in an easy victory (they thought that the Ju-87s were flying without fighter escort), or something else.

It is exceptionally dangerous over the field of battle to disregard even the most basic regulations of flying and conducting aerial engagements. Front-line veterans of ground troops well understand a single, somewhat crude, but hard-learned truth: disregard for the rules of conduct at the forward edge, light and sound discipline, and proper use of the terrain for concealment can very quickly lead to death.

The aviators had their own specific rules in this realm, but they all boiled down to one thing: strict observance of the various security and safety measures that maximally excluded undesirable and, at times, wholly serious consequences.

On 18 September a pilot of the 104th Guards Fighter Regiment, Senior Sergeant Petr Maslov, after accomplishing his combat reconnaissance mission, on the return route flew near Voskresenka at near treetop level. He came under intense fire from enemy anti-aircraft artillery. His Airacobra was set on fire and upon striking the ground was turned into a burning inferno, as was the pilot.

The cause of this pilot's death and the loss of the aircraft was Maslov's disregard of a basic rule of aviators: "Do not conduct low-altitude flight over populated areas and other places inhabited by enemy troops!" These areas always have well-organized anti-aircraft defenses. And there was no necessity for this pilot to violate that basic rule.[3]

Battles were being fought in the area around and north of Melitopol in the last days of September 1943. Squadron after squadron took off into the sky, flew to the forward edge, and from the march entered into heavy air combat with enemy fighters and bombers.

The twenty-seventh of September turned out to be quite intense. The 16th Guards Fighter Regiment shot down seven enemy aircraft without losing one of its own. The 100th scored four kills, but the aircraft of one of its aces, Boris Glinka, was set on fire and Glinka was seriously wounded. This was an experienced, brave, high-scoring aerial warrior. How did this happen? What was the cause of his misfortune in this battle?

It was an engagement with a modest group of bombers. However, a fighter pilot must employ flexible, thoughtful tactics in any situation. The neglect of the basic rule was fraught with a terrible outcome. Nine Ju-87s were flying toward our forward edge with four escort Messerschmitts. This was not a significant enemy force. Boris divided his six-ship flight into two subgroups. Glinka led two pairs of P-39s in an attack on the dive bombers, and Vasiliy Sharashenko and his wingman Aleksandr Trufanov engaged the Bf-109s. Several minutes later there was one less Messerschmitt. They had set one on fire. This aircraft struck the ground in several burning pieces.

The bombers continued their flight in a tight formation. They would soon cross the front line. Then, though Glinka's subgroup might prevent them from executing their precision dive bombing against our troops, their ordnance would strike our ground force positions even if dropped aimlessly. This was unacceptable. Let them present this "gift" to their own troops.

Glinka ordered his Airacobras to conduct a frontal attack. This direct attack permitted them to gain several valuable minutes and to intercept and defeat the enemy over his territory. If the Airacobra pilots of the 100th Fighter Regiment had taken the time to gain altitude, the air battle would have commenced and flowed over the positions of our own advancing infantry and tanks.

In principle, the selected tactical method was correct. However, the experienced ace committed the crudest mistake. His four aircraft did not have the maximum possible speed when they began the attack. The compact formation of nine enemy aircraft was able to establish a dense frontal fire screen. The experience of multiple similar attacks had shown that such a barrier was completely penetrable, without losses, but only at high speed.

A result was quick in coming. Glinka's Airacobra was shot up and set on fire. A bullet struck Boris in the left shoulder, seriously wounding him. Overcoming fierce pain, he managed to land the aircraft on its belly near a cavalry unit before the fire reached his fuel cells. He received immediate medical treatment.

After his leader left the battle, Vasiliy Sharashenko took command of the group and the Airacobra pilots managed quickly to shoot up the enemy formation. Three Ju-87s did not return to their airfield.

Glinka was transported to the Mariupol hospital on 28 September. At his request, his escorts took him by the airfield at Volodarskoe to see his comrades. The pilots and mechanics surrounded the ambulance. Each of them pressed the hand of the courageous ace and wished him the most rapid recovery and return to his combat family.

Aleksandr Pokryshkin regarded his wounded comrade with exceptional feeling. He hugged him and expressed his heartfelt regret for what had happened. Of course there was great regret that in this period, when the Red Army aviators were driving the Germans to the west, this remarkable, fearless pilot had been taken from their ranks.

Pokryshkin asked Boris how this had happened. Glinka freely admitted that he had led four Airacobras in a frontal attack on Ju-87s without sufficient speed to penetrate the fire screen. He was in a hurry to disrupt their bombing raid. Glinka asked the medics to take him to the hospital. As the ambulance departed it was obvious to everyone that he was in pain.[4]

For some time that day the aviators discussed among themselves the cause of this misfortune. A wizened aviator at the controls of a high-speed fighter did not push it to its limit and now lay in a deadly trap. Glinka, and all the other pilots, had known for some time that the gunners on the bombers could launch hundreds of large-caliber bullets at the attacking Airacobras in a second. When an attack was launched on the enemy, a pilot had to turn his aircraft into a "meteor."

Boris Glinka returned to the 9th Guards Fighter Division after his recovery. He was named commander of the 16th Guards Fighter Regiment and ended the war in the ruins of Berlin.

Adjusting Artillery Fire

The war brought the fighter pilots many surprises. On the evening of 4 October 1943, air reconnaissance detected an accumulation of enemy railroad rolling stock at Yakimovka and Melitopol stations. The command of the 28th Combined Arms Army, lacking its own artillery spotter aircraft, submitted a written request to the commander of the 9th Guards Fighter Division, General Ibragim Dzusov, to dispatch aircraft for adjusting the fire of heavy artillery.

The ground commanders were confident that their petition would receive a positive response (after all, everyone was working toward the common goal of defeating the hated enemy). In connection with this, the army command sent along with the request a map with a set of target reference points marked on it. The artillery liaison officer was prepared to issue detailed instructions to the crews designated to execute this unusual mission.

The representative of the "big guns" asked the air division commander to assign a pair of aircraft to each long-range artillery battery. The artillery units planned to conduct fire simultaneously with two batteries, one firing at each station. So that the element of surprise would be maintained, the air division commander agreed to send a pair of Airacobras to each area, one fighter to adjust the artillery fire and the other to provide cover.

The division commander handed the mission over to the 100th Guards Fighter Regiment and the pairs of fighters were quickly named: Lieutenant Vasiliy Bondarenko with Junior Lieutenant Vyacheslav Antonov, and Lieutenant Ivan Babak with Junior Lieutenant Nikolay Novikov. The officers quickly arrived at division headquarters to receive their instructions from the artillery liaison officer.

The preparation of the Airacobra pilots for this complex and at the same time important mission was begun. The honor of the blue shoulder boards (which all aviation officers wore) demanded exact performance from each aviator. There were a multitude of issues to address, including signals between the aviators and the artillerymen that indicated the pilots' preparedness to adjust fires, the beginning of registration and then on-target fires, the cessation or completion of fires, and the end of adjustment activity. Safety measures discussed included the direction and maximum trajectory height (altitude) of the fired rounds. An air corridor was defined into which the fighters could not fly, in order to prevent an accidental collision between aircraft and artillery rounds.

The bulk of these efforts lay on the shoulders of the pair leaders, Vasiliy Bondarenko and Ivan Babak. The task of their wingmen was to enable the pair leaders to accomplish the artillery fire adjustment mission in any air situation by providing them reliable protection against possible Messerschmitt attacks.

Preparation of the crews consumed three hours. None of these fighter pilots had ever before adjusted artillery fire from an aerial platform. The Airacobra pilots of 100th Guards became the pathfinders in this complicated task.

The air crews returned to their unit and discussed the mission with fellow pilots. The jokes began flowing almost immediately: "Vasiliy, check your airspace carefully. An artillery shell is smaller than a 'bandit,' but an encounter with it is three times more dangerous!" "Ivan, are you going to apply for duty with the 'gunners' after you complete your duties as forward observer?" There was laughter and then more ribbing.

Two pairs of Airacobras took off at dawn the next morning to reconnoiter the target area. They had to ascertain the situation before artillery fires were launched at the stations. The reconnaissance pilots did not detect any changes on the steel roads. The strings of rolling stock were still in place. The artillery rounds would not be wasted.

It was time to begin the combined efforts of the fighter pilots and artillerymen. Each pilot had a 1:50,000 topographic map with target reference points marked on it. This duplication was undertaken in the event that for any reason one of the aircraft of a pair was unable to begin or continue the artillery adjustment mission (damaged by antiaircraft fire or downed in air combat). Each Airacobra pilot tuned one of his radio receiver-transmitters to the frequency of "his" firing battery.

The spotter aircraft launched, rapidly arrived in the area of the command and control point that served the artillery batteries, and established contact with the artillery commander. After this the P-39s headed toward Melitopol and Yakimovka at an altitude of 3,280 to 4,920 feet. Upon arriving at these locations the pilots sent out the agreed-upon signal: "Prepared for work!" Several seconds later, the response came back from the artillerymen: "Beginning registration fire!"[1]

During their deployment into firing positions, artillery units normally sent forward observation posts to the front line. These forward observation posts were established for the purpose of reconnoitering the enemy, locating targets, and adjusting fire. Observation posts could be primary or supplementary (forward and flank). Although collocated with front-line units, these posts remained under the command of their respective artillery formations. In this particular case, the Airacobra pairs of Bondarenko and Babak were serving as frontline (aerial) observation posts.

Later, after returning to their airfield, the Airacobra pilots provided their comrades with a detailed description of their joint combat activities with the artillerymen. It made sense for the other pilots to learn the nuances of such an unusual mission. The aviators' services might become necessary to the artillerymen on a future occasion. "The experience of one is the accomplishment of all!" The inviolable frontline requirement had been fulfilled.

[Bondarenko:] Our pair was orbiting in the area of Melitopol station, an important junction of rail lines and highways. A significant grouping of enemy anti-aircraft artillery was providing coverage over the target. We had to fly continuous anti-aircraft avoidance maneuvers (rapid changes of course, speed, and altitude) in order to reduce the probability of a hit. All the time we had to hold in the zone east of the rail yard, forcing enemy anti-aircraft gunners to fire into the sun. To some degree this blinded the crews and reduced the effectiveness of their fires. At the same time, the sun helped us see the target area better and spot the round impacts.

The first two registration rounds landed somewhat north of the station (in quadrant two), but even in this the artillerymen did a good deed. The rounds struck an enemy anti-aircraft artillery battery. I reported to the fire control center the coordinates of these rounds and simultaneously congratulated them for the destruction of the anti-aircraft guns.

The second pair of 152mm rounds exploded in the central quadrant. "Target covered!" was my immediate report to the guns. After a brief pause, over the ensuing five minutes a hurricane of fire landed on the station and its approaches. Freight cars and station structures were set on fire. Ammunition began to cook off. Fire quickly spread along the train. We spotted several tank cars in quadrant three and requested fires over there. The artillerymen delivered their ordnance and new fires broke out.

My wingman, Vyacheslav Antonov, intently searching the sky around us, was covering me from above. At times he pointed out new targets to me.

[Ivan Babak:] When we returned from division headquarters to our unit, we examined in detail the possible nature of our actions over the target. We realized that the sun would be behind us and also did not neglect anti-aircraft avoidance maneuvers. Our registration rounds on Yakimovka station landed right in the heart of the target. The artillerymen destroyed approximately fifteen freight cars containing various cargoes, damaged a water tower, and set the station building on fire. Large, strong obstacles of rolling stock were formed on the track lines. I think that movement on this railroad will be paralyzed for at least thirty-six to forty-eight hours.

The anti-aircraft fire was especially strong in the area south of Yakimovka. To shift the fire of the long-range guns there would have meant significantly weakening fires on the station. This was not an appropriate measure. Nikolay Novikov undertook, in principle, a risky and impermissible decision. He dropped down to treetop level and silenced the enemy position with a short burst of cannon and machine-gun fire. After his pass he rose into the heavens like an arrow and took up his wingman position. Such a violation of the normal order of a pair's combat formation and coordination within the pair was normally inexcusable. One circumstance justified his actions: no enemy fighters had appeared in the zone of our work. Had this happened at that exact moment, the accomplishment of the assigned mission might have been compromised.

Fortunately, the artillery strike on the target was completed in a brief period of time. The batteries fired sixteen rounds each and inflicted substantial damage on the Germans.

The airborne forward observers received the signal "fires completed!" They could return to their base. As they had agreed before departing on the mission, the pairs of Airacobras "unloaded" by strafing the station, pouring lead on rolling stock not touched by the artillery strike. This action added new flames to the fires already burning.

The command of 100th Guards Fighter Regiment was attentively monitoring the situation in the zones of action of the P-39 pairs. Eight additional fighters were on the airfield in readiness for immediate launch to assist Bondarenko and Babak.

This example shows that there were not insurmountable obstacles to the goal of destroying the enemy. A way out of a difficult situation had been found. Close, although not prolonged, unification of the efforts of the Airacobras and heavy artillery gave remarkable results.

The command of 28th Army declared its thanks to the pilots of 100th Guards Regiment for outstanding accomplishment of the combat mission, and particularly to Lieutenant Vasiliy Bondarenko.[2]

Air strikes were renewed against these particular targets by evening of the same day, this time with bombers. Two Pe-2s destroyed German rolling stock at the stations and along the tracks. The flow of cargo had been disrupted on an important railroad line, forcing the enemy to find bypass routes. He had to expend priceless time for the subsequent movement of troops and materiel.

More Battles

After his defeat at the Mius River in August and September 1943, the enemy was retreating to the west under pressure. He managed to create a new defensive line along the Molochnaya River with nodes of resistance at Vasilevka, Karachekrak, Terpeniye, Melitopol, Ivanovka, and beyond, along the west shore of Molochnoye Lake.

By breaking through the enemy's defenses south of Melitopol and reaching a line at Veseloye, formations of the 4th Ukrainian *Front* created a threat of encirclement of German forces in that area. This forced the enemy to abandon positions on the Molochnaya River and withdraw his forces to the west side of the Dnieper River.

The combat actions of the advancing Soviet Army formations were characterized by fierce battles to break through enemy defenses in the first half of October and rapid westward movement to pursue a retreating enemy in the second half of that month. In this situation, the enemy launched air strikes against our ground formations with isolated groups of bombers in the areas of Melitopol and west of Bolshoy Tokmak. At times the Germans brought air assets from other sectors of the front for this purpose.

The 9th Guards Fighter Division was providing support for the 4th and 5th Guards Cavalry Corps, and also the 4th Mechanized Corps. Units of the 9th Guards relocated three times in the course of this mission, from Rosovka airfield network to Kaykulak, from Kaykulak to Veseloye, and from Veseloye to Lyubavka.

At the beginning of October the division's regiments had a total of forty-eight serviceable Airacobras (16th Regiment twenty, 100th Regiment twelve, and 104th Regiment sixteen) and twenty-two unserviceable P-39s (nine, nine, and four, respectively). The regiments had sixty-seven combat-ready pilots (thirty-four, nineteen, and fourteen) and twenty-seven pilots not ready for combat (wounded, sick, and insufficiently trained in piloting skills; two, eight, and seventeen, respectively).

The division flew 1,614 aircraft sorties and fought 68 air engagements in accomplishment of its assigned missions in October. Total losses to the units due to enemy activity were 18 aircraft and twelve pilots, at a cost to the enemy of 65 aircraft losses of all types. Thus, each P-39 lost in combat cost the enemy 3.6 destroyed aircraft.[1]

This relatively high ratio of kills to losses is explained in part by the fact that in this period an RUS-2 radar set with operators was assigned to the division. This apparatus detected enemy aircraft approaching the front line and rapidly transmitted the incoming data to the division headquarters. The presence of such an effective means of technical reconnaissance permitted the 9th Guards Division to have two groups of fighters in constant readiness on airfields, one consisting of twenty to thirty and the other of twelve to twenty P-39s. Our employment of such large groups of fighters forced the enemy to avoid using large bomber formations, noticeably reducing his air activity.[2]

Here is how the RUS-2 radar station was used by the division. Data received from the radar regarding enemy aircraft was transmitted by telephone to a plotting board in division headquarters. From there the information was immediately dispatched by radio to the ground vectoring station, and simultaneously the required number of groups of covering aircraft were launched. Ground vectoring station "Tiger" directed the patrols that were approaching the front line toward specific air targets.

On 7 October, the ground vectoring station directed two pairs of P-39s from 100th Guards Regiment, led by Guards Captain Mikhail Petrov, to the location of four Bf-109s (over Mordvinka). Petrov and his wingman were flying at an altitude of 14,760 feet. The second pair, led by Ivan Babak and flying at 13,125 feet, looked up and saw two "bandits" attempting to attack Petrov and his wingman from above. Babak shot down the lead Messerschmitt with an attack from below and left. In turn his wingman, Junior Lieutenant Petr Guchek, coming in from above and behind, took out the second Bf-109 from a range of 110 to 80 yards.

At this time, Petrov's pair observed an additional two Messerschmitts at an altitude of 16,400 feet. Petrov and his wingman immediately climbed toward them from their rear. Petrov attacked one of them at almost point-blank range. His salvo was precise and penetrated the Bf-109's fuel cell. The enemy fighter exploded in flight. "Tiger" confirmed all three downed enemy aircraft. Petrov's group returned to their airfield at full strength.[3]

In all probability, the enemy had managed to establish by aerial reconnaissance or radio intercepts that a radar set capable of detecting aircraft in flight was operating on this particular sector of the front. To reduce the effectiveness of the radar, the enemy began to approach the front line at low altitudes. This indeed complicated the work of the RUS-2 operator, but data continued to be acquired (at closer ranges) and transmitted simultaneously to the plotting charts both at division headquarters (for the launching of fighters) and at ground vectoring station "Tiger" (for guiding the patrols). This duplicative process saved valuable time.

On 22 October, six P-39s of 16th Guards Fighter Regiment were launched on the basis of radar sightings. Their leader—Guards Senior Lieutenant Andrey Trud—contacted the ground vectoring station and received a report regarding the course of approximately fifty Ju-87s escorted by eight Bf-109s. The bombers were "sneaking" toward the front line at an altitude of 9,840 feet.

The combat formation of Trud's group was split into two subgroups: a strike flight of four Airacobras and a covering flight of two Airacobras. The patrol's main forces conducted the first attack head on, upon the completion of which they were, in turn, attacked by six Bf-109s. After fending off the enemy fighters, the four Airacobras turned around and launched their second strike from behind into the rear of the enemy bomber formation. At that moment a pair of "bandits" began to dive on Trud's P-39s from above. Junior Lieutenant Viktor Zherdev's covering pair blocked their path and sent the lead Messerschmitt down in flames.

One had to be exceptionally smart in such rapidly unfolding, intense engagements with an experienced enemy. A pilot needed only to permit the smallest reduction in speed in a maneuver to immediately find himself under heavy and accurate enemy fire. Something like this happened with Junior Lieutenant Sergey Kleymenov. His Airacobra slowed for just an instant in a turn after the first pass (perhaps the pilot feared entering a spin) and was caught in a heavy tracer stream from a Messerschmitt. Sergey had managed to shoot down only two enemy aircraft in his brief career. The life of yet another defender of the Motherland who longed for the day of victory had ended prematurely.

Witnessing the destruction of four of their escort fighters, the German bomber crews did not risk further danger. They dropped their high-explosive ordnance southwest of Burchak and in a disorderly manner dove and turned back toward their own territory.[4] Combat experience gained by spilled blood and at the price of many lives was and will always be a good teacher.

An example of passive air combat by the crews of six Airacobras of 104th Guards Fighter Regiment occurred on 24 October. Senior Lieutenant Aleksandr Lukantsev was leading this group. His mission was to provide support to ground troops in the Mikhaylovka area. The entire patrol was comprised of relatively inexperienced pilots who did not have a single downed enemy aircraft to their personal credit. For example, Aleksandr Lukantsev had flown fifteen combat sorties by this day and had been the leader during two aerial engagements. Grigoriy Khatavskiy had flown ten missions but had not participated in a single battle. Leonid Golidze's numbers were twenty and zero; Mikhail Likhovid twenty-eight and three, Vladimir Stepanov twenty-four and two, and Vladimir Klimov eight and one.

The pairs and groups displayed low levels of activity on the whole. They conducted two engagements with clear numerical superiority over the opposing Messerschmitts. The altitude of these engagements was significant: the first occurred at 19,690 feet and the second at 16,400 feet. The pilots were inadequately trained for combat actions at these heights. This was the origin of the sluggishness in their attacks on the enemy.

The events in the coverage zone unfolded in the following manner. During the approach to the zone, the flight leader received information from the ground vectoring station that no enemy had been detected in this area. The patrol reached its mission airspace and began orbiting. Two Bf-109s appeared from the south and were immediately engaged. But the actions of the left-flank pair (Golidze and Khatavskiy) were so passive that one of the "bandit" pilots managed to get in behind the pair and fire up Grigoriy Khatavskiy's aircraft. The junior lieutenant was wounded, bailed out of his aircraft, and landed in the hospital. He did not return to the unit after his recovery.

The attacking enemy aircraft departed to altitude unpunished and then disappeared toward German lines. This pair was probably flying a reconnaissance mission. Beginning with the detection of the enemy, Aleksandr Lukantsev committed a gross error. With a threefold numerical superiority, he failed to attempt to "squeeze" the Bf-109s from all sides and destroy them with no particular difficulty. Lukantsev did not draw the correct conclusion from the engagement just completed, did not instruct his crews by radio, and did not demand from them decisive offensive actions in the future.

Ground vectoring station "Tiger" was concerned and ordered the patrol to continue flying their mission but to be more vigilant and stubbornly attack the enemy, even a superior enemy force. This firm requirement of the division commander (he was at the ground vectoring station) came out of a relatively simple, but wise ancient rule: "A rapid, powerful attack on the enemy gives you a threefold superiority. You anticipate the enemy, you stun his forces, and in the end— you win!"[5]

No more than twenty-five minutes had passed. The patrol dropped down to 16,400 feet, where it detected a second pair of Messerschmitts. They were attempting to take up a suitable position in relation to our patrol. Likhovid and his wingman disrupted their plan by forcing the "bandits" into a steep turn. Mikhail, reaching a position above and to the rear, shot down the leading Bf-109.[6]

The misfortune of Mikhail Likhovid's first encounter with the enemy was particularly distressing. He drew the correct conclusions from it and pledged to fight the enemy stubbornly, actively, and boldly, and constantly to study his comrades' skillful actions. He kept his promise and before his tragic death in 1944 was credited with sixteen personal and eleven shared kills.[7]

Free Hunting

In the spring of 1943, an order of the Supreme High Commander was published that required aviation units to dispatch their best pilots on "free hunt" on particularly important enemy lines of communication. In fighter units, these free hunt missions were flown, as a rule, by a pair of fighters, and in ground attack and bomber units by single crews in poor weather conditions.

The free hunt was a relatively difficult combat action associated with enormous risk for pilots. Every aviator who was sent out on such an important mission knew the slogan, "Without risk there will be no victory!" The primary mission of the free hunt was to find the enemy, destroy him with a sudden attack, and then quickly disappear. The aviators constantly strove to see much but themselves remain invisible to the enemy.

The profile of the free hunt was characterized by flights behind the enemy front line to depths of sixty to ninety miles, and sometimes more. This deep penetration by the "hunters" into enemy airspace was accompanied by loss of radio communication with the ground vectoring station. There was no one to apprise them of the situation in the target area and adjacent zones. In the enemy's rear they could not anticipate any support in an emergency situation. The pair's only hope lay in the strength of the two pilots.

Preparation for the free hunt included the study of a number of issues: the ground and air situation; and the region of the upcoming actions (presence of enemy airfields, types of aircraft based on them, and most favorable approaches to them for a stealthy attack). During this preparation the "hunters" considered also the circumstance that each enemy airfield was protected by anti-aircraft assets, and on these airfields were fighters that were on alert, prepared to launch in mere minutes (on the order of three to five).

The hunter pilots selected reference points (linear and area) and studied their configuration and the relief of the terrain. They determined a flight route that would ensure a surprise arrival at the target and the safest route of subsequent flight (over a lake, bay, swamp, mountains, and so on) after the attack. Key elements to the success of the free hunt were good cooperation between the hunter pair members, their exceptional moral and psychological qualities, and their aircraft's reliability. The P-39 Airacobra met this reliability standard.

It was the regiment commander who most frequently assigned the mission for the free hunt. In the mission statement he indicated the area of the pair's actions, the existing ground and air situation, to the degree that it was known, and any current information obtained from aerial reconnaissance. Frequently the hunters received the mission to destroy a specific target. In this case, they personally selected the route, altitude, and speed of the flight, and the direction of the target run.

Typical targets for the hunters were enemy aircraft on the ground and in the air, rail rolling stock, truck columns and individual vehicles (especially those that might be carrying important persons), combat equipment, animal transport, and enemy personnel.

Crews designated for the free hunt carefully prepared for the mission. They studied in great detail the peculiarities of the mission area on the map: the rail and road network, their directions of travel and to what populated areas they led, and the specific features of each of these (bridges, intersections, tunnels, viaducts, and so on). Should their aircraft compasses malfunction, the pilots could quickly take a course to their own territory by means of these easily recognizable features.

In October 1943 the free hunt was conducted primarily against rail traffic. In view of the existence of a single rail line from Zaporozhe to Genichesk, the destruction of steam locomotives and rolling stock on this line was not too difficult. This led to delays, and at times the complete cessation of movement for German trains.

A pair of Airacobras was sent out to execute this mission. Sometimes two pairs were dispatched for a sixty-mile section of rail line. They operated in the following manner. Two P-39s began their search for targets at the north end of the zone while the other pair began in the south. This diverted the attention of enemy early warning posts. When required, the hunters could quickly rally to support each other.

On frequent occasions, the hunt was conducted continuously for the entire course of a day. The first pair, as a rule, launched for their hunting mission at dawn. Reconnaissance of the rail line was begun from one end of the designated sector. After the destruction of any discovered targets, the Airacobras returned to their airfield for rearming and refueling. Upon landing, the pilots reported the results of their actions, defined precisely the sector of the rail line they had overflown, and identified the location of any enemy they had detected and destroyed.

The second pair began working the route at the point where the first pair left off. Upon discovering and destroying a new target, they returned home. This pattern continued throughout the day, as long as there was sufficient ambient light to fly and identify targets. In all, from four to six pairs of Airacobras participated (eight to twelve aircraft). In addition to disrupting movement on the rail lines of communication, the rotational attacks of the hunters permitted the crews to inspect the results of previous strikes.

The procedures of the free hunt changed daily, both in their tactical methods and in time, so as not to establish a pattern. Patterned combat activity inescapably would allow the enemy to implement effective countermeasures and, consequently, inflict unjustified losses on the Airacobra pilots.

Dense overcast presented almost ideal conditions for hunting rolling stock along the railroad because it prevented the interference of enemy fighters. In these conditions the altitude of the hunters' flight varied within the range of 985 to 1,970 feet. If the pilots dropped down lower, it was difficult for them to acquire and lay on the target. This might require a second pass. The radius of an aircraft's turn was significantly enlarged in unfavorable weather conditions. In addition, valuable time would be expended and, more importantly, the element of surprise would be lost.

The methods of attack used against steam locomotives and tank cars varied: strafing from the rear or front of the train; at unloading platforms and sidings with embankments or cuts; and more distant from stations, which were more frequently covered by anti-aircraft assets. Frequently, the hunters attacked rolling stock from the right or left at almost right angles to the direction of travel. Experience showed that an approach at near-right angles was most effective in that it rendered anti-aircraft gun crews, mounted on platform cars, less effective because of the rapid displacement of the aircraft in space. Enemy gun crews could not easily conduct aimed fires and were forced to put up barrier fires. According to reports and observations of air crews, the projectiles of the 37mm aircraft cannon penetrated the boilers and completely disabled locomotives. The steam escaped and frequently the boiler itself exploded.

The following data speak to the overall effectiveness of the free hunt method for the period from 23 September to 1 November 1943: eight locomotives and twenty-three tank cars were destroyed and countless others were damaged; sixteen wheeled vehicles were destroyed; four airfields were reconnoitered (containing an aggregate eighty aircraft of various types); three fuel and ammunition dumps were destroyed; and four artillery firing locations were strafed. A total of seventy-five aircraft sorties were flown (16th Regiment thirty-four, 100th thirty-one, and 104th ten).[1] Here are some typical examples of free hunt missions.

On 8 October, a pair of Airacobras (Mikhail Likhovid and Vasiliy Drygin) of 104th Guards Fighter Regiment launched early in the morning to reconnoiter in a zone over Akimovka, Grigorevka, and Genichesk. The pair observed a train with six tank cars at Butlyug station. Mikhail well understood that such an important target on a single rail line, which supplied the enemy's Melitopol grouping, of course would have an organized anti-aircraft defense. If they attacked it head on they might not return home. With his wingman, Likhovid agreed to take advantage of the cloud cover for a stealthier approach. They gained altitude and flew toward the west to avoid enemy air observation posts. Flying some fifteen miles deep into enemy territory, the pair turned 180 degrees and, moving from one cloud to another, flew toward Butlyug station. This was a judicious decision. All the attention of the enemy observation posts was focused toward the front line, not the German rear.

The stealth of the hunters and their approach from the least dangerous direction permitted them to break through to the strafing target with no difficulty. Deployed abreast, they executed an "eagle strike" of several seconds' duration. Cannon and machine-gun bursts penetrated the loaded tank cars. Something ignited the spilled fuel and towering flames reached into the sky. The fire burned at this station for the next two days. It engulfed not only all six tank cars but also spread to cars standing nearby, station outbuildings, and warehouses. The black column of smoke in the sky over Butlyug station became an excellent reference point for pilots of various units.

The 9th Guards Fighter Division operated mainly in the interests of the left wing of 4th Ukrainian *Front* during November 1943. Because of poor weather conditions and insufficient enemy air assets, the air situation was characterized by a small number of aerial engagements. Insignificant numbers of enemy fighters participated in them. Apparently the German command was giving particular attention to opposing the formations of 3d Ukrainian *Front,* which was advancing on the Kriviy Rog axis.[2]

As before, the division continued actively to free-hunt across a broad zone and to a significant depth of the enemy dispositions. On 3 November, a pair of P-39s of Captain Gregoriy Rechkalov and Junior Lieutenant Nikolay Chistov (16th Guards Fighter Regiment) sortied on free hunt in the area of Bolshoy Tokmak and Melitopol. On the approaches to the latter the Airacobra pilots discovered six He-111s escorted by two Bf-109s at an altitude of 13,125 feet.

In his first pass, coming out of the sun from above and behind, Captain Rechkalov shot down the trailing Heinkel from a range of 110 yards. His wingman covered his actions. After this successful strike the hunters flew back into the sun and were not detected by the enemy. The surprise that they had achieved and their skillful concealment permitted the Airacobra pilots to conduct a second pass at a well chosen moment. While re-forming, one Messerschmitt became separated from its leader. Chistov took advantage of the situation and with a steep dive set fire to the "bandit" with an attack from above and behind.[3] Once again, both P-39s maneuvered from out of the sun and a few moments later took a course back to their airfield.

On 19 November, Senior Lieutenant Mikhail Likhovid and Lieutenant Nikolay Kireev of 104th Guards Fighter Regiment flew in the sector Armyansk–Vonka station from 1522 until 1600. Some 220 yards from the station they observed a Fieseler-Storch aircraft preparing to take off. The two Airacobras launched an attack. Hits on the fuselage did not set the small aircraft on fire. It continued to move toward a takeoff area. A second head-on pass finally destroyed the target.

In Mikhaylovka they found two heavily loaded trucks and began to strafe them. During his recovery from the dive, Likhovid felt a hit and his Airacobra made a half-turn. The aircraft was not responding to aileron inputs. Mikhail maintained his course with the throttle control and raced toward Soviet-occupied territory. He made a belly landing on the island Churyuk. Upon inspection of the aircraft he found two direct hits by anti-aircraft rounds. One was in the right wing at the aileron mounting point, and the other was on the leading edge in the middle of the left wing, closer to the fuselage. Three anti-aircraft artillerymen from the 7th Battery of the 674th Anti-aircraft Regiment approached the site of the forced landing in a vehicle. By evening Likhovid had been delivered to Novo-Nikolaevka, and from there to his unit. The fighter remained under guard of the anti-aircraft artillerymen until a technical team arrived at the island the next day to begin the recovery operation.[4]

A pair of P-39s flown by Lieutenant Iosif Grafin and Junior Lieutenant Nikolay Klimov from the 104th Guards Fighter Regiment was flying a free hunt in the area of Dzhankoe and Ishun on 26 November. The Airacobra pilots worked rapidly and boldly, conducting reconnaissance of the target from an altitude of 5,250 feet. They discovered up to fifty rail cars and a working steam locomotive at Vonka station. The pair dropped down to treetop level and strafed the targets, disabling the locomotive immediately and setting several of the freight cars on fire.

But they also came under anti-aircraft fire. The two pilots left the danger zone without climbing and continued their search for new targets. Six miles north of Vonka they spotted two trains of up to thirty freight cars. One of the trains was accompanied by a locomotive. The pilots "hosed down" the freight cars with cannons and machine guns, blowing up the locomotive. They flew on to reconnoiter the next station up the line, Ishun, where they found and strafed up to twenty freight and flat cars on sidings with no visible means of locomotion.[5]

By the end of November, formations of the 51st Combined Arms Army and 19th Tank Corps of 4th Ukrainian *Front* had occupied a line from Turetskiy Val to Armyansk and beyond along the north shore of the Sivash as far as Genichesk.[6] Soviet troops forced the strait in the area of Kos and Russian Island and captured a beachhead along the line Urzin, Ashkadan, Biyuk-Kiyat. The enemy was now cut off in the Crimea.

The enemy began operating transport aviation (Ju-52 aircraft) to provide supplies to this isolated grouping. The RUS-2 radar detected frequent flights of these transports from Odessa to the Crimean Peninsula. Initially these flights were made in groups of five to six aircraft.

To combat these Ju-52s, division reconnaissance aircraft were ordered to operate as "hunters" and destroy them on their routes across the Black Sea. This mission was largely flown by pilots of the 16th Guards Fighter Regiment.

The weather was quite poor on 20 December, with heavy black rain clouds obscuring the sky. In this kind of weather, the commander of 16th Guards Regiment, Guards Major Aleksandr Pokryshkin, along with his irreplaceable wingman Georgiy Golubev, decided to go out on the mission.

Pokryshkin recalls: "I had dreamed about these flights while we were still in the Kuban. I rounded up some fuel drop tanks, hoping that they would enable us to intercept targets at great range out over the Black Sea. I was always attracted to the free hunt flight profile. These flights were characterized by intense actions and great risk, but the results could also be very significant."[7]

During the preflight preparation, maintenance personnel discovered that the radio transmitter was not working in Pokryshkin's "100." The regiment commander did not want to wait for repairs to be made. They had to hurry before the weather improved. According to the regiment maintenance officer, Vladimir Savin's Airacobra was completely flight ready. Aleksandr Pokryshkin sortied to the free hunt in this aircraft.

Pokryshkin's pair flew over land and then into the coastal area of the Black Sea, consuming fuel from the auxiliary tanks while saving their main tanks. This procedure was required: an empty auxiliary tank did not cause rupture of the fuel delivery lines during high-stress maneuvers in aerial combat or rupture and burn if it were struck by enemy fire.

The "hunters" crossed the coastline west of Skadovsk. As far as they could see the sea was raging in a force-9 storm.[8] They flew through dense overcast at an altitude of 330 feet. Their route extended out over the Black Sea some sixty to ninety miles from land, the aircraft flying a "twisted ribbon" search pattern first from north to south, then from south to north. This pattern enabled them to inspect a relatively large airspace. They peered at the dull horizon and the dense tufts of hanging clouds. In places their aircraft were drenched by saltwater spray. The vertical corridor between the dense overcast and the dark waters of the sea was no more than 330 feet in height. It was in this very corridor that German transports were crossing from the Crimea to Odessa and back.

The pair had already searched for twenty minutes and had not found a single target. They flew across the waves at an altitude of 165 feet. Pokryshkin was in the lead, followed by Georgiy Golubev to his right rear. The wingman spotted a heavily loaded Ju-52 up ahead. He gave a brief report to his commander of the transport's direction of flight and altitude. Pokryshkin gave the command to Golubev to attack the enemy plane.

The wing of Georgiy's Airacobra almost touched the waves as he made a slight turn. He closed on the Ju-52, and "55" (the tail number of Golubev's aircraft) fired a long burst into the left engine. A black plume of smoke extended back in the aircraft's wake, followed quickly by bright flames on the wing. The attacking Airacobra caught up to the tri-motor on a parallel course. The enemy aircraft, increasingly engulfed in fire, dropped toward the water and then caught its fixed undercarriage in a wave. It nosed over and in an instant disappeared beneath the cold water. This Crimean "visitor" did not return home.

With fuel remaining in their tanks, the pilots continued the mission. Another ten minutes passed. Pokryshkin spotted a Ju-52 headed toward the Crimea. The Airacobra pilots came at it from below, barely clearing the tops of the waves. The Guards major "stitched" the transport with the fires of two wing-mounted heavy machine guns from close range. For some reason the nose-mounted cannon and heavy machine guns were silent. But even this reduced portion of lead was sufficient. The ponderous aircraft exploded. Its burning pieces were extinguished as they fell into the dark sea.[9] Their work completed, the two pilots turned toward home.

At the airfield Pokryshkin discovered the cause of his primary weapons' malfunction. It turned out that Vladimir Savin's aircraft had not been flown for an extended period of time. During the winter the ammunition had become wet and at the required moment of combat this now frozen ammunition caused the cannon and heavy machine guns to jam. The armorers learned an uncomfortable lesson. The regiment, which had been equipped with Airacobras eight months previously, was now in its first winter with this aircraft. The maintenance and support units had no experience maintaining the fighters in these conditions.

The "gods of fire" [unit armorers] made no such mistakes in the future. If for any reason a P-39 did not sortie for an extended period of time in cold and wet weather, then the weapons were periodically reloaded. The possibly wet ammunition was removed and replaced with dry ammunition. It was extra work that took some time, but these were not significant factors when compared to the importance of functioning guns in air-to-air combat. After the ammunition was replaced, the cannon and machine guns were always test-fired.

The year 1943 was drawing to a close. During his fourth hunting sortie over the Black Sea, Aleksandr Pokryshkin survived an incident that almost cost him his life and did bring an end to his favorite mission profile. As during previous flights, the weather was quite bad, with a strong wind, sticky wet snow, and a heavy overcast hanging over the white-capped sea. Soon after his arrival in the designated mission area Pokryshkin encountered a Ju-52 flying at an altitude of not more than 230 feet. At times its profile disappeared from his field of view as it moved in and out of the overcast. Pokryshkin approached it from behind and below and fired on it with all weapons. As the aircraft dropped rapidly toward the waves, Pokryshkin fired one more burst into its belly. At that instant he passed within two or three yards of the falling transport's tail and disappeared into the overcast. This was a most dangerous near miss. The celebrated ace had almost been killed in a collision between his Airacobra and the Junkers. Despite his combat success, the regiment commander's mood was foul. He could as easily have died as lived.

Without any hesitation or malicious intent, Golubev described this, yet another of many free hunts, to his comrades in the regiment, not sparing any details of his commander's near miss. As these things always do, the story somehow reached the commander of the 8th Air Army, Lieutenant General Timofey Khryukin. Two days later Pokryshkin was summoned to his headquarters. He received a good scolding and was categorically forbidden to conduct any more free hunts. The air army commander ordered him to fight only over land, and always as part of a group of fighters.

In the first days of the new year the army command and staff organized a conference of fighter pilot hunters in Agalman. It was conducted under the overall supervision of Major General Evgeniy Savitskiy and Guards Major Aleksandr Pokryshkin.[10] The best ace pilots had been invited to this conference: Twice Heroes of the Soviet Union Vladimir Lavrinenkov, Dmitriy Glinka, Aleksey Alelyukin, and Amet-Khan Sultan; and Heroes of the Soviet Union Aleksey Reshetov, Boris Glinka, and Mikhail Komelkov.[11]

The conference was convened to discuss the experience accumulated by these hunter pilots, to work out the most effective method of preparing aviators for this special combat mission, and to recommend improved tactical methods for fighters. The pilots shared their personal experiences in destroying various targets on the ground and in the air, discussing both their successes and failures on their free hunt missions.

This conference lasted for three days. The assembled materials were carefully analyzed, the necessary conclusions drawn, and the recommendations sent out to aviation units. The air army commander's order required subordinate commanders to review the considerable experience of the celebrated hunters with their own air crews and particularly with those pilots whom they had selected for this most dangerous method of destroying the enemy.

Over the Perekop

In November 1943 the forces of the 4th Ukrainian *Front* continued their offensive in the direction of Kherson and Crimea and liberated the left bank of the Dnieper River along its lower course. They captured a beachhead on the eastern portion of the Crimean Peninsula and laid a pontoon bridge across the Sivash.

The 9th Guards Fighter Division provided coverage to the 51st Combined Arms Army for the entire month. During this period the fighter regiments flew a total of 834 mission sorties. All of these sorties were flown by the 16th and 104th Guards Regiments, as the 100th Guards Regiment was undergoing reconstitution and training. The division was based at airfields at Askaniya-Nova and Krestovskiy. Because of poor weather conditions, the larger engagements were fought in the second half of November. On 15 November, the two active regiments (16th and 104th) had sixteen and ten operational aircraft, respectively, twenty-four and fifteen combat-qualified pilots, and eight and eleven pilots not combat-qualified.[1]

Special attention was given to preserving the crossing site across the Sivash and preventing bombardment of units crossing over into Crimea. The commander of the 8th Air Army, General Timofey Khryukin, arrived at the 16th Guards Fighter Regiment on 10 November. After listening to a report from its commander, Guards Major Aleksandr Pokryshkin, regarding the status of his unit, the general assigned the mission: "Your regiment is responsible for covering the beachhead on the Sivash and the crossing site. The conditions for ground units there are exceptionally difficult. There are few bridging assets available. You must do everything to prevent air strikes on our forces."

Pokryshkin recalled this conversation with the air army commander:

I told the general, "We can cover the crossing sites in a timely manner and fend off attacks only by simultaneous commitment to battle of main forces or the entire regiment, and only if we stop patrolling from dawn to dusk in small groups. I need to hold the regiment in a fist until it is time for combat, and then inflict a powerful blow. The squadrons will remain on alert, ready for immediate launch until the enemy has been spotted.

This method is possible only if I have access to a radar set and appropriate radio communications with it, and the approval of the division staff for this method of operation. Under these conditions, the regiment can successfully execute the mission that you have assigned." The general responded, "You will receive the radar and the instructions will be issued to division headquarters"[2]

Intensive training began in the squadrons for the difficult upcoming combat mission. The staffs and pilots conducted several exercises to resolve various tactical issues. The chiefs of services prepared their subordinates to accomplish their support and maintenance tasks in quick order.

On 12 November a group of specialists deployed a radio transmitter and an RUS-2 radar set near the regiment commander's command post. They installed a plotting board in the command post to display the radar inputs. Simultaneously, Arkadiy Fedorov's squadron was transferred to a makeshift airfield at Novo-Pokrovka, only ten miles from the crossing site.[3] This was in effect an ambush at the very shore of the Sivash. The mission of this squadron was to maintain flights on alert to respond to visual detection or launch commands from the regiment command post. In addition, two groups of eight fighters each remained on alert at Askaniya-Nova, at readiness levels 1 and 2.

The regiment commander and staff, along with the air crews, studied the configuration of the RUS-2 and its ability to detect enemy aircraft. The regiment headquarters personnel needed to know what the apparatus was capable of detecting. The air crews needed to check out this new device and evaluate its worth by its achievements. The RUS-2 considerably aided the pilots of the airfield alert groups. Before they got this equipment, they sat in the cabins of their aircraft for long periods of time, in tense anticipation of the signal to launch. These periods of sitting were frequently in vain. Now only the group at readiness level 1 had to remain in their aircraft.

Based on the data received from the RUS-2, twelve to fourteen Airacobras could be dispatched to the coverage area by the time of the approach of the German bombers. The P-39s did not have to maintain a constant presence over the crossing site. This placed the enemy in a difficult situation. There were several occasions when the bombers turned around or shifted to a secondary target.

The responsible division staff officer or commander of the unit that had scrambled a group of fighters in response to a radar sighting monitored the group's actions and followed the situation in the coverage zone. This was easily accomplished by tracking the group leader's radio commands and the instructions transmitted from the ground vectoring station. The unit commander could redirect the patrol in the air toward German bombers if they broke off to another area or turned around.[4]

At the end of each flying day the regiment and division staffs developed map overlays showing the enemy bombers' routes to targets. Careful study of these overlays and the situation reports on the plotting charts derived from RUS-2 data enabled the operations staff to avoid scrambling groups of Airacobras in response to isolated enemy aircraft and instead to focus on groups of bombers. In order to increase the effectiveness of the command and control of fighters based on RUS-2 data, regiments and the division continuously were ordered to maintain officers at the plotting boards and relieve these officers frequently. In this manner they would gain the necessary experience, acquire knowledge regarding the tactics of enemy aviation, and maintain continuous accounting for our own airfield basing area and the zones where our fighters engaged enemy bombers and their escort fighters.

Eight P-39s were parked at Askaniya-Nova airfield at readiness level 1 on 17 November. The leader of this group was the commander of 16th Guards Fighter Regiment, Guards Major Aleksandr Pokryshkin. Information arrived at the command post from the radar station indicating that a large group of enemy bombers was approaching the crossing site. Two red rockets fired into the air signaled the launch of this group. Three minutes later the Airacobras took off, gained altitude, and turned toward the Sivash. Their combat formation was the familiar "bookshelf." The crews suddenly heard the voice of General Khryukin in their headphones. "Airacobra pilots, remember! Not one bomb should fall on the crossing!" This did not happen every day. To be fighting the enemy within eyesight of the air army commander entailed increased responsibility.

In turn, squadron commander Arkadiy Fedorov at the forward airfield received a command from the regiment headquarters to launch his on-call flight. Markers on the target plotting chart showed the locations of Ju-87s and our fighters. Pokryshkin's group received instructions from "Tiger" to go to a particular quadrant to make the intercept.

Viktor Zherdev made a brief radio report to his leader: "Ahead to the left and below, large formation of bombers!" Pilots in that sector spotted three nine-ship formations of bombers. They were flying in their favored "echelon right" formation, which gave enemy pilots significant time to re-form, make a half-turn, and dive on the target. They preferred to drop their bombs from an altitude of 4,920 to 3,280 feet.

"'40' [Aleksandr Klubov and Nikolay Chistov]! This is '100.' Cover us. We are attacking!" commanded Pokryshkin. Led by their regiment commander, the four Airacobras dove out of the sun into the lead formation of nine bombers. The other four-ship group (Klubov–Chistov and Viktor Zherdev–Viniamin Tsvetkov), led by Klubov, attacked the enemy fighter escort and distracted them by battle. They dispersed the "bandits" into a large airspace and then quickly turned back toward the second echelon of Ju-87s.

The two groups of Airacobras launched an almost simultaneous attack on a large portion of the approaching enemy bombers. Rear-facing gunners in the Ju-87s put up a fierce barrage of fire. Pokryshkin's group broke through this barrier at high speed and burst into the bomber formation. Two Ju-87s quickly went down in flames, trailing black smoke. Executing a right turn, the Airacobras climbed toward the sun to get into position for a second "eagle strike."

Zherdev's group shot down one Ju-87 but was itself attacked by a pair of Bf-109s. Pokryshkin saw it coming. "'25'! This is '100'! Messerschmitt on your tail!" He raced to assist his subordinates. The Germans, having spotted the P-39s diving toward them, halted their approach to Zherdev and, with a left turn and rapid decrease in altitude, dove under Pokryshkin and his wingman Golubev.

This was Pokryshkin's "formula of terror," put into practice. "Speed, maneuver, and fire!" defeated the enemy, helped a comrade, and launched a renewed attack on the second echelon of now eight Ju-87s. During all of this, the group leader [Pokryshkin] managed to monitor the actions of the other pairs. Every second was valuable in this kind of high-speed, intense aerial engagement.

The turning point in the battle had been reached when the bomber formation was broken up. The remnants of the first nine bombers showed the way. They turned around, dove toward the ground, and dropped their ordnance without reaching the crossing site. The detonations of these bombs raised large fountains of salty Sivash water.

As before, the battle continued at a high tempo. Engines revved under heavy loads; the cannon and machine-gun barrels disgorged streams of fire. The fuel levels in the Airacobras' tanks were drained lower with each passing minute and the end of the battle was still not in sight. Soon they would have to request a "33" (depart for home). The third echelon of bombers, which had not yet been attacked, could possibly break through to the crossing site.

"Tiger, Tiger! This is *Sotka* ['100,' Pokryshkin's call sign]. Launch Fedorov's squadron!" Pokryshkin requested. His four-ship group needed to break off pursuit of the bombers of the first group. They needed to give a quick assist to Klubov, whose flight was being chased by six Bf-109s. With a rapid gain of altitude ("Be above, and not below, the enemy!"—Pokryshkin held strictly to this rule) and a rush at the Messerschmitts, Pokryshkin went to his comrades' aid. A pair of "bandits" appeared above them, threatening the counterattack of Pokryshkin's Airacobras.

The battle burned with new energy, now at two levels. At the upper level Konstantin Sukhov and Andrey Trud attacked the Bf-109s, fending them off the regiment commander. The pilot of one Messerschmitt would have liked to live longer. Below, Pokryshkin, Zherdev, and Klubov visited themselves upon the second and third echelons of Ju-87s. One after the other, two dive bombers spun all the way to the ground.

Having received data from the RUS-2, ground vectoring station "Tiger" quickly gave another alert. The air situation was becoming more complicated by the minute. The enemy, in all probability, intended to ram through our crossing site cover by sending in wave after wave of bombers. The division command understood the enemy's intent and launched patrol after patrol to the Perekop area.[5] Arkadiy Fedorov's squadron was already on station above Pokryshkin's eight aircraft. Hurrying to assist Fedorov was a group of six P-39s from Askaniya-Nova, led by Guards Captain Grigoriy Rechkalov.

Consuming their last available liters of gasoline, Pokryshkin and his subordinates made one final pass at the bombers. With a burst of speed the Airacobras penetrated into the rear of the third echelon of Ju-87s. A stream of cannon and machine-gun fire from the P-39s silenced the rear gunners of two Ju-87s. The latter, trailing smoke, splashed into the waters of the Sivash.

Their available fuel at an end, the eight aircraft commanded by Pokryshkin dropped down, closed up into a tight formation, and broke away for their airfield. Below them the crossing was operating normally, supporting the movement of infantry and trucks. Despite considerable effort, the enemy had not penetrated to the pontoon bridge. The Airacobra pilots of the 16th Fighter Regiment had put a "wall" in their path. The score for this battle: seven Ju-87s, one Bf-109, and one P-39. Klubov and Zherdev had been especially outstanding in this battle, each downing two bombers.[6] The P-39 crews passed their tough examination before the eyes of the air army commander with excellent marks and he conveyed his appreciation to them after they landed.

Despite his significant losses, the enemy continued his stubborn attempts to break through to the crossing site, changing his tactics and methods. Enemy aircraft began to approach the Sivash at low level. They were difficult to detect on the far approaches to the bay, and as a consequence, aircraft parked at Askaniya-Nova airfield were delayed in launching. The main burden of defeating these enemy raids fell on the squadron of Arkadiy Fedorov (Novo-Pokrovka airfield).[7] If the situation in the air required the reinforcement of Fedorov's group, help was quickly sent from the regiment's main basing area.

On 20 November the Germans simultaneously threw up to forty Ju-87s at the crossing site, escorted by six Messerschmitts. Fedorov's squadron went up to engage them first. The forces were not equal. The pilots understood that they had to delay the enemy for a period of time until help arrived. Each of them fought boldly and confidently. Conducting battle in the vertical plane, the Airacobra pilots were able to disperse the compact bomber formation somewhat. Breaks appeared in the dense fire of their rear gunners. Airacobras flew through these breaks at maximum speed and attacked from the inside of the enemy formation. Fedorov's pilots fought like lions and shot down six Ju-87s and two Bf-109s.

The enemy did not give up. He found a crack in the wall through which his bombers could reach the Sivash to bomb the crossing sites. Taking advantage of bad weather and darkness, the Germans began to raid in large and small groups at the end of November. Three echelons of nine Ju-87s each raced toward the crossings on the evening of 27 November. Pavel Eremin's squadron launched to defeat the enemy bombers over the Perekop and shot down eleven of the twenty-seven bombers. The ground forces commander sent a special message of thanks to the Airacobra pilots for this effort.

November 1943 was a severe test for the pilots of the 16th Guards Fighter Regiment. On average, seventeen of the regiment's authorized thirty-two pilots were combat-capable throughout the month. The pilots experienced the heaviest load in the last ten days of November, when normal flying weather prevailed. Enemy aviation immediately conducted more raids on the Sivash crossing sites and against ground units in the area of Ash-Kadak and Russian Island. A particularly difficult day was 27 November, when Airacobra regiment units flew fifty sorties.

Pokryshkin's unit suffered light combat and noncombat losses during this month. One Airacobra was shot down, and an Il-2 Shturmovik executing a landing collided with a P-39 on the ground in its revetment, destroying the P-39. The loss of only these two aircraft was a clear indication of the high level of training of squadron personnel. The regiment fought eighteen air battles in November, in which 25 Soviet and 130 German aircraft participated.[8]

December 1943 was a normal working month for the Airacobra pilots. They covered the ground forces on those same lines of the Perekop and actively conducted free hunts and reconnaissance in Crimea. At the beginning of the month the regiments had the following aircraft on hand: 16th Guards, twenty Airacobras, ten of which were combat ready; 104th Guards, fifteen P-39s, eight of which were combat ready; and 100th Guards, ten aircraft for training flights.

The 104th Regiment was displaced to Askaniya-Nova on 13 December, leaving only the 100th Regiment at Krestovskiy. On 20 and 21 December the 9th Guards Fighter Division received sixteen new P-39s: 16th Guards eight aircraft, 100th Guards six aircraft, and 104th Guards two aircraft. At the end of 1943 these fighters were not yet combat ready due to poor flying conditions (fog, low ceiling) during the last two weeks of December.

Only a few of the several aerial engagements over the Perekop in December bear mention. On 8 December, operating closely with the RUS-2, a group of ten Airacobras led by Captain Pavel Eremin and Senior Lieutenant Andrey Trud engaged ten Ju-87s escorted by four Bf-109s. The well-coordinated actions of the strike group (six P-39s led by Eremin) and the cover group (two pairs of P-39s led by Trud) prevented the bombers from reaching their target. The Luftwaffe lost four Ju-87s and one Bf-109. All the Airacobras returned safely to land at Askaniya-Nova.

On 17 December two pairs of Airacobras led by Pavel Eremin (cover group) and six P-39s led by Arkadiy Fedorov (strike group) conducted an intense lopsided battle south of Urzhiy with forty bombers accompanied by ten Messerschmitts. The enemy outnumbered our forces five to one. The persistent and calculated attacks of the Airacobra pilots and the close cooperation between and within the two groups yielded remarkable results. Ten minutes into the fight the enemy had lost six bombers and two fighters. Eremin's group had suffered no losses.

Unfortunately, on three occasions the Airacobra pilots were unable to prevent the enemy from bombing ground forces on the Sivash crossing site. On 27 December, at 1305, the RUS-2 detected a large group of enemy bombers heading toward the Sivash. None of the 9th Guards Fighter Division regiments could launch aircraft because of below-minimum weather conditions at their airfields. The ceiling at Askaniya-Nova was under 200 feet. Taking advantage of these weather conditions over the Airacobra bases and the evening darkness, the enemy executed two unopposed air strikes on our ground forces between 1730 and 1835 that evening.[9]

The 9th Guards Fighter Division flew 465 combat missions in December, distributed in the following manner: 16th Regiment flew 256 and the 104th flew 16 missions to provide coverage for the 51st Combined Arms Army; these two regiments flew 15 and 130 reconnaissance sorties, respectively; and 16 and 6 free hunt sorties, respectively. The 9th Guards Fighter Division did not suffer any combat or noncombat losses of aircraft during the last month of the long and intense year of 1943.[10]

The actions of 9th Guards "Mariupol" Fighter Division units over the Perekop, in close coordination with the RUS-2 radar station, were exceptionally productive. The unprecedented assignment of a radar station to a single air regiment (the 16th) enabled this regiment to defeat multiple enemy attempts to launch air strikes at the ground forces' most important object of enemy interest—crossing sites over the Sivash. The RUS-2 made sixty intercepts of enemy aircraft groups of various composition between 23 October and 23 December. Launching sorties based on this data, Airacobra crews fought twenty engagements with large groups of German aircraft.[11]

In addition, the presence in the division and regiment of an efficient means of detecting enemy aircraft in the air and determining the relative size of enemy formations permitted our air staffs to economize on scarce aircraft and engine resources. Without the RUS-2 radar apparatus, the division would have expended some eighty aircraft sorties per day. When this radar set was available, a maximum of sixty-two missions sorties were flown on the most intense day of combat activity (27 November). Practice showed that maintaining close and timely coordination with the RUS-2 operators permitted the division and regiment staffs to mass fighter resources when necessary and put twelve to sixteen aircraft in the air. These powerful patrols inflicted serious losses on the enemy.[12]

Relocation to New Airfields

One of the most important and difficult missions of logistic services was the problem of timely preparation of new airfields and the concomitant rapid relocation of aviation units to these airfields. An examination of the experience of 9th Guards Fighter Division provides insight into both the positive and negative aspects of this problem.

During the Great Patriotic War this division traveled a lengthy combat path: its air echelon (personnel and aircraft of aviation units that relocated to a new airfield by air) covered some 3,800 miles, and its ground echelon (aviation unit personnel and equipment that relocated to a new airfield by rail and wheeled vehicle) 5,550 miles. The 9th Guards Fighter Division relocated to a different airfield on sixty-four occasions in the twenty-six months between March 1943 and May 1945. This frequency of displacement placed an enormous burden on the supporting logistical organizations, which were required in the shortest possible time to prepare the necessary number of airfield networks, deploy a portion of aviation logistic support units to them, and create reserves of materiel for both supporting and supported units.[1] The successful accomplishment of all these tasks depended first of all on the timely and organized relocation of the airfield service battalion (BAO).

A 27 January 1943 order pertaining to logistical support of 4th Air Army (to which the 216th, later 9th Guards, Fighter Division was assigned) levied the following requirement for displacement of logistical support units. "The BAOs must relocate to new airfields immediately upon release from supporting aviation units. Battalions must follow directly behind forward ground formations, maintaining continuous communications with the headquarters of these formations. Designate and reconnoiter movement routes and crossings at water obstacles ahead of time as instructed by RAB chiefs. Establish communications with re-basing BAOs by control points, using the radio and liaison officers."[2]

It must be noted that there were other problems associated with the use of airfield service battalions. For example, the workload this placed on an organizational entity was enormous. The established norm was one BAO servicing two single-engine regiments or one two-engine regiment.[3] In practice, the ratio was quite different at times. In October 1943, 691st BAO of 8th Air Army (to which 9th Guards Fighter Division belonged at that time) supported an aviation corps and division, two fighter regiments, and a separate squadron. In this case, the service battalion commander was required to have contact with five aviation commanders, to whom he was subordinated for countless logistical support issues. Of course, this created a certain number of difficulties for all parties concerned.

From early 1944 until the end of the Great Patriotic War, RABs in air armies were attached in operational subordination to commanders of aviation corps for specific periods of combat operations. This command relationship ensured careful planning of the RABs' employment, rational preparation and conduct of dislocation of fighter units, and displacement of the required numbers of BAOs.

Combat experience permitted commanders to define and solidify in practice two methods of airfield relocation. In the literature this is sometimes referred to as "airfield maneuver." The first means was by advance teams. Sent out from the BAO, an advance team was configured so as to be capable, while separated from the parent battalion, of ensuring uninterrupted combat activity for one air regiment.[4]

The second method was to employ a reserve battalion. The chiefs of logistical services of air armies always attempted to have this element of aviation-technical support. However, without exception, in any offensive operation of the third period of the war (January 1944 to May 1945), all air armies had fewer airfield service battalions than there were aviation units. Take, for example, 16th Air Army. By the beginning of the Berlin operation, it had seventy-two BAOs to service ninety-six aviation regiments. Of these aviation units, nineteen two-engine regiments were each supported by a single service battalion. These service battalions designated advance teams that departed for the new basing locations of their supported units.

The remaining seventy-five regiments, which were equipped with single-engine aircraft, were maintained in full combat readiness by fifty-two service battalions. Because thirty-eight of these battalions were servicing two regiments each, the chief of logistic services was able to hold fifteen BAOs in reserve. This permitted him to accomplish their timely dislocation to the areas of intended construction (rehabilitation) of airfields.[5] The planning norm was one airfield-engineer battalion for two landing fields. The local populace, and sometimes nearby troop units, were frequently drafted to assist the engineer unit.

In the course of battles in the Kuban, 216th Air Division was based on Popovicheskaya airfield for almost five months (28 February to 16 June 1943). The dirt runway permitted the Airacobra pilots to execute takeoffs and landings of their fighters, but when the rains came, the airfield became unsuitable for combat flying. In early April, when enemy air activity began to increase, the P-39s were unable to scramble to intercept them because of the saturated soil. Only five days later, on 8 April, did the airfield dry out sufficiently to permit flight operations to resume.[6]

By the beginning of May, the division had increased to four regiments (16th, 42d, 57th Guards, and 45th Fighter Regiments). It had to be dispersed and began to conduct combat operations from three airfields: Popovicheskaya, Krasnoarmeyskaya, and Slavyanskaya.

One BAO supported each regiment. There were no interruptions in the accomplishment of assigned missions that could be attributed to these battalions. They provided the aviation units with all necessary materiel and technical supplies.[7]

From 1 August 1943, 9th Guards Fighter Division (16th and 100th Guards Regiments), on order of the commander-in-chief of the Red Army VVS, was subordinated to 8th Air Army of Southern *Front*. On this same day the division was displaced to the Mirskoye, Filinskiy, Alekseevka, Tuzlovka airfield network (northeast of Taganrog). Six Pe-2 aircraft of 270th Bomber Division led the flight of the first echelon of fighters from Slavyanskaya airfield (west of Krasnodar).

The commander of 8th Air Army designated nine Li-2 (named for B. P. Lisunov, this was a Soviet-built Douglas DC-3 produced under license) aircraft to move the ground echelon and division headquarters to the new airfield. This transfer required thirty-six sorties over a period of two days. The first priority was to relocate the division headquarter's operations group with its wire communications and advance teams of the regiments' technical staff, which together fully supported the reception and servicing of the flying echelon. The division headquarter's wheeled transportation and 19th Separate Guards Communications Company arrived at the new airfield two days later with the main command and control assets. The bulk of the division had completed the movement by 1800 on 1 August. The regiments' pilots acquainted themselves with the area of anticipated combat activity on the following day.

On 14 August the division headquarters received, through 8th Air Army, a telegraphic instruction from Stavka of the Supreme High Command regarding transfer of 9th Guards Fighter Division from Southern to Southwest *Front*.

For clarification of all issues regarding movement to new airfields, the deputy commander, Guards Lieutenant Colonel Aleksandr Rykalov, flew to the headquarters of 17th Air Army, where he received all the necessary instructions. However, they could not be fully implemented. While the transfer operation was still in its initial stages, the 17th Air Army commander received new orders and passed them along by radio. The 100th Guards Fighter Regiment was to move to Svatovo airfield, which conflicted with an earlier instruction to fly to Novoaleksandrovka airfield. As a result, the regiment's aircraft landed at Svatovo (forty miles southwest of Kupyansk), and its technical component, acting in accordance with the initial order, was transported by air to Novoaleksandrovka airfield.

Both of these airfields were already overcrowded. Two full-strength regiments were already parked at Novoaleksandrovka, and an even larger number of aircraft at Svatovo. In light of this situation, the decision was made to land the 100th Guards Fighter Regiment at Kremennaya airfield (fifty miles south of Svatovo). Despite the fact that this airfield was absolutely unsuitable for Airacobra flight operations, all the regiment's aircraft were sent here. The single aircraft mishap of the entire rebasing operation occurred at this airfield.

During the relocation the division headquarters and communications company commander committed a series of errors that quickly revealed themselves at the new airfields. Insufficient communications personnel and equipment had been dispatched on the initial air transports. This prevented establishment of timely communications at Kremennaya and Svatovo airfields. The lack of a radio transmitter (it was still en route) created difficulties in initial command and control of the regiments.

That insufficient consideration was given to receiving the division into 17th Air Army is confirmed by the fact that there were no BAOs at the arrival airfields when the regiment's aircraft began to arrive. BAO advance teams began to arrive only on the following day, 17 August. Thanks to the foresight of the division command, units were supplied with both fuel and ammunition and quickly began to perform their combat mission. These important materials were transported by air from the previous airfields by reducing the number of personnel transported in the first sorties.[8]

The rebasing of 216th Fighter Division from airfields in the Kuban to the Donbass region and its subordination to 8th Air Army, then 17th Air Army in the Svatovo area, and subsequently back to the 8th Air Army clearly demonstrated that if airfields were prepared by BAOs for full-scale air operations, then fighter regiments would be in a condition to accomplish any assigned missions within three to four hours after concentration on the new airfields.[9] This was achieved by prior dispatch of functionally capable operations groups with the required communications assets, and also the transfer by transport aircraft of command-technical personnel and a single basic load of ammunition before the arrival of the flying echelon.

Combat operations of Soviet ground forces south of Taganrog were developing rapidly in the second half of October 1943. Units of 9th Guards Fighter Division were covering the offensive of 4th and 5th Guards Cavalry and 4th Mechanized Corps. The fighter regiments had to move to new airfields several times, sometimes shifting fifty to sixty miles. This required precision and flexibility in the efforts of logistic organs. Unfortunately, the RAB and BAOs were often unable to support such frequent and rapid movements from one region to another and the combat operations that immediately followed. For example, on 29 October, 100th Guards Fighter Regiment flew to Veseloye airfield (twenty-five miles northwest of Melitopol), and 702d BAO, which was servicing this airfield, was not prepared to receive the Airacobras.

In October a method was widely employed by which advance teams of a BAO moved behind forward advancing ground units to reconnoiter and prepare subsequent airfields. This method yielded good results.[10]

For almost the entire month of June 1944, one of the regiments of 9th Guards Fighter Division—100th Guards—worked in the Jassy area from Likhneshti airfield. It was serviced by an advance team from 495th BAO. This unit was unable to provide the regiment with a steady supply of GSM. In addition, because of the lack of engine oil, or its unsuitability for use (contaminated by sand or metal filings, low viscosity), combat operations were interrupted for five hours on 3 June.[11] The poor quality of engine oil also led to cases where aircraft returned to their airfields without accomplishing the assigned mission due to overheated engines. Interruptions in the delivery of lubricants led to irregularity in the distribution of the combat effort to the fighter squadrons in the regiment.[12]

On 18 June this same regiment was transferred to Prizhani airfield, where not everything was satisfactory regarding its logistical support. For two days no one from the service organizations appeared in the area where the regiment was based. Only late on 19 June did an advance team from 436th BAO arrive, but this unit was not in a condition to support the regiment. It had only 2,000 liters of gasoline and a single 1.5-ton truck. The battalion's remaining personnel were still on the road and a portion of its component was supporting the operations of 304th Fighter Division at Yampol airfield. Units from 428th BAO replaced this understrength advance team on the following day. Deploying in six hours, they immediately began to support 100th Fighter Regiment with all categories of materials and supplies.

Another regiment of 9th Guards Fighter Division—16th Guards—was moved to Tedireni airfield, where it remained from 1 to 18 June 1944. A positive aspect of its rebasing was that an advance team of 495th BAO moved the entire equipment component and headquarters to the new airfield in thirty-six hours. But there were also some problems. The regiment's units in this and subsequent cases had to land on a field that was not fully prepared for use (not all aircraft had shelters, the runway was insufficiently leveled and packed). The RAB had installed their own personnel and offices in the living quarters that had been prepared for the air crews. They quickly began to prepare other accommodations for the aviators, but were exceedingly slow in equipping them. The pilots had to sleep on bare cots without bedding for four days. The battalion's technical department failed to arrange timely delivery of engine oil to the squadrons. Airacobras were intermittently unable to fly because of this oversight. Food, especially for the air crews, was prepared in a monotonous and bland manner.[13] Many of the truck drivers in 495th BAO did not have driver's licenses. This led to delays, sometimes for three to four hours, of the convoy at military police checkpoints during the movement of the technical personnel and supplies.

In late June 1944, 9th Guards Fighter Division had to execute a transfer between *fronts,* from Second Ukrainian *Front* to First Ukrainian *Front,* to participate in the Lvov–Sandomir operation (13 July to 30 August 1944). RABs, BAOs, and other logistical units also supported the transfer of aviation formations from one *front* to another. The statistics speak eloquently to the success of this effort. In the month of July 1944, ten RAB directorates, sixty-five BAOs, and more than twenty other logistical units were transferred between *fronts.*[14] They subsequently accepted responsibility for and prepared for combat employment of the transferred aviation formations and units.

On the basis of an order from the USSR People's Commissariat of Defense, a 26 June classified telegram from the general staff of the Red Army, and a 29 June order of 5th Air Army, on 29 June the commander of 7th Fighter Corps (to which 9th Guards Fighter Division was assigned) issued an oral combat order to the commander of 9th Guards Fighter Division. The division was released from 5th Air Army of the Second Ukrainian *Front* and assigned to 2nd Air Army of First Ukrainian *Front,* with concomitant transfer to airfields in the area of Sitno-Berestechko.

In accordance with this instruction, the bulk of the technical staff and headquarters was to be moved by railroad from the station at Vereshti. On 4 July, in order to conceal the concentration of the aircraft, the air echelons were to fly to rear-area airfields of the Starokonstantinovka airfield network of 2d Air Army (eighty-five miles from the front line). Then, on 13 July, the aircraft were to fly in and around the area of the new bases and anticipated combat operations. After this they were to fly in small groups to designated airfields: Krupets (4.2 miles from the front line), Mikhaluvka (7.5 miles from the front line), and Ivashuki (Sitno) (9 miles from the front line).

Teams were sent out from each regiment for support at rear airfields and reception of aircraft at forward airfields. Eight Li-2 sorties, two for each regiment and two for division command and control, were moving these teams.

The main component of technical specialists and headquarters property was concentrated for loading at Vereshti station (thirty miles from Stefaneshti airfield) from 1 to 4 July. Approximately forty to forty-five technical personnel remained in the regiments, one-half of whom were designated for work at the forward airfields and the other half at rear airfields. A staff officer headed up each group.

On 1 July the division's forward command and control team, headed by the deputy chief of staff, departed for the new airfield in two trucks. This team included representatives of all staff departments and two officers from the operations-intelligence department, and a portion of the communications company with the necessary equipment for wire and radio communications. This column arrived at the new location after traveling 270 miles in two days.

Additional instructions came down on 3 July: immediately transfer the technical personnel to the division's forward airfield network. The number of transport sorties was increased to twenty to carry out this order. The technical personnel, who had already arrived at the railroad station with their equipment, were hurriedly returned to their garrisons by truck. The technical personnel and their gear were delivered to the forward airfields at Mikhaluvka and Ivashuki in sixteen Li-2 sorties from 3 to 8 July. A third landing field, Krupets, was unsuitable for use because it was subject to enemy artillery fire. Groups of from two to four Airacobras covered the transport aircraft during this move.

The technical specialists were landed at Granovka airfield, twenty miles from the front line, to conceal the movement of these personnel and to protect the air transport assets. Trucks were later used to carry them to their designated airfields.

The railroad echelon (205 personnel, primarily young specialists, and headquarters property) departed Vereshti station on the night of 4 to 5 July and arrived at the destination station Verba (twenty miles from the forward edge) on 10 July. Trucks were used the following night to move the personnel and headquarters property to their designated airfields.

The deputy division commander and an operations group of two officers departed for the rear airfield on 7 July to receive units. The regiments' flying echelon and the technical teams for servicing aircraft were moved on Li-2 aircraft to Starokonstantinovka airfield network on the following day. 16th Guards Fighter Regiment and the division command and control went to Kuzmin and the 100th and 104th Guards Regiments went to Vorontsovtsy. Bombers and ground-attack aircraft (*shturmoviki*) of various formations of 2d Air Army occupied most of the available space at both of these airfields.

The movement of the flying echelons of the division's units was accomplished in the following manner. The deputy commander of 16th Guards Fighter Regiment conducted a weather reconnaissance flight along the route in an Airacobra at dawn on 8 July and confirmed the readiness of Kuzmin and Vorontsovtsy airfields to receive the aircraft. It was determined that the transfer could begin. The regiments began to move to the Starokonstantinovka area at 0800, in groups of four to eight aircraft with fifteen- to thirty-minute intervals between groups. The last P-39 landed at the new airfield at 1900. To conceal this movement, radio transmissions between aircraft and also with ground stations were categorically forbidden. Two exceptions to this procedure were allowed: a lost pilot could request a heading, and in the event of the appearance of enemy aircraft.

The necessity to work in two directions (on front-line and rear-area airfields) significantly complicated the activity of the division staff for commanding and controlling its subordinate regiments. From 1 to 7 July, its departments were divided into two parts: the main component supported the organization of the movement to the Novokonstantinovka airfield network and controlled its execution, while the operations group took care of preparations for the receipt of aircraft at the forward airfields. Over 7 and 8 July, it became necessary to supervise activity in three locations: the main headquarters element and communications company at the forward airfield, the small operations group (two personnel) using four switchboards from BAO and RAB communications assets at Stefaneshti airfield, and a second operations group (also two personnel) with a transmitter and a rear-area communications company team at Novokonstantinovka airfield network. After accomplishing its mission, the communications team was transferred forward by a division liaison aircraft. This organization of the headquarters' activity provided the division commander with uninterrupted and relatively reliable command and control of the regiments during their movement to new airfields.[15]

The fly-around of the area of anticipated combat actions that was planned for 8 to 10 July was not conducted because of a gasoline shortage. Only out of the acute necessity to provide cover for a concentration of the northern shock group of First Ukrainian *Front* forces did

104th Guards Fighter Regiment fly to its airfield at Ivashuki late on 10 July. From here the regiment's squadrons began to familiarize themselves with the area of their anticipated combat actions. The rebasing of 16th and 100th Guards Regiments was delayed because of deteriorating weather on 11 and 12 July. They were able to reach Mikhaluvka only late on 13 July. The flight was conducted at low altitude in small groups of four to six aircraft. This permitted the regiments to accomplish their concentration in relative secrecy. A portion of the group (potential flight leaders) was able to conduct a fly-around of the area while en route.

Two accidents occurred in the division during the entire period of relocating to new airfields: one during landing because of a sudden downpour; the other the result of an engine fire that caused the engine to seize.

And so, as experience showed, the use of a rear-area airfield network with designation of primary airfields near the front line was an effective practice. This method ensured favorable conditions for maneuver and at the same time allowed for complete secrecy in the creation of an aviation grouping on the axis of an upcoming offensive.

Never before or later did the division's regiments relocate so often as in July 1944. The 9th Guards Fighter Division moved six times between 8 and 28 July—three times before the start of the Lvov–Sandomir operation and three times in the first period of the offensive of forces of First Ukrainian *Front*. To the credit of the personnel of the BAO supporting the division, they fully accomplished their missions in these difficult conditions. Aircraft of 9th Guards Fighter Division worked from Mikhaluvka airfield with the commencement of combat operations on 13 July. Seven days later the division had to displace forward because its coverage area was now some sixty miles from the runways. Because of the lack of reconnaissance data and prepared airfields, all regiments were concentrated at one place, Neznanuv (thirty-five miles due west of Mikhaluvka).

Personnel and headquarters property were transported by cargo trucks of 23d RAB and 379th BAO. Because of a shortage of wheeled vehicles, eighty-two personnel and headquarters property of 100th Guards Fighter Regiment remained at Mikhaluvka airfield. These personnel were flown to Smolintse airfield by Po-2 aircraft of 8th Air Army only on 24 July.

The division remained at Neznanuv for all of four days. Notification of the requirement to move came just two days after the division's arrival at this location. The ground forces continued relentlessly to develop their breakthrough into the enemy's defenses. This forced the 9th Division command to send the division's check pilot and gunnery officer out in Po-2 aircraft to reconnoiter airfields in the designated area. After two days of searching, they found a landing strip near the village Guyche (4.2 miles northeast of Rava-Russkaya). In the future, the same method was employed during the selection of new basing sites. This permitted subordinate fighter units to move more quickly behind advancing ground force formations.

The small size of the Guyche airfield and the lack of other suitable landing strips nearby conditioned the transfer to this airfield of only two regiments (16th and 104th Guards Fighter Regiments) on 24 July. 100th Guards Fighter Regiment remained in the Neznanuv area, prepared to relocate to the west as soon as the situation required. Thus, a new method of relocating fighter units spontaneously (without planning) was born—leapfrogging forward—after the advance of ground forces and the discovery of suitable new landing fields.

On 26 July the 100th Guards Fighter Regiment was shifted to the selected airfield at Smolintse, a straight-line distance of approximately sixty miles. The ground echelon and various headquarters and supply property were relocated by RAB wheeled vehicles and Po-2 aircraft of 8th Air Army. Again, because of the limited size of Smolintse airfield, only 16th Guards Fighter Regiment was relocated here. 104th Guards Fighter Regiment remained at Guyche, prepared for a jump to the west to remain in close proximity to the ground forces. This "leapfrog" repositioning of its units permitted the division to provide continuous coverage to the combined arms formations that were leading the offensive at a high tempo. The aviators did not want to fall behind their comrades in the ground forces.

The division had to fly its combat missions across almost the entire zone of the *front* offensive. The shortest distance to the front line was eighteen to thirty miles, and to the northern flank, where air coverage was also needed, was fifty to eighty miles. These somewhat difficult conditions of the operational ground and air situation demanded exceptional precision from the fighter division staff in the supervision of subordinate units. Command and control were exercised in the following manner. Advance teams capable of directing the regiments' combat actions at new airfields were formed from the division headquarters and communications company. Representatives of all departments and services and two operations-intelligence department officers were assigned to these temporary organizations. The deputy chief of staff of the division (or the operations-intelligence department chief) headed up this team.

The advance team of the communications company had the minimum necessary amount of wire communications equipment for rapid establishment of telephone communications in the selected displacement area and a powerful radio transmitter-receiver (11-AK[16]). The radio was used to communicate with the communications company headquarters and the headquarters of 7th Fighter Corps. This team was maintained on a permanent basis, prepared at a moment's notice to move forward and carry out its work in the designated location.

The main part of the division headquarters began relocating using its own wheeled transportation assets immediately upon receipt by radio of a report from the advance team regarding the selection of its next site. Two operations-intelligence department officers, and sometimes the chief of staff, remained at the old headquarters site along with a rear group from the communications company. Using a powerful RSB-F transmitter, this group ensured the exchange of information with the new airfield and the transmission of combat instructions received from higher headquarters at the old address.[17] This group of communications specialists simultaneously maintained a minimal quantity of wire communications in working order, left there for controlling the regiments' takeoffs. These wire communications were pulled out upon departure of the last units of the flying echelon. Having dispatched all the squadrons to the new airfields, the division headquarters group departed immediately behind them on liaison aircraft.[18]

The measures undertaken by the division command that were necessary to provide the regiments with suitable airfields were not always sufficient to resolve this complex problem. Frequently the fighter units were located a significant distance from the ground troops they were supporting. For example, the Airacobras' takeoff and landing strips were some 25 to 30 miles from the areas of combat actions for just the first four of nineteen days of the offensive operation of First Ukrainian *Front*. Because of this, patrol groups were able to loiter over the target areas for thirty to thirty-five minutes. For the next eleven days, this distance was increased to 40 to 50 miles. The P-39s worked in the covering zone for twenty to twenty-five minutes. During the remaining four days, the areas of combat actions were 70 to 80 miles from the division's primary airfields, and 100 miles from the 104th Guards Fighter Regiment. In this situation, groups of fighters were able to cover the ground forces for not more than ten minutes. The Airacobras made many forced landings during this period because they ran out of fuel while returning to their airfields.[19]

During the Lower Silesia offensive operation (8 to 24 March 1945), our ground forces captured Buntslau (on the bridgehead across the Bober River). An airfield was found and prepared at Aslau, eight miles northeast of Buntslau, for basing the 9th Guards Fighter Division's regiments. This airfield had hangars for the aircraft and taxiways but lacked an airstrip. In view of the above-freezing temperatures and the thawing of the soil, this airfield was not suitable for use by Airacobras. A search of the surrounding area did not reveal any other landing fields that met the requirements for fighter plane operations.

The Breslau–Berlin autobahn passed not far from the airfield. The division commander, Guards Colonel Aleksandr Pokryshkin, decided to use this road surface as a runway. This was a unique occurrence in the Great Patriotic War. At this locale the autobahn was seventy-five feet wide and consisted of two concrete strips, each thirty-one feet wide. Between them ran a fourteen-foot-wide median of vegetation.

To prepare the autobahn to serve as a runway, the trees and bushes had to be cut down and crushed rock or planks placed in the median area, thus joining the two roads together into a single surface. The 7th Engineer Battalion of 23d RAB, the airfield-technical company of 299th BAO, and the troops of this and 388th BAO began work at 1200 on 16 February 1945. They cut down the vegetation and reinforced the soil with sand and crushed rock over a stretch of almost 4,000 feet of autobahn median, without removing the frozen upper layer of soil. This was a crucial construction error that soon manifested itself.

By the evening of 17 February, 4,500 feet of autobahn was prepared for use as a runway by Airacobras. A short piece of concrete road 26 feet wide led from the autobahn to the taxiways. The landing strip was used for flight operations without limitations before 23 February, while there was no significant thaw. With the arrival of warm days, the center portion of the runway (the former median) began to show signs of being water-logged. The soil began to swell. Takeoffs and landings became more difficult and at times were halted entirely.

In their haste to construct a makeshift runway, the engineer troops had removed vegetation and laid down sand and crushed rock on the frozen soil and smoothed it out. They should have removed the upper layer of frozen soil, put down a base of sand, and rolled it out. Then they should have brought in gravel and leveled and packed it. The unfortunate construction troops had to come back on 26 February and repair their work. They reinforced the ground with bricks in order to prevent additional soaking of the artificial covering.

A number of lessons were learned during the ten days that the autobahn was used for a runway. Its limited width of 75 feet, considerably less than the minimum-required 200 feet, and increased elevation above the surrounding terrain excluded rollout and taxi beyond the boundaries of the constructed strip and complicated takeoffs and landings. The orientation of the autobahn in this sector did not coincide with the direction of the prevailing winds, requiring aircraft frequently to take off and land with crosswinds that were sometimes relatively strong. It was impossible to launch a pair of aircraft, and in particular to land a large group, because the location of the taxiways was such that time was required for the taxi of each landing aircraft and, at most, a pair of aircraft.

All these circumstances required careful organization of flight operations during the use of the autobahn. The takeoff detail was augmented with duty officers (regulators) on the taxiways.[20] One of these officers directed the taxi of aircraft on taxiways from the hangars, and a second was positioned at the conjunction of the taxiways and the autobahn. His responsibility was to prevent the movement of a P-39 from the taxiway onto the autobahn-runway when other fighters were landing or taking off.

A takeoff position was laid out for a distance of 500 to 650 feet from the end of the runway. With westerly and southwesterly winds, takeoffs were conducted to the northwest. When winds were from the east and southeast, takeoffs were conducted to the southeast. In the first case, the Airacobras began their takeoff roll immediately upon entry from the taxiway. In the second case, the aircraft were forced to taxi to the far end of the runway to begin their takeoff roll.

Special attention was given to takeoff markers that indicated the direction and strength of the wind. Smokepots, ignited on one side or the other of the runway depending on wind direction, were used to signal this information. A tower was also erected in the center of the airfield on which was flown a streamer. The landing "T" was laid out not according to wind direction, as was normally the practice, but along the landing strip to indicate the touch-down area, and for aircraft arriving from other airfields, also the direction of landing.[21]

During the Berlin operation (April 1945), 9th Guards Fighter Division supported the combat actions of 4th Guards Tank Army of First Ukrainian *Front*. On 16 April, two of the division's regiments (16th and 104th Guards) were based on the Burau airfield, which was quite limited in size. The sandy soil of the landing strip greatly complicated the Airacobras' work. A thick cloud of dust was raised during takeoff of the first pair of aircraft, enveloping all the following aircraft. These and other dangerous shortcomings of this airfield led to the relocation of 104th Guards Fighter Division to the Kunau area.

The mobile forces' offensive was developing rapidly. By 20 April, the fighters' zone of coverage was some 85 to 95 miles from their airfields. In these conditions, the P-39 could loiter over the ground formations for only ten to fifteen minutes. The division was assigned to the airfield at Neuhausen (7.2 miles southeast of Kotbus) on 21 April. Two regiments of La-5s were already stationed at this base, which was 60 to 65 miles from the front line. After inspecting this area, it was clear to Guards Colonel Aleksandr Pokryshkin that because the airfield was already crowded, only two regiments could be repositioned here. Advance teams of 16th and 100th Guards Fighter Regiments (each on four ZIS-5 trucks[22]) and division command and control personnel departed for Neuhausen airfield on the morning of 22 April. Flying echelons arrived at the new base on this same day. From here these two regiments continued to cover the advance of formations of 4th Guards Tank Army. 104th Guards Fighter Regiment remained at Kunau airfield.

A new instruction arrived on the evening of 22 April. The main body of 2d Air Army was redirected to support forces operating on the Dresden axis, which had been assigned the mission to link up with the Allies—the American 4th Army—in this area.

In this situation, and in connection with the insignificant opposition of enemy air units around Berlin, the commander of the air army ordered the division to dispatch one fighter regiment to support the advancing forces. Yuterbog airfield was designated for this regiment. The remainder of the division continued to support the combat actions of 4th Guards Tank Army.

Guards Colonel Pokryshkin made the decision to move 104th Guards Fighter Regiment, located at Kunau, to Yuterbog on 23 April. Advance teams and the flying component were already at the new airfield by noon of that day. Three Li-2 sorties were allocated for rapid movement of the technical staff and their equipment. These aircraft moved sixty-six personnel on 24 April. The remaining technical specialists arrived in Yuterbog by routine ground transportation.[23]

Thus, 9th Guards Fighter Division operated in two directions in the final days of the Great Patriotic War. The combat actions of its two regiments (16th and 100th Guards) on the Dresden axis is of some interest. Airacobra pilots had to carry out their assigned missions in relatively difficult atmospheric conditions: dense smoke from fires in the forests and along the front line. Visibility on some days was reduced to 1,600 to 2,000 feet. The smoke rose up in the atmosphere to 5,000 feet, at times closing the airfield. P-39s returning from missions frequently were diverted to neighboring airfields.

As before, the division's main body was stationed a significant distance (95 to 105 miles) from the front line. In addition to limiting the loiter time of the fighters over their targets to not more than ten minutes, this completely excluded the possibility of increasing the strength of patrols should there be an encounter with large groups of enemy aircraft.[24]

The Airfield—the Aviators' Home

In addition to the landing strip, every airfield had a command post for the regimental commander, two personnel bunkers for thirty-six men each (the pilots), one bunker for the maintenance personnel, and thirty-six revetments for aircraft (twelve per squadron). This was the necessary minimum for basing a single fighter regiment. Depending on the duration of a regiment's stay at a given airfield, continuous effort was made to develop the airfield infrastructure. Personnel bunkers were constructed for the BAO personnel, storage bunkers were dug into the ground for all types of ordnance, GSM, and equipment. Fire protection measures of various forms were carefully organized.

In accordance with a regulation of the State Committee of Defense (13 February 1943), reaction detachments consisting of twenty to twenty-five men, armed with submachine guns, machine guns, and hand grenades, were created in the BAO at each airfield for combating enemy airborne assaults. Two-wheeled vehicles were dedicated to support their maneuver.[1]

Regiments of the 216th Fighter Division remained at Popovicheskaya airfield more than five months. During this time the basing district was equipped with a whole complex of facilities to house the technical personnel, cover the aircraft, and store the materiel and equipment. The air crews lived in requisitioned quarters in Popovicheskaya, where the division headquarters was also located. The developed wire communications network permitted the rapid delivery of necessary instructions to the regiment and squadron commanders at their billets. On the airfield itself were several bunkers where the pilots could spend the day (preflight and postflight rest periods).

The division headquarters continued to work intensely at night. Staff sections were organized and operated in shifts. This was required for the simple reason that the division received its mission for the upcoming day from the air army staff, as a rule, at 0200 or 0300. Based on this mission statement, the division staff developed its own combat instructions and distributed them to regimental liaison officers an hour before dawn. It was not necessary to distribute this document to subordinate units earlier than this because their commanders and staffs were resting. At the same time, this method provided a higher level of physical security regarding the next day's activities.[2]

From the second half of May 1943, 216th Fighter Division operated from the following airfield network: 16th Guards and 45th Fighter Regiments were at Popovicheskaya, 42d Fighter Regiment was at Krasnoarmeysk, and 57th Guards Fighter Regiment was at Slavyansk. In mid-July the entire division flew to Slavyansk airfield. There the air crews were quartered in local municipal buildings (schools, clubs, *kolkhoz* and *sovkhoz* facilities) of the named villages, which were carefully guarded. Maintenance personnel stayed on the airfields proper.[3]

In view of the frequent flights from one place to another, when the division displaced to the regions northeast and west of Taganrog (the summer months of 1943), all the regiments' personnel were housed on the airfields in tents, makeshift shelters, and repair shop vans. Fighter pilots could not be housed in village settlements, which the Germans had almost completely burned and demolished with explosives during their retreat. What remained suitable for housing had been occupied by ground forces.[4]

Special concern was shown for living conditions, particularly for the air crews, in the fall and winter months. The frequent dislocation of units sometimes prevented the construction of personnel accommodations on airfields. In response to this, the division command requested assistance from the air army commander in reserving a certain amount of living space in villages around airfields (even those heavily damaged) by giving priority to fighter regiment air crews over ground troops.[5]

Although in a number of cases this request was granted, frequently it could not be, especially in areas closer to the front line. The density of advancing forces was too great when compared to the small supply of inhabitable quarters in settlements that had only recently been liberated. Air crews sometimes had to be quartered in tents, for which there was an inadequate supply of heaters. The priority for these creature comforts went to the fighter air crews and staff personnel.

Over the course of November 1943, the forces of Fourth Ukrainian *Front* continued their offensive on the Kherson–Crimea axis and completely cleared the left bank of the Dnieper in its southern reaches of enemy troops. Attempts of 51st Army and 19th Tank Corps to break into Crimea from the march were unsuccessful. By the end of the month formations of 51st Army occupied the line Turetskiy Val–Armyansk, and beyond along the northern shore of Sivash Inlet as far as Genichesk. Our troops forced the Sivash in the area of Arabatskaya Strelka Spit and Russian Island and seized a bridgehead along the line Urzhin–Ashkadon–Biyus-Kiyat.[6]

Over the course of the month, 9th Guards Fighter Division was operating in support of the formations of the left wing of Fourth Ukrainian *Front*. Flight operations were reduced during this period, for two reasons: the heavy fog that enveloped the airfield in the mornings had a tendency to lift somewhat by midday, forming a dense overcast; and the enemy lacked adequate aviation forces. As a consequence of these two factors, there were relatively few air battles on this sector of the Soviet–German front. The enemy transitioned to the employment of bombers in groups of five to six aircraft, which attempted to take advantage of the poor weather conditions (clouds and evening twilight).

The regiments of the 9th were disposed as follows: 16th Guards Fighter Regiment at Askaniya-Nova and 100th and 104th Guards Fighter Regiments at Krestovskiy. Leaving behind seven Airacobras for training new pilots, 100th Guards Fighter Regiment soon transferred the remainder of their aircraft to the division's other regiments. The 100th was then sent to the airfield at Kharkov for reconstitution.

Only the 16th Guards Fighter Regiment conducted active combat actions in November and December, preparation for the liberation of the Crimea that was launched from 8 to 12 December 1944. An RUS-2 radar station was assigned to the regiment for this period. The regiment's air crews were housed in facilities at Askaniya-Nova Nature Preserve, while the maintenance personnel occupied well-equipped accommodations at the airfield. The command of 702d BAO expended considerable effort to provide the aviators with normal living and working conditions. Even a club bunker was constructed. When the commander of 8th Air Army, General Timofey Khryukin, visited the regiment on 14 November, all the unit's personnel were assembled in this club.

The Airacobra pilots were especially careful regarding the flora and fauna of the preserve—an unusual national treasure. This corner of the Ukrainian land was indeed a paradise, a place of exceptional beauty and wildlife. Great flocks of birds almost continuously crowded the skies over the pilots' heads. A chorus of bird cries filled the air all day long. The coming of nightfall did not quiet their voices. Geese, ducks, and other fowl plied the surrounding lake waters and then flew to the Sivash and Sea of Azov. The preserve's beauty was further enhanced by hundreds of unique trees that had been brought into Askaniya-Nova from various countries of the world.

In the May and June 1944 battles around Jassy, Romania, the fighter regiments of 9th Guards Fighter Division were based on airfields at Stefaneshti and Todireni some forty-five to thirty miles from the front line. The 100th Guards Fighter Regiment flew to Prizhani (eighteen miles from the forward edge) in July.[7]

Before I comment on the issue of housing the unit personnel in these areas, I want to emphasize the following two circumstances. The 6th Tank Army achieved high rates of movement during the conduct of the Uman–Batoshani offensive operation (3 March to 17 April 1944) during the spring thaw. The German–Romanian forces had just recently suffered a large-scale defeat in the Korsun–Shevchenkovskiy encirclement (24 January to 17 February 1944). Fearing another encirclement, they were hurriedly withdrawing beyond the Southern Bug River, intending to organize a stable defense at that line. The tankers of General Andrey Kravchenko's 6th Tank Army disrupted the plan of the Hitlerite command.

The enemy was hoping that he would manage to delay the advancing Soviet forces at the Dnestr River. He was not that lucky. Rapidly developing their success, forces of the Second Ukrainian *Front* forced the Prut River from the march on the night of 28 March and brought combat operations onto Romanian territory. The formations of the *front* moved some 125 to 155 miles in the course of the offensive. They crossed six rivers—Gornyy Tikich, Southern Bug, Dnestr, Reut, Prut, and Siret—in the spring runoff and thaw and liberated Uman, Vapnyarka, Pervomaysk, Batoshani, and hundreds of other settlements. In this situation the enemy was unable in the course of his retreat to turn the territory he had abandoned into a "wasteland," as he had done in other regions. The large and small towns, villages, and settlements were preserved almost undamaged.

And the second circumstance. In the first week of April 1944, the entire populace of a sixty-mile zone along the front was evacuated to the rear, to recently liberated regions of Moldavia and Ukraine. "Field-garden teams" created in Soviet Army troop units showed enormous concern for the preservation of the crops planted in the field gardens of the *kolkhoz* and *sovkhoz* workers.[8]

In this situation (undamaged, unpopulated villages and settlements), there were no problems with housing the air crews and maintenance personnel of the fighter regiments. The warm spring and summer weather permitted the billeting of personnel on airfields in tents, shelters, and simply underneath aircraft and vehicles. This practice was widespread during the days of intense combat actions for the Airacobra crews in late May and early June 1944.

The following facts attest to the complexity of the situation in this period. By the beginning of the battles around Jassy, 30 to 40 percent of the pilots in the division's units were inexperienced and had not participated in a single aerial engagement. These air battles were conducted by large groups of fighters on both sides. Thus, the inexperienced fighter pilots found themselves in a difficult situation. Each operational aircraft was expected to fly, on average, 6.6 sorties.[9]

In the combat path of the 9th Fighter Division the second most difficult period (after the Kuban) for its units was at the beginning of the Lvov–Sandomir operation by forces of First Ukrainian *Front* (13 July to 30 August 1944). The difficulties were manifold. As has already been noted, the fighter regiments were forced to make frequent flights from one basing area to another, and they did not stay at any airfield for long. The ground forces' rapid forward movement required that aviation keep up, in order to provide uninterrupted and effective air coverage of ground operations.

Of course, given such frequent dislocations there could be no question of the aviators' complete comfort at any given airfield. The personnel of the BAO that was servicing the regiments did everything possible under the circumstances to create the necessary comforts of home for the air crew and maintenance personnel. Unfortunately, they did not always succeed.

In July the basing districts for the 9th Guards were in the areas of western Ukraine that had been annexed to the Soviet Union in September 1939.[10] In a number of its regions some of the population were hostile, putting it mildly, to the Soviet Army. The masters of the surrounding forests were the Banderovs—groups of bourgeois nationalists.[11] On any given night they were capable of launching an attack or some other type of diversionary activity. They committed atrocities on Ukrainian and Polish soil: they burned villages, shot the civilian inhabitants, and killed air crews who executed forced landings in territory under their control.[12]

The rear-area situation immediately behind the front line in any Ukrainian region was unfavorable. The division command undertook broad-scale measures to protect and defend airfields and places where air crew and maintenance personnel lived. They required around-the-clock guard posts in all units. All civilian personnel who appeared in the zone of an airfield were detained and counterintelligence organs made an appropriate investigation.

Then came Poland and Germany. The stationary airfield network in these foreign lands was reasonably developed. Of course, during their retreat the fascists attempted to render all its elements, particularly the landing strips, unusable. With some exceptions, airfield contonement areas remained in satisfactory condition. After some preparatory work, they were used for housing the air crew and maintenance personnel, along with headquarters and their staffs. As if in reward for their many years of meager wartime subsistence, in the end aviators were billeted in towns and villages in houses and apartments, two to three pilots or mechanics per room. These accommodations had almost all the conveniences.

There was a down side to this. Aviation units frequently had to fly to other forward airfields whose accommodations were not equal to their own. But they dealt with this as the war was moving toward a final victory on a broad front.

There were also exceptionally dangerous cases that could have cost the lives of many Airacobra pilots. For example, during the Lvov–Sandomir operation (in mid-July 1944), 100th Guards Fighter Regiment was transferred to Edzhuyuv in Poland. This particular German-built airfield had a beautiful wide runway and taxiways, comfortable living quarters, and an adequate number of hangars. All of these facilities were in good repair. The tank troops' rapid breakthrough had prevented the Germans from carrying out their customary demolition tasks.

Air crews occupied apartments in brick buildings, taking rooms in pairs (lead and wingman). Maintenance personnel found themselves places on the airfield in well-appointed bunkers, at the entrance to which were hand-lettered painted signs—*Min nyet* [no mines]. Regimental signal personnel immediately turned their attention to one unusual feature in the equipping of these accommodations. On the wall opposite the doors they found the carefully cut ends of wires. The Airacobra pilots attempted to use these wires for communications by joining them in various combinations to their communication devices. Nothing worked, however.

There was more. On the runway they discovered many patches carefully filled with cement and arrayed in a chessboard fashion. Some thought that these were patched craters, the result of bombs dropped by British, American, or even Soviet bombers. All became clear a few days later. A local civilian came to the airfield. With difficulty (gestures and mimicry) he explained to the aviators that the runway had been mined. The explosives had been placed in the carefully arranged bomb craters, and the wires in the personnel bunkers were intended to detonate the demolition charges. Apparently, the sudden appearance in this area of the advancing Soviet tanks had disrupted the crafty enemy plans. The airfield remained intact.

The command of the 100th Guards Fighter Regiment and the division were taught an object lesson.[13] These mistakes were not made in other locales after this incident was publicized. Before a unit settled into a selected air base complex, specialists thoroughly checked them for demolitions. These inspections also were expanded to clear mines, high explosives, and bombs that might have been concealed in the dirt.

When division units were deployed on German territory (airfields at Aslau, Rogazen-Korbus, and Grossenhein), Airacobra pilots of all categories were quartered in German airfield garrisons that were located close to the runway and hangars. The barracks and maintenance buildings were guarded around the clock. This is how combat actions proceeded on enemy territory. They required redoubled vigilance.

The protection of airfields was an important mission of airfield-technical support, one of the basic branches of VVS logistics. Aircraft parking ramps, headquarters, and materiel-equipment storage facilities were guarded and defended by the service personnel (mechanics, technicians, and so on), staff personnel, and BAO troops. The Red Army did not have any special airfield security units. In addition to their normal daytime duty requirements, at night the engineering-technical personnel had the additional responsible mission of guarding and defending the airfield itself.

Airfield protection was accomplished in accordance with standing operating procedures. A defense plan was drawn up. This document included an order to the airfield garrison, a calculation of the forces and means available, a coordination table of the fighter unit covering the airfield and the air defense forces, a sketch of the defenses (with a brief legend), and a plan for carrying out specific measures. This component of the overall plan included signal instructions and specified the actions the airfield service personnel and aircraft crews were to take upon being alerted of a ground, air, or chemical attack.

The BAO commander or the chief of the advance team servicing the regiment, who was the deputy chief of the airfield garrison, was appointed as the chief for ground defense. A strong reserve force with wheeled transportation was placed at the disposal of the chief for ground defense. In the event of an enemy ground attack against the airfield, this reserve provided for rapid reinforcement of the threatened sector. The reserve was positioned in the area of the unit CP.

The headquarters of the Red Army VVS issued a directive on 6 May 1943 that laid down the basic requirements for airfield security and defense. These requirements remained in force for the remainder of the Great Patriotic War.

1. Unit headquarters and staffs were to be situated compactly, in public facilities, isolated from the local populace. If such facilities were not available, staffs were to be allocated work space in bunkers.

2. All the personnel of the BAO and airfield-technical teams and headquarters were to be used for airfield defense. So as to remain available, these BAO units and airfield-technical teams were to be housed in bunkers or tents near the airfield.

3. All units, headquarters, and teams were to develop and publish for all of their personnel instructions for alert procedures for ground, air, and chemical attack.

4. Storage facilities for GSM, ammunition, food provisions, and supplies were to be cordoned off by barbed wire. Boxes of sand and barrels of water were to be positioned nearby, along with a supply of buckets, boat hooks, axes, shovels, and so on.

5. A pass was required for access to the airfield and the headquarters. A control point was set up at the perimeter to monitor access. Without permission of the unit duty officer, local authorities were prohibited from offering overnight lodging in facilities where troops were billeted.

6. The BAO was to create reaction forces consisting of twenty to twenty-five men, armed with machine guns, submachine guns, and hand grenades,

to combat enemy airborne assaults. The reaction forces were to be provided two trucks.[14]

When the RUS-2 radar apparatus became more widely available for monitoring the air situation, a new procedure was introduced for covering airfields with fighter aircraft. From dawn to nightfall every day, a pair of Airacobras in each regiment was designated at readiness level no. 1 and another pair at readiness level no. 2. Upon signal from the radar station, these aircraft sortied to fend off enemy air attacks.[15]

Speaking frankly, the forces and means that the regiments and BAO could designate for resolution of the vital airfield defense mission were clearly inadequate. They were also poorly armed. They had to resort to removal of cannons and machine guns from battle- or accident-damaged P-39s and employment of these weapons on the ground to reinforce the firepower of the airfield garrisons (see Figure 1).

Aleksandr Pokryshkin described an interesting example of this in his memoir:[16] "The landing strips for 16th Guards Regiment were near Lyubachuv (in the Rava-Russkaya area). Banderovs fired into our airfield on the first night. No one was wounded and no damage was inflicted, but several shots fired from the surrounding forest deprived all our people of sleep for the entire night. We had to pack dirt under the main gear and level the aircraft with the horizon so that, if necessary, we could conduct fire from the machine guns. Technicians and mechanics sat in the cockpits and from time to time fired into the woods."

The problems associated with protecting airfields against enemy air attacks received constant attention, but the assets for this mission were also inadequate. On 13 February 1943, the State Defense Committee adopted a resolution concerning the formation of thirty-four airfield anti-aircraft regiments for the VVS.[17] Unfortunately, units at forward airfield basing regions did not see these anti-aircraft regiments in 1943 or 1944.

Perhaps this explains a subsequent directive from Red Army VVS headquarters (20 September 1943) that required weapons taken from unserviceable aircraft to be used for anti-aircraft defense of airfields. The weapons of choice in this regard were the heavy machine guns and 20mm cannons (from early Airacobras). They were used for airfield defense almost to the end of the war, as long as ammunition supplies for these weapons remained (see Figure 2).[18]

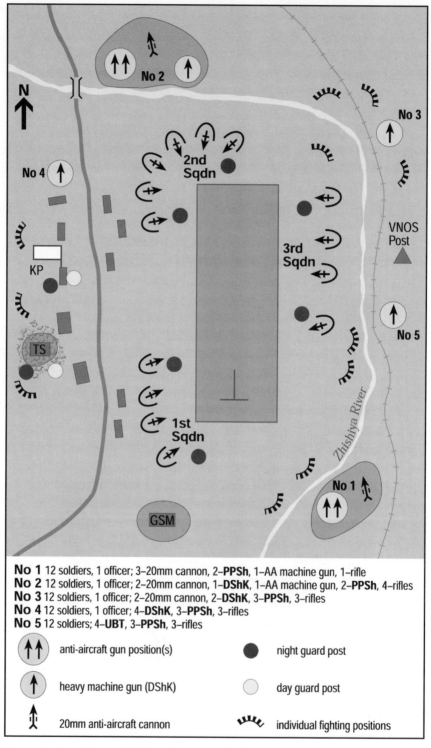

No 1 12 soldiers, 1 officer; 3–20mm cannon, 2–**PPSh**, 1–AA machine gun, 1–rifle
No 2 12 soldiers, 1 officer; 2–20mm cannon, 1–**DShK**, 1–AA machine gun, 2–**PPSh**, 4–rifles
No 3 12 soldiers, 1 officer; 2–20mm cannon, 2–**DShK**, 3–**PPSh**, 3–rifles
No 4 12 soldiers, 1 officer; 4–**DShK**, 3–**PPSh**, 3–rifles
No 5 12 soldiers; 4–**UBT**, 3–**PPSh**, 3–rifles

anti-aircraft gun position(s)   night guard post

heavy machine gun (DShK)   day guard post

20mm anti-aircraft cannon   individual fighting positions

Figure 1. Guarding and defending an airfield, 16th Guards Fighter
Regiment in Todirena, Romania (May 1944).

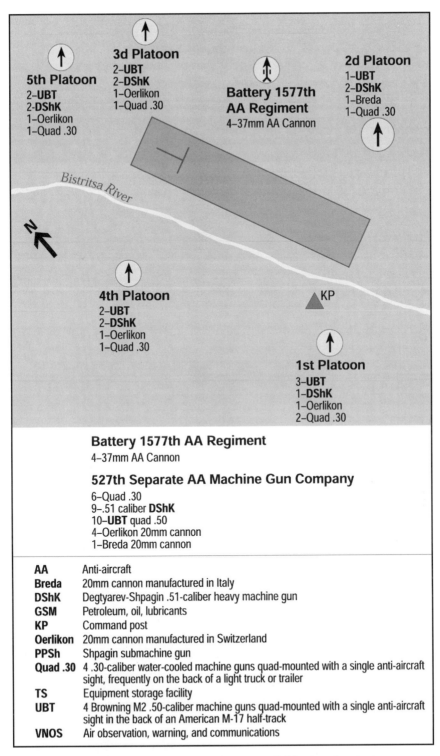

5th Platoon
2–UBT
2–DShK
1–Oerlikon
1–Quad .30

3d Platoon
2–UBT
2–DShK
1–Oerlikon
1–Quad .30

**Battery 1577th
AA Regiment**
4–37mm AA Cannon

2d Platoon
1–UBT
2–DShK
1–Breda
1–Quad .30

Bistritsa River

N

4th Platoon
2–UBT
2–DShK
1–Oerlikon
1–Quad .30

KP

1st Platoon
3–UBT
1–DShK
1–Oerlikon
2–Quad .30

Battery 1577th AA Regiment
4–37mm AA Cannon

527th Separate AA Machine Gun Company
6–Quad .30
9–.51 caliber **DShK**
10–**UBT** quad .50
4–Oerlikon 20mm cannon
1–Breda 20mm cannon

AA	Anti-aircraft
Breda	20mm cannon manufactured in Italy
DShK	Degtyarev-Shpagin .51-caliber heavy machine gun
GSM	Petroleum, oil, lubricants
KP	Command post
Oerlikon	20mm cannon manufactured in Switzerland
PPSh	Shpagin submachine gun
Quad .30	4 .30-caliber water-cooled machine guns quad-mounted with a single anti-aircraft sight, frequently on the back of a light truck or trailer
TS	Equipment storage facility
UBT	4 Browning M2 .50-caliber machine guns quad-mounted with a single anti-aircraft sight in the back of an American M-17 half-track
VNOS	Air observation, warning, and communications

Figure 2. Anti-aircraft defense of Smolintse Airfield (28 July 1944).

Documents Tell the Story

A person who has lived on this earth has an obligation to leave something behind, whether something hardly worth noticing or something profound. There have been some who have bequeathed to their offspring something grandiose, that has even brought fame and glory to their own name. Such a person was Aleksandr Pokryshkin, an innovator in the sphere of aerial combat tactics for fighters. He delivered into the hands of his own unit comrades, and later to all the fighter pilots of the Soviet Army, a powerful weapon for victory over the enemy. Much has been written and said regarding his remarkable formula of battle ("Altitude, speed, maneuver, fire!"), his design of combat formations, and other issues.

This chapter presents some official documents concerning Pokryshkin's theories. These documents will contribute to a broader understanding of the tactical methods employed by Soviet fighter pilots in Airacobras who engaged the German-fascist invaders.

New methods of combat employment for the P-39 that were used in the first aerial combat in the skies of the Kuban yielded tangible results. The commander of 216th Fighter Division, Major General Aleksandr Borman, saw with his own eyes how his subordinates, operating in a nonroutine manner, sent German aircraft plummeting to earth in flames. General Borman, located at the main vectoring radio station, observed scores of air battles. He carefully analyzed them and drew specific conclusions that he put in writing. This document was submitted to the commander of 4th Air Army.

I have reached the conclusion that we must change the basic psychology of our pilots. We have persistently hammered into them the method of defensive battles of the early days of the war, where comrades took courage from physical or visual contact with each other. In today's combat environment this is a great evil. Our pilots have to feel a freedom to maneuver, so that they no longer move in swarms and drone like bees. Our pilots must begin to feel that their strength is in pairs.

We must liquidate their imaginary illness—the fear of becoming lost in the airspace. A decisive change is required. We must instill confidence in our pilots, beginning first of all with regimental commanders. Fearing losses, in all circumstances they are sending groups of four, eight, or twelve fighters out on missions and are not allowing the pair leader to take any initiative. The commanders of these groups, in turn, fearing that they will lose sight of their groups, lead them in dense combat formations that preclude free maneuver. They act as simple guardians of their wards and do not engage in any creative leadership activity.

As a rule, it is easier for a pair to engage in combat, maneuver, and when necessary, disengage from combat.[1]

As this document illustrates, the issue was stated clearly and succinctly. A vital requirement had emerged to change the tactics of air combat ("Fight by the old methods and you won't make it to Berlin," the combat veterans said), to construct combat formations differently. The concept of fighting in pairs as a combat entity had to be skillfully introduced in units. Pilots' psychology had to be changed; they had to be taught to operate creatively, energetically, and nonroutinely. An offensive spirit had to be instilled in the pilots.

Here is a second, somewhat wide-ranging document. It was authored by the chief of staff, 9th Guards Fighter Division, whose commander was Aleksandr Pokryshkin.

To the chief of staff, 7th Guards Fighter Corps (21 May 1944)

CHARACTERISTICS OF AIR COMBAT TACTICS
of Twice Hero of the Soviet Union
Guards Lieutenant Colonel A. Pokryshkin

Active participation in the course of the entire Great Patriotic War in combat operations has helped Pokryshkin not only master completely the tactics of air combat but also develop his own personal tactical methods.

The basic principle of Guards Lieutenant Colonel Pokryshkin in his combat activity as a fighter pilot is to detect the enemy in a timely manner, so as to be the first to attack and in so doing defeat the enemy. In addition, a keystone of his successful air battles is his great desire to fight, skillful control of his aircraft and armaments, and excellent knowledge of tactics and the capabilities and characteristics of his own and enemy aircraft. Comrade Pokryshkin possesses all these qualities to perfection.

Skillfully controlling the maneuver and fire of his own aircraft, he always emerges victorious in battle. The most important rule for him in an aerial engagement, no matter what situation he might find himself in, is to conduct aimed fire. His law is to fire from a short distance and only using the sight. If possible, Comrade Pokryshkin never commences fire from extended ranges because the first burst does not harm the enemy and at the same time gives away the firing aircraft's position.

Carefully executed maneuvers have great significance in air combat. A properly conducted maneuver allows the pilot to achieve a position in the air from which he can rapidly attack the enemy or gain a better firing position. In executing maneuvers, Pokryshkin always attempts to preserve the unity of the pair.

During the conduct of an air battle with a group of enemy Ju-88 and He-111 bombers, the goal of Pokryshkin's group maneuver is always to disperse their formation. Knowing that the frontal armaments of these bombers is significantly weaker than their rear armaments, Comrade Pokryshkin conducts the first group attack head on at a slight angle of attack. Attacking the bombers, he preserves the combat formation of his group—a line formation—with pairs at relatively the same altitude. Completing the first pass, the group of fighters passes through the enemy formation and turns around, either all to the same side or by pairs in various directions, if the decision has been made to get the enemy in a "pincers."

With the advantage gained by a high-speed climbing turn, he rapidly closes with the enemy in a dive and makes a second pass, but this time from the rear. This tactic almost always succeeds in breaking apart the enemy formation and permits the fighters to engage individual enemy aircraft with relative ease.

In air combat with enemy fighters, Comrade Pokryshkin always plans the maneuver of his group so that the enemy, in seeking to escape the attack of one group, falls under the fire of a second group. Guards Lieutenant Colonel Pokryshkin achieves this result by correct echelonment of his aircraft in altitude. By this skillful maneuver he manages to subject the enemy to fire of the group positioned at a higher altitude, to draw the enemy into the zone of our anti-aircraft artillery fire, to break up the enemy combat formations, or to cut off a portion of the enemy force and thus achieve local superiority.

The art of Pokryshkin in aerial combat is manifested in his ability to achieve tactical superiority in the process of closing with the enemy. During the approach he strives to be above the enemy and to approach undetected. To achieve surprise he closes from the direction of the sun or from sectors of blind spots for the enemy aircraft, and when flying below enemy aircraft he takes advantage of the backdrop of the terrain. Comrade Pokryshkin also skillfully employs broken clouds as protection against enemy observation.

In individual aerial engagements, Comrade Pokryshkin is an adherent of maximum exploitation of tight maneuver in the vertical plane (steep dive, vertical climb), especially in proximity to enemy aircraft that are attempting vertical maneuvers. The sharpness or tightness of the maneuver makes it possible to take advantage of the delayed enemy reflex, and subsequently to defeat him.

Attacking an enemy fighter, Comrade Pokryshkin always takes up a starting position that permits him to execute a half roll or turn of his aircraft to arrive behind and above the enemy.

In order to achieve greater surprise during an attack, he seeks a position that places the enemy at an angle of 70° to 80° relative to his own movement axis. He seeks this angle because the German fighter has an armor shield at the rear of the cockpit that makes it difficult for the enemy pilot to observe the sector at the indicated angles.

Pokryshkin considers the most favorable altitude to be 2,300 to 4,920 feet above the enemy aircraft. From this start position he can transition his aircraft into a dive, striving to remain somewhat behind the enemy aircraft so as to come out of the dive at a range of 330 to 220 yards. He covers this distance at increased speed and, approaching to within 110 to 80 yards, captures the enemy aircraft in his sight, and opens fire simultaneously from all his weapons until he has closed to a minimum range. Then he executes a sharp high-speed turn and bank.

At high speeds for breakaway from the enemy he resorts to such methods as steep climb and bank, Immelman with turn, and also a climbing spiral in cases when the enemy attacks from the rear and is close.

If the enemy is forced to flee, Comrade Pokryshkin catches up to him from above. Upon encountering a reconnaissance aircraft, he first cuts off the enemy pilot's path to cloud cover, then forces him into an engagement.

Upon an unexpected encounter with German aircraft at close range, he launches an immediate attack with the greatest possible energy and takes the initiative of the battle into his own hands.

Chief of staff, 9th Guards Fighter Division
Guards Lieutenant Colonel Abramovich[2]

Fierce land and air battles were being waged in the area north of Jassy, Romania, in late May 1944. The German–Romanian command had decided to liquidate a Soviet bridgehead on the west bank of the Prut River. Units of 9th Guards Fighter Division participated in an intense eight-day period of combat operations. During this time the division's fighters conducted fifty-two air battles, an average of six to seven battles each day. The first two days were particularly active. Over this entire period, only one battle ended without Soviet air victories. The relative fighter strength of the two sides in these battles was two to one in favor of the Soviet fighters.

Of the enemy aircraft that participated in the combat, approximately 65 percent were fighters and 35 percent bombers, which indicates the designation of significant forces to provide protection to the bombers. The 9th Guards Fighter Division suffered losses of twenty aircraft destroyed and twelve pilots lost; an additional eighteen P-39s were damaged in combat or mishaps, and twelve pilots were wounded.[3]

A general conference was conducted on 12 June 1944 to discuss the lessons of this operation. Here are the conclusions presented at this conference by the commander of 9th Guards Fighter Division, Guards Lieutenant Colonel Aleksandr Pokryshkin.

The young pilots of the 104th Guard Fighter Regiment showed themselves to be the best in the division. This regiment had the fewest losses and were effective against the enemy. There were cases in the 16th Guards and 100th Guards Regiments when, fearing their unpreparedness, the young pilots did not seek combat. This shifted the entire load of combat missions to the more experienced pilots. But young pilots cannot acquire combat experience by avoiding these opportunities.

When we are allocated fuel for training flights, we must expend it in such a way that each individual pilot receives an allocation. No one will be left out. By the time of the next major commitment there should not be a single unprepared pilot in the regiments.

I have heard talk of insufficient time for development of missions, when the signal has been given to scramble to provide support to ground troops. We are fighter pilots, not bomber pilots. They have assigned us the mission to provide this support. We should form groups in the regiments to perform this task and determine the required combat formations. This group in each regiment should always be prepared to launch.

The enemy has begun to operate in large combined groups of fighters and bombers. We also initially accomplished our combat missions in large groups. The experience we gained indicates that we should consider covering a single area with two patrols of six to eight aircraft each. Both of these patrols should be echeloned by altitude and cooperate with each other, supporting each other.

Because we have so many young and relatively inexperienced pilots, our pairs are somewhat weakly bonded. Therefore in training we must first place special emphasis on the development of the actions of a pair in sharp maneuvers at combat speeds. When flying with an inexperienced wingman, pair leaders must keep in mind that sometimes they must accommodate themselves to the younger pilot, until his training level has improved. Failure to make this adjustment can lead to separation of the wingman and his subsequent loss.

The nature of the actions of the enemy fighters (in groups of four to six aircraft) underscores that we should work out and practice the actions as flights (four aircraft) by pairs, so that both pairs carry out the same mission and do not operate independently.

There have been aircraft losses (both combat and noncombat) that were the fault of the pilot. When these pilots return to us, we receive them with open arms, as though they were some kind of heroes. We fail to point out to them their mistakes and we do not demand explanations. We need pilots who are destroyers of enemy aircraft, not destroyers of their own aircraft.

Our curse in operations is our tendency to wander. We have suffered many losses because of this. Navigational training in our units is not up to standard. All you navigators must carefully analyze every occurrence of loss of orientation and take measures to eliminate them. When we lose orientation, we seem unable to recover it. A pilot became lost and flew at treetop level until he ran out of fuel. Naturally, he found nothing, he saw nothing, and he was unable to select a suitable landing site.

When you lose orientation, get some altitude and do not fly until your tanks are empty. When five to seven gallons remain, find a place to land—gear down if possible, but on the belly if not.

Now a few words about combat tactics. When you are patrolling in an assigned area at the mission altitude, fly so that during your approach to the front line you gain altitude above the specified altitude. Come down to the specified altitude using the sun or clouds for *maskirovka*. You will gain surprise and speed and can attack an enemy aircraft higher or lower than yourself. In the coverage area, fly at combat speed, developing that speed not by forcing your engines but through altitude loss. Area-coverage patrols should be structured in a manner that will protect the assigned region against enemy air attacks. Sometimes our groups become distracted and venture far forward or to the flank, permitting enemy bombers to penetrate to our ground force positions.[4]

The final document contains the conclusions of the commander of 7th Fighter Corps, Major General of Aviation Aleksandr Utin.

From my own observations, the observations of other officers and generals, and the results of your combat actions in the operation, it can be concluded that the combat capability of the division is high.

I have no complaints to voice to the division regarding its combat actions. You fought more frequently over the enemy's territory, and this is what was required.

In the future I must consider that sometimes I will need to vector a group to a specific point toward which enemy bombers are flying. Moreover, while I may not have visual contact with either our own patrol or the enemy group, I will indicate only a location to which the patrol should fly and make subsequent vectoring adjustments. The problem with this type of action is that our pilots are quite unfamiliar with the area, are fumbling with their maps, and asking how to find the designated point. As a result, they are late in arriving. We must correct this deficiency. When an operation is in progress on a narrow sector of the front (and this was the case in this instance), the pilots must commit to memory the distinctive features of the locale and be able to find them quickly both on the map and on the terrain.

Three factors contributed to the division's losses in the battles you just fought:

1. The units' pilots have not fought for some while, and after a six-month break were immediately forced to operate in a very intensive air campaign.

2. A whole group of old pilots fought "too well," that is, they got carried away. They rushed in too quickly, without employing cunning and restraint.

3. Disengagements from combat were disorganized. I saw individual aircraft and pairs disengaging. Disengagement from combat should be accomplished as a group.

Improper disengagement, besides losses, leads to unauthorized self-directed departure from the battlefield. There were cases when just as an aerial battle was developing, one or two crews removed themselves and circled north of my KP [command post]. They did not identify themselves and did not respond to my radio calls. When the engagement was completed, they rejoined their group and flew home. This indicates poor control. It is necessary to determine who these pilots are and take immediate corrective measures. If it turns out to be a young pilot, be careful in evaluating his actions. It could be that he is not a coward, but is simply not accustomed and is timid in his first combat. This is natural. If we do not monitor him and correct this tendency in a timely manner, he will become an unintentional coward and a traitor.

From my observations of the air battles I can say that when we fought in groups of four and six fighters, we had no losses. As soon as we lost our cooperation and began to fight in pairs and then single aircraft, the group began to suffer significant losses.

Just as ineffective are large groups. We cannot fight with eight aircraft in a single group. This complicates command and control and reduces maneuver. The best group size for battle is four or six planes, no more.

The Germans have an old method—"Create a threat from every direction!" Enemy fighters fly about in groups: four to six FW-190s, four Bf-109s in pairs. But there are many of these groups. They loiter at all altitudes across a broad front. Therefore they can mass better and deliver an attack from all directions. This is another indicator that we must break up our cumbersome groups into several smaller groups.

A patrol of fourteen to sixteen aircraft should operate over the battlefield in groups of four to six fighters. When a larger group is employed, the separation between aircraft is greater. Sometimes, for no particular purpose, the leader turns a group in a flanking maneuver. Pairs become separated, lose coordination with each other, and suffer losses.

The wingman, of course, answers for the safety of his leader in combat, but sometimes a leader loses his combat wingman. If this happens too often, you must investigate the cause of such losses. If a pilot does not demonstrate the capability to lead a patrol, redesignate him as a wingman. If he abandons his comrade in combat, court martial him for cowardice.

A word about alert sorties. Some complaints have been made here to the staff that insufficient time is allocated to prepare for takeoff. But you are fighter pilots, not bomber pilots. A group should be prepared for combat missions well in advance of alert. If the day's mission has been announced as "cover ground troops," for example, no special preparation is required. If the mission will be combined groups and they are hastily designated, the regimental commander is at fault.

Bear in mind that in the upcoming days, when you are being rebased to new airfields that are twice as close to the front line as you are today, I will be using you to respond to requests for close air support. Be prepared for this.

There are two things I do not like in your combat actions:

1. Poor radio discipline. The flight leader is on the radio with me and carrying out my orders. But just as soon as the fight begins, something unimaginable frequently comes up on the net. Everyone is talking, shouting, and cursing. Sometimes several pilots push their transmit button at the same time, creating a noise and preventing anyone from understanding anyone else. I cannot control the battle amid such poor radio discipline. And I do not understand why you do this. It is impossible to use the radio direction finder. It should receive an interrogation from you, resect your position, and give you an azimuth. But what can you hear through such noise?

You must conduct yourselves with the strictest procedures on the air.

2. Noncombat losses. We are suffering much higher noncombat losses than combat losses. If we did not have these noncombat losses, we would be in outstanding condition. Among our noncombat losses most of them are on account of inattention. You fly until all of your fuel is expended, until the motor cuts out, you land where you fall, you destroy aircraft.

Everyone knows that if he becomes lost, while he has a fuel supply he should choose a landing spot and put the aircraft down carefully. I categorically require that when you lose orientation, do not lose altitude but gain it and at a medium altitude reestablish orientation. Reduce the cases of becoming lost to zero.

I hope that all these deficiencies will be corrected and in the upcoming operation the division will fight even better.[5]

PART THREE

May 1944 to May 1945

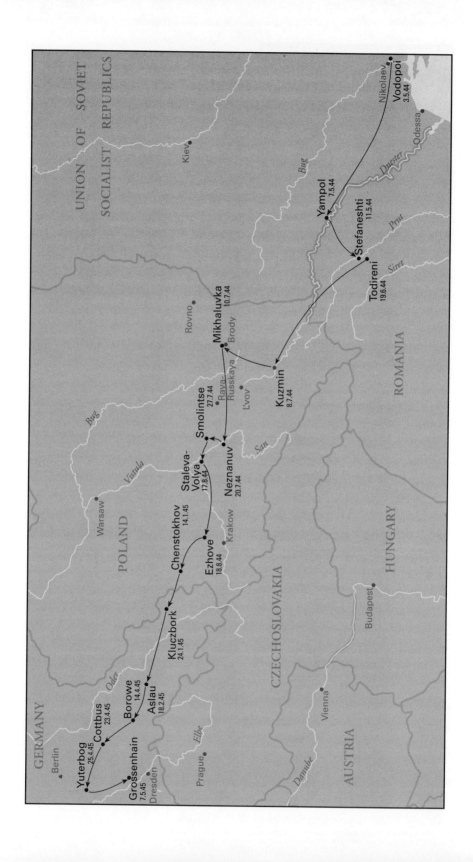

Three Years Later

There was a lull in combat activity on the left flank of the Soviet–German front from March through August 1944. Both sides were on the defense. The 9th Guards Fighter Division spent almost six months preparing for upcoming combat operations. By mid-May, its units had displaced to Stefaneshti airfield in Moldavia. The division commander, now Twice Hero of the Soviet Union Aleksandr Pokryshkin, supervised the division's relocation.

Wartime roads! It had to happen. After almost three years, the 9th Guards had returned to the place, the very same airfield, where flight commander Pokryshkin had greeted the dawn of 22 June 1941—the beginning of the war. It was symbolic. However, few of the veterans who launched in response to the alarm—genuine, not training—on that long ago Sunday morning were returning. Among them were Pavel Kryukov, Ivan Vakhnenko, Andrey Trud, Grigoriy Rechkalov, and Aleksandr Pokryshkin. The same was true among the maintenance personnel. Heady with countless air battles, all of them were adorned with glittering rows of medals on their chests, and their division commander with two Gold Stars. Many officers were wearing considerably higher rank insignia.

On 18 May the squadrons of the regiments began familiarization flights around the operational area. They would be engaging the enemy as part of the 5th Air Army (commanded by Colonel General Sergey Goryunov), subordinated to the 2d Ukrainian *Front*. At the beginning of the third week of May, intelligence information indicated that the enemy was preparing for an offensive in the area of Jassy, Romania. By this time, the 9th Guards units had the following combat strengths: 16th Regiment, forty-one serviceable aircraft and thirty-one combat-ready pilots; 100th Regiment, forty-one and thirty; and 104th Regiment, thirty-nine and twenty-eight, respectively.[1]

At 0440 on 30 May, the enemy launched an offensive from the Jassy area with the forces of six divisions (four tank, one infantry, and one mountain infantry) in the general direction of Kyrpitsa. The goal of this attack was to liquidate a Soviet formation on the west bank of the Prut River. The German-Romanian forces had significant artillery and tank strength on the ground, supported by massed air formations. Stubborn, around-the-clock battles continued until June 6. After suffering great losses, the enemy was forced to abandon his assigned missions. Both sides remained at their previously held defensive positions.

Three objective circumstances predetermined the nature and results of the fierce duels in the skies of Moldavia and Romania. As has already been pointed out, the 9th Guards Fighter division had not participated in combat operations for a protracted period of time. This could not help but reflect on its combat effectiveness. Nothing substantially new had been added to its earlier experience and, in fact, the combat hardening of the division's air crews had been interrupted. But changes had occurred in the air forces of both Germany and the Soviet Union. The fighter units of both sides were now formed around new equipment that to some degree had transformed the tactical methods of conducting aerial engagements.

The squadrons of all the regiments contained a large number of young pilots who lacked front-line experience (30 to 40 percent of available personnel).[2] The morale of these air crews was exceptionally high. The war was coming closer and closer to the borders of fascist Germany. By the beginning of the battles at Jassy, 1,154 days of the Great Patriotic War had passed. Victory was just around the corner!

The morale and combat capabilities of fighting men and women of all arms and branches of the armed forces was an important, but not the only factor in achieving success in the mortal struggle with the enemy. Having begun the offensive, the German-Romanian command threw large numbers of aircraft, both bombers and fighters, into the fight. They were pursuing a decisive goal: to defeat the Soviet defense in a short time with a powerful attack of ground and air forces, and to the degree possible liquidate the bridgehead on the right (west) bank of the Prut River.

The enemy sent large groups of Ju-87s and Ju-88s out on these missions, escorted by up to twenty Bf-109s and FW-190s. Large groups of Airacobras (ten to sixteen aircraft) were also operating from our side. However, lacking the experience of air combat in such strong patrols, our pilots achieved fewer kills in air battles than their numbers would suggest.

The developing situation demanded adjustments in the construction of the combat formation of the Soviet fighter groups. Its basic element became not the pair, as it earlier had been, but the flight (four aircraft). The commanders of this low-level unit also lacked experience in commanding and controlling such an element in aerial engagements. The aggregate of these enumerated internal and external factors of the developing situation was revealed in the intense weeks of battles east of Jassy and above the Prut River.

The first fierce encounters with a powerful air enemy after the aviators' long "vacation" occurred on 30 May. For his own part, each combatant had clearly established goals and tried, in spite of every obstacle, to accomplish them. Ten Airacobras, led by Captain Pavel Eremin, were covering ground forces in the area of Vulturuy and Skulyany from 1245 to 1330. The weather was excellent: clear and calm. The P-39s reached their designated sector at low altitudes (6,560 to 4,920 feet), which complicated the enemy's detection of them by both technical means and visual observation.

The pilots saw almost continuous flashes of artillery and tank fire on the hills beyond the Prut River; the forward edge was covered in dense smoke. A stubborn, bloody battle had ignited and was raging below. The ground vectoring station provided the patrol with information regarding the absence of the enemy on the approaches to their coverage zone. Not wasting any time, Eremin led his group to altitude, concentrating it in three elements: two four-ship flights (attack and cover), and two Airacobras in the "hunter" role (the brothers Ivan and Vasiliy Onishchenko). The latter flew to the flank of the main body's combat formation. This pair would catch individual enemy aircraft that were attempting to break away from the combat. If the situation required, they could quickly rejoin the crews engaged in direct fighting with enemy aircraft.

After some time, the Airacobra pilots observed the approach from the southwest of up to forty Heinkels, in groups of six to eight aircraft and escorted by eighteen to twenty Messerschmitts and Focke-Wulfs at an altitude of 13,125 feet. Employing the altitude advantage of his attack flight above the approaching armada, Pavel Eremin shot down one bomber at a range of forty to thirty yards from above and behind. However, the enemy also displayed a high level of activity. Four FW-190s attempted to trap Eremin's P-39. The pair of Lieutenant Viktor Nikitin boldly engaged them in battle. Nikitin managed to catch a Focke-Wulf in his sight and sent it plummeting to the earth. But

Nikitin's aircraft took a number of hits, one of which penetrated his oxygen tank, exploding it.[3] The P-39 was damaged and its pilot hurriedly departed to an airfield.

In turn, Senior Lieutenant Nikolay Starchikov's subgroup attacked a flight of Hs-129s from two sides: from behind and below and from the flank and behind.[4] This rapid attack led to some confusion of the enemy gunners. Their tracer streams, fired too late, caused no harm to the Airacobras that were approaching the bombers. The result was encouraging: three enemy aircraft exploded, and a fourth—set on fire—went into a spin trailing flames. And so, one destroyed bomber each was added to the battle scores of Starchikov, Viktor Priymachenko, Aleksandr Torbeev, and Mikhail Novikov. Priymachenko's P-39 incurred serious damage in the course of the attack. Viktor reported by radio that he was executing a forced landing.

After this successful attack on the bombers, Starchikov's covering subgroup engaged the escort fighters in battle. Starchikov shot down one "bandit" with an attack from above and behind. The active and highly effective maneuvers of the Airacobras led by Starchikov dispersed the columns of bombers. Four or five of them dumped their bomb loads and turned back. The brothers Onishchenko did not ignore the moment of change in the air situation. Ivan led his pair into a dive and set one Hs-129 on fire from close range. The remaining bombers drastically reduced their altitude and, taking cover in the relief of the terrain, abandoned the engagement area. After a brief interlude, Vasiliy Onishchenko fell into a tracer stream while being engaged by four FW-190s. His reduction gear began to fail. Without hesitation, the lieutenant made a forced landing.

The momentum of the situation in the battle zone had changed somewhat, unfortunately not in our favor. The intact bombers trailed off toward German lines and circled, in anticipation that their fighters would clear a path to the target for them. This demonstrated that the enemy would strive for active operations. And as if in confirmation of the given circumstance, the Messerschmitts and Focke-Wulfs hurled themselves at Eremin's group with increased frenzy from all sides. From strident offensive tactical methods the Airacobra pilots transitioned to the defensive. The enemy had managed to seize the initiative. A real danger was posed of our losses increasing.

Division commander Aleksandr Pokryshkin continued attentively monitoring the battle from his position at the ground vectoring station. The experienced ace understood the threat posed by the rapidly occurring changes at altitude. He ordered a standby patrol to launch and take up a station from which he could subsequently direct them to assist the Airacobra pilots who were now in an unequal battle. Eremin issued the command for gradual withdrawal from the engagement.

Pokryshkin later wrote, "To observe an air battle from the ground and actively intervene in its conduct was an entirely new responsibility for me. I encouraged the engaged pilots and reported the situation to those approaching the front line. And I worried."[5]

At 1315 the commander of 3d Squadron, 16th Guards Fighter Regiment, Aleksandr Klubov, led eight Airacobras to the aid of Eremin's group. On recommendation of the division commander, 3d Squadron commander and his subordinates flew six miles into enemy air space and from there rushed toward the designated zone. This maneuver provided two advantages: the achievement of surprise, and blocking of the enemy's path of withdrawal into his own rear.

Klubov employed a sudden attack initiated from an axis totally unanticipated by the enemy. He deployed his group across a broad front and attacked the bombers rapidly over a large space. The sky was cleared of three bombers. Distracted in the fight with Eremin's Airacobras, the enemy fighters did not interfere with the actions of the newly arrived patrol. The German bombers, jettisoning their ordnance, plummeted toward the ground, attempting to evade pursuit by low-level flight. Some of Klubov's pilots sought to pursue them, but their leader sternly ordered them to resume their positions in the group's combat formation. Klubov ordered the covering subgroup to gain altitude and his own four-ship flight to go after the Bf-109s and FW-190s decisively.

A "carousel" of fighters formed. A Focke-Wulf got on the tail of Captain Klubov and opened fire. Fortunately, the tracer stream missed. Lieutenant Nikolay Karpov came to the assistance by attacking the enemy from above and behind. His burst only damaged the FW-190 and did not force it to the ground. The Focke-Wulf headed toward Jassy in inverted flight. In this rapidly gyrating vortex of aircraft from both sides, the young pilots (Nikolay Belozerov, Mikhail Buzuev, Nikolay

Khotskiy, Aleksey Poddubskiy) became separated from their pair leaders and displayed some indecisiveness at the most intense moments of the battle. This was purely a reflection of their inexperience.

The fact must also be emphasized that the pair leaders, primarily experienced pilots (Aleksandr Klubov, Nikolay Karpov, Vladimir Petukhov, Nikolay Trofimov), during the prolonged period of inactivity had grown hungry for the hunt for more "bandits" and bombers, and at times forgot about their subordinates. Therefore it is not surprising that the two losses in this flight happened to untested pilots (Buzuev and Khotskiy). Karpov turned out to be the most effective in the as yet unfinished engagement. He shot down one and damaged another FW-190. The enemy suffered three destroyed and three damaged aircraft.[6]

A number of shortcomings that reduced the effectiveness of the Soviet pilots were noted at the postflight debriefing of Klubov's group. First was the fact that in such an intense situation of the battle, Klubov had been unable to hold his flights in a "fist," both the attack subgroup and the patrol as a whole. They spread out in pairs that were poorly coordinated one with the other. The leaders were intent on the destruction of enemy aircraft, forgetting in this that they were required at the same time to give appropriate guidance and direction to the fight of their subordinates. Once contact was established with the enemy escort fighters, for all practical purposes the battle was fought at a common altitude. The attack and covering subgroups were joined together and transformed into a single fighting unit. The leader of the group for some reason ignored the experience already gained and more than once confirmed in practice—the conduct of the battle in the vertical dimension. The more so since the enemy generally avoided this tactical method.

All the above enumerated mistakes of the construct of the battle formation, command and control of subgroups and flights, and violation of recognized tactical imperatives during accomplishment of the assigned combat missions were direct causes of the loss of two Airacobras. Despite these failures, however, modest losses were inflicted on the enemy.

On the afternoon of 30 May the coverage of ground units was being accomplished by units of 100th Guards Fighter Regiment. Ten P-39s led by Senior Lieutenant Aleksey Trufanov were orbiting in the area of

Vulturuy and Kyrpitsa from 1420 to 1525. They encountered eighteen bombers escorted by eight Bf-109s and two FW-190s at an altitude of 11,485 feet. The enemy had an almost three-times superiority of forces over our patrol. This fact had a bearing on the outcome of the engagement. The basic combat formation of this patrol was pairs. A majority of the pilots of the 100th Guards Fighter Regiment had not yet been trained to conduct battle in flights of four aircraft. Training and more training was required.

Captain Ivan Svinarenko and his partner, Junior Lieutenant Vladimir Gurov, attacked the first group of Ju-87s from the front and above. They encountered heavy fire by the enemy's wing guns and turned away. During this evasive maneuver the wingman's aircraft began to smoke and then lost altitude in a steep dive. Gurov did not respond to radio calls.

The second pair (Lieutenant Konstantin Shvetsov and Junior Lieutenant Vladimir Lisogor) attacked the same group of bombers from above and right, firing long cannon and machine-gun bursts. The bomber formation began to break up. A portion of the bombers jettisoned their loads. Meanwhile, Svinarenko and Vladimir Gurov attacked the second group of nine Ju-87s. The pair was able to down one of them.

The subgroup of Senior Lieutenant Aleksey Trufanov (six P-39s), positioned behind and above the already attacking P-39s, engaged in a furious battle with the ten escorting German fighters. Employing a frontal attack, Trufanov set the lead Bf-109 on fire with his first burst. The second pair (Lieutenant Petr Guchek and Junior Lieutenant Vyacheslav Ananev) did not lag behind the group leader. These pilots chased after a pair of Messerschmitts from two directions. Insufficient forethought prevented the completion of this attack. Chased by an FW-190, Guchek's Airacobra entered a spin. Ananev dove after the Focke-Wulf and sent a burst of cannon fire into the "bandit" from a position above and left of the FW-190 at a range of 110 yards.

The Airacobra pilots conducted the engagement with the Messerschmitts and Focke-Wulfs "holding on to the enemy by the teeth," that is, at close range. This method tied up the enemy fighters and deprived them of freedom to maneuver. At the same time, in a majority of cases the P-39s' firepower was devastating at this range. One must give the German pilots their due. They did not back down in this developing situation but continued to resist fiercely, at times turning the tables on the Soviet fighters. Lieutenant Vasiliy Bondarenko and his partner Junior Lieutenant Petr Begunov attacked two Bf-109s. The pair leader brought his Airacobra into a head-on attack with a left turn and on a closing course shot down the lead "bandit."

Senior Lieutenant Vasiliy Shkatov and Lieutenant Konstantin Shvetsov engaged three additional enemy fighters 660 feet higher. As the situation unfolded, both young pilots were left without the support of their more experienced colleagues. This was a leadership failure on the part of their group and subgroup leaders. Despite the unequal odds, Shvetsov managed to damage a Messerschmitt. However, fresh German reinforcements arrived several minutes later. The German fighters swirled around the Airacobras with renewed energy and isolated the aircraft of Shvetsov and Shkatov. These two young airmen did not return to their base that day. The phrase "did not return from combat mission" appeared in the pertinent headquarters accountability documents opposite their last names. Some hope remained that they might reappear. The fortunes of war were unpredictable.

And so 30 May—the first intense combat day—came to an end. The lessons of this day can be examined. Unfortunately, they turned out to be irreconcilable. The division commander and his staff understood the need to take immediate corrective measures. Pokryshkin issued instructions to summon the regiment and squadron commanders to a conference. Together they had to determine the causes of several unsuccessful initial air battles, listen to the experienced pilots, and take genuine positive steps to address the noted deficiencies. This was standard practice in the flights, squadrons, and regiments. On this occasion, the problem had to be addressed at the division level. Efficiency in the resolution of any issue, the more so of such an important matter for subsequent operations, was a standard approach in Pokryshkin's command style. Long days of intense air clashes lay ahead of his division.

After a careful, two-hour discussion of fundamental issues in the combat actions of their fighter units, the assembled commanders reached several unanimous opinions. Patrols had to be strengthened numerically. Experienced pilots had to be designated as group leaders. The pair remained the basic combat formation and the flight (two pairs) only as an exception. These elements were to be controlled by pilots who had participated in no fewer than five to six air battles. Co-ordination and cooperation in the air were also emphasized.

At the conclusion of the conference Pokryshkin asked the Airaco-bra pilots to recall the battle-tested tradition of the 9th Guards Fighter Division to attack the enemy boldly without consideration of his num-bers, to remember that the Airacobra was superior to any German fighter in firepower, and to employ the tactical methods of employing the P-39 that had been confirmed in many fierce air battles.

The chief of the division political section, Guards Lieutenant Colonel Dmitriy Machnev, considered it necessary to remind the pi-lots, "Look at the map of the course of combat operations on the So-viet–German front. The hour of total liberation of our Motherland from the German scum is near. The closer we approach the lair of the fascist beast the more ferocious his resistance will become. This means the strength of our attacks should be doubled or even tripled."[7]

On 31 May, as before, the conflagration at the convergence of the two sides' ground forces was very fierce. The situation in the air was no less intense. The enemy continued to send out significant groups of bombers in support of his ground forces, escorted by large groups of fighters. Raids were conducted simultaneously at several targets on our side. There were air engagements from morning to night.

On this day the division commander instructed that 104th Guards Fighter Regiment be the on-call unit. The 16th and 100th Guards Fighter Regiments were, for the most part, engaged in developing tactical meth-ods by flights and had dispatched several pairs of P-39s on free hunt.

In the period from 0645 to 0800 the commander of the 104th Guards Fighter Regiment, Guards Lieutenant Colonel Kryukov, led fourteen Airacobras to the Skulyany-Larga zone. Pavel Kryukov had encountered the enemy here in the first days of the war. Two groups of enemy aircraft appeared in this same area almost simultaneously: six Bf-109 and FW-190 fighters for clearing out the airspace (at 14,765 feet), and ten Ju-88s es-corted by ten "bandits," all flying 1,640 feet above the lead fighter group.

Kryukov's combat formation consisted of three flights of four air-craft (led by Kryukov, Major Nikolay Novikov, and Captain Aleksey Zakalyuk) and a pair of hunters led by Captain Mikhail Komelkov. The aviators leading the subgroups had personal experience of six, six, nine, and ten air battles, respectively.

The fight took on an active offensive nature from the first moment. Kryukov directed his own flight of four at the Ju-88s. An attack from behind and below set one of the bombers on fire. Lieutenant Iosif Grafin raced after a Bf-109 and when he came within range shot his cannon at it from behind. The enemy aircraft lost its propeller and, emitting smoke, disappeared in a steep dive.

Captain Zakalyuk's flight took on the enemy fighter escort, attacking from behind and out of the sun. The forces were unequal. The group commander should have reinforced Aleksey's flight with Komelkov's pair, but this did not happen. Zakalyuk shot down the Messerschmitt, which spun all the way to the ground. Two Airacobras (Junior Lieutenants Nikolay Klimov and Leonid Yazov) fell under heavy fire in a brief but fierce encounter with the Bf-109s and FW-190s and were shot down.

Major Nikolay Novikov's subgroup attacked the trailing bombers. The enemy aerial gunners put up a heavy curtain of fire, causing the P-39 pilots to respond with their own return fires at extended range. Two Ju-88s were damaged, immediately dropped their bombs, and went into spiraling dives. Subsequently masking themselves in the folds of the terrain, they turned away to the southwest.

Unfortunately, this flight did not avoid losses either. Nikolay Novikov's aircraft was smoking heavily and, without any radio transmissions, left the engagement zone in a steep vertical dive. Ivan Mikhalin's Airacobra received damage to the propeller and skin. This was his fourth battle in his first month at the front. He was fortunate to get away with moderate damage.

It was the fifth combat sortie on the last day of May, from 1515 to 1625. Sixteen Airacobras launched in four flights, the flights led by the deputy regiment commander Captain Mikhail Komelkov, assistant regiment commander for aerial gunnery Captain Aleksandr Rumm, Captain Aleksey Zakalyuk, and Lieutenant Ivan Mikhalin. They were orbiting above Balturia at 8,200 to 9,845 feet. Beginning in the morning and throughout the day the enemy attempted to penetrate into our positions at medium altitudes, making early detection by our RUS-2 radar set somewhat problematic.

At the conclusion of the patrol the pilots spotted fourteen bombers escorted by ten Bf-109s one to two miles north of Jassy, at the same altitude as the P-39s. The ground vectoring station "Steel Zhdanov" had not detected their presence. Komelkov gave the command to turn the flights toward Jassy and to attack the approaching enemy aircraft. The enemy had overall superiority in numbers of aircraft, however, and more importantly, he had fewer fighters. In addition, when the battle was over enemy territory, bombs jettisoned by the bombers would fall on the heads of German, not Soviet, troops.

The patrol launched a simultaneous attack on the bombers and fighters with two subgroups of eight aircraft each. Rumm led the first and Komelkov the second. The bombers immediately began to dump their bomb loads. The Airacobra pilots executed the majority of their attacks from above and behind, which permitted them to achieve results in a single pass. Komelkov chased a Bf-109 to the ground and shot it at point-blank range. Flying at treetop level, Rumm shot up a Ju-88. Zakalyuk set a Messerschmitt on fire from a range of fifty-five yards. Junior Lieutenant Viktor Samsonov executed an unsuccessful attack on a bomber. The rear gunner hit him with a precise burst that damaged his P-39's propeller, holed the starboard aileron, and jammed his flaps. The pilot requested permission to disengage.

In Zakalyuk's flight, Grigoriy Turyanskiy's Airacobra was also forced to abandon the engagement zone. His rudder and horizontal stabilizer received bullet holes, making control of his aircraft difficult.

The enemy lost six aircraft (three bombers and an equal number of fighters) as a result of a brief, dynamic battle. Two P-39s were damaged.[8]

Enemy aviation activity remained at a relatively high level at the beginning of June. In connection with this, the squadrons of 9th Guards Fighter Division were also operating at a high operational tempo. For example, the 16th Guards Fighter Regiment flew an average of 34 sorties per day during the first week of June. The regiment flew 245 combat sorties for the entire month, an average of slightly more than 8 per day.[9] The 100th Guards Fighter Regiment flew 371 combat sorties in June, losing twelve P-39s (from 30 May to 6 June 1944).[10] The 104th Guards Fighter Regiment flew 157 combat sorties during this same period (87 of which were flown in the first ten days) and fought 45 aerial engagements. For comparison, this same regiment flew 178 combat sorties in May.[11]

In the early part of June, when German and Romanian ground forces were attacking Soviet defensive positions, Soviet pilots frequently fought against superior enemy air forces. Here are some typical engagements from this period. June began with a lopsided encounter between ten Airacobras of the 100th Guards Fighter Regiment and an enemy force several times larger. The leader of the patrol was Guards Major Mikhail Petrov. The coverage area was east of Jassy at an altitude of 13,125 feet. The enemy lost a total of eight aircraft (four FW-190, two Ju-87, and two Bf-109). Guards Junior Lieutenant Petr Begunov did not return from this mission.

The composition of the formation of P-39s predetermined the success of the engagement. Behind the sticks of five P-39s were pilots who had the experience of countless engagements with the enemy. Each of them had some downed enemy aircraft to his credit: Mikhail Petrov seven, Vasiliy Sapyan five, Vasiliy Bondarenko four, Petr Guchek seven, and Grigoriy Sanyut two.

During the approach to Jassy the patrol encountered fifty Ju-87s escorted by sixteen Bf-109s and six FW-190s at an altitude of 11,485 to 13,125 feet. The enemy bombers were in a wedge formation in groups of nine aircraft echeloned one behind the other, with 550 to 880 yards of horizontal and 655 to 985 feet of vertical separation. Petrov's group consisted of two flights (one led by the group leader and the other by Junior Lieutenant Sanyut) and a cover pair (Junior Lieutenants Vasiliy Sapyan and Petr Guchek).

Petrov's flight launched its first attack on four FW-190s. Vasiliy Bondarenko downed a Focke-Wulf with three long bursts into its tail section from above and behind. Petr Begunov conducted a flank attack on a second "bandit" from above and behind, also successful. The Focke-Wulf went south at treetop level.

Then Petrov's pilots began repeated attacks on the bombers. Mikhail Grigorevich damaged the motor and right wing of a Ju-87 with an accurate burst from behind. The bomber spun all the way to impact. At this time Petr Guchek was dueling with an FW-190. He shot down the Focke-Wulf from the right rear with one burst. Ivan Mamaev managed to catch the same "bandit" in his sight and also fired at him.

Bondarenko rapidly directed his flight at the bombers and their immediate fighter escorts. These attacks were normally conducted from the rear into the tail, from the left rear, or from above and behind. Mikhail Petrov, Ivan Mamaev, and Konstantin Shchepotkin each increased their personal scores of downed enemy aircraft by one Ju-87.

In the course of the battle, Bondarenko, having evaded the fire of an FW-190, found himself in a closing course with another Focke-Wulf. He boldly closed with the enemy and at 220 yards fired at him with all weapons. The German fighter burst into flames and, rapidly losing altitude, disappeared into the overcast.

Upon setting up for a follow-on attack, Grigoriy Sanyut came under fire of two Bf-109s. He dove under them, his Airacobra responding poorly to the controls. The junior lieutenant reported by radio to Petrov that he was damaged and he took a course to the airfield. With enormous difficulty he stretched out his glide path to the nearest landing field and successfully landed his damaged fighter.[12]

A group of twelve Airacobras in 100th Guards Fighter Regiment was designated to execute the assigned mission in the afternoon of 3 June. The leader was Ivan Babak. He well understood that the success of any engagement depended on three most important factors: composition of the patrol group; careful preparation for combat; and skillful, coordinated actions in the air. Babak, together with Dmitriy Glinka (both from the regiment command group), determined the combat formation of the group: a strike group (six P-39s: Ivan Babak, Mikhail Petrov, Grigoriy Dolnikov, Aleksandr Zaytsev, Grigoriy Petrushev, and Konstantin Shchepotkin); a cover group (four Airacobras: Dmitriy Glinka, Vasiliy Sapyan, Ivan Mamaev, and Yuriy Obraztsov); and a hunter pair (Petr Guchek and Vyacheslav Ananev).

During preparation for the flight the subgroups received specific tasks for their actions. The subgroup leaders provided detailed guidance to each pilot. Especially important were each pilot's place in the combat formation, close coordination within pairs, and the highest vigilance at every stage of the flight.

The group launched at 1750 and was to patrol until 1840 over the area of Movilena and Zakhotka. Approaching the coverage zone, Babak queried the ground vectoring station "Steel Zhdanov" regarding the air situation. No enemy aircraft had been detected. Several moments later the ground vectoring station commanded, "Drop down under the overcast in the area of Epureni!" The attack subgroup immediately executed the order, while the covering subgroup remained above the overcast. The pair of Guchek and Antonev was positioned some 1,640 to 1,970 feet above Dmitriy Glinka's subordinates. This three-tiered construction of the patrol's combat formation permitted them to control a significant area of altitude in the overcast conditions. An undetected approach by the enemy was practically impossible.

Arriving in the area over Epureni, Guards Major Guchek reported to the ground vectoring station a group of enemy bombers and fighters approaching from the southwest. He did not report their altitude or number. Although the overcast was scattered, it complicated the determination of these necessary reporting elements at that range. The ground vectoring station responded that it had not acquired the enemy aircraft.

Dmitriy Glinka led his subgroup to engage the enemy. The Airacobra pilots quickly noted that Ju-87s were already diving from behind the overcast. Guards Major Glinka gave the command immediately to attack the enemy aircraft. Simultaneously his pilots confirmed their targets. Glinka's first flight went after the bombers and his second flight the fighters.

The hunters acted with exceptional speed. Masked by the clouds, they approached close to the covering "bandits." Guchek fired on a Bf-109 at point-blank range. Two Messerschmitts pounced on Guchek, but Vyacheslav Ananev was looking out for his pair leader. Beating off their attack, he passed through a Messerschmitt's cannon and machine-gun tracer stream. At this time the attack subgroup was attacking the bombers. Babak and Dolnikov each downed a bomber on their first pass.

The fight between the enemy fighters and the hunters was very difficult. Guchek requested assistance and Petrov's pair joined them. Petrov made a quick pass at a Bf-109 and set it on fire. The two joined pairs tied up all six escorting "bandits." They dove into the overcast. Guchev and Petrov, patrolling over the engagement zone, had been astute. The slight numerical superiority of the Messerschmitts and their ability to gain cover in the clouds created opportunities for active engagements.

The pair of Sapyan and Obraztsov was covering the attack of Glinka's subgroup. Glinka's pilots had downed two Ju-87s and one FW-190. Active, coordinated attacks by the subgroups and included pairs had enabled them to inflict telling losses on an enemy force four times their own strength.

On 4 June 1944, ten Airacobras of the 16th Guards Fighter Regiment sortied from 1625 to 1730 to patrol in the area of Larga station. Their subsequent air battle occurred at low to medium altitudes (4,920 to 6,560 feet). Several aspects of this patrol's combat actions merit examination. Among its pilots was the regiment commander, Guards Major Boris Glinka, but he was not the group leader. That responsibility fell on Guards Captain Aleksandr Klubov. He was an experienced ace pilot. The regiment commander and his wingman, Nikolay Kudrya, were assigned the role of hunter. Glinka's assumption of this role gave complete independence to the leader of the eight-ship patrol. The main body was further subdivided into one flight of four and two pairs. The leader of the four-ship flight was Nikolay Trofimov, who had close coordination with his pilots.

On the near approaches to the patrol zone, the pilots were vectored by ground station "Steel Zhdanov" to an approaching enemy force of sixteen Ju-88s and eight Bf-109s. The bombers were in an echelon right formation. Four "bandits" made an attempt to sweep the skies before the enemy bombers reached their intended strike zone. Glinka advised Klubov not to disperse his forces. Glinka's own pair would engage the lead enemy element. Conducting heavy barrier cannon and machine-gun fire, the hunters forced the Bf-109s toward Jassy. Boris Glinka was trying to ensure freedom of maneuver for the patrol's main body at the moment of its commitment to battle.

Captain Klubov and his wingman, Fedor Kutishchev, conducted a vigorous frontal attack on the bombers, forcing the enemy flight to jettison its ordnance before reaching the target and to depart to its own lines in disarray. Klubov's pair attacked the second flight of Ju-88s in the same manner, forcing it also to drop its bombs prematurely. The group leader conducted the next successful attack from above and behind, causing one bomber to fall out of the formation.

Several intense minutes of maneuvering passed. The situation was further complicated by the appearance of eight additional enemy fighters. The pairs led by Klubov and Aleksandr Ivashko and the four-ship flight of Nikolay Trofimov engaged the Messerschmitts and Focke-Wulfs in battle despite the enemy superiority in numbers (twelve Bf-109s and six FW-190s versus eight Airacobras). In the increasingly difficult situation, Boris Glinka joined his hunter pair to the group's main body with an attack from above, out of the sun.

The coordination of these actions and the attack against the enemy escort from various axes had some results. Glinka shot down an FW-190, Ivashko a Bf-109, and Trofimov an FW-190. The overall outcome of this aerial engagement was one Ju-88, two Bf-109s, and three FW-190s destroyed, and two bombers damaged. Klubov's group landed at their airfield at Stefaneshti with no losses. The mission had been successful due to careful preparation, continuous command and control of subordinates before and during the course of the engagement, and maintenance of a tight combat formation throughout the period of the mission.

The enemy broke off his offensive on 6 June. Air battles in the Jassy area had been a unique test of the combat readiness of the Guards 9th Fighter Division's regiments after a significant hiatus in combat activity. The ensuing operational pause at the front allowed them to work out many issues of fighter unit tactics and to examine and determine the causes of a number of unsuccessful engagements with a powerful enemy. The positive results of battle for the unit as a whole were handed down to individual pilots.

Air crew tactical conferences were conducted in the regiments for this purpose from 15 to 22 June. The staggered scheduling of these meetings ensured the attendance at each meeting of all aviators who performed the duties of flight leader or higher. The division command played an active role in all regiment conferences. The principle, "Learn from the successes and mistakes of others," remained fundamental for all fighter pilots. The mutual exchange of good habits acquired in combat with the enemy enriched the front-line aviators. "I will study your experience from yesterday's fight. Tomorrow it will be my own!"

As a rule, the weeks of battles over Jassy were fought with an enemy superior in number and highly active. The engagements occurred, for the most part, at medium altitudes. This was connected with the fact that bombing strikes were being conducted on the nearest troop targets in the interests of the attacking German and Romanian formations. The enemy was using artillery smoke rounds to designate targets for the bombers. This was at the same time a good reference marker for our fighter patrols. Our pilots could figure out where the enemy bombers intended to drop their loads. Flight leaders brought their Airacobra forces to probable flight routes into the intended target areas in order to intercept the bombers before they reached their drop zones. The battles were fiercely fought from the first shot fired because the enemy was escorting with significant numbers of fighters (from fifteen to twenty).

It became acutely necessary to send out patrols in large numbers to cover defending Soviet ground units. The situation demanded that the basic combat formation be not the pair but the flight of four aircraft. The results were excellent in those squadrons where the combat actions of four-ship elements had been successfully developed. The continuous maintenance of a compact formation of the group and its subgroups, along with close cooperation within and between these temporary formations, played a significant role.

Young pilots (who constituted 40 percent of the units) acquired the skills of fighting against a relatively strong enemy, which had a positive influence on the results of air battles in subsequent offensive operations. Analysis of the majority of the engagements showed that the most effective were attacks against enemy aircraft from above and behind and from below and behind at shallow attack angles. In this case the target would remain in the sight of the attacking fighter for a longer period of time than at steeper attack angles.

Pilots strove to destroy the enemy on the first pass, conducting precise cannon and machine-gun fire from all weapons simultaneously at ranges of from 165 to 55 yards, infrequently out to 220 yards. Rich experience was accumulated in conducting the "free hunt," both directly over the battlefield of ground units and in the enemy's deep rear. In the first case, the "hunter" pair launched for their mission some five to ten minutes ahead of the patrol's main body. Passing several times at significant altitude and high speed, and not detecting the enemy in the designated coverage zone, the "hunters" would extend their penetration to six to nine miles into enemy territory and search there for enemy aircraft approaching the front line. After a rapid attack the "hunters" would return to their initial coverage zone.

Upon receiving the mission to "hunt" deep in enemy territory, the pair designated for this mission profile sortied ten minutes ahead of the coverage group and went to an altitude of 16,405 to 19,685 feet. Their subsequent hunt was conducted from 70 to 185 miles deep into enemy territory.

He Flared Like a Comet

The examples of self-sacrifice of soldiers, sergeants, and officers in the Great Patriotic War are countless. These heroic acts were committed for a variety of reasons, great and small: to save a commander or a comrade in battle; to facilitate or continue an attack (as when soldiers covered a bunker embrasure with their bodies); to save the lives of civilians or preserve towns and villages (when an aircraft was shot down or an aircraft accident occurred in the sky above a populated area). In the latter two cases, the pilot did not abandon his damaged or disabled aircraft but rather stayed with it until the last moment, guiding it away from towns and villages. Frequently this prevented the pilot from saving himself by parachuting to safety. These pilots perished along with their fighter or bomber. They gave their lives so that their combat comrades and innocent civilians could move forward toward the day of victory.

In early March 1944 a group of pilots (thirty-six men—three squadrons) from the 9th Guards Fighter Division was dispatched to the Caucasus to pick up and ferry back Airacobras. These aircraft were arriving in the Soviet Union in a steady stream by Lend-Lease, through Iran as before. Guards Major Pavel Kryukov of the 100th Guards Fighter Regiment was placed in command of the group.

A rather intense period of ten days was allocated to resolve all the necessary tasks involved in receiving the aircraft and confirming their mechanical condition, both on the ground and in the air. The pilots were to fly the Airacobras from the point of issue to their airfield in Chernigov [approximately sixty miles northeast of Kiev]. The weather did not favor the pilots, particularly in the northern Caucasus region. Clouds, fog, and at times rain would complicate their flight. But these men, whose hands had been overworked by the war, kept a firm grip on the control stick. The Airacobra pilots were hurrying homeward in order to reconfigure their aircraft for combat more quickly and permit more time to train new pilots for the difficult battles that still lay ahead.

Kryukov planned and maintained a march route with the fewest possible landings. The magnitude of these "jumps" from one airfield to the next was limited by the fuel supply in the Airacobras' tanks. The crews landed, refueled, rested at night, and took off again at first light. They did not anticipate any delays that might disrupt the rapid tempo of their ferrying operation. These aircraft were much needed at the front.

The pilots flew in squadron-size subelements. Kryukov led the first, Guards Major Nikolay Lavitskiy the second, and Anatoliy Komosa the third. The planned flight altitude was 6,560 to 9,845 feet, depending on ceiling and visibility in any overcast they might encounter. A speed was selected that favored fuel economy.

Gudermes station was visible ahead. The tracks were jammed with train after train of tank cars bearing hundreds of tons of various fuels. Aviators, tankmen, infantrymen, and artillerymen were waiting for this fuel at the front lines. Everyone who was actively fighting the enemy required fuel.

Only the squadron commanders were using their transmitters. Everyone else was on radio listening silence. Strict radio discipline was being maintained. Nothing portended catastrophe. The P-39s were new and their engines were working rhythmically. Suddenly the slightly worried voice of Nikolay Lavitskiy was heard, calling to Kryukov. "My engine is smoking!"

"Make an emergency landing!" the leader instructed him.

A few terse moments later came a more worried report, "I have an engine fire!"

"Put it down! Land!" demanded Kryukov. There was no other way out. Lavitskiy needed to make a belly landing at any available spot. There was no time left to select the best landing area. The pilots of the second squadron were particularly concerned. They could see the flames from Lavitskiy's aircraft, but they could do nothing to help him. What advice could they offer? Despite the crisis situation, none of the Airacobra pilots broke radio silence and, consequently, did not interfere with the dialog between Kryukov and Lavitskiy.

The situation became more critical with each moment. Flames engulfed the entire engine compartment of the aircraft and were showing on both sides. Lavitskiy could not find even the smallest flat spot in the mountainous terrain suitable to crash-land his aircraft. In a few more minutes he would be unable to see the ground through the thick smoke now swirling around his cockpit.

Kryukov now issued an order to Lavitskiy to bail out. The 2d Squadron commander replied, "I'm side-slipping my aircraft. All I see below me are tank cars with fuel." He was coughing as he spoke from the thick smoke. That was his last transmission. Perhaps the fire had burned its way through to the transmitter, which was mounted behind the motor in the rear fuselage. Most likely in this critical, rapidly deteriorating situation, the pilot was totally consumed by another concern. He did not want his heavily burning aircraft to crash into Gudermes station. This would set off a chain of explosions and fires in the tank car rolling stock that filled all the tracks into and out of the station. The celebrated ace gave no thought to his own fate in the developing situation. With all his strength he tried to prevent a disaster, to save the equipment, fuel stocks, and the populace of Gudermes.

The incident had begun when the Airacobra was flying at 6,560 feet. Had they been higher, Lavitskiy might have been able to glide away and fall somewhere distant from the railroad station. Now the flaming aircraft was being carried toward the center of the settlement. Witnesses of his last gasp later recounted what happened. The P-39 was trailing thick black smoke. Lavitskiy certainly had trouble seeing and perhaps did not know where the ground was. Risking his own aircraft, Nikolay Iskrin flew in close to Lavitskiy's Airacobra. He was troubled by what he observed. The cockpit was full of smoke and the pilot was not visible. While the P-39 was responding to controls the Airacobra pilot extended its guide path, attempting to make it across the strings of tank cars on the tracks below.

The "burning comet" departed to the northwest. When it had flown past the station, the fighter began to lose altitude rapidly. Then it went over on its left wing and slashed into the ground at full speed. Fountains of fire and sparks erupted in all directions. Iskrin made several orbits over Lavitskiy's crash site. Merciless flames were devouring pieces of the fuselage and wings. Red tongues of fire licked at the deformed cockpit. There was nothing to be done to save Lavitskiy. The hero ace had died.

Iskrin reported his observations to the flight leader. Kryukov, choking back tears and grief, ordered Iskrin to assume command and catch up to the main body of the 2d Squadron. Pain gripped Nikolay Iskrin's heart. A friend with whom he had flown wingtip to wingtip in combat on more than one occasion, who had killed Germans in scores of engagements, had been turned into a falling comet along with his Airacobra. He was no longer among the living Airacobra pilots and his combat comrades were unable even to give him the traditional aviators' farewell salute. Their P-39s were not carrying ammunition for their weapons.

Iskrin made several more orbits above this tragic piece of ground, then guided his aircraft to the northwest. The Guards lieutenant made himself a promise. After the victory, if he remained alive, he would visit this final stop along the front line road of the hero, ace, and good man, Nikolay Lavitskiy.

Yet another heavy loss had been sustained, now on the downhill run toward the finish line of triumphal victory. What irony that it did not happen in the heat of battle at the front but in the deep rear, along a ferry route. The 9th Guards Fighter Division lost a remarkable pilot who had been recognized with his country's highest military award for downing eleven enemy aircraft.[1] Had Lavitskiy lived, the enemy would have lost many more aircraft before war's end. Fate has its own laws!

Nikolay Lavitskiy was burned to ashes in a fire at Gudermes on 10 March 1944. Let the pages of this book remain a living memorial to this Hero of the Soviet Union, an invincible aerial warrior, one of the millions who perished defending the Motherland.

The Chase

This is a humorous combat episode. A pair of Airacobras of 16th Guards Fighter Regiment (Junior Lieutenants Vladimir Petukhov and Mikhail Novikov) received a mission: early on the morning of 28 May 1944, penetrate into the enemy rear at high altitude and conduct a free hunt in the Roman–Bakeu zone to destroy enemy aircraft. They were to reconnoiter the Roman landing fields on the return leg to their own airfield.

The combat mission area was sufficiently complicated. A large enemy airfield (bombers and fighters) was located in Roman, and it had a well-organized system of anti-aircraft defense. This circumstance forced the hunters to maintain an altitude of no less than 13,125 feet. German pilots rarely attained this altitude over their own territory, but there were occasional exceptions in combat situations.

Scattered and in places dense clouds permitted the Airacobras to hide safely and, when necessary, take up a concealed position for launching an attack on an air target. The hunters had to display calm nerves, patience, and still more patience in the enemy's back yard. They had to be vigilant and await the enemy until their fuel ran out. On this day their efforts were rewarded, and then some!

About thirty minutes had passed and the enemy had not yet made an appearance. Two covering Bf-109s were circling over Roman airfield. Finally, an FW-189 "Rama" appeared from the southeast, 3,280 feet below the P-39s. All indications were that this aircraft was flying toward Soviet positions for visual, but more likely photographic reconnaissance. To this point the German aircraft did not have any fighter escort, normally provided by a pair and sometimes four Messerschmitts or Focke-Wulfs. Perhaps the escorting of the "Rama" would commence upon its approach to the forward edge.

It was not easy to shoot down this agile and armored aerial platform. Petukhov issued instructions. "We will attack in pair out of the sun. I will fire at the motors and you, Mikhail, at the gondola [the large glassed-in crew compartment]. Forward!"

For the enemy airmen, the attack was, if one can use the expression, a "double surprise"—deep in their own territory and out of the sun. The Germans did not see the Airacobras until the moment their aircraft came under withering cannon and machine-gun fire. In the blink of an eye the "Rama" was turned into a burning torch and fell out of the sky. With this shootdown the hunters had lost the element of surprise. They could now anticipate the appearance of the Messerschmitts covering the airfield or, perhaps, the on-duty flight.

The hunter leader issued a new command: "Drop down! We will take a pass over the airfield and then home!" With a dive out of the sun, the P-39s dropped down over the town of Roman. At treetop level and high speed they zoomed the length of the runway and apron, full of bombers and fighters (no fewer than forty aircraft), then climbed skyward. Enemy anti-aircraft gunners opened fire but it was already too late. Their tracer streams fell far behind the Soviet pair.

Petukhov and Novikov had accomplished their mission and now needed quickly to return to their own base. Darting from cloud to cloud, they held a course to the east. Jassy passed by on their left. Suddenly the two pilots spotted an FW-190 in front and below. Petukhov radioed to Novikov, "Cover me—I'm attacking!" Petukhov dove on the Focke-Wulf in an "eagle strike." Its pilot, having seen the Airacobra diving on him, hurried toward the town with a hard right turn and drop. Having gained sufficient speed in the dive to overtake the FW-190, Petukhov raced after him.

The range was closing with each second: 440—220—165 yards. Petukhov was attempting to close with the Focke-Wulf to get a sure kill. Dacha cottages flashed by below. Jassy was nearby. The smoke haze in the air could help the enemy fighter to escape. The junior lieutenant advanced the throttle lever and his Airacobra surged forward. The German, perhaps with the back of his head, sensed that at any moment the Airacobra's fiery tracer stream would pass through his aircraft's fuselage. He pitched his fighter to the side. A cannon burst from the P-39 passed close by. The German understood that he might not evade the follow-on cannon and machine-gun salvo of the Airacobra, which was clinging tightly to his tail.

Up ahead, on a small hill, stood the walls of a large Orthodox church. The German pilot headed straight toward this building. The junior lieutenant rotated his P-39 slightly to the right in order to bypass the religious structure. He passed the site and then lost sight of the FW-190. At that moment he heard Novikov's voice in his headphones: "The German held at the church! He is circling it!"

Petukhov turned his fighter around with a hard turn. He could not believe his own eyes. The Focke-Wulf was circling the sanctuary, pressed close to its walls. The German had stood his FW-190 on its left wing with its back toward the church. Petukhov observed that the German pilot had gained two advantages with this maneuver: he had a reasonably good view of the airspace in all directions and thus could spot anyone approaching him; and the body of his aircraft was positioned between himself and any source of gun fire.

Diving on the Focke-Wulf from behind and above, the junior lieutenant opened fire. He missed by a wide margin. The significant magnitude of the German fighter's lateral displacement in the arc of the circle afforded it some protection. Petukhov made a second pass, this time with a more horizontal approach, trying to catch the FW-190 in the tail and shoot it down from close range. This also proved too difficult. In its maneuvering and turning flight the enemy aircraft remained in the aiming sight for too brief a period. The linear tracer stream arrived at the aimpoint too late, the target having already "turned the corner." As before, the enemy remained untouched.

The young officer clenched his teeth, then ordered his wingman "Cover me! I am going to chase him. Maybe I can get and hold him in my sight!" Petukhov's burning desire to add one more trophy to his shelf overcame his reason.

The furious and futile chase continued for perhaps thirty minutes. Just as before, several bursts fired by Petukhov missed their mark. Two times Mikhail Novikov recommended abandoning the chase in order to return to base. The flight commander ignored his comrade's entreaties. He was consumed by the thrill of the chase—he would catch his prey no matter what the cost. "Continue to cover me! Watch the sky!" the flight leader responded to his wingman's pleas.

Finally the end came. At full speed, the Focke-Wulf separated from the orbit around the church and fell to the earth. Petukhov, out of surprise, drove his Airacobra upward into the sky. He made a circle over the downed FW-190, now engulfed in black smoke. Petukhov made a low-level pass and fired a long burst into the stationary target. Bright flames broke out around the Focke-Wulf. Both Airacobras now orbited above the burning FW-190. Its pilot was nowhere to be seen, having apparently gone down with his aircraft. Great joy overcame the

Guards junior lieutenant. He led his wingman up to altitude and together the "hunters" turned eastward, toward their airfield.

Petukhov and Novikov gave a detailed report at the regiment regarding the accomplishment of their mission. Guards Major Boris Glinka quietly listened to his subordinates. They brought in the developed but still wet film from the gun cameras of Petukhov and Novikov. This was documentary confirmation of both downed enemy aircraft. Glinka and the staff officers inspected Novikov's film with great interest. This film had a few frames of the carousel around the church.

Here, in the headquarters, in front of everyone, the celebrated ace Boris Glinka labeled the actions of Petukhov as reckless. He repeated this at a later enlarged discussion for passing on the lessons of recent battles, in order to discourage other pilots from similar thoughtless pursuits. Fortunately, this escapade ended without any punishment by the enemy. It could have ended in a totally different way. Two Airacobras were in enemy-controlled territory at low altitude. If a pair, or in a worse case a foursome of enemy aircraft had made an appearance, the over-eager hunters would have met the same fate as the "chased-down" Focke-Wulf.

Discussing this incident, the two comrades could not stop pondering the perplexing questions. "Why did not the enemy pilot, after he fell into the 'mess,' summon help? What caused him to go down? Did he run out of fuel?" This was the most likely cause of his crash. The P-39s themselves landed with nearly dry tanks.

This highly unusual case brought to the staff of the regiment a unique problem, a puzzle really. How should this downed German aircraft be recorded in the appropriate documents and in the pilot's personal logbook? There was no problem concerning the "Rama." But what about the FW-190? It could not be recorded that it was shot down. After some pondering, they decided to record in pencil, "Chased in a circle until it fell."

The regiment commander, Boris Glinka, although he reprimanded them for their recklessness and risk taking, recommended both Petukhov and Novikov for awards: Orders of the Patriotic War—first degree for Vladimir Petukhov and second degree for Mikhail Novikov. Petukhov never learned of his award. He did not return from a mission on 31 May 1944.[1]

Look, See, Find

Ignoring the vitally important precept "Stay alert!" even for a single moment is fraught with serious consequences. This is particularly true in a rapidly unfolding air battle between a fighter aircraft and a powerful and cunning enemy.

On 28 May 1944, a pair of Airacobras (Lieutenant Vladimir Stepanov and Junior Lieutenant Aleksandr Zakharov) of the 104th Guards Fighter Regiment was assigned the mission to ascertain the location of our ground forces at the front line in the area of Khodora. The weather conditions were moderately complicated, with scattered clouds and visibility from 1.2 to 2.5 miles. The patrol approached the mission area and began orbiting at an altitude of 6,560 to 8,200 feet, inspecting the terrain below to determine the location of the two sides' battle lines. The wingman, junior pilot Zakharov, was following some 440 yards behind his commander. He committed a blunder, however. All of his attention, like that of his leader, was concentrated on study of the ground situation. He should have also been inspecting the sky above and the flanks and rear. He should have maintained all-around observation—the most important factor in flight safety and consequently also in the accomplishment of the mission.

Several minutes of combat patrolling passed. Misfortune was not long in coming. Two Bf-109s came diving out of the overcast. They rained a hail of fire on Zakharov's P-39. Stepanov hurriedly turned back to assist his wingman, but the decisive seconds that determine the outcome of an engagement had already been squandered. Zakharov's fighter, enveloped in tongues of fire and smoke, disappeared into the low-hanging overcast.

Stepanov remained alone to face a superior enemy. Now everything depended on the pilot's skill. The enemy was considerably more adroit than the young Airacobra pilot. Stepanov did not take his eyes off the Messerschmitts that had just shot down his wingman. They made a large-radius turn, preparing for a follow-on attack on his own aircraft. It turned out that this was a distracting maneuver deliberately undertaken by the enemy. The Guards lieutenant took the bait. He should have reduced his speed and sought cover in the cloud bank just beneath his aircraft. Rather, he took up a waiting posture, and paid for it.

Unexpectedly for Stepanov, two additional Messerschmitts fired on him from above and behind. Their tracers literally enveloped his P-39. In an instant his fighter was heavily damaged but, fortunately, not set on fire. His engine began to miss and his radio failed. The hapless pilot dove his Airacobra downward with a right turn and disappeared into the dense overcast. This maneuver saved him from attack by either enemy pair and certain death. In truth, hesitation in the conduct of any counter maneuver would have been fatal. Had he accomplished such a maneuver just moments earlier, he probably would have remained undamaged.

Masked by clouds, Stepanov flew to his own territory. His engine oil pressure fell dramatically just before the Allison seized. He landed the Airacobra on its belly some two miles from the forward edge, on a hill west of Dumbrovits. In all likelihood, the enemy had good observation of his landing area, because almost immediately it was bracketed by indirect fire. The Airacobra was riddled by shrapnel and the right wing was heavily damaged. The closest Soviet unit did not refuse the pilot's request. The commander of the 442d Rifle Regiment was instructed to haul the crippled fighter to Novyye Khermeneshti and there to place a guard on it. The fruit of poor vigilance was three combat losses in a single flight, one of them irreplaceable.[1]

To see but remain unseen was a mandatory requirement for hunters, particularly over enemy-held territory. On 25 August 1944, from 1000 to 1045, a pair of hunters (leader Captain Aleksandr Klubov and wingman Sergey Ivanov) from the 16th Guards Fighter Regiment reached the "working" zone—Sandomir, Lagun, Keltse, Mologosh, and Khmelnik. They spotted a lone enemy fighter at 13,125 feet in the area of Keltse. The two hunters immediately slipped into the clouds and took a closing course with their prey. They did not rush their approach, carefully masking themselves with clouds and overcast.

Klubov guided Ivanov into an attack on the "bandit." The wingman struck from the front at an angle. The enemy aircraft flashed by underneath the Airacobra. It turned out that this was a new German fighter, the Bf-110.[2] The rear gunner opened up with a solid stream of barrier fire. The hunters' first pass ended in failure. They could not allow this priceless trophy to get away. They had to destroy it at any cost.

Klubov informed Ivanov, "We will pursue! Attack from the left and right rear. Full throttle!" The Airacobras deployed and began their chase. Klubov stitched the gunner's compartment with a long burst from 110 to 85 yards. At that instant the now dead gunner ceased firing. Ivanov planted his tracer stream in the motors, setting them on fire.

The Messerschmitt began slowly rotating to the right, presenting its entire underbelly to the P-39s' guns. Klubov finished off the German newcomer in a second pass. The Bf-110 turned over on its back. The junior lieutenant slashed out at the twin-engined fighter a third time, delivering the coup de grace. Seconds later the "bandit" hit the earth.

Whenever two pilots simultaneously or sequentially shot up and destroyed an enemy aircraft, each of them received credit for half an enemy aircraft. The monetary bonus for destruction of a fighter (1,000 rubles in the closing period of the war) was split between them.[3]

This remarkable result in finding and destroying the target was achieved by close and continuous coordination between the RUS-2 radar station and the aircraft. Airacobras that were equipped with the SCh-3 [*svoy-chuzhoy* (friend-foe)] device were especially adept at working with the radar, which could differentiate the Airacobra from the enemy aircraft based on the signal emanated by this device.

On the morning of 21 March 1945 the RUS-2 detected significant activity by small groups of enemy aircraft. At 1332, the radar station picked up a flight of enemy aircraft fifteen miles west of Kraybau airfield, heading east. Upon receipt of this report, the on-call pair (Captain Aleksey Lukantsev and Junior Lieutenant Yuriy Golberg) from 104th Guards Fighter Regiment sortied at 1325.

Orbiting on the northwest approaches to Kraybau at an altitude of 2,300 feet on the edge of a cloud cover, they received information on the approach of an enemy group. The patrol detected four FW-190s on an intersecting course, flying in pairs echeloned right. The Airacobras' sudden attack broke up the enemy formation. Taking advantage of the scattered clouds, the trailing enemy pair broke off the engagement with a hard right turn.

The remaining pair of Focke-Wulfs entered the fray. The lead FW-190 darted in under Lukantsev's P-39 just as he exited a turn and momentarily got on the Airacobra's tail. However, the interval between Lukantsev and the German was significant. Lukantsev immediately evaluated the situation. The enemy pilot had not opened fire on account of the excessive range and was in fact attempting to close. Lukantsev could not turn inside the Focke-Wulf because of the already tight radius of the turn. He radioed to Golberg, "I will lead the Focke-Wulf to you—shoot him!"

At this time Golberg was under the cloud skirt. He spotted the FW-190 in front of him in its turn. Without hesitation Golberg dove on it from above and in front at a shallow attack angle. He fired a long burst with all weapons from a range of 165 to 45 yards. The tracer stream cut across the German fighter's engine compartment, setting the aircraft on fire. Its pilot bailed out and was captured. He was a lieutenant, a deputy commander of the 2d Group, 76th Fighter Squadron.

Long-range search and support against unanticipated enemy attacks on our reconnaissance aircraft and hunters was accomplished by providing these pilots with reports regarding the presence of enemy aircraft in their airspace. The close merging of the efforts of the radar station and the P-39s greatly increased the effectiveness of the Airacobras in executing their assigned missions at altitudes of 4,920 to 6,560 feet and ranges of up to 18 to 21 miles into enemy-controlled territory. This coordination was especially important when there was no ground vectoring station in a particular sector of the front.

The hunters queried the division command post regarding the "working" zone. A division staff representative ordered the RUS-2 to inspect the sector in question and report by radio to the air crews if any enemy aircraft were detected. For its part, the radar station scanned the airspace over enemy territory periodically (every five to ten minutes) and was permitted to report anything it detected directly to the leader of the hunters or reconnaissance group, and at the same time to the division command post.[4]

This procedure emerged and was practiced in the closing months of the war. It permitted a high level of efficiency in the passing of radar intelligence to its consumers and to command and control organs. The latter could husband fighter resources more carefully and surge when necessary.

At the Western Border

There was hardly a sector of the front to which a fighter aviation division of the Reserve of the Supreme High Command was not sent. Only a short time ago the 9th Guards Fighter Division had arrived in Moldavia to be assigned to the 2d Ukrainian *Front*. Now it had been reassigned to the 1st Ukrainian *Front*. It was slated to participate in the Lvov–Sandomir offensive operation (13 July to 30 August 1944).

On 10 July the regiments were transferred to the airfield at Mikhaluvka. This was a new, relatively complicated operational direction in several respects: the deployment of aircraft; the difficult conditions of orientation to the new terrain; and unfavorable weather. Despite all of this, the aviators began flying combat missions in the second half of July. The following data confirm this: The thirty-one serviceable aircraft in 16th Regiment flew an average of 30.7 aircraft sorties during the month. The regiment's squadrons flew from 80 to 100 mission sorties on some days (101 on 13 July; 80 on 16 July; 90 on 21 July; and 89 on 22 July).[1] In twenty-seven flying days 100th Fighter Regiment pilots flew from 18 to 38 sorties in coverage of ground forces (Mikhail Petrov 18, Ivan Babak 22, Grigoriy Dolnikov 29, Vasiliy Bondarenko and Viktor Parshev 38 each).[2] Combat flight operations were intense on particular days. For example, a combat-ready aircraft and pilot flew on average 3.5 sorties on 14 July, and more than 2.6 sorties on 15, 16, 21, and 22 July.[3]

The activities of enemy air forces, in comparison with the recent battles around Jassy, were characterized by several peculiarities. Just as earlier, a pair of Bf-109s or foursome of FW-190s was dispatched to clear the airspace. These aircraft did not immediately engage the Airacobras but flew on the flank. Just before the arrival of their bombers the German fighters began their attacks, attempting to distract the P-39s to prevent their unhindered access to the bombers.

The Focke-Wulfs frequently were used for ground attack missions. They appeared in flights of from six to ten aircraft carrying external bomb loads. They dropped this ordnance on their targets by diving, making two or three passes. After each pass they gained altitude and resumed their position with the covering group.

Bombers appeared in large numbers, as a rule in the morning and evening. During the day they attempted to conduct strikes in small groups covered by four to six pairs of fighters. In bad weather, taking advantage of the overcast, the bombers appeared over the target in groups of up to fourteen aircraft without fighter escort.

The complicated geographical conditions of the mountainous and forested region of western Ukraine and the distinctive tactics of the enemy air forces required some adjustments to the planning for the use of Soviet fighter units. These adjustments were implemented on a squadron-by-squadron basis. A schedule of combat sorties was established on the basis of a division combat order. The group leader received his mission from the regiment commander. In turn, he passed specific mission instructions to each pilot in the squadron and flight. At the lowest levels the air crews carefully worked out their tactical actions in the coverage zone.

When it was necessary to redirect a patrol that was already in the air, this was accomplished by the ground vectoring station. Supplementary missions were transmitted to the group leader from the regiment command post.

As has already been noted, the mountainous and forested terrain and unfavorable weather conditions made it difficult to determine the location of aircraft. In the period from 13 to 31 July 1944, there were nine flying days, eight limited flying days (missions could be flown only in portions of these days), and two nonflying days. There were frequent losses of orientation.[4] To solve this problem the division established a beaconing station, however its operators lacked sufficient experience in its operation in the latter half of July. This situation improved considerably in August, by which time the beaconing station functioned well when the units of the 9th Guards Fighter Division were based at a given airfield for at least five or six days.

Mistakes were made in the displacement of the beaconing station to the area of the new landing fields. The beaconing station executed a movement to the assigned position in the daytime, when the regiments were conducting flight operations. Consequently, it was unable to render assistance to the pilots upon their loss of orientation. It was quickly realized that for greater effectiveness, the beaconing station should be repositioned at night.

Yet another practical conclusion was drawn on the basis of the experience of employing the beaconing station in the first three or four days of the operation. It was recognized as effective to have on duty at the beaconing station an aviation officer who was well versed in the tactics of fighter aircraft. He would be able to control the work of the beaconing station crew for issuing correct azimuths. On some days the enlisted personnel working the station gave incorrect directional responses to pilots requesting assistance, which led the Airacobras astray.[5] These deficiencies were rapidly corrected.

On 17 July the beaconing station was repositioned together with regiment advance teams who were departing for new airfields. The movement was conducted at night, without interruption in supporting flight operations. The issue of officers performing duty at the beaconing station was also resolved in a positive manner. It should be noted that any problem that arose in relation to the support of combat actions of the fighter units was resolved by the division staff and appropriate chiefs of services in the shortest possible time.

Air crews received the strictest instructions: do not contact the beaconing station without the utmost need; frequent, unnecessary appeals to the station's crew led to cluttering of the air waves. Since a crew might stray from its route at any moment, it might not be able to establish contact with the station. At the same time, instructions were issued that ground and airborne communications assets were to repeat azimuths issued by the station to disoriented fighter pilots. This would be of great assistance to them in finding their way home.

The forces of 1st Ukrainian *Front* began the breakthrough of the enemy's defenses on 13 July 1944. On this day the 9th Guards Fighter Division had the mission to cover the combat formations of 3d Guards Combined Arms Army with continuous patrolling in the areas of Bluduv, Svinyukhi, and Porvanche. An additional assigned mission was to support the forces of the 13th Army in the area of Gorokhov, Tsekhuv, Podbereze, and Stoyanuv.

All of the division's regiments provided from eight to fourteen aircraft from 0430 to 2130 daily for continuous support of these missions. The coverage zones were located some thirty-five to forty miles from the 9th Guards Fighter Division's airfields. The flight to and from the coverage zones took approximately twenty-five minutes in each direction. Therefore, during the mission planning it was recognized that each patrol could not loiter in the mission area for more than twenty-five minutes.[6]

When during the course of the offensive the distance to the coverage regions was extended beyond forty-two miles, the patrols could remain in the assigned coverage zones no longer than twenty minutes. Therefore, three patrols were required to provide one hour of continuous coverage over the battlefield. When the distance from the airfields to the coverage zone exceeded sixty miles, the number of patrols per hour was increased to four. This led to a situation in which the division, though operating at full-strength in aircraft and at maximum sortie rate, had to limit the size of its patrols to four to six aircraft. This force was clearly inadequate for successful accomplishment of the assigned missions.

During the morning and evening hours, when enemy air activity sharply increased, and particularly during the breakthrough of his initial defensive belt, the commitment of mobile groups, and the struggle for a bridgehead on the western bank of the San River, the patrols were increased to twelve to sixteen P-39s. This surge in the size of fighter groups, achieved by a reduction in group size during the day, was justified in practice. As a rule, these groups had to conduct aerial engagements with superior enemy forces, but even in these cases the Airacobra pilots inflicted significant losses on the enemy.[7]

The most intense days of the operation were 14, 15, 16, and 18 July, and particularly 14 and 16 July. Division units flew 297 combat sorties with a total flight time of 270 hours 23 minutes on 14 July, and 210 sorties and 165 hours 45 minutes on 16 July.

Taking increased enemy air activity into consideration, coverage was provided in groups of from twelve to sixteen aircraft at the beginning and end of the day. The combat formations of these groups were echeloned in two or three layers stacked from 2,000 to 6,560 to 11,485 feet.

The pilots of 9th Guards Fighter Division clearly made their presence known from the first days of combat actions in the Lvov–Sandomir operation. Well-armed aviators with a rich experience of the most fierce struggles with an enemy in any strength appeared on this sector of the Soviet–German front. The Airacobra pilots of the 9th Guards Fighter Division once again found themselves on a central and main axis of the Great Patriotic War. Along with the ground forces, the air crews took a giant step closer to the enemy's capital—Berlin.

On 14 July 1944, six Airacobras of the 16th Guards Fighter Regiment were covering ground forces in the zone over Svinyukhi and Bluduv. The weather permitted limited flight operations, with scattered cumulus clouds, haze, and visibility of 1 to 1.2 miles. The combat formation was a foursome (leader Viniamin Tsvetkov, wingmen Viktor Zherdev, Mikhail Buzuev, and Nikolay Kudinov) and a pair of hunters (regiment commander Boris Glinka and his wingman Nikolay Kudrya).

The group flew out to the coverage area, where they observed four Bf-109s whose apparent mission was to clear out the airspace. Unfortunately, the cloud cover limited visibility. In these conditions the Soviet pilots would have to be extremely attentive and vigilant. They strictly observed the rule of "all-round observation," each one of them without exception monitoring the situation in the zone and on all the approaches to it. But the leader of the group and all its participants committed an inexcusable blunder. It turned out that the enemy had a two-tiered combat formation, the lower foursome of which was in sight, and the upper pair (cover, or "hunters") of which were hidden close by in the clouds.

Having spotted the enemy, Major Glinka and his wingman dove in the attack. All the aviators' attention at this time was concentrated on the targets that had been selected for destruction. The wingman Nikolay Kudrya in his turn made an error in covering his commander. He was following a short distance behind Glinka, hoping to catch one of the "bandits" himself with fire. In the limited visibility, according to veterans, Nikolay should have been positioned to the left or right rear of his leader at a distance of 220 to 330 yards. Then he would have been able to block the path of the attacking Messerschmitt.

The enemy had fooled our pilots. At the moment of Boris Glinka's attack a pair of Messerschmitts launched their own strike on the regiment commander from out of the sun. Kudrya had neither the time nor the maneuver space to prevent disaster. Glinka's Airacobra was set on fire, the pilot was wounded, and he bailed out. He landed in Soviet-occupied territory and was transported to the hospital.[8]

Courage and bravery are very important in combat, but they are futile in the absence of reasoned actions. An example of the union of these three factors is an engagement with the enemy in the early evening hours (1850 to 1955) of 15 July by twelve Airacobras of the 100th Guards Fighter Regiment. The deputy commander of 9th Guards Fighter Division, Guards Lieutenant Colonel Leonid Goreglyad, was in command of this group. The patrol was orbiting over an area six miles east of Gorokhov and Stoyanuv at altitudes from 9,845 to 10,500 feet. The ground vectoring station of the commander of 7th Fighter Corps broadcast information regarding the approach of up to forty enemy bombers escorted by no fewer than twenty Focke-Wulfs. The armada of Ju-87s was flying at an altitude of 4,760 feet, with the FW-190s circling to the right and left above it. From this position the enemy bombers would not have to waste time repositioning for their bomb runs. The bombers were beginning to work their targets directly from their approach route.

Goreglyad's group took good advantage of the enemy's method of operation. Its significant altitude advantage over the enemy permitted the group to select the best attack position (out of the sun) and, in launching their "eagle strikes," achieve the maximum speed of the Airacobras not through engine revolutions but with the aid of gravity. These two advantages of altitude and speed played an important role in the engagement with a superior enemy force.

The group leader acted appropriately in the developing situation. He divided his flight into two powerful subgroups, six Airacobras in each. "Beat the enemy not with extended fingers, but with a tightly closed fist." The results were not long in coming. The strike group of six Airacobras under Goreglyad's command dove on the diving Stukas, whose formation was in a wedge. This facilitated a simultaneous attack on a broad front and the massing of cannon and machine-gun fires. Almost all of the components of Pokryshkin's "formula of terror" were present.

Goreglyad shot up a Ju-87 from above and behind at a range of eighty to forty-five yards. He pulled his P-39 up into a steep climb and then turned 180 degrees for a second pass, again in the rear. A second bomber fell to his guns. While Goreglyad's formation was attacking the bombers, the escorting Focke-Wulfs attacked the subgroup of Guards Lieutenant Colonel Vladimir Bobrov.

Although the dive bombers were easy prey, the situation required that Goreglyad and his group come to the aid of their comrades.

Goreglyad commanded his subordinates, "Right turn ninety degrees! Attack the Focke-Wulfs!" With an upward climbing maneuver the deputy division commander's subordinates linked up with Bobrov's six aircraft. The enemy clearly had not counted on so rapid a reaction from the Airacobra pilots who were engaging the Ju-87s. Perhaps he supposed that the Airacobra pilots would stay with the Stukas until the end of the engagement. Goreglyad attacked and set one FW-190 on fire. In a brief, intense period the Soviet pilot had destroyed three enemy aircraft (two bombers and one fighter). This was an excellent example of maximum employment of positional superiority over the enemy, skillful actions of pilots, and the maneuverability of the P-39.

The pilots of Bobrov's group also displayed good offensive tactics. They conducted the first attack on the bombers. Bobrov poured a heavy burst into the cockpit of a bomber from a range of 165 to 110 yards. It turned over and dropped toward the earth like a stone. The other pilots of Bobrov's group did not lag behind their commander. Guards Lieutenant Grigoriy Turyanskiy caught a Ju-87 from below and behind. Bobrov achieved a "double" when he sent a second Stuka to its final resting place.

Guards Lieutenant Nikolay Veretennikov (Goreglyad's wingman) also shot down a Ju-87 with a top attack. When Veretennikov pulled out of his attack, his P-39 passed through the tracer stream of the rear gunner of another bomber. The Airacobra's right wing was damaged and the motor began to labor. Veretennikov was wounded in the left shoulder. Forced to disengage, he belly-landed his Airacobra with difficulty and was carried to a hospital. Veretennikov returned to the regiment on 16 August, after recuperation.[9]

The fervor of the attack by Bobrov's subgroup continued. Guards Junior Lieutenants Genadiy Voroshilov and Ivan Mikhalin shot down a bomber and a fighter, respectively. The pair of Guards Captain Aleksandr Rumm and Junior Lieutenant Iosif Grafin displayed a particularly high level of action and persistence in the engagement. Guards Lieutenant Colonel Goreglyad encouraged his pilots for their outstanding performance.[10]

Their fuel was running low. The decision was made to disengage and the command ("33") was issued over the radio. The enemy bombers had been dispersed and were fleeing westward singly and in groups. The escort fighters prevented pursuit by the Airacobras through defensive maneuvering. The Airacobra pilots did not make a concerted effort in this vein, having only sufficient fuel in their tanks to return to their own airfields. Just to be sure, the deputy division commander gave an order forbidding any pilot from engaging in pursuit of the retreating enemy aircraft.

Close cooperation between the two subgroups and the pairs within them, the exceptional bravery of each participant in the battle, and the maximum employment of the capabilities of the fighters and their armaments yielded stunning results. Together they had destroyed six Ju-87s and two FW-190s with the loss of a single P-39.[11]

An exceptionally large and successful air battle was fought on the afternoon of 16 July 1944. Twelve Airacobras of 16th Guards Fighter Regiment engaged sixty Ju-87s and four Hs-129s escorted by eight FW-190s. The enemy bombers were formed in columns of nine and the escorting fighters were in two wedges of four.

Several aspects to this engagement made it noteworthy. The commander of the 9th Guards Fighter Division, Guards Lieutenant Colonel Aleksandr Pokryshkin, was a participant. It was an explosive engagement, literally and figuratively, from start to finish: in the rapidity with which the events unfolded and in the tempo of the Soviet pilots' attacks—one immediately following the other, depriving the enemy of freedom of maneuver. The attacks were launched simultaneously and successively from various directions, which led to dissipation of the enemy's attention and effort. The group consisted of the most experienced aerial warriors (three Twice Heroes of the Soviet Union, Aleksandr Pokryshkin, Grigoriy Rechkalov, and Aleksandr Klubov, and one Hero of the Soviet Union, Andrey Trud). The remaining participants were battle-tested. Later the division's pilots recalled this engagement as the "battle of aces."

At 1940 a group of P-39s under the command of Guards Captain Grigoriy Rechkalov sortied to cover the cavalry-mechanized group of General Viktor Baranov. The patrol's combat formation consisted of three subgroups (four fighters in each). Captain Rechkalov was the leader of the strike foursome, Andrey Trud led the support subgroup, and Aleksandr Pokryshkin led the top cover subgroup. The "bookshelf" was extended upward with a vertical spacing of 1,310 to 1,640 feet between the first and second layers and 1,970 to 2,300 feet between the second and third layers.

In employing this formation the division commander ensured for his subordinates complete freedom of action upon encountering the enemy and took upon himself the role of supporting their actions. At the same time, it permitted Pokryshkin, within recognized limits (not violating the multitiered structure of the formation), to act independently. Most of all, he could lead his own subordinates to the most rapid reinforcement of the other two groups in the course of the battle.

At the end of the patrol (at approximately 2010), in the area of Sushko, the Airacobra pilots observed an approaching group of enemy bombers flying at an altitude approximately 5,000 feet below their own. The enemy fighter escort was positioned in pairs 2,300 to 2,625 feet above the bombers. Upon detecting the Airacobras, the Germans reformed into a single file and then began to circle, dropping their ordnance without aim.

Taking advantage of their favorable start positions, the P-39 strike and cover subgroups simultaneously rushed into the attack on the bombers. Andrey Trud's foursome engaged the Focke-Wulfs. The Airacobra pilots were operating by a method that had been proven in previous combat: a lightning strike against all (or a large portion) of the enemy forces to tie them down in combat and deprive them of the ability to maneuver.

Pokryshkin's foursome launched a frontal attack from above on the bombers that had formed the defensive circle. His Airacobras burst inside their combat formation and concentrated fire from close range (80 to 55 yards) at two or three enemy aircraft. Then with a high-speed turn they departed the enemy "carousel" and struck it again from another direction. In four passes Pokryshkin shot down an Hs-129 and Turchenko an FW-190. On the last pass the division commander shot down his second aircraft, a Ju-87, with a shallow attack angle from a range of 110 to 80 yards.

The enemy fighters attempted to catch the P-39s in their sights at the moment the Airacobras pulled out of the circle. But Pokryshkin fooled the enemy each time, leading his subordinates to the side of the circle away from the Focke-Wulfs.

Rechkalov's strike group was attacking the second group of nine enemy bombers, who also had formed a defensive circle. They attacked from below and behind, penetrating the enemy formation from the inside. With tracer streams from all guns, firing from close range,

Senior Lieutenant Ivan Vakhnenko, Junior Lieutenant Andrey Ivanov, and Captain Grigoriy Rechkalov each increased their personal score of destroyed enemy aircraft.

Andrey Trud's foursome was fully engaged in the battle when it "crossed fiery swords" with the covering fighters. The enemy's two-times superiority did not frighten or deter the pilots of this group. They managed to prevent the FW-190s from reaching the patrol's main body, which was in turn engaging the bombers. The Luftwaffe pilots were thus engaged on "two fronts."

Each side suffered losses in this lopsided battle: Trud sent one Focke-Wulf careening to the earth, while the Germans downed the Airacobra of Guards Senior Lieutenant Aleksandr Ivashko with a lucky shot. The seriously wounded pilot managed to execute a belly landing, and though he was taken to a hospital, he died a short time later.[12]

Because of the decisive and organized actions of Rechkalov's group, the enemy suffered telling losses: seven Ju-87s, one Hs-129, and two FW-190s were destroyed and one Focke-Wulf was damaged.[13]

At the postflight debriefing of this combat action the Airacobra pilots' attention was focused on the issues whose resolution had secured this great success: careful preparation for the assigned mission; effective construction of the patrol's combat formation; timely adoption of a rational decision for a rapid attack against almost the entire enemy armada (in depth and altitude); and the compact and combined actions of the foursomes and pairs in each subgroup.

The Airacobra pilots had disrupted the enemy's plan by preventing him from reaching his bombing target. He was forced to drop his ordnance load without aim and, after suffering great losses, to turn back.

Airacobra pilots did not always manage to fight their air battles so successfully. An example of insufficient organization occurred in an aerial engagement between seven Airacobras of the 16th Guards Fighter Regiment and seventy Ju-87s, six Bf-109s, and eighteen FW-190s on 25 July. The enemy had unquestioned numerical superiority. The patrol of P-39s was providing cover over river crossing sites in the area of Nelepkovitse and Yaroslav from 1950 to 2045 on that day. It was later discovered that this large force of enemy aircraft was only the first echelon. Several miles west of the engagement area was another similar force of enemy bombers moving in the same direction.

In the unfolding situation Guards Captain Pavel Eremin should have directed his subordinates to undertake defensive actions while he immediately requested assistance. He did not do this. Without regard for the unfavorable odds, the Airacobra pilots rushed into battle with the dense formation of enemy aircraft. Eremin's flight executed its first attack from the front, without success. They immediately turned around to attempt a second pass, this time at the rear of the enemy formation. They managed to set one Ju-87 on fire. A second Stuka went down in a third pass from the rear. Attacking from behind and below, the pair of Lieutenant Ivan Onishchenko and Junior Lieutenant Mikhail Novikov shot down two bombers. The third pair of P-39s attacked from above and behind. Lieutenant Viktor Nikitin set an FW-190 on fire.

The advantage of surprise achieved by the ill-considered actions of our handful of fighters was exhausted in just a few moments. The initiative then passed over to the German pilots, who were aided in their countermeasures by the dispersion of Eremin's formation in frontage and height. The battle assumed a piecemeal nature, with each pair of Soviet fighters isolated and engaged by a superior enemy force. Two FW-190s attacked Nikitin. Their fires damaged his tail assembly and his aircraft began to fall, out of control. The lieutenant bailed out of his Airacobra and landed in enemy-held territory. Fortunately, he touched down near a patch of woods and was able to hide for a day until the arrival of advancing Soviet troops.

Misfortune awaited yet another Airacobra pilot, Junior Lieutenant German Babkin. An FW-190 attacked him in a turn and his oil tank was punctured. The temperature of his engine quickly shot up to a critical level. He belly-landed his P-39 and was delivered back to the airfield unhurt.

The engagement was fought in a disorganized manner for a large portion of its duration. During the attack on both the bombers and fighters Eremin's group was dispersed in pairs whose actions were uncoordinated. The enemy's numerical superiority prevented the patrol from disengaging in an organized fashion, and the Soviet pilots straggled back to their airfield.

The greatest mistake of the patrol's commander was that he rushed into the first attack without requesting assistance from the regimental command post.[14] The battle was over quickly. The ground vectoring station was working with other groups and did not keep good track of Eremin's seven aircraft.

A Gift from the Bell Factory

The battlefield performance of combat equipment that was delivered to the Soviet Union through Lend-Lease was of interest not only to our own technical specialists but also to the American firms that produced the equipment. I recall that there were American factory representatives in the Soviet mechanized corps equipped with Sherman tanks in which I served. While researching in the archives of aviation units, I did not find any evidence of similar representatives. There may be such evidence in the archives of the air army staffs. Detailed reports concerning various deficiencies, shipping damage, and factory defects of the Airacobras were sent to this level of command and control. It was common knowledge that the governments of the anti-Hitler coalition had diplomatic missions in Moscow.

But by one means or another, Bell Aircraft Corporation received reports and complaints on the P-39 regarding various modifications, performance problems with components of the aircraft, the portions of the fuselage that were subject to deformation when overstressed, and so on.

The names of the pilots who fought the Germans with the Airacobras was no secret either. The American mission in Moscow had detailed information regarding these men. These names were made available by the headquarters of the Soviet Army Air Force at the request of the mission staff.

I raise this issue in order to introduce a single, very interesting document preserved in the archival files of 9th Guards Fighter Division. This document is dated 6 October 1944, and reads as follows:

The president of the Bell firm (USA), which produces the Airacobra aircraft, has awarded engraved watches with congratulatory letters signed in English to Three Times Hero of the Soviet Union Guards Colonel Pokryshkin, A. I.; Twice Heroes of the Soviet Union Guards Major Glinka, D. B., and Guards Captain Rechkalov, G. A.; Heroes of the Soviet Union Guards Major Glinka, B. B., Guards Major Vishnevetskiy, K. G., Guards Captain Klubov, A. F., Guards Senior Lieutenants Babak, I. I., and Trud, A. I., and Guards Captain Komelkov, M. S. (all of whom had shot down twenty or more enemy aircraft as of 24 June 1944 while flying the Airacobra).[1]

These valuable gifts found their way to the aviators at the front. They were presented to them by the commander of the 2d Air Army, General Stepan Krasovskiy. Unfortunately, Major Konstantin Grigorevich Vishnevetskiy, the deputy commander of 9th Guards Fighter Division for aerial gunnery service, never learned of this unusual gift from our ally in a common struggle. On 30 July 1944 he was representing the 9th Guards Fighter Division with the ground troops and perished in an enemy air raid. The division command arranged for this watch to be presented to his family.

The deputy commander for aerial gunnery service of the 16th Guards Fighter Regiment, Guards Captain Aleksandr Fedorovich Klubov, did not check the time for too long on his Bell watch. A freak accident took the life of this fearless ace on Turen airfield. He deserves several words regarding the last day of his life at the front. On 1 November 1944, Guards Captain Klubov was conducting a training flight on the La-7, a fighter that was unfamiliar to him and that he had not yet mastered. He did not fully extend the flaps while landing. The aircraft, carrying excessive speed, careened past the end of the runway and flipped over when one of its wheels dug into the soft dirt. The aircraft broke up and the pilot was killed.[2]

This entire incident occurred in full view of many of Klubov's comrades. Many rushed to his aid, including the division commander, Aleksandr Pokryshkin. Despite the frantic efforts of a doctor to save him, Klubov died in Pokryshkin's arms next to his aircraft.[3] He was buried in Lvov on the Hill of Glory. About six weeks after the conclusion of the war, an order was published by the Presidium of the USSR Supreme Soviet. Aleksandr Klubov was awarded his second gold Hero of the Soviet Union star, posthumously.[4]

After the death of Aleksandr Pokryshkin in 1985, his widow Maria placed his "Bell" watch in the Central Museum of the Soviet (now Russian) Army in Moscow, where it remains on display to this day.

Flights from the Autobahn

Between 1 and 31 March 1945, 9th Guards Fighter Division, then assigned to the 2d Air Army (commanded by General Stepan Krasovskiy), participated in the Upper Silesia offensive operation of the 1st Ukrainian *Front*. The division's mission was to provide coverage for formations of the 53d Combined Arms and 3d Guards Tank Armies.

With the capture by the advancing forces of Buntslau, an airfield was found and made ready for reception of aircraft at Aslau (eight miles northeast of Buntslau). This airfield had hangars and aprons, but no suitable takeoff and landing strip. The above-freezing temperatures and thawing soil made the existing grass field unusable for flight operations. A search for other airfields or landing strips in the area was unsuccessful.

A stretch of the Berlin–Breslau autobahn that passed near the Aslau airfield attracted the attention of our aviators as a possible substitute runway for the Airacobras. The division commander, Guards Colonel Aleksandr Pokryshkin, made the unusual decision to convert a portion of this roadway into a takeoff and landing strip. This novel solution to the landing field problem had never been tried before, though I understand that later, during the Cold War, many autobahns in the western zone of Germany were designed and prepared for use as emergency airfields.[1]

Although the combat actions of the squadrons of two regiments (16th and 104th Guards Fighter Regiments) continued from this hastily prepared concrete strip into the second half of April 1945, the most intense period of use was the first week of March. Over the course of approximately six weeks, 334 aircraft sorties were launched from this location that resulted in fourteen aerial engagements. Only two of these engagements did not result in downed enemy aircraft.

The heavy moisture content of the soil around the concrete strip and powerful wind gusts (for example, up to thirty-six mph on 2 March) that blew across the roadway significantly complicated, and at times altogether prevented, combat operations of the division's regiments.[2]

On 1 March 1945 the division's regiments had the following aircraft strengths: 16th Guards, thirty Airacobras; 104th Guards, twenty-seven Airacobras; and 100th Guards, thirty Airacobras, for a total of eighty-seven aircraft. Of the division's 114 available pilots, 96 were considered combat-ready. An additional 6 pilots had sufficient combat experience but had recently returned from hospitalization for wounds and required some refresher training.[3]

The 9th Guards Fighter Division pilots had to conduct extremely intense, but at the same time relatively successful air battles on 3 and 7 March. On 3 March, sixty of the planned sixty-eight sorties were flown with good results. The cancellations resulted from poor flying weather conditions. Four aerial engagements occurred on that day in which five enemy aircraft were destroyed with the loss of a single Airacobra.

A group of eight P-39s of the 104th Guards Fighter Regiment sortied under the command of Guards Captain Mikhail Komelkov. The enemy force they encountered consisted of two Bf-109s and six FW-190s, a force equal in size to the Soviet flight. Thanks to close coordination between the pairs, the good use of signals from the ground vectoring station, and excellent organization of the battle, the Airacobra pilots downed three enemy fighters (one Messerschmitt and two Focke-Wulfs) without any losses.

On 7 March the 9th Guards Division pilots flew forty-nine of fifty-eight planned combat sorties, poor weather again leading to flight cancellations. Three enemy aircraft were shot down with no losses on our side in three aerial engagements conducted on that day. Once again the aviators of 104th Guards Fighter Regiment were successful. Six P-39s, led by Guards Major Aleksandr Polukhin, clashed with the same number of enemy fighters. Polukhin had properly organized his search for the enemy: a pair of hunters flying under the cloud cover spotted the enemy fighters and quickly reported to the group commander. A rapid and surprise attack brought good success: three "bandits" did not return to their airfield. Our patrol had no losses.

On the first day the autobahn was used as a landing strip, ten aircraft were temporarily put out of commission with punctured nose wheel and main landing gear tires. Personnel of the 299th Airfield Service Battalion, the unit responsible for preparation of the landing strip, had not cleaned the concrete of small, sharp pieces of rock and gravel. The division staff officers bore a share of the responsibility for having failed to ensure the readiness of the highway for use as a runway.

On the morning of 8 March the enemy began an offensive in two sectors (2.4 miles south of Kozel and 3.6 miles north of Ratibor) with the forces of two infantry divisions, one mountain infantry division, and a mechanized division, supported by a regiment of assault guns and thirty-five tanks. His intention was to push our formations back to the east bank of the Oder River.

Heavy fighting continued throughout the entire day. The enemy made minor headway on some axes and was able to compress some of the defending units. By 1800 the battle had ebbed and the sides dug in and improved positions where they stood. The observation post of the 9th Guards Fighter Division was deployed with the command post of the 52d Army in an effort to ensure continuous coordination with the ground units. An RUS-2 radar set and a ground vectoring station were placed at this observation post with direct wire communications with the division headquarters. All this facilitated the mission to cover the defending forces and conduct aerial reconnaissance to a significant depth of the enemy dispositions.

After some regrouping, on 15 March following an artillery and air preparation the left flank of the 1st Ukrainian *Front* (21st, 4th Tank, and 52d Armies and 7th Mechanized Corps) went over to the offensive on the Nesse–Neustadt axis. The 6th Combined Arms Army attacked westward from the area south of Kozel. Having broken through the enemy defense and successfully advanced, on 18 March Soviet formations encircled a large grouping of German forces southwest of Opeln and over the next two days liquidated this force. Following this success the ground forces of 1st Ukrainian *Front* went into an operational pause, during which they prepared for a new operation.

The air battles did not let up, though, even for a day. As before, the RUS-2 apparatus remained at the disposal of the commander of 9th Guards Fighter Division. It was used with great success on 31 March. At 1215 on that day, the radar detected a large group of enemy aircraft some twelve to fifteen miles southwest of Lauben, heading east. Based on this report, at 1220 the on-alert flight of 100th Guards Regiment sortied from the autobahn to engage this enemy force and a radio warning went out to a pair of hunters from 104th Guards Regiment, led by Guards Lieutenant Nikolay Anishchenko. This pair of hunters was able to execute a surprise attack on a group of fourteen FW-190s, while the on-alert patrol engaged the other enemy group of twenty FW-190s. All the enemy fighters were carrying external bombs for attacking our ground forces. The Airacobra of Guards Senior Sergeant Konstantin Panov (100th Guards Regiment) did not return from this flight.[4]

In this late period of the war the aviators of the 9th Guards Fighter Division encountered and successfully overcame still another genuine problem. They helped substantially to expand the Airacobra's combat capabilities. Having witnessed the Germans' successful employment of the FW-190 in the ground-attack role, the 9th Guards pilots were tasked to attempt the same with the P-39. The first step in this direction was taken on 23 March, when a pair of hunters sortied, each carrying a single FAB-100 [100-kilogram fragmentation bomb]. After that date, the majority of P-39 hunters and reconnaissance aircraft sortied carrying a bomb and used it against ground targets.

Careful preparation of both the aircraft and pilots was required, with some preliminary practice in dropping bombs on a training range. The first step was to design the bomb rack and attach it to the aircraft. When this device had been successfully tested, the pilots studied the behavior of the P-39 in the dive-bomber role. Guards Colonel Aleksandr Pokryshkin flew some of the test flights himself, after which he personally instructed his air crews in the proper techniques of bomb release from the Airacobra. The lack of dummy bombs and the limited availability of service ordnance did not allow for prolonged preliminary training on a test range. A number of pilots had their first experience in this new role directly against enemy targets.

The first combat tests, conducted on 23 March as part of a free hunt mission, yielded poor results. The principal cause of the ineffective bombing was the high release altitude (9,845 to 11,845 feet) and the aircraft pullout after bomb release (7,220 to 8,200 feet). In some instances the FAB-100 was dropped during the pullout from the dive or even afterward. On this first day of dive bombing with the P-39, some of the ordnance fell as far as 1.2 miles from the aimpoint.

As a result of an analysis of these mistakes and discussion with all of the air crews, the effectiveness of bombing attacks increased almost daily. Once they had become convinced of the safety of dive bombing (some of them feared the bomb would fall into their own propeller), pilots significantly lowered the altitude at which they began and pulled out of their dive and increased the steepness of the dive. They learned to release the bomb before pulling the P-39 out of the dive, which brought success in this new method in the closing days of March 1945.

On 25 March, a pair of fighters from the 16th Guards Fighter Regiment, led by Guards Major Pavel Eremin, were flying a reconnaissance mission in the area of Lauban, Fridland, and Levenberg from 1520 to 1605. Each aircraft was carrying an FAB-100. Flying at an altitude of 8,200 feet, the Airacobras encountered four Bf-109s and avoided contact by gaining altitude and flying toward the sun. The pair leader observed a group of structures that resembled supply dumps north of the town of Lauban and decided to attempt to drop his bomb. Eremin took his P-39 up to an altitude of 9,845 feet and with a left turn put his Airacobra into a sixty-degree dive on the target. Simultaneously he ordered his wingman, Guards Lieutenant Petr Ketovo, to fall in behind him and drop his own bomb on the same target. They released their bombs at 4,920 feet and pulled out. Coming out of their dives, the pair observed the direct hit of Eremin's bomb on one of the buildings. A fire started that several minutes later led to a large explosion. The wingman's bomb sailed over the target and caused no damage. Having heard the explosion and seen enormous columns of smoke from a distance of nine miles, ground forces confirmed the destruction of an ammunition dump.[5]

Two Airacobras of the 16th Guards Fighter Regiment, under the command of Guards Senior Lieutenant Vasiliy Bondarenko, were conducting a free hunt in the area of Miskau, Shpremberg, and Richan from 1610 to 1735 on 31 March. They crossed the front line at an altitude of 11,485 feet and continued their flight at that altitude. In an opening through the clouds on the eastern outskirts of Konsdorf (west of Shtremberg) they observed an enemy airfield on which there were approximately fifty twin-engined and single-engined aircraft. Approaching from the southwest, the hunters re-formed into a column, one aircraft 550 yards behind the other. They dove at an angle of sixty to seventy degrees and released their bombs at 6,560 feet at the ramp and taxiways.

Coming out of their dive and having regained altitude back up to the base of the clouds, Bondarenko brought his pair around to inspect the results of their strike. They observed that a large explosion had occurred in the area of the hangars, starting a raging fire. The column of smoke from the explosion and fire already reached up to 3,280 feet.

The conclusion drawn from these experiences was that the best altitude for a fighter to enter a dive for bombing was 6,560 to 4,920 feet. The FAB-100 bomb should be dropped at an altitude on the order of 3,280 to 1,970 feet, with the Airacobra in a fifty-to-seventy-degree dive. If these parameters were observed, the speed of the aircraft upon pulling out of the dive would be 300 to 320 miles per hour and the bomb would fall exactly on the aimpoint.

In poor weather conditions the dive had to begin at altitudes below 4,920 feet and the ordnance dropped so that the aircraft could pull out of the dive no lower than 985 feet. Depending on the altitude at the start point of the dive, the pilot sought to reduce the angle of the dive to a minimum of thirty degrees.[6]

A number of measures were taken from the first day of flight operations on the autobahn to conceal the exact location of the landing strip. Tractors were used to pull several German gliders forward. When all the Airacobras were on the ground and concealed, these gliders were towed out onto the "runway." The P-39s, meanwhile, were quickly taxied into the woods and carefully camouflaged. Trucks were periodically driven along the autobahn to make it look like a normal road.

The enemy looked for the airfield from which the Airacobras were operating for more than two weeks and did not find it. On one March morning a Messerschmitt appeared above the airfield. The aircraft was alone and was having some kind of problem. It did not circle but came straight in to make a low-level inspection of the landing strip. The Airacobra pilots then realized that the German pilot was familiar with this site and, seeing five German gliders parked on the edge of the taxiway, suspected nothing. Pokryshkin's men did nothing to scare off this German fighter, and it landed. They disarmed the pilot the moment his aircraft stopped moving and quickly sent the captured prisoner off to the air army headquarters for interrogation.

The activeness of the Airacobras during the battles on the approaches to Gerlits (mid-March to early April) forced the German command to search more energetically for our concealed front-line airfield. On one occasion an enemy diversionary who had been inserted by parachute was captured outside the Aslau airfield. In the course of his interrogation it did not take long to learn that the purpose of his insertion was to reconnoiter the area of the P-39s' landing fields.

On 18 March 1945 a pair of P-39s flown by Guards Captain Aleksey Lukantsev and Lieutenant Yuriy Golberg was flying cover over the autobahn. Golberg was a relatively inexperienced combat pilot who had only a few engagements under his belt. The weather conditions were somewhat complex, with low cloud cover and frequent rain showers. The pair was patrolling back and forth over the airfield under the bottom edge of the overcast (altitude 2,625 to 3,280 feet). Suddenly six FW-190s dove through a break in the clouds. They did not spot our patrol. Their primary mission, as it later became clear, was to search for the unknown airfield.

The Airacobras attacked rapidly from above. From the opening shots the battle was exceptionally fierce. The left-flank Focke-Wulf went down, shot by Lukantsev. The enemy's superiority made him extremely aggressive. At one moment in the battle the Airacobra leader and his wingman became widely separated. Golberg noticed that Lukantsev, who was attacking his next FW-190, did not see the enemy fighter that was closing up on him from behind. In another moment or two this Focke-Wulf's guns would hurl a deadly portion of lead.

Yuriy, executing an unbelievable maneuver (he later failed in an attempt to repeat it), came out below the Focke-Wulf on a closing course and opened fire from a range of 110 yards. His cannon tracer was precise. The enemy aircraft exploded in mid-air and its pilot was thrown clear of the wreckage like a sack. He opened his parachute and landed on the airfield that he was supposed to be reconnoitering. The prisoner turned out to be ace Hauptmann Bruno Borm, who had been awarded the Iron Cross and had nine American Flying Fortresses and several British fighters to his credit. This was his first and last sortie on the Soviet–German front. This Luftwaffe pilot could not believe that a young Soviet pilot had shot him down, stating, "Only Pokryshkin could have downed me." But when Golberg showed the maneuver of his own and the enemy aircraft with hand motions, the German hung his head. This was the one!

Enemy air reconnaissance later began to appear over Aslau with more regularity. They were interested in the intensive movement along the highway and, of course, were still looking for the hated "secret" airstrip. They finally found it. On 7 April (from 1635 to 1640) two

He-111s and six FW-190s from behind some clouds and from an altitude of 9,845 to 11,485 feet made a bombing attack on Aslau airfield. They dropped approximately thirty bombs on the hangars, the P-39 parking ramp, autobahn landing strip, and local air defense artillery positions. The bombing was effective. The 16th and 100th Guards Regiments lost four damaged P-39s each; in the 104th Guards Regiment one Airacobra was set on fire and nine others received considerable damage from flying shrapnel. Three of the nine required significant repair effort.

Senior Lieutenant Viniamin Tsvetkov, a squadron commander in the 104th Guards Regiment, was mortally wounded. The chief of PARM-1, Senior Technical Lieutenant Yakov Boldyrev, was also killed, and Technical Lieutenant Nikolay Markitanov was wounded.[7]

Two Airacobras were in the air during the air raid. Lieutenants Boris Likhonos and Vyacheslav Berezkin were conducting gunnery training. Likhonos received the order to attack the enemy fighters that were bombing the airfield. Likhonos, having broken through the overcast, observed four FW-190s departing to the southwest. He pursued the enemy aircraft and closed to within firing range from above and behind. The trailing Focke-Wulf began trailing smoke but continued to hold its previous course, albeit losing altitude. Due to a shortage of ammunition in their feed trays, the Airacobra pilots broke off the pursuit. According to the air observations of Vyacheslav Berezkin and the pilots of 16th Guards Regiment from the ground, it was determined that the damaged FW-190 fell burning to the earth some nine to eleven miles southwest of Aslau.[8] From this unlucky day forward a stronger fighter patrol was maintained continuously over the airfield. As a rule, the enemy suffered losses on the way to Aslau and his plans to attack the runway on the autobahn were disrupted.

At noon on 10 April, a flight led by Guards Senior Lieutenant Aleksandr Torbeev (16th Guards Regiment) was covering the division basing area. They were flying back and forth in the "pendulum" manner at altitudes from 9,845 to 16,400 feet. The enemy was employing a somewhat new tactical method. His aircraft were working in two groups. One, orbiting at altitudes from 9,845 to 13,125 feet, had the mission to attract the Airacobras' attention and lure them off to the side. At the same time, the second group, flying much lower, at 2,625 to 4,920 feet, attempted to break through to their intended targets and attack them with bombs.

In connection with this, the commander of 9th Guards Fighter Division ordered that strengthened patrols of two subgroups be sent out for airfield coverage. The first subgroup was to attack the enemy patrols, engage them in battle, and deprive them of the opportunity for free maneuver during the engagement. The second subgroup was to be operating at altitudes of 4,920 to 6,560 feet, no higher. Its primary mission was to destroy the enemy bombers and ground-attack fighters. Aircraft from this group were categorically forbidden to enter the fray with enemy aircraft operating at higher altitudes.[9]

At the conclusion of a patrol mission in the Buntslau area, a group of Airacobras led by Aleksandr Torbeev spotted six FW-190s flying below and to their right, heading east. Four of them were flying at 9,845 feet in a right echelon. A pair of Focke-Wulfs followed behind them some 1,640 feet higher. Having seen our P-39s, the Germans turned to the left and dropped their ordnance aimlessly northwest of Aslau. At this moment the group leader's pair was closest to the enemy aircraft. Aleksandr Torbeev ordered his wingmen Ivan Vakhnenko and Nikolay Koryavin to cover him. He attacked the third enemy pair from the right and above, without success.

A mistake committed several minutes earlier now came to bear. Our patrol had not utilized the overcast for concealment. This had permitted the German pilots to spot them early, jettison their bombs, and prepare themselves psychologically for battle. This was no small advantage in an aerial engagement.

The first miss did not dishearten the Airacobra pilots. Having turned around 180 degrees, Torbeev managed to get directly behind the same pair of FW-190s. He sent one of them to the earth with a burst of fire from a range of 110 to 65 yards. The pilot bailed out and was captured. Vakhnenko and his wingman attacked the right-flank pair of Focke-Wulfs, which immediately dove into the overcast. In the unfolding situation (almost equal forces and disruption of the enemy bombing of Aslau airfield) the enemy fighters abstained from aerial combat and sped away into the upper layer of clouds.[10]

Battles were being fought from morning to evening. The German sky was ablaze and the ground shook from bomb strikes and massed artillery fires. The war had arrived at German towns and villages. In a single combat mission a group of six Airacobras from the 100th Guards Fighter Regiment, led by Guards Major Dmitriy Glinka, fought three extremely intense and successful engagements on 18 April. The time of their mission was 1320 to 1435, in the area of Shtromberg. Flying at an altitude of 8,200 feet, the group spotted twelve Focke-Wulf 190s flying below them, covered by four Bf-109s. The enemy aircraft were attacking Soviet ground troops.

Glinka ordered all the patrol's aircraft to attack the enemy simultaneously. Leading the charge, Glinka burst into the circle of Focke-Wulfs and from the inside, attacking from above and the right, fired rounds into one of the "bandits." The FW-190, attempting to evade the fire, twisted sharply and then broke into a spin. It did not recover and spun all the way to the earth. Despite their numerical superiority, the Germans did not accept battle. Singly and in pairs, they stopped their bombing and raced back toward their own airfield at treetop level.

Recovering from the attack and having gained altitude, Glinka's group received a report from the ground vectoring station that ten FW-190s were bombing ground troops in an area 1.2 to 1.8 miles north of Shtromberg. The celebrated ace quickly led his subordinates to that area. Upon arriving, the Airacobra pilots discovered Focke-Wulfs in a circle attacking the advancing Soviet units from an altitude of 6,560 feet.

Six P-39s rushed toward the diving German fighters from above. On this occasion they also struck from inside the enemy's circular combat formation. Glinka set a Focke-Wulf on fire with a burst fired from above and right at a range of fifty-five yards. Jettisoning their remaining bombs, the enemy pilots dispersed and quickly departed to the west.

No purpose was served by chasing the fleeing enemy. Pursuit would only burn up precious fuel and expend critically needed ammunition. At this moment something unexpected happened. One of the Focke-Wulfs turned 180 degrees and flew toward the departing Airacobras at top speed. Guards Lieutenant Nikolay Klimov, in turn, executed a similar maneuver. These two enemies were rapidly closing. A head-on attack such as this portended many possibilities. Even if the tracer streams of savage, point-blank fire passed close by, the intact aircraft occasionally lost control at the moment when they were at a critical distance one from the other. Veterans knew from their own experience. Pilots in this circumstance stopped breathing and their heart pounded.

The two aircraft were headed toward each other like meteors. Neither pilot changed his course. They collided with a horrendous noise. The Airacobra emerged without a wing and the FW arced downward, its tail section having fallen off. Neither pilot bailed out. Both fighters fell and broke into small pieces over a square kilometer of enemy soil, one on each side of a small stream. Klimov apparently lost consciousness upon impact with the Focke-Wulf, while the German was cut up by the P-39's propeller. His Iron Cross was sprayed with blood. Soviet ground troops buried the German pilot where he fell. They carried Klimov from the battlefield so that he could be buried in his home district with full military honors.

This ramming incident in the fourth year of the war sent a shock wave through the 9th Guards Fighter Division, which had not experienced such an event for approximately eighteen months. This was the last ramming case in the combat "biography" of the celebrated fighter formation.[11] An order regarding this tactic had been promulgated by the commander-in-chief of the Red Army VVS on 23 September 1944. This order proscribed the ramming tactic except in exceptional cases and as an extreme measure.[12]

The situation demanded yet additional actions by the aviators. After the ramming incident, Guards Major Glinka's group was directed by the ground vectoring station at an enemy for the third time in this sortie. Two Messerschmitts had appeared. Dmitriy Glinka sent two P-39s to altitude to provide cover and ordered the remaining four to attack the enemy. The enemy pilots were experienced. They managed twice to evade cannon and machine-gun bursts from the Airacobras. Only in the third pass did the P-39s have success. Glinka and Grigoriy Dolnikov found their targets. Two Messerschmitts were turned into burning, falling heaps.[13]

Mistletoe

The German command attempted with every kind of contrivance to prolong the agony of its criminal regime. One such attempt was the employment on the approaches to Berlin of a "new weapon"—a piggyback combination of two aircraft the Germans called the "Mistel" [mistletoe]. The pilots of the 9th Guards Fighter Division were among the first to encounter this strange flying machine.

The presence in the division of the RUS-2, its appropriate positioning, and reliable wire communications between the radar set and command and control organs that enabled timely passing of the latest reports of enemy air activity all facilitated the timely launching of on-alert fighters to provide cover over Aslau airfield and the autobahn landing strip. One example of a successful response to a radar sighting was the sortie of a group of three Airacobras of 100th Guards Fighter Regiment on 11 April 1945.

At 2008 the radar operator detected up to twelve enemy aircraft at a range of fifty miles on a heading of 280 degrees, flying at an altitude of 9,845 feet. The radar operator passed this report by land line to the on-duty chart attendant at the 9th Guards Fighter Division command post, who in turn informed the operations-intelligence duty officer.

Because the airfield cover patrol was at this same time engaged with three FW-190s in the sky southwest of Buntslau, an order was issued to launch the on-alert flight of 100th Guards Fighter Regiment, which was at readiness level no. 1. Guards Major Mikhail Petrov, Guards Lieutenant Grigoriy Sanyut, and Guards Junior Lieutenant Nikolay Kochkin sortied at 2010.

Using reports received from the RUS-2 and his radio, the duty officer vectored Petrov's group toward the enemy aircraft (in the zone west of Halbau, 2.4 miles from Aslau airfield). This was 6 to 7 miles from the front line, on the Soviet side. Major Petrov, now in the air, continued to maintain radio communications with the ground vectoring station at division headquarters and received updated location reports on the enemy aircraft.

Upon arriving over Halbau, Petrov, who was flying at an altitude of 9,845 feet, spotted a Ju-88 to the left and 1,640 feet below. The enemy bomber was flying due east in some scattered clouds, escorted by four Bf-109s. The fighters were formed in two pairs echeloned right, 2,300 to 2,625 feet above the bombers and trailing it 330 to 550 yards.

Having alerted his wingmen, Petrov conducted the first attack from above and behind at a shallow angle. But he was unable to close with the bomber because he was himself attacked by the Messerschmitts. Guards Lieutenant Grigoriy Sanyut fended off this attack on his leader. When the Bf-109 began to seek altitude, Sanyut caught him with a killing burst from a range of fifty-five to thirty yards. The enemy aircraft fell on fire all the way to the earth, trailing a plume of black smoke.

Mikhail Petrov pulled his Airacobra out of the uncompleted attack with a high-speed left turn and then looked around. He again spotted the Ju-88 but could not believe his eyes. Attached to the top of the enemy bomber's fuselage with long struts was a Bf-109 fighter—a double-decker flying "monster" or, as Soviet pilots later called it, a *karakatitsa* [cuttlefish]. The engines of both aircraft were working.

The guards major attacked the target a second time out of a right turn from above and behind and from a range of 135 to 75 yards set the left engine or fuel cell of the Ju-88 on fire. Several seconds later the bomber began to lose altitude rapidly, went over into a dive, and fell toward the earth. When it was still 985 to 1,640 feet above the ground, the Bf-109 separated from it. The left side of the Messerschmitt's motor was on fire. Its pilot attempted to make a hard left turn, but the aircraft lay over on its back and, as the flames spread along the fuselage, disappeared into the thick haze. None of the P-39 pilots observed the point of impact due to the poor visibility.

Continuing its fall detached from the Bf-109, the crippled bomber disappeared into a forest. This was confirmed by soldiers and officers of the 175th Regiment, 58th Guards Rifle Division. The division chief of staff, Colonel Boris Abramovich, and several officers inspected its crash site. The crater formed by the explosion of the Ju-88 was 10 yards in diameter and approximately 5 yards deep. The pine trees in a radius of 55 to 220 yards from the crater were bent over and some flattened to the ground and burned. In addition, the two radial engines, two propeller hubs, one propeller blade, and pieces of aluminum skin and fuel cell material were found at distances of 220 to 2,200 yards from the Ju-88 crash site. No signs were detected of any crew mem-

bers from the bomber, leading those who examined the case to con-
clude that the bomber was being controlled by the Messerschmitt pilot. Later, we learned from the interrogation of captured enemy pilots
that the Germans had named this exotic aerial machine the "Mistel"
[mistletoe].[1]

Several soldiers in the rifle regiment who were in positions as far as
660 yards from the crash site received minor burns. The stories of
some of these infantrymen suggested that the explosive force of the
downed bomber exceeded that of a 1,000-kilogram aviation bomb.[2]

The crash site of a second "TNT bomber," either shot down by another group of fighters or more likely by anti-aircraft fire, was discovered not far from the rifle regiment position. This Ju-88 had gone
down some five to ten minutes before the aircraft shot down by
Guards Major Mikhail Petrov. The ground troops had not seen this
bomber separate from its fighter.

Thanks to the timely detection by the RUS-2 operator of a group of
enemy aircraft, the prompt scrambling of the on-alert patrol flight, its
subsequent vectoring to the enemy, appropriate construction of
Petrov's combat formation, and decisive attack by the Airacobra pilots,
two Bf-109s and one Ju-88 had been destroyed. All Airacobras returned to their airfield.

In connection with the appearance of this new type of enemy aircraft at the front, the division's air crews were issued instructions regarding methods of shooting it down. Upon encountering this
combination aircraft, pilots were to conduct attacks only from above,
commencing fire first at the fighter aircraft attached to the top of the
Ju-88. A successful strike against the Messerschmitt or its pilot would
leave the bomber uncontrolled and it would go down by itself. Attacks
from the bottom were not advised because there was considerable
danger of detonating the explosives with machine-gun and cannon
fire. The shock wave from the explosion or shrapnel from the aircraft
itself would likely damage the attacking fighter.[3]

The sky over Berlin was thick with smoke; the air smelled heavily
of ashes. The forests, towns, and villages were burning. "But it was
easy to breathe!" recalls a 9th Guards veteran, "because we sensed that
if not today, then tomorrow this horrible war would be over!" Their joy
could not be measured. Aviators fought the enemy and did not tire. All
their energy was used to drive the enemy into his grave.

There was another unusual encounter by the Airacobras during the battles on the approaches to the lair of the fascist beast. On 16 April, eight P-39s of the 16th Guards Fighter Regiment, led by Guards Captain Nikolay Trofimov, were orbiting over Soviet ground forces in the area of Klein Bademayzel and Klein Zarkhen. They encountered and engaged four FW-190s.

The pair of Guards Lieutenant Petr Tabachenko attacked a single Focke-Wulf from the left rear and at close range. It appeared that their first bursts found the target. At the second burst the Focke-Wulf began a steep climb. While at the apex of a left half roll, the German fighter lost its momentum and fell through, burning. At that moment Tabachenko was quite close to the damaged enemy fighter. He was unable to turn away and collided with the falling FW-190, losing the right wing from his P-39. The lieutenant bailed out of his stricken fighter and landed by parachute among Soviet troops.

The pieces of the two damaged fighters, many of them on fire, rained down toward the earth in all directions. The lack of vigilance of the pair of Guards Senior Lieutenant Viktor Nikitin proved expensive for one of its pilots. A heavy piece of aircraft metal struck and shattered Nikitin's canopy. Although not injured by the missile, Nikitin was hurled from his cockpit by the force of the airstream. He also landed by parachute among Soviet troops.[4]

This particular incident was analyzed in great detail at the postflight debriefing with all of the regiment's pilots. Tabachenko's fundamental mistake was that after attacking the enemy from close range, he should have immediately pulled away to the flank. Nikitin's error was his failure to maintain visual awareness of the upper hemisphere. He and his wingman were watching the collision of two combat machines and failed to consider the danger to themselves from falling debris.

The Airacobra as Shturmovik

Large-scale offensives by the Red Army on the main axis (in Belorussia) in the summer of 1944 led to a fundamental change in the strategic situation on the Soviet–German front. All branches of the Soviet Armed Forces still had to redouble their pressure on the enemy for the most rapid accomplishment of his defeat and the victorious conclusion of the war. This required the employment of the combat capabilities of the troops with maximum effectiveness and the search for new methods of employing available equipment on the ground and in the air.

One document from the headquarters of the Red Army VVS is of some interest in this regard. It is a directive from the deputy commander of aviation dated 7 September 1944, "Regarding the employment of fighter aircraft for defeating ground targets."

At the present time, when our air forces have garnered and are maintaining unquestioned air superiority, all the conditions have been created for the broadest employment of fighters for defeat of enemy ground targets with bombs and machine-gun and cannon fire.

I remind all of you that the bomb racks on our fighters were not placed there by accident and not for decoration, but so that these aircraft can be used for daylight bomb attacks on enemy personnel and equipment on the battlefield.

Beginning on 10 September 1944, you will indicate in a separate line of your daily reports submitted to the air army staff the number of sorties flown by fighters carrying bombs.[1]

Fighter regiments of the 9th Guards Fighter Division frequently executed close air support missions (bombing and strafing) against enemy ground targets in the Berlin offensive operation (16 April to 8 May 1945). These fighters employed not only their on-board weaponry (37mm cannon and machine guns) but also fragmentation and cluster bombs. The primary ground targets for air strikes by Airacobras were enemy personnel and combat equipment, excluding armored vehicles. Only the FAB-100 was capable of disabling armored vehicles. Soviet fighter units equipped with the P-39 did not have armor-piercing ammunition for the 37mm cannon, and the standard issue high-explosive round was not suitable for combating armored targets.[2]

Had the P-39 come supplied with armor-piercing ammunition for the cannon, it could have attacked the engine compartment covers and turret tops of German tanks and assault guns. The thickness of the armor plate on these vehicles varied in the range of 15 to 30 millimeters. Standard 37mm armor-piercing rounds (had they been available for the P-39) were capable of penetrating armor of a thickness from 1 to 1.5 times their own diameter (37 to 55 millimeters).

Fragmentation aviation bombs destroyed targets by the shock wave of their detonation and partly by the shrapnel fragments from the body of the bomb. These bombs were equipped with contact fuses and therefore detonated upon striking the ground or some other hard object.

A cluster bomb was aviation ordnance in the form of a thin-walled bomb filled with air-delivered mines or bomblets. The bomblets were dispersed by an expelling or explosive charge ignited (detonated) by a proximity fuse at a specified altitude above the target.[3]

The P-39s employed RRAB-70 (*rotatsionnaya rasseivayushchaya aviabomba* [rotary-dispersing aviation bomb], 70-kilogram) ordnance in the battles around Berlin. A single container of this ordnance type contained thirty-five to forty bomblets weighing 1.5 to 2 kilograms each. The container had a small windmill device. After bomb separation from the aircraft this windmill began rotating and at a specified altitude triggered a mechanical detonating device that blew open the bomb cannister. The bomblets were dispersed into the air and spread out over the area of the enemy target.

On 24 April, formations of the 1st Belorussian and 1st Ukrainian *Fronts* came together southeast of Berlin, completing the encirclement of the enemy's Frankfurt–Gubensk grouping. On 25 April the forces of these two *fronts* joined west of the capital of the Reich, completing encirclement of the entire Berlin grouping. Formations of the 5th Guards Army met in the vicinity of Torgau with units of the First American Army approaching from the west on this same day.

Regiments of the 9th Guards Fighter Division played an active role in the destruction of these encircled German forces from 26 April to 8 May. The division had 102 Airacobras on hand at the end of April, of which eighty-eight were serviceable and fourteen were unserviceable. Of the 103 assigned pilots, 91 were in units and considered combat-ready; 6 were deemed not combat-ready. A total of twenty-nine P-63 Kingcobra aircraft had arrived in the division during the month of

April, received from the 6th Reserve Aviation Brigade. In addition, one P-39 had returned from a major repair shop. The 16th and 100th Guards Regiments were based at Neuhausen airfield and the 104th Guards Regiment at Yuterbog.[4]

Combat against the encircled enemy was conducted in poor flying weather conditions, with exceptionally heavy overcast, a ceiling of 985 to 1,315 feet, and visibility of 1.2 to 1.8 miles. At 1130 on 2 May, an enemy group of more than 500 men broke through the encirclement ring in the vicinity of Lukkenwald and attacked the airfield garrison at Yuterbog, where the 104th Guards Fighter Regiment was stationed. The regiment personnel took up defensive positions all around the airfield and engaged the enemy with concerted fires of rifles, submachine guns, trophy *panzerfausts,* and small caliber anti-aircraft guns.[5] Individual groups of enemy infantry managed to penetrate to within 550 yards of the landing strip. Despite heavy enemy small arms fire, four P-39s led by Guards Lieutenant Vasiliy Onishchenko were able to take off.

The Airacobras flew out on a combat mission, each aircraft carrying a single RRAB-70 with contact detonation fuses. Approaching the target area in pairs, they observed an accumulation of enemy personnel and equipment about one kilometer to their right. Deploying to their right, Onishchenko's group, one fighter at a time, dropped their containers from an altitude of 985 feet in horizontal flight. The lethal radius of the bomblets was 25 to 50 yards for personnel and 25 to 30 yards for equipment, primarily wheeled vehicles. After dropping its container, each Airacobra entered a tight circle with an interval between aircraft of 275 to 330 yards and at a glide angle of fifteen to twenty degrees made eight to ten strafing passes, until all cannon and machine-gun ammunition was expended. The P-39s did not experience any losses to enemy anti-aircraft fire.[6]

Units of the 24th Rifle Corps came to the assistance of the aviators defending the airfield against ground attack. As a result of the combined actions of the airfield garrison and the hurriedly arriving infantry, the majority of the enemy group that broke out of the encirclement was destroyed; the remainder were taken into captivity.

The commendation extracted below, sent by the commander of the 24th Rifle Corps to the commander of the 9th Guards Fighter Division, is testimony to the effectiveness of the actions of the 104th Guards

Regiment's air crews, who flew frequent ground-attack sorties against the encircled enemy, particularly at the end of April 1945.[7]

The air division, comprised of the 104th and 16th Guards Fighter Regiments, operated in close coordination with the 24th Rifle Corps in the liquidation of an encircled enemy force in the area of Barut and Lukkenwald in the period from 26 April to 2 May 1945. As a result of the energetic combat actions of the division's air crews, who conducted intense ground attacks and reconnaissance of the enemy in coordination with corps forces, the enemy suffered the following losses: 8,152 soldiers and officers killed; 35 tanks, 54 armored transporters, 74 guns of various caliber, 386 trucks, 72 motorcycles, 98 machine guns, and 12 radios destroyed; 16,734 soldiers and officers were captured. A significant portion of the enemy losses were as a result of the skillful actions of the air crews of your division, who sortied to execute combat missions during the poorest weather conditions (low ceiling, smoke from fires in the operations area).

Commander, 24th Rifle Corps
Hero of the Soviet Union
Guards Major General D. Onuprienko
3 May 1945

The Last Combat Sorties

After the Berlin operation, Army Group Center and a portion of Army Group Austria continued to resist on the territory of Czechoslovakia. More than 900,000 men, equipped with 9,700 guns and mortars, 1,900 tanks and assault guns, and 1,000 aircraft had not laid down their arms.[1]

A people's uprising broke out in Prague on the morning of 5 May, for the suppression of which the German command brought in large numbers of troops of Army Group Center. In response, the forces in revolt appealed to the Soviet Army and the Allies for help. The situation demanded that the enemy be defeated as quickly as possible and that the uprising be supported.

The plan of the Soviet command was to launch several powerful attacks on axes converging on Prague, surround and isolate the enemy grouping in smaller pieces, and thus liberate the Czechoslovakian capital. Forces were allocated from the 1st Ukrainian *Front,* operating in southern Germany, and the 2d Ukrainian *Front,* located in the Brno area of central Czechoslovakia.

During the Prague operation (6 to 11 May 1945) the 9th Guards Fighter Division was based with all regiments at the Grossenhain airfield network. Groups of four to eight Airacobras continuously patrolled on the first day of the operation to cover units of the 13th Combined and 4th Guards Tank Armies, which were attacking on the main axis of 1st Ukrainian *Front.* From 8 to 10 May the division covered only the tank army, which was moving rapidly toward Prague and then participated in its liberation.

The P-39s' combat actions were conducted at the limit of their operational radius (over ninety miles). The average duration of a flight was seventy to eighty minutes. Division pilots shot down four enemy aircraft in two aerial engagements, one of these directly above the city. The Germans ceased their air attacks on the city from the moment of the appearance of the Airacobras in the sky above the Czechoslovakian capital.

The division flew 386 sorties in the first ten days of May 1945. An additional 5 sorties were canceled because of equipment failures. On

2, 4, 9, and 10 May, intense days, there were 86, 78, 86, and 105 sorties, respectively.

A jubilant human tide—the citizenry of Czechoslovakia and Soviet troops—were celebrating on the ground. The great, long-awaited day of victory had arrived, but air battles were still being waged in the skies around the city. The enemy was continuing to resist and had to be defeated. The pilots of 9th Guards Fighter Division continued to go out on missions.

Two of the most intense days were 9 and 10 May. On the morning of 9 May, Guards Senior Lieutenant Georgiy Golubev and Guards Lieutenant Vyacheslav Berezkin were patrolling over Prague. The weather was excellent, with partly overcast skies and scattered, blinding white clouds. The pair leader spotted a German twin-engined Dornier-217 bomber, flying from west to east.[2] Golubev began to catch up to it, with peaceful intentions. Perhaps the Germans had decided to turn it over to us. He could assist them in reaching the airfield and executing a safe landing. Or so thought Golubev.

Suddenly, the Dornier bristled with muzzle flashes. A long tracer stream flowed from its top turret. Georgiy led his pair out of the beaten zone with a left maneuver. The Airacobras were undamaged. The German air crew was still at war! Didn't they know that the war was over? Golubev fired several warning bursts but the enemy continued on his course. The Airacobra pilots caught up to the Dornier, gained a little altitude, and indicated with a machine-gun burst the direction for landing. Undoubtedly the fascists understood what was required of them but they would not give up. The aircraft continued to follow its previous course and fired back yet again. Georgiy Gordeevich made no further "requests" of the German crew. A precise cannon burst tore into the Dornier, which went down somewhere in the hills, burning.

Another engagement occurred on the same day. Six Airacobras of 100th Guards Fighter Regiment, under the command of Vasiliy Pshenichnikov, were executing a mission to cover Prague from 1657 to 1800. The Airacobras were orbiting at 4,920 feet. A command came from the ground vectoring station: "To your right is an FW-189 Rama. Attack it!"

Pshenichnikov examined the indicated sector. Indeed, there was a German reconnaissance-spotter aircraft, circling at an altitude of 1,640 feet. By all indications, the crew was inspecting and photographing the positions of Soviet troops. The Airacobra leader attacked the Focke-Wulf from the right rear out of a right turn. He fired the first burst at a range of 440 yards—too far out and in haste. The rounds missed. Pshenichnikov closed to within 110 yards and fired a second stream of tracers into the Rama's fuselage. The enemy aircraft stubbornly refused to go down. A third cannon and machine-gun attack, this time from 55 yards, slashed into the Focke-Wulf. The aircraft exploded in midair, hurling out a single parachutist. The remaining crew, along with their Focke-Wulf, crashed to the earth on the outskirts of Prague.[3]

Unfortunately, sorties also resulted in losses on the side of the 9th Guards Fighter Division. But these were equipment losses only; the pilots survived. A group of four P-39s sortied on 10 May, led by squadron commander of the 16th Guards Fighter Regiment, Guards Senior Lieutenant Konstantin Sukhov. He was accompanied by Junior Lieutenants Nikolay Kudinov, Fedor Kutishchev, and Aleksey Senichev. The patrol took off at 1430 to fly cover over the Czechoslovakian capital. They were orbiting in their assigned zone; the air situation was quiet with no enemy in sight. The aircraft of Kutishchev and Senichev, which had high-time engines, expended their fuel load. These two pilots reported that fact to the flight leader, Sukhov, who for unexplained reasons did not take any rapid measures for return to their distant airfield. They continued the flight, and only after a second low-fuel warning did Sukhov lead the group home to Grossenhain.

Another ten to fifteen minutes of flight passed. The Airacobras entered a zone of reduced visibility. The fuel gauges in the aircraft of Kutishchev and Senichev were at critical levels. They could not continue flying on the intended route and had to land immediately and so dropped to minimum altitude, separating themselves from the remaining pair of P-39s. As the two pilots reached an area twelve miles west of Dresden, Senichev's engine began to sputter as it burned the last drops of fuel.

Guards Junior Lieutenant Kutishchev decided to land at the Dresden airfield. He ordered his wingman—Senichev—to come in behind him. A tense seven to eight minutes later the engine in Senichev's P-39 suddenly died. The pilot glided his aircraft in for a wheels-up landing. As it happened, the terrain was not flat. His aircraft received significant damage. In fact, it was deemed unrepairable and later dis-assembled for spare parts. The lucky Senichev escaped with several minor injuries. Kutishchev continued his flight more successfully. The little fuel he had remaining enabled him to find a more suitable landing place. He dropped his landing gear and safely put the Airaco-bra on the ground.[4]

After 10 May 1945, every single cartridge and round of every air-craft was accounted for. They became peacetime ammunition stocks. The cannons and machine guns had seen their last wartime use.

APPENDIX A

Order of the People's Commissar of Defense No. 294 of 8 October 1943

[Extract from the] REGULATION regarding decorations and monetary awards for personnel of the Red Army VVS, long-range aviation, PVO fighter aviation, and the Navy VVS

I. Fighter aviation

1. Fighter aviation pilots are recommended for official decorations:
    a. For personal destruction of enemy aircraft in aerial combat or on airfields: for an initial award, three bombers or reconnaissance aircraft personally destroyed or four destroyed aircraft of other types, or six aircraft destroyed on the ground; for a subsequent award, for each additional four bomber or reconnaissance aircraft personally destroyed or five destroyed aircraft of other types, or six aircraft destroyed on the ground; for the highest award, the rank Hero of the Soviet Union, for ten personally destroyed bomber or reconnaissance aircraft or fifteen personally destroyed aircraft of other types; for the highest award, the rank Twice Hero of the Soviet Union, for thirty personally destroyed aircraft of all types; for the highest award, Three Times Hero of the Soviet Union, for fifty personally destroyed aircraft of all types.
    b. For destruction of railroad rolling stock and disorganization of railroad shipping on enemy territory: for an initial award, six destroyed locomotives or four train derailments caused by aircraft attacks; for a subsequent award, for each additional eight destroyed locomotives or six derailed trains caused by aircraft attacks.
    c. For combat sorties to accompany *shturmoviki,* bombers, torpedo bombers, reconnaissance aircraft, and artillery spotter aircraft, and also for combat sorties to provide cover for ground forces on the battlefield, naval bases, lines of communication, and other facilities, for thirty successful combat sorties; for subsequent awards, for each subsequent thirty successful combat sorties.
    d. For combat sorties in close air support and troop reconnaissance: for the first award, for twenty successful combat sorties; for subsequent awards, for each subsequent thirty successful combat sorties.

Note: This regulation was promulgated by Stalin's signature as Commissar of Defense of the USSR on 8 October 1943. Source: *TsAMO RF,* Collection 2, index 920266, file 7, sheets 399, 400, 402–405.

2. Fighter pilots are to be recommended for official decorations for personal destruction of enemy aircraft during night actions in accordance with paragraph 1 of this instruction, with the proviso that the number of destroyed aircraft is reduced by one-half.

3. The recommending of the leader of a pair for an official decoration for aircraft shot down in personal aerial combat conveys the right to recommend for decoration his wingman, if by his actions the wingman ensured the success of his leader in combat.

4. Commanders of subunits, units, and formations,[1] in addition to decorations received for personal victories, are to be recommended for official decorations:

    a. For skillful command of subordinate units, the actions of which contribute to the successful defeat of the enemy in combat or the operations of ground forces or the navy.

    b. A squadron commander (including separate squadrons), under whose command the squadron has destroyed twenty-five aircraft in aerial combat or on airfields, in the process not losing more than ten of his own aircraft.

    c. A regiment commander, under whose command the regiment has destroyed sixty aircraft in aerial combat or on airfields, in the process not losing more than ten of his own aircraft.

Note 1. A fighter combat sortie that is to be counted for purposes of decoration is a flight that contains an engagement with an aerial enemy or a flight that extends into the zone of the enemy's anti-aircraft fire or over enemy combat formations.

Note 2. If it cannot be established who personally shot them down or if they are destroyed by the simultaneous attacks of two or more pilots, aircraft downed in group aerial engagements are divided equally and counted as a partial destroyed aircraft for each individual pilot who participated in the group battle.

XI. Aircraft destroyed in aerial combat or on the ground, and also damage inflicted on the enemy are to be documented by one of the following indicators:

    a. With written confirmation from ground troops, vessels, partisan detachments, or the reports of the agent network.

    b. With written confirmation of downed aircraft from the local populace, verified by organs of local authority.

    c. With photographs that confirm the destroyed aircraft or damage inflicted on the enemy.

    d. With confirmation by VNOS [*vozdushnoye nablyudenie, opoveshcheniye, i svyaz,* air observation, warning, and communication] posts and other systems of observation and reporting.

    e. With written confirmation from two or more crew members of aircraft operating in the given group, or of a crew sent out for the purpose of inspecting a successful bombardment in conditions when another form of confirmation is not possible.

   f. By personal report of an individual hunter-fighter or *shturmovik*-torpedo bomber, upon confirmation by his regimental commander.

XIII. Monetary awards to air crews of all forms of aviation (except long-range aviation) for successful combat actions

20. Air crew members of all types of aviation (except long-range aviation), notwithstanding their recommendation for official decorations, are paid monetary awards for successful combat actions:

   a. To the pilot and navigator who are part of a crew: for 30 successful combat sorties, 2,000 rubles; for 50 successful combat sorties, 3,000 rubles; for 80 successful combat sorties, 4,000 rubles; for 120 successful combat sorties, 5,000 rubles. All remaining crew members are to receive an amount equal to 30 percent of the award received by the crew commander.

   b. A member of a crew who personally destroyed an enemy aircraft is awarded: for each enemy bomber, reconnaissance, or transport aircraft destroyed, 1,500 rubles; for each aircraft of other type destroyed, 1,000 rubles.

   c. The pilot and navigator of an air crew are to receive 750 rubles for each enemy locomotive destroyed or train derailed. All other crew members are to receive 500 rubles each.

   d. For sinking an enemy destroyer or submarine, the pilot and navigator are to receive 10,000 rubles each and all remaining crew members 2,500 rubles each.

   e. For sinking an enemy transport, the pilot and navigator are to receive 3,000 rubles each and all remaining crew members 1,000 rubles each.

   f. For sinking an enemy patrol vessel or minesweeper, the pilot and navigator are to receive 2,000 rubles each, and all remaining crew members 500 rubles each. For sinking an enemy barge, tugboat, or armed schooner, the pilot and navigator are to receive 1,000 rubles each, and all remaining crew members 300 rubles each.

XV. Official decorations and monetary awards to engineering-technical personnel of the Red Army VVS, long-range aviation, PVO fighter aviation, and the Navy VVS

1. Mechanics (technicians) who work directly on aircraft are to be recommended for official decorations:

   a. For outstanding preparation and launching of aircraft for the accomplishment of a combat mission in time periods established by the command: for the initial award, 100 aircraft launches, and when servicing type U-2, R-5, and MBR-2 aircraft,[2] for 250 aircraft launches; for subsequent awards, for each subsequent 100 aircraft launches, and when servicing U-2, R-5, and MBR-2 aircraft, for each subsequent 250 aircraft launches.

Special services mechanics, technicians, and armorers are to be recommended for their initial and subsequent awards if the aircraft serviced by them (in accordance with their specialties) have accomplished the following quantity of combat sorties: for fighter and ground-attack aircraft, 750 aircraft sorties; for short-range bombers and close reconnaissance aircraft, 400 sorties; for heavy and long-range bombers and long-range reconnaissance aircraft, 300 aircraft sorties; for U-2, R-5, and MBR-2 aircraft, 1,500 sorties.

2. Supervisory engineering-technical personnel of aviation units are to be recommended for official decorations: aircraft technician, for 200 aircraft sorties; senior squadron technician (engineer) and his deputies for armaments and special services, 750 aircraft sorties; senior regimental engineer and his deputies for armaments and special services, 1,500 aircraft sorties.

3. In addition to official decorations, aviation unit engineer-technical personnel are paid monetary awards for outstanding maintenance, stockage, and preservation of equipment:

a. For each 100 aircraft sorties: 1,000 rubles to an aircraft mechanic (technician); 400 rubles to an aircraft engine mechanic; 600 rubles to other technical personnel (armorers, instrument repairmen, electricians, radio repairmen, and special equipment repairmen).

Note. The monetary award of 600 rubles allocated for "other technical personnel" is distributed by the unit commander, taking into consideration the volume of work of each specialist and the reliability and functionality of the armaments, instruments, and systems that are serviced by each specialist as an individual.

b. If 75 percent of the aircraft mechanics (technicians) of a flight/ squadron receive monetary awards, the supervisory engineer-technical personnel of the flight/squadron receive monetary awards: 1,500 rubles for a flight aircraft technician; 2,000 rubles for a senior squadron technician (engineer); 1,500 rubles each for the deputy squadron engineers (senior technicians) for armaments and special equipment.

c. If 50 percent of the aircraft mechanics (technicians) of a regiment receive monetary awards, the supervisory engineer-technical personnel of the regiment receive monetary awards: 2,500 rubles for the senior regimental engineer; 2,000 rubles each for the deputy senior engineers for armaments and special equipment.

Note 1. When an aircraft is unavailable for employment for reasons not associated with the technical personnel (destroyed in air combat, destroyed by the enemy on the ground or as a result of an accident, and also during replacement of components, dislocation of personnel, or re-outfitting with new equipment), previous sorties of the aircraft are counted toward the norm established by this regulation.

Note 2. The payment of monetary awards for preservation of equipment and accident prevention to personnel of flight training institutions, instructional-training institutions, and reserve units of the Red Army VVS, long-range aviation, and the Navy VVS is conducted in accordance with a special regulation.

Note 3. Official decorations and monetary awards for the technical personnel of repair units (PARM-1 [*podvizhnaya aviaremontnaya masterskaya,* mobile aircraft repair facility], 3, 10 PAM [*podvizhnaya aviatsionnaya masterskaya,* mobile aviation repair facility], SAM [*statsionarnaya aviatsionnaya masterskaya,* stationary aviation repair facility])[3] for high-quality repair of equipment are conducted in accordance with a special regulation.

> Commander-in-chief of the Red Army VVS
> Marshal of Aviation Novikov
> 30 September 1943

Notes

1. In Russian, *podrazdeleniy, chastey,* and *soedineniy,* in this context squadrons, regiments, and divisions.

2. The R-5 was a two-place reconnaissance-bomber aircraft from the Polikarpov design bureau. The MBR-2 was a short-range maritime reconnaissance aircraft.

3. The PARM and PAM, while similar in title, performed their work at different echelons of maintenance.

APPENDIX B

Soviet Aces Who Flew the P-39 Airacobra

The table below contains the names of Soviet pilots who compiled lifetime scores of at least fifteen kills and who flew the P-39 Airacobra for some portion of their Great Patriotic War service. Unless otherwise indicated, all kills were achieved in the Great Patriotic War, though not necessarily while flying the P-39.

	Individual + shared kills	Missions/aerial engagements	Unit	Last military rank
Alelyukhin, Aleksey (H2)	40 + 17	~600/258	9th GFR	Major general
Amet-Khan, Sultan (H2)	30 + 19	603/150	9th GFR	Lieutenant Colonel
Arkhipenko, Fedor (H2)	30 + 14	467/102	129th GFR	Colonel
Babak, Ivan (H)	33 + 4	300/	16th GFR	Captain
Balyuk, Ivan (H)	25 + 5	500/	54th GFR	Colonel
Bashkirov, Viktor (H)	18	>300/	907th FR	Colonel
Batyaev, Vasiliy (H)	19 + 7	639/234	88th FR	Colonel
Baykov, Georgiy (H)	15	252/50	9th GFR	Colonel
Bekashonok, Mikhail (H)	18 + 4	170/50	129th GFR	Major
Bobrov, Vladimir (H)	43 + 24	577/159	129th, 104th GFR	Colonel
Bykovets, Leonid (H)	19 + 4	220/	28th GFR	Colonel
Chepinoga, Vladimir (H)	23 + 1	100/37	508th FR	Major
Chistov, Nikolay	19	~300/	16th GFR	Colonel
Delegey, Nikolay (H)	15 + 3	>200/	508th FR	Lieutenant Colonel
Dmitryuk, Grigoriy (H)	18	206/37	19th GFR	Major General
Dokashenko, Nikolay (H)	15 (11 in Korea)	NA	17th FR	Colonel
Dolgushin, Sergey (H)	17 + 11	422/	30th GFR	Lieutenant General
Dolnikov, Grigoriy (H)	15 + 1	160/42	100th GFR	Colonel General
Edkin, Viktor (H)	15 + 3	294/53	72d GFR	Colonel
Egorov, Aleksey (H)	24 + 7	271/66	212th GFR	Lieutenant Colonel
Eliseev, Vladimir	15	256/	67th GFR	Colonel
Elizarov, Sergey (H)	17 + 8	200/70	9th GFR	Major

Note: H, Hero of the Soviet Union; H2, Twice Hero of the Soviet Union; H3, Three Times Hero of the Soviet Union; FR, Fighter Regiment; GFR, Guards Fighter Regiment; GFD, Guards Fighter Division.

Source: Extracted from Nikolay Bodrikhin, *Stalinskiye sokoly* [Stalin's eagles] (Moscow: NPP Delta, 1997), app. 2.

	Individual + shared kills	Missions/aerial engagements	Unit	Last military rank
Eremin, Pavel (H)	22	NA	16th GFR	Colonel
Fadeev, Vadim (H)	17 + 3	~400/51	16th GFR	Captain, killed in battle, 5 May 1943
Fedorov, Arkadiy (H)	24 + 3	600/	16th GFR	Colonel
Figichev, Valentin (H)	21	612/	205th FR	Colonel
Filatov, Aleksandr (H)	20	300/	30th GFR	Captain
Galchenko, Leonid (H)	24 + 12	410/90	145th, 609th FR	Colonel
Glinka, Boris (H)	31	200/	100th, 16th GFR	Colonel
Glinka, Dmitriy (H2)	50	300/100	100th GFR	Colonel
Glotov, Nikolay (H)	16	203/33	129th GFR	Colonel
Golovachev, Pavel (H2)	31 + 1	457/125	9th GFR	Major General
Golubev, Georgiy (H)	15	300/70	16th GFR	Colonel
Goreglyad, Leonid (H)	15	132/53	22nd GFR	Major General
Grachev, Ivan (H)	18 + 8	203/94	191st GFR	Major, killed in battle, 14 September 1944
Grafin, Iosif (H)	19	200/	104th GFR	Senior Lieutenant, killed in battle, 28 April 1945
Guchek, Petr (H)	18 + 3	242/56	100th GFR	Senior Lieutenant, killed in battle, 18 April 1945
Gulaev, Nikolay (H2)	57 + 3	240/69	129th GFR	Colonel General
Kamozin, Pavel (H2)	35 + 13	200/70	101st GFR	Major
Karasev, Aleksandr (H)	30 + 11	380/112	9th GFR	Major General
Karlov, Valentin (H)	18 + 4	172/44	129th GFR	Colonel
Karmin, Aleksandr (H)	19 + 14	221/31	129th GFR	Colonel
Khramov, Nikolay (H)	18 + 4	327/113	NA	Colonel
Klubov, Aleksandr (H2)	31 + 19	457/95	16th GFR	Captain, killed in crash, 1 November 1944
Kobyletskiy, Ivan (H)	17 + 9	465/95	54th GFR	Lieutenant Colonel
Komelkov, Mikhail (H)	32 + 2	321/75	104th GFR	Colonel
Komosa, Anatoliy (H)	19 + 4	383/	2d Air Army	Major
Korolev, Ivan (H)	18 + 11	500/	9th GFR	Colonel
Kovachevich, Arkadiy (H)	26 + 6	520/150	9th GFR	Lieutenant General
Kozhevnikov, Anatoliy (H)	25	211/62	212th GFR	Lieutenant General

	Individual + shared kills	Missions/aerial engagements	Unit	Last military rank
Kryukov, Pavel (H)	22	650/	16th GFR	Major General
Kukharenko, Aleksey	15	>300/	Northern Fleet	Colonel
Kuznetsov, Nikolay A. (H)	25 + 12	252/150	57th GFR	Major General
Lavitskiy, Nikolay (H)	22 + 2	250/>100	100th GFR	Captain, killed in crash, 10 March 1944
Lavrinenkov, Vladimir (H2)	35 + 11	448/134	9th GFR	Colonel General
Likhovid, Mikhail (H)	16 + 11	208/44	104th GFR	Senior Lieutenant, killed by Banderovs, 12 August 1944
Lukyanov, Sergey (H)	15 + 19	360/70	100th GFR	Colonel
Lusto, Mikhail (H)	18 + 1	169/36	129th GFR	Colonel
Mariinskiy, Evgeniy (H)	20	200/60	129th GFR	Colonel
Matsievich, Vasiliy (H)	16 + 6	NA	26th GFR	Colonel
Mazurin, Fedor (H)	19 + 2	250/50	28th GFR	Colonel
Melnikov, Evgeniy (H)	16 + 5	405/95	54th GFR	Colonel
Mikhalev, Vasiliy (H)	22 + 2	~150/50	508th FR	Colonel
Mikhaylik, Yakov (H)	17 + 6	316/73	54th GFR	Colonel
Mironov, Sergey (H)	18 (2 in Finland)	400/	153d GFR	Colonel General
Mironov, Viktor (H)	15	350/	19th GFR	Captain, killed in battle, 16 February 1943
Nikiforov, Petr (H)	18 + 4	297/69	129th GFR	Colonel
Nikitin, Aleksey (H)	19 + 5	238/73	28th GFR	Colonel
Novichkov, Stepan (H)	29	315/	67th GFR	Lieutenant Colonel
Novikov, Aleksey (H)	22	~500/	17th FR	Major General
Pasko, Nikolay	15 + 1	265/32	28th GFR	Colonel
Petrenko, Evgeniy	15 + 1	293/75	20th FR, Northern Fleet	Colonel
Pokryshkin, Aleksandr (H3)	59 + 6	~650/156	9th GFD	Marshal of Aviation
Rechkalov, Grigoriy (H2)	56 + 6	450/122	16th GFR	Major General
Rents, Mikhail (H)	18 + 5	250/56	30th GFR	Colonel
Semenishin, Vladimir (H)	23 + 7	~300/	104th GFR	Lieutenant Colonel, killed in battle, 29 September 1943
Semenov, Aleksandr (H)	23 + 15	240/65	322d FR	Lieutenant General
Sergov, Aleksey (H)	17 + 7	~500/	508th FR	Major General

	Individual + shared kills	Missions/aerial engagements	Unit	Last military rank
Sgibnev, Petr (H)	19	319/39	78th FR, Northern Fleet	Captain, killed in battle, 3 May 1943
Sharenko, Vasiliy (H)	16 + 4	~300/ ~70	NA	Major, killed in battle, 30 July 1944
Shchirov, Sergey* (H)	17	400/	267th FR	Colonel
Shestakov, Lev (H)	29 + 45 (8 in Spain)	~600/130	9th GFR	Colonel, killed in battle, 4 March 1944
Shevelev, Pavel (H)	17 + 2	258/78	67th GFR	Colonel General
Shishkin, Yakov (H)	18	244/	32d FR	Colonel
Sirotin, Vyacheslav (H)	21	~300/	17th FR	Major
Smirnov, Aleksey (H2)	34 + 1	427/72	153d FR	Colonel
Snesarev, Vladimir	16 + 8	314/40	11th GFR, Black Sea Fleet	Colonel
Starchikov, Nikolay (H)	18 + 1	489/80	16th GFR	Major
Sukhov, Konstantin	22	297/68	16th GFR	Colonel
Timofeenko, Ivan (H)	23 + 6	435/105	9th GFR	Colonel
Trofimov, Nikolay (H)	15 + 11	~400/75	16th GFR	Lieutenant General
Trud, Andrey (H)	24 + 1	600/	16th GFR	Colonel
Tvelenev, Mikhail (H)	18 + 28	420/130	9th GFR	Colonel
Vilyamson, Aleksandr (H)	18 + 6	382/66	104th GFR	Colonel
Vishnevetskiy, Konstantin (H)	20 + 15	200/	104th GFR	Major, killed in ground accident, 30 July 1944
Zakalyuk, Aleksey	19 + 14	596/65	104th GFR	Lieutenant Colonel
Ziborov, Vasiliy (H)	20	180/38	72d GFR	Colonel

*For reasons that are not explained in the source document, this pilot's Hero of the Soviet Union rank was later revoked.

APPENDIX C

Lineage of 216th (9th Guards) Fighter Division

Division commanders

Major General Vladimir Illarionovich Shevchenko (May to October 1942)

Major General Aleksandr Vladimirovich Borman (October 1942 to May 1943)

Major General Ibragim Magometovich Dzusov (May 1943 to April 1944)

Colonel Aleksandr Ivanovich Pokryshkin (April 1944 to May 1945)

Honors

216th Fighter Division was redesignated as 9th Guards Fighter Division on 17 July 1943. The division was awarded the Order of Bogdan Khmelnitskiy 2d Degree on 9 August 1944, the Order of the Red Banner on 5 April 1945, and the Order of Lenin on 28 May 1945. The division received the honorific titles "Mariupol" on 10 September 1943, and "Berlin" on 2 May 1945. The division was mentioned in orders of the Supreme High Commander on twelve occasions.

Regiments of the division

55th Fighter Regiment was redesignated 16th Guards in June 1942. Order of Aleksandr Nevskiy, honorific title "Sandomir."

45th Fighter Regiment was redesignated 100th Guards Fighter Regiment on 18 June 1943. Orders of Aleksandr Nevskiy and Bogdan Khmelnitskiy 2d Degree, honorific title "Generokhovsk."

298th Fighter Regiment was redesignated 104th Guards Fighter Regiment on 24 August 1943. Order of Aleksandr Nevskiy, honorific title "Krakow."

NOTES

The information contained in this book is derived from a number of sources. After each combat flight of a patrol group, in the postflight debriefing, the pilots reported in detail regarding their actions (positive and negative). All these reports were written down by the squadron adjutant. In addition, a pilot confirmed by his own written report the combat results of his wingman or other fellow pilots (how many and by what method enemy aircraft were damaged or shot down) and in what area the aircraft fell. Several pilots made these confirmatory reports after a mission.

All these documents have been preserved in the files of the fighter regiments in the Central Archive of the Ministry of Defense of the Russian Federation (TsAMO RF). They constitute the official basis for counting pilots' personal and shared scores of enemy aircraft destroyed. This score was carried over into regiment documents and to the pilot's personal logbook.

Collectively, all these materials from the squadrons served as a basis at regiment headquarters for the end-of-day combat report regarding squadron activities in the course of executing their assigned combat missions. This report was passed up from regiment to division headquarters at a specified time each day.

Fighter regiment and division files at the archive also contain some sketches showing the conduct of interesting, intense, and lopsided aerial engagements, and tables of subordinate unit sortie data. The regiment reports contain detailed information pertaining to the time and place of actions, the composition of patrol groups (how many and what type of aircraft, pilots' last names), the altitude at which the engagement occurred, the weather conditions, what pair or pilot, at what target aspect, from what direction attacked the enemy (or from what direction the enemy attacked our fighters), from what range fire was initiated, the result of the fight (how many of what type aircraft were damaged or destroyed), where the aircraft fell, and who could confirm the result of the battle. Ammunition expenditure by caliber was also listed for each engagement.

At the end of each report was a section showing the number of aircraft on hand, the number of aircraft ready for missions the next day, and information regarding personnel. This category included the number of pilots in the regiment, the number of pilots capable of flying assigned combat missions, and the number of pilots sick, on leave, and on temporary duty.

Division staff used regiment combat reports for compiling daily operations summaries, which were submitted to air corps or air army headquarters by a specific time each day. The division operations summary contained information in all the categories listed above, but compiled by regiment. All these operations summaries (day after day) are preserved in the archival files of 216th (9th Guards) Fighter Division.

Division staff developed and submitted to higher headquarters summaries concerning the combat activities of the regiments for the past month. These division summaries also described in detail various aspects of the daily routine of subordinate units, their air battles, and results achieved. Information was also provided regarding the movement of equipment (what aircraft and how many were received from or sent to repair facilities or other units).

These summaries laid out the nature of the actions of enemy aviation: the new tactical methods of his fighters and bombers, information regarding the concealed enemy airfield network, and so on. Along with this, the reports from division made note of deficiencies in the combat actions of subordinate units and the measures being taken to correct them. Various suggestions were made regarding issues of command and control of fighters in the air and on the ground, and regarding the rebasing of the regiments.

At the end of the year the division staff submitted a summary regarding the combat actions of its units for the preceding twelve months. This year-end summary document reflected on such issues as the type of missions the regiments executed and in what period, the names of operations, how many aircraft sorties were flown for each assigned mission, the number of damaged and destroyed enemy aircraft, and our own losses in aircraft and pilots.

Each technical service that supported aviation activities compiled daily and monthly reports and summaries. These documents from logistic units addressed issues of supply of everything necessary for the accomplishment of combat missions. They reflect the difficult work of the airfield service battalions that supported the regiments.

In turn, senior engineers of the regiments and division compiled daily maintenance reports and, at the end of the month, a summary of maintenance support. These documents discussed deficiencies in operating the aircraft, the nature of breakages in P-39 components and how they were repaired, Airacobra accidents and their causes, how and where battle- and accident-damaged aircraft were repaired, and what supply commodities were delivered late or were of low quality (as was frequently the case with engine oil).

In regiments, and later at the division, tactics conferences were convened after the completion of an operation or during an operational pause in the actions of ground forces. The command and air crews of 9th Guards Fighter Division regiments and neighboring aviation units were invited. This facilitated the exchange of experience and the rapid dissemination of new tactical methods. The themes of these regiment and division conferences included discussions of battles in recent operations, the positive and negative aspects of fighter unit actions, and the causes of losses in air battles.

Summaries of these conferences are preserved in archival files of regiments and the division. These summaries include presentations made by pilots and the conclusions of the commanders present, significant analytical material, instructive materials of battle participants (of a positive and negative nature), and their suggestions on various tactical and command and control issues. Occasionally, after such conferences regiment and division orders were issued that described actions to be taken to correct noted deficiencies.

Technical conferences were also held in regiments and at the division, at which engineer-technical personnel of various ranks shared their experiences of employment and repair of the Airacobras. Presenters at these conferences suggested methods and procedures for correcting observed mechanical deficiencies.

The archival documents of the 216th (9th Guards) Division contains much detailed material regarding the combat employment of the RUS-2 radar apparatus that was attached to the division and to 16th Guards Fighter Regiment.* Also available are materials regarding tactical issues, such as the "free hunt" over the Black Sea and behind enemy lines, adjusting artillery fire, and employment of the Airacobra as a fighter-bomber. These subjects are covered in this book.

Issues of radio communications are addressed throughout the archival documents, including positive and negative aspects of the work of aircraft and ground stations.

The deputy regiment commander for political affairs submitted a daily political report to the political section of the division staff. This report covered the political and morale condition of unit personnel, measures of a Party and Komsomol nature conducted in the unit (conversations, lectures, meetings, conferences, how many combat leaflets were printed and distributed that publicized combat feats in recent battles with the enemy, and the results achieved by all of the above), extraordinary incidents (aircraft accidents, causes, who was killed or wounded), disciplinary incidents, and other aspects of unit life. Almost every political report contained a brief description of the feats of the Airacobra pilots, including ramming incidents, lopsided battles with the enemy, the results of combat, and who received what awards.

Generalized materials of these regiment reports plus the division's own measures were laid out in the pages of the political report submitted by the division chief of political affairs. This report was sent to higher level Party organs (the air corps or air army political department, depending on the subordination of the division at the time the report was submitted).

In addition to all of these reports, the archival files contain a large quantity of orders and supporting documents for awards and recommendations. These materials describe the feats for which pilots and other personnel were recommended for and received medals and orders.

The massive volume of preserved archival materials made it possible for me to describe in detail every aerial engagement of the fighter units. In the interests of time and space, I have selected the most interesting and instructive, those that demonstrate the capabilities of the Airacobra and the mastery and courage of the pilots-*inomarochniki*.†

A number of books have been written by 9th Guards Fighter Division veterans that describe various activities in which the authors played a role. I have studied these memoirs in detail and compared them with archival documents. This is an absolute, self-imposed requirement. I have been able to converse with veterans of these units regarding their combat experiences. I have also checked their stories against archival documents. Unfortunately, there are a

*In Russian, *radiolokatsionnaya usovershenstvovannaya stantsia* (improved radar set). [JG]

†This compound Russian word is formed from the two words *inostrannaya marka*, which mean "foreign mark or brand." The label *inomarochnik* (plural *inomarochniki*) was attached to all personnel of the Soviet Armed Forces who operated foreign-made equipment during the war, even so far as to be noted in their personnel records and stamped in their identification booklets. [JG]

number of gaps and areas of confusion or conflict (time, place, combat results, and so on), and even distortions, both in the memoirs and in the stories of the war veterans. In these cases I have used the archival documents as ground truth and have inserted references (endnotes) in the text.

Prologue

1. In the Soviet Army, as in many other armies, the right flank of a formation was a place of honor.

2. In Russian, *Reserv Verkhovnogo glavnogo komandovaniya.*

3. "Mariupol" and "Berlin" were honorific titles that the unit had received by war's end. [JG]

4. "Donbass" is a shortened form of "Don basin," the name given to a region of Russia and Ukraine, north of the Sea of Azov, drained by the Don River. It is most noted for coal production. [JG]

5. "The Kuban" is a name given to a region of Russia drained by the Kuban River. This river flows northwestward out of the Caucasus Mountains, passes through the major city Krasnodar, and empties into the Sea of Azov at Temryuk Bay. [JG]

6. *Velikaya Otechestvennaya voyna 1941–1945* [Great Patriotic War 1941–1945] (Moscow: Sovetskaya entsiklopediya, 1985), 434.

7. Other period photographs show P-39s still in the United States with red stars on a white disk with no blue field. Upon arrival the Soviets painted over the white disk with olive drab paint, leaving the star red. [JG]

8. See, for example, Edward R. Stettinius, Jr., *Lend-Lease: Weapon for Victory* (New York: Macmillan, 1944), 1; and Robert Huhn Jones, *The Roads to Russia: United States Lend-Lease to the Soviet Union* (Norman: University of Oklahoma Press, 1969), 13.

9. Jones, 37.

10. Rick Mitchell, *Airacobra Advantage: The Flying Cannon* (Missoula, MT: Pictorial Histories, 1992), 15.

11. Mitchell, 18; Robert F. Door, "Bell Airacobra Variants: P-39 Airacobra and P-63 Kingcobra," *Wings of Fame* 10 (1998): 118; and Birch Matthews, *Airacobra! Bell Aircraft Corporation 1934–1946* (Atglen, PA: Schiffer Military/Aviation History, 1996), 264–265.

12. Yefim Gordon, "P-39 in the USSR," *Wings of Fame* 10 (1998): 144–151, 144. Another recent source suggests that sixteen aircraft arrived in Arkhangelsk on 31 August, but does not specifically identify them as Airacobras. They could have been P-40s. See V. Roman, "The Airacobra Aircraft in Soviet Aviation," *Journal of American Aviation Historical Society* 43, no. 4 (Winter 1998): 282–296, 283.

13. Admiral William H. Standley reported seeing P-40s and Airacobras parked on the airfield at Abadan during an inspection trip in late March 1942. This strongly suggests that P-39s were being shipped in quantity by this date. Jones, 110–111.

14. "Crating Airacobras," *Bellringer* [Bell Corporation factory newspaper] 1, no. 10 (September 1941): 21; and "Airacobras in Cellophane," *Bellringer* 4, no. 6 (May 1944): 21.

15. According to Roman (290), the Soviets established an assembly team here of approximately 300 engineers and laborers.

16. Two articles that provide a detailed glimpse of the Lend-Lease effort in Iran are John N. Greely, "Iran in Wartime," *National Geographic Magazine* (August 1943): 129–155; and Harvey Klemmer, "Lend-Lease and the Russian Victory," *National Geographic Magazine* (October 1945): 499–512.

17. The use of this route from the U.S.–Canadian perspective is described in great detail in Blake W. Smith, *Warplanes to Alaska* (Blaine, WA: Hancock House, 1998).

18. Matthews, 284.

19. Richard C. Lukas, *Eagles East* (Talahassee: Florida State University Press, 1970), 233, for the figure 4,750; and *Lend-Lease Shipments, World War II*, U.S. War Department, 31 December 1946, gives the figure 4,423. The Soviet Union received approximately 2,000 P-40s and 2,300 P-63s over the course of the war.

20. The official factory weekly newspaper, *Bell Aircraft News*, contains such headlines as "Correspondent Says Russians Use P-39s in 'True Role as Fighters'" (July 15, 1944) and "Airacobra-Flying Russians Top All War Aces" (July 29, 1944). Another factory publication, the monthly *Bellringer*, contains like titles: "'AIRACOBRAS are Clearing Soviet Skies!" (July 1943); "His Score—59 Nazis" (June 1944, reprinted from *Time*). These and other similar articles in both publications emphasize the use of the P-39 in air-to-air combat.

21. Echelons of Red Air Force commanders above the air army level were responsible for ensuring the manning and training of the air force and its personnel, the procurement, supplying, and maintaining of aircraft, and other doctrinal, personnel, and technical support issues.

22. In fact, the Russian term for "ground support" and "close air support," as this mission is understood by Western readers, is *shturmovaya aviatsiya* [ground-attack aviation]. The Soviet Air Force had an outstanding aircraft purpose-designed for this role, the Il-2 *Shturmovik*, which was assigned to regiments with the *shturmovaya aviatsiya* mission and designation.

Transition Training

1. The full English text of this order that was read, but not published in writing, to Soviet units in late July 1942 is found in Dmitriy Loza, *Fighting for the Soviet Motherland* (Lincoln: University of Nebraska Press, 1998), app. B.

2. Rations in wartime Soviet Union varied in caloric value with one's location and duties, with frontline soldiers at the upper end of the scale and civilians in rear areas at the lower end. [JG]

3. *Pokryshkin v vozdukhe i na zemle. Sbornik vospominaniy odnopolchan* [Pokryshkin in the air and on the ground. Collection of his comrades' recollections] (Novosibirsk, 1994), 144.

4. In fact, the doors were a product of the Hudson Motor Car Company, manufactured under contract to Bell Aircraft Corporation. Mitchell, 13. [JG]

5. A spin is a spontaneous or induced rotation of the aircraft around its longitudinal axis at a critical attack angle (autorotation) with simultaneous loss of altitude in a spiral of small radius. Aircraft spins come in different

forms: by type—normal and inverted; by direction of rotation—right and left; by angle of incline of the longitudinal axis of the aircraft—steep (angle of incline greater than fifty degrees), shallow (angle of incline from fifty to thirty degrees), and flat (angle of incline less than thirty degrees); by nature of rotation—unrecoverable and recoverable. The aircraft can go into a spin spontaneously because of pilot error or the spin can be induced to familiarize the pilot with peculiarities of the behavior of the aircraft in a spin and to train the pilot in techniques of entering and departing from a spin. The rearward center of gravity of the P-39 led to frequent spinning of the aircraft, especially in the hands of young and inexperienced pilots.

6. In Russian, *"Doma i ugly pomogayut!"* [JG]

7. The traditional homeland of the Ossetian peoples was in the Caucasus range, midway between the Black and Caspian seas.

The Skies of the Kuban

1. TsAMO RF, collection 20046, index 1, file 18a, sheet 19.
2. Ibid., sheet 137.
3. Ibid., sheets 18, 25.
4. Ibid., sheet 137.
5. Ibid., sheet 19.
6. TsAMO RF, collection 739, index 90613, file 5, sheet 165.
7. TsAMO RF, collection 362, index 20272, file 1, sheets 243–247.
8. *Shturmovik* (plural, *shturmoviki*), though a generic Russian term that refers to a ground-attack fixed- or rotary-wing aircraft, in this context was normally applied to the Il-2. This single-engined two-place attack aircraft had a maximum speed of 251 mph, a range of 475 miles, and a bomb payload of 1,321 pounds. It was armed with two wing-mounted 23mm cannons, two 7.62mm machine guns in the forward fuselage, and a rear-mounted 12.7mm flexible machine gun. [JG]
9. TsAMO RF, collection 362, index 13812, file 2, sheet 96.
10. Flight and gunnery training of air crews included a whole set of measures directed at training aviation unit personnel. Flight training encompassed the aggregate skill level of the air crews and the degree of training proficiency of units in the conduct of combat operations in various situations. This was the principal component of combat proficiency, the most important indicator of combat readiness. Aerial gunnery readiness was the proficiency of the air crews in the employment of their aircraft weaponry. It consisted of study of the theory and practice of the skills of aerial gunnery and bombing.
11. Circumspection, caution, foresight in actions. Applied to military aviation terminology: look with both eyes; constantly observe in all directions to find the enemy; detect the enemy before he sees you.
12. TsAMO RF, collection 739, index 14708, file 4, sheet 169.
13. TsAMO RF, collection 20046, index 1, file 18, sheet 19.
14. Ibid., sheet 25.
15. Ibid., sheets 13–14.
16. Ibid., file 18a, sheets 18–19.

On the Left Wing of the Soviet–German Front

1. It is common in European culture to refer to the right and left banks of rivers. When standing with one's back toward the river's source and facing downstream, the left bank is the land on the left and the right bank is the land on the right. "Left-bank Ukraine" is therefore the land on the east (left) bank of the Dnieper River (which flows north to south). [JG]

2. ADD [*aviatsiya dalnego deystviya* (long-range aviation)] was a branch of the VVS redesignated in February 1942 from long-range bomber aviation. All ADD units were directly subordinated to Stavka VGK and were employed for deep strikes against enemy military, industrial, and political targets, and in support of *front* and strategic ground operations. See *Sovetskaya voyennaya entsiklopediya* (Moscow: Voyenizdat, 1977), 3:91, *sv. dalnyaya aviatsiya* [long-range aviation].

3. TsAMO RF, collection 20046, index 1, file 18a, sheet 17.

4. *Istoriya Velikoy Otechestvennoy voyny* [History of the Great Patriotic War] (Moscow: Voyenizdat, 1954), 3:388.

5. TsAMO RF, collection 319, index 4798, file 47, sheet 81.

First Air Battles

1. The reason for this echeloned introduction of units into combat, according to the testimony of 9th Guards veterans, was the delay in the ferrying of the fighters from Iran. Either the assembly of the aircraft at Teheran was slow or unforeseen delays occurred in the ocean voyage of the vessels transporting the aircraft from America.

2. It may be no coincidence that five of these eight pilots became Heroes of the Soviet Union, Dmitriy Glinka achieving that honor twice. Koval (ten individual and three shared victories) and Kudrya (ten individual victories) were killed in May 1943, and Lavitskiy (twenty-two individual and two shared victories) in March 1944. Berestnev retired at the rank of lieutenant general in 1961 and died in 1980. Glinka retired at the rank of colonel in 1960 and died in 1979. [JG]

3. DB, the first letters of his name and patronymic—Dmitriy Borisovich—was his call sign. His brother Boris—BB—served in the same regiment.

4. The Petlyakov-2 was a twin-engined dive bomber. Powered by two Klimov liquid-cooled engines, it had a maximum speed of 335 mph, range of 932 miles, and bomb load of 2,645 pounds. It was armed with two nose-mounted machine guns and two dorsal- and ventral-mounted flexible machine guns. [JG]

5. TsAMO RF, collection 20046, index 1, file 13, sheet 73.

6. Ibid., sheets 76, 78.

7. Ibid., sheet 80.

8. Ibid., sheet 83.

9. Ibid., sheet 86.

10. Ibid., sheet 87.

11. The actual Russian used here and many other places in the manuscript is *stervyatnik* (carrion crow or vulture), a common Russian slang term for en-

emy aircraft during the war, used in the same manner as Western pilots used the term "bandit." [JG]

12. TsAMO RF, collection 20046, index 1, file 13, sheet 113.

13. In Russian, *"Sam pogibay, a tovarishcha vyruchay!"* [JG]

14. TsAMO RF, collection 20046, index 1, file 13, sheet 89.

15. Ibid., sheet 88.

The New Methods Win Out

1. *Pokryshkin v vozdukhe i na zemle,* 93.

2. Aleksandr Pokryshkin, *Nebo voyny* [The sky of war] (Moscow: Voyenizdat, 1966), 235.

3. TsAMO RF, collection 20046, index 1, file 13, sheets 111–117.

4. In Russian, *Otvagoyu polny i opyt est. Krushit vraga—stavyat sebe za chest.* [JG]

5. The LaGG-3 was a single-seat fighter with a top speed of approximately 350 mph at 16,400 feet. Although heavily armed (one 20mm cannon and two 12.7mm machine guns), it was no match for an experienced pilot in a Messerschmitt Bf-109. [JG]

6. TsAMO RF, collection 20046, index 1, file 13, sheet 110.

7. Ibid., file 88, sheet 51. The flight manual for the P-39Q recommends that pilots not exceed 475 mph in a dive, with a stated maximum dive speed of 523 mph. *Pilot's Flight Operating Instructions for Army Model P-39Q-1 Airplane,* reprinted as *Flight Manual for P-39 Airacobra* (Appleton, Wisc.: Aviation, 1978), 16, para. 15a. [JG]

8. TsAMO RF, collection 20046, index 1, file 18, sheet 3; file 77, sheets 164, 167.

9. *Sovetskiye VVS v Velikoy Otechestvennoy voyne 1941–1945* [Soviet VVS in the Great Patriotic War 1941–1945] (Moscow: Voyenizdat, 1968), 159.

10. Quoted in Pokryshkin, *Nebo voyny,* 262–263; TsAMO RF, collection 20046, index 1, file 77, sheets 154–156.

11. TsAMO RF, collection 2, index 920266, file 399, sheet 403.

12. TsAMO RF, collection 20046, index 1, file 13, sheet 118.

13. Ibid., file 88, sheets 40, 44.

14. Ibid., file 13, sheet 139.

15. Ibid., sheet 108.

16. Ibid., sheet 118.

17. Ibid.

18. TsAMO RF, collection 100th Guards Fighter Regiment, index 207601, file 1, sheet 103.

19. TsAMO RF, collection 20046, index 1, file 13, sheet 118.

20. Another source indicates that Sergeant Bezbabnov was also piloting a P-39, and either he or Mikhail Petrov was shot down by famed German ace Erich Hartmann on this evening combat. See V. Roman, "The Airacobra Aircraft in Soviet Aviation," *Journal of American Aviation Historical Society* 43, no. 4 (Winter 1998): 292. Examination of Hartmann's record indicates that his seventh credited victory was an Airacobra shot down in the vicinity of Taman on 15 April 1943 between 1455 and 1555. See Raymond F. Toliver and Trevor J. Con-

stable, *The Blond Knight of Germany* (Blue Ridge Summit, Pa.: Tab Books, 1985), 290. Hartmann estimated that he shot down a total of thirty-three Airacobras (p. 301). The time difference between the Soviet and German accounts can be explained by the different time standards the two sides used in maintaining official journals in field units. [JG]

21. TsAMO RF, collection 100th Guards Fighter Regiment, index 207601, file 1, sheets 103–104.

The Sky Was Ablaze

1. TsAMO RF, collection 20046, index 1, file 18, sheets 44–45.

2. Later this tail number would be changed to "100" and remain with the decorated ace until war's end.

3. TsAMO RF, collection 20046, index 1, file 13, sheet 121; file 18, sheets 17–18.

4. TsAMO RF, collection 20046, index 1, file 13, sheet 124.

5. Ibid., sheet 128.

6. Ibid., file 77, sheet 200.

7. Ibid., sheet 215.

8. Ibid., file 18, sheet 3.

9. Ibid., file 13, sheet 134.

10. At both readiness levels, 1 and 2, the Airacobras were fully refueled and rearmed, oxygen tanks topped off, and all systems and instruments tested and checked. At readiness level no. 1, the aircraft was parked in a revetment or under camouflage (where possible). The pilot was sitting in the aircraft with parachute on. The motor was kept warm by periodic starting, the radio was turned on, and during hot weather the right door was kept open for ventilation. The aircraft's crew chief was nearby, prepared to assist the pilot as required. The aircraft was expected to take off within two to three minutes of a launch order, normally indicated by a flare fired from the control tower and confirmed by telephone from the tower to the aircraft parking area. At readiness level no. 2, the pilot waited with other pilots in a dugout, ready shack, or tent. The crew chief remained close to the aircraft with other maintenance personnel. Upon signal to launch or to come up to readiness level no. 1, the pilot took his seat in the aircraft, turned on the radios, and put on his parachute. As soon as the readiness level no. 1 aircraft launched for a combat mission, readiness level no. 2 aircraft were redesignated as readiness level no. 1 and another group of aircraft assumed readiness level no. 2.

11. TsAMO RF, collection 20046, index 1, file 13, sheets 130–131.

12. Ibid., sheets 124–125.

13. *Sovetskiye VVS v Velikoy Otechestvennoy voyne 1941–1945*, 188.

14. *Istoriya Velikoy Otechestvennoy voyny Sovetskogo Soyuza 1941–1945* [History of the Great Patriotic War of the Soviet Union 1941–1945] (Moscow: Voyenizdat, 1964), 3:389.

15. TsAMO RF, collection 20046, index 1, file 18, sheets 14, 45.

Wild Vadim

1. Valeriy Pavlovich Chkalov (1904–1938) was a famous Soviet military test pilot. He was most noted for a sixty-three-hour nonstop flight from Moscow across the North Pole to Vancouver, Washington, in a monoplane with two other Soviet pilots in 1937. He was killed while flight-testing an aircraft in December 1938. [JG]

2. Built by Polikarpov, this monoplane fighter had a maximum speed of 326 mph at sea level, a range of 435 miles, and was armed with two .30 caliber machine guns in the upper forward fuselage and two wing-mounted 20mm cannons. [JG]

3. At this time Soviet industry manufactured and distributed folding meter sticks made of metal or wood. Tape measures of thin flexible metal did not appear until after the war.

4. Georgiy Golubev, *V pare s "Sotym"* [Wingman for "100"] (Moscow: DOSAAF, 1974), 82. Golubev finished the war with 252 missions and 12 victories. He retired at the rank of colonel in 1977.

5. Arkadiy Fedorov was later named commander of 16th Guards Fighter Regiment. By the war's end he had flown more than 600 missions and was credited with 24 personal and 4 group victories. He retired at the rank of colonel in 1955 and died in March 1992. [JG]

6. TsAMO RF, collection 20046, index 1, file 13, sheets 111, 115, 119, 121, 124, 125, 129, 134.

7. Ibid., sheet 121.

8. Ibid., file 77, sheet 215. By the war's end, Andrey Trud had flown more than 600 combat missions and was credited with 24 personal and 1 group victory. He retired at the rank of colonel in 1972.

9. Golubev, *V pare s "Sotym."*

10. Soviet decorations for valor were serial-numbered and could therefore be traced to their rightful holder through archival records. As this passage makes clear, it was not unusual for Soviet pilots to wear their decorations into combat. [JG]

11. *Geroi Sovetskogo Soiuza: Kratkiy biograficheskiy slovar* [Heroes of the Soviet Union: Brief biographical dictionary] (Moscow: Voyenizdat, 1988), 2:636.

12. Pokryshkin, *Nebo voyny,* 268–269.

13. In the Hall of Heroes at each of these memorials are listed in alphabetical order the last names only of Heroes of the Soviet Union, and in Moscow also Heroes of the Russian Federation, who were awarded this high rank for bravery and heroism displayed in combat with the German-fascist occupiers.

Pass the Experience Along

1. The aphorisms at the beginning of both of the first two paragraphs rhyme in the original Russian: (1) *Boevoy opyt svoy i protivnika—izuchat, i v povsednevnuyu praktiku deystviy—vnedryat!*; (2) *Ne tolko naydennyy effektivnyy sposob boya svoy znay. No obyazatelno ego drugomu odnopolchaninu pereday!* [JG]

2. Ibragim Dzusov was commanding the 9th Guards Fighter Division at this time. He went on to command the 6th Guards Fighter Corps before the

end of the war. Dzusov was awarded the rank Hero of the Soviet Union on 29 May 1945, and retired in 1955 at the rank of major general. He died in October 1980. [JG]

3. *Sovetskiye VVS v Velikoy Otechestvennoy voyne 1941–1945,* 159.

4. *Pokryshkin v vozdukhe i na zemle,* 109.

5. In Russian, *Soldatskaya pravda* and *Listok perednego kraya. Sovetskiye VVS v Velikoy Otechestvennoy voyne 1941–1945,* 159.

Combat Successes and Losses

1. TsAMO RF, collection 20046, index 1, file 18, sheet 17; file 13, sheet 134.

2. Ibid., file 18, sheets 35, 36, 44.

3. Ibid., sheets 45, 46.

4. Ibid., sheet 44.

5. Type-83 and -85 engines were used in P-39 M, N, and Q models. [JG]

6. TsAMO RF, collection 20046, index 1, file 88, sheet 70; 100 Guards Fighter Regiment collection, index 207601, file 1, sheet 20.

7. TsAMO RF, collection 20046, index 1, file 18, sheet 80. The UTI-4 (*uchebno-trenirovochnyy istrebitel*) was a training variant of the P-39 with a seat and controls installed in the nose, forward of the standard cabin.

8. The Blue Line was a German defensive belt on the approaches to the Taman Peninsula between the Azov and Black seas. It was eighty-two miles long and twelve to fifteen miles deep. It consisted of two defensive lines, and the intersecting positions, villages, and heights on these lines were turned into strongpoints. *Voyennyy entsiklopedicheskiy slovar* [Military encyclopedic dictionary] (Moscow: Voyenizdat, 1983), 201.

9. Grigoriy Rechkalov, Sergey Lukyanov, and Aleksandr Pokryshkin were all squadron commanders.

10. TsAMO RF, collection 20046, index 1, file 18, sheet 49.

11. Ibid., file 88, sheet 67.

12. Ibid., file 78, sheet 262.

First Priority—the Aircraft

1. This definition is from *Illyustrirovannyy aviatsionnyy slovar dlya molodezhi* [Illustrated aviation dictionary for youth] (Moscow: DOSAAF, 1964), and *Voyenno-aviatsionnyy slovar* [Military-aviation dictionary] (Moscow: Voyenizdat, 1966).

2. This enumeration of personnel was introduced in April 1942 and, with insignificant changes, prevailed until the end of the Great Patriotic War. *Sovetskiye VVS v Velikoy otechestvennoy voyne 1941–1945* [Soviet VVS in the Great Patriotic War 1941–1945], no. 7 (Moscow, 1965), 12; TsAMO RF, collection 20046, index 2, file 42, sheets 37, 63.

3. In Russian, *podvizhnaya aviaremontnaya masterskaya.* A number following this acronym differentiated a PARM by its subordination, equipping, and level of repair authorized. [JG]

4. Konstantin Sukhov, *Eskadrilya vedet boy* [The squadron fights] (Moscow: DOSAAF, 1983), 109. Sukhov finished the war with 297 combat missions and 22 personal victories. He retired at the rank of colonel in 1975.

5. Grigoriy Dolnikov, *Letit stalnaya eskadrilya* [The iron squadron flies] (Moscow: Voyenizdat, 1983), 178.

6. TsAMO RF, 100th Guards Fighter Regiment collection, index 207597, file 3, sheet 1.

7. TsAMO RF, collection 20046, index 1, file 88, sheet 34.

8. Ibid., sheet 42.

9. Ibid., sheet 44.

10. Ibid., sheet 51.

11. Ibid., file 77, sheet 100.

12. Ibid., file 88, sheet 70.

13. The P-39's landing gear was raised and lowered by a twenty-four-volt, three-quarter horsepower electric motor, driving the assembly through a forty-to-one reduction gear. The clutch was designed to slip at an output torque of 700 inch pounds. Clutch slippage could have been caused by improper adjustment or if the gears were mechanically frozen or combat damaged. [JG]

14. In Russian, *batalon aerodromnogo obsluzhivaniya*. [JG]

15. TsAMO RF, collection 20046, index 1, file 18, sheet 39.

16. Ibid., sheet 53.

17. Ibid., sheets 88, 125.

18. The Allison V-1710-85 engine in the P-39Q had a single-speed, single-stage, gear-driven supercharger. *Flight Manual for P-39 Airacobra* (Appleton, Wisc: Aviation, 1978), chart on 22. [JG]

19. TsAMO RF, collection 20046, index 1, file 18, sheet 125.

20. Ibid., sheets 121, 126.

21. Ibid., sheet 126.

22. Ibid., sheet 128.

23. Ibid.

24. Ibid.

25. TsAMO RF, 16th Guards Fighter Regiment collection, index 206874, file 3, sheet 5.

26. TsAMO RF, 100th Guards Fighter Regiment collection, index 207599, file 1, sheets 5, 6.

27. Although the spark energy for the Allison engine was generated by a magneto, it was routed to the proper spark plug by a distributor. [JG]

28. TsAMO RF, 100th Guards Fighter Regiment collection, index 207599, file 1, sheet 57.

29. Ibid.

30. TsAMO RF, 16th Guards Fighter Regiment collection, index 206874, file 2, sheet 52.

31. *Sovetskiye VVS v Velikoy otechestvennoy voyne 1941–1945*, 286.

32. Ibid., 323.

33. TsAMO RF, 16th Guards Fighter Regiment collection, index 206874, file 2, sheets 143, 144, 146.

34. Almost 33 percent of the fighter aircraft support for the Berlin operation were Lend-Lease P-39 Airacobras. [JG]

35. TsAMO RF, collection 20046, index 1, file 39, sheets 223–226.

Logistical Support

1. TsAMO RF, collection 35, index 283223, file 98, sheets 56–57.

2. *Razvitiye tyla Sovetskikh vooruzhennykh sil 1918–1988* [Development of logistical support of Soviet armed forces 1918–1988] (Moscow: Voyenizdat, 1989), 165.

3. *Maskirovka* is a Russian term that describes a complex set of measures (camouflage, concealment of objects by camouflage means, construction of dummy objects, and others), which when applied to airfields was conducted with the purpose of hiding airfields from enemy air reconnaissance and air attacks, preventing the detection of airfields through radio and radar devices, and also misorienting the enemy regarding the exact location of airfields.

4. In Russian, *rayon aerodromnogo bazirovaniya*. [JG]

5. *Sbornik dokumentov. Sovetskiye VVS v Velikoy otechestvennoy voyne 1941–1945* [Collection of documents. Soviet air forces in the Great Patriotic War 1941–1945], no. 4 (1959): 18.

6. The Po-2 was a single-engined biplane utility aircraft.

7. *Inzhenerno-aerodromnoye obespecheniye aviatsii v Velikoy otechestvennoy voyne 1941–1945* [Airfield engineer support of aviation in the Great Patriotic War 1941–1945] (Moscow: Voyenizdat, 1952), 14. This souce hereafter cited as *Airfield engineer support*.

8. TsAMO RF, collection 290, index 201841, file 1, sheet 189.

9. *Trudy Voyenno-vozdushnoy akademii* [Works of the military-air academy], no. 8 (94), 97.

10. For example, in May 1942 in the Karelian *Front* an airfield was made usable in rapid fashion with the installation of a wood VPP (runway). Some 65,500 cubic yards of forest products were used in this effort. The planking, placed down over a peat bog, permitted aviation units of 7th Air Army to conduct combat operations in any weather. *Airfield engineer support,* 146.

11. The common American term for this item was "pierced steel plate," or "PSP." According to an official postwar report, 50,451,000 square feet of landing mat were delivered to the USSR through the Lend-Lease program. This area of landing mat was sufficient to construct 240 landing surfaces with a width of 100 feet and a length of 2,100 feet. *Lend-Lease Shipments, World War II*. Section II, Engineers. U. S. War Department, 31 December 1946, 2. [JG]

12. *Airfield engineer support,* 165.

13. TsAMO RF, collection 35, index 225933, file 1, sheets 56–57, 72–73.

14. TsAMO RF, collection 319, index 20523, file 4, sheet 63.

15. TsAMO RF, collection 327, index 102981, file 3, sheets 95–96.

16. The P-39's Allison V-12 engine burned a higher octane fuel than did Soviet-manufactured aircraft. Additives shipped from the United States were added to Soviet-produced gasoline to produce the required high-octane mixture. All ammunition for the P-39's 37mm cannon and .50 or .30 caliber ma-

chine guns was manufactured in the United States and delivered to the Soviet Union by a combination of sea and overland routes. [JG]

17. TsAMO RF, collection 20046, index 1, file 18, sheet 107.

18. Ibid., sheet 126.

19. Ibid., sheets 84–85.

20. Ibid., sheet 120.

21. Ibid., sheet 121.

22. A fuel inventory sheet was supposed to be maintained at each fuel storage container. The entries on this sheet included the quantity and type of fuel, a qualitative statement (whether the fuel contained additives), and who checked the fuel and when it was checked. The fuel storage container was to be measured with a stick on a regular schedule. The same procedures applied to containers that were used to store motor oil and other fluids used for the Airacobras.

23. TsAMO RF, collection 20046, index 1, file 26, sheet 125.

24. TsAMO RF, collection 16th Guards Fighter Regiment, index 206784, file 2, sheet 327.

Command and Control of Fighters

1. TsAMO RF, collection 346, index 5953, file 1, sheets 304–307.

2. *Start-stopnyy telegraph* (start-stop telegraph). This was a set that automatically turned on when a subscriber contacted it and automatically stopped when the subscriber ended its transmission. It was capable of 2,000 words per minute. Its range was 42 miles in a field cable environment, 90 miles with a pole wire line, and 370 miles with a permanent line.

3. TsAMO RF, collection 20046, index 1, file 18a, sheets 19–20.

4. Ibid., sheet 36.

5. Ibid., sheet 37.

6. TsAMO RF, collection 302, index 4205, file 24, sheets 218–219.

7. TsAMO RF, collection 920266, file 7, sheet 351. Bear in mind that the primary role of reserve regiments was training new pilots and transitioning pilots to new aircraft types.

8. *Radiostantsiya avtomobilnaya telegrafnaya* (truck-mounted radio and telegraph set). This set operated in the 2,500–12,000 kHz bands and was used for both voice and code transmissions. Its range was 1,240 miles in telegraph mode and 370 miles in voice mode. The set was carried on three trucks, one each for the transmitter, receiver, and power supply.

9. TsAMO RF, collection 302, index 21851, file 7, sheet 43.

10. TsAMO RF, collection 20046, index 1, file 18, sheet 118.

11. Ibid., sheet 129.

12. Ibid., sheet 130.

13. TsAMO RF, collection 302, index 4196, file 48, sheet 167.

14. Ibid., sheets 168–169.

15. TsAMO RF, collection 20046, index 1, file 18a, sheet 56.

16. Ibid., file 26, sheet 112.

Navigational Support

1. TsAMO RF, collection 20046, index 1, file 32, sheet 138.

2. This variant of the P-39 was designated the TP-39. This aircraft was created by installing a factory-supplied modification kit on an existing P-39. The guns in the nose compartment were removed and an instructor seat and limited controls placed in front of the existing cockpit. The pilot in training sat behind the instructor and had the full range of flight controls and instruments. See Mitchell, *Airacobra Advantage*, 38. [JG]

3. TsAMO RF, collection 20046, index 1, file 22, sheet 20.

4. Ibid., file 26, sheet 33.

5. Ibid., file 29, sheet 123.

6. Ibid., file 26, sheet 132.

7. Ibid., file 39, sheet 194; file 26, sheets 132, 184.

8. Ibid., file 39, sheet 194.

9. Ibid., file 26, sheets 132, 184.

A Wingman's Feat

1. Golubev, *V pare s "sotym,"* 97.

2. TsAMO RF, collection 20046, index 1, file 18, sheets 2, 18, 105, 133. *GAZ* is an acronym for *Gorkiy avtomobilnyy zavod* [Gorkiy Automobile Plant].

You Won't Get Away!

1. TsAMO RF, collection 20046, index 1, file 18, sheet 110.

2. "21" was Tsvetkov's tail number and call sign.

3. Meaning "frame," this Russian nickname was applied to the Focke-Wulf 189 because of its twin-boom construction. Designed primarily for reconnaissance, it carried its crew in a central nacelle that was heavily armored. The aircraft had a maximum speed of 218 mph and was armed with two dorsal-mounted 7.9mm machine guns, two rear-mounted 7.9mm machine guns, and one forward-firing 7.9mm machine gun in each wing root. [JG]

Over the Molochnaya River

1. Nikolay Trofimov flew 341 combat missions by the end of the war and was credited with fourteen personal and eleven shared victories. He was awarded the rank Hero of the Soviet Union on 27 June 1945. Trofimov retired as a lieutenant general in 1982. [JG]

2. Konstantin Sukhov flew 250 combat missions and was credited with twenty personal victories by the war's end. He was awarded Hero of the Soviet Union on 27 June 1945. Sukhov retired at the rank of colonel in 1975. Pavel Eremin, who flew the B-25 before transitioning to the Airacobra, finished the war with more than 300 missions and twenty-two individual kills. [JG]

3. TsAMO RF, collection 20046, index 1, file 18, sheet 105; file 18a, sheets 47–48.

4. SMERSH is the Russian acronym for *smert shpionam* (death to spies). It is the official name of an element of the NKVD that was present in all military units at specified levels. Its mission was to root out spies, prevent desertions, and in every way possible ensure the political loyalty of all military personnel. The instruction to examine "skin and hands" is the commander's way of suggesting to SMERSH personnel that the pilot had been tortured by the Germans, and that in itself should be some testament to his loyalty.

5. For personal heroism and courage displayed in combat with the German-fascist invaders during the Great Patriotic War, for high results in combat preparation of his troops, for the mastering of complex combat equipment and in connection with the sixtieth anniversary of the Soviet Army and Navy, by order of the Presidium of the Supreme Soviet of the USSR of 21 February 1978, Grigoriy Dolnikov was awarded the rank Hero of the Soviet Union. Colonel General Grigoriy Dolnikov passed away in 1992. His wife Valentina Mikhaylovna now lives in Moscow. The delay in awarding him the rank Hero of the Soviet Union may have been a result of his having spent three months in German captivity in late 1943 and three more months as a partisan in early 1944.

Covering an Amphibious Landing

1. TsAMO RF, collection 20046, index 1, file 18, sheet 105.
2. Ibid., file 31, sheet 104.
3. Ibid., file 18, sheet 110.
4. Ibid., sheets 110–111.
5. Ibid., sheet 111.
6. Aleksandr Pokryshkin, *Poznat sebya v boyu* [Recognize oneself in combat] (Moscow: DOSAAF, 1986), 349.
7. TsAMO RF, collection 20046, index 1, file 18, sheet 115; file 18a, sheets 50, 52.

A Costly Mistake

1. By the time of his death, Semenishin was credited with twenty-three personal and seven shared victories in approximately 300 sorties. [JG]
2. TsAMO RF, collection 20046, index 1, file 18; collection 104th Guards Fighter Regiment, index 20781, file 1, sheets 102, 107.
3. TsAMO RF, collection 20046, index 1, file 18, sheet 107.
4. Ibid., sheets 47, 48, 54, 64.

Adjusting Artillery Fire

1. The maximum range of the 152mm [towed] gun was 28,000 yards (approximately sixteen miles) and the mass of a projectile was 48.8 kilograms [107 pounds]. The gun's rate of fire was three rounds in four minutes. [JG]
2. TsAMO RF, collection 20046, index 1, file 18a, sheet 53.

More Battles

1. TsAMO RF, collection 20046, index 1, file 18, sheet 116; file 18a, sheets 48, 54.
2. Ibid., file 18, sheet 118.
3. Ibid.
4. Ibid.
5. Like so many others, this aphorism rhymes in Russian: *Bystriy, moshch-nyy na vraga nalet—tri preimushchestva tebe daet: protivnika uprezhdaesh; ego voinstvo oshelomlyaesh; v itoge—pobezhdaesh!* [JG]
6. TsAMO RF, collection 20046, index 1, file 18, sheet 118.
7. On 12 August 1944, while preparing an aircraft for evacuation from a forced-landing site in Lvov Oblast, Likhovid and two maintenance personnel were captured by a group of Banderov guerrillas, soaked in gasoline, and set on fire. He was awarded the rank Hero of the Soviet Union posthumously on 27 June 1945. [JG]

Free Hunting

1. TsAMO RF, collection 20046, index 1, file 18, sheets 52, 53.
2. Ibid., sheet 123.
3. Ibid., sheet 126.
4. TsAMO RF, collection 104th Guards Fighter Regiment, index 20781, file 2, sheet 113.
5. Ibid., sheet 118.
6. The Sivash is a brackish body of water on the northeast side of the Crimean Peninsula. It is separated from the Sea of Azov by a long, narrow spit of land known as the Arabatskaya Arrow. The water of the Sivash has a heavy mineral content. [JG]
7. Pokryshkin, *Poznat sebya v boyu*, 365.
8. This is a reference to the Beaufort Scale. At force 9 the wind speed ranges from forty-one to forty-seven knots (seventy-five to eighty-eight kph) and is described as a "strong gale." [JG]
9. TsAMO RF, collection 20046, index 1, file 18, sheet 136; file 18a, sheet 66.
10. General Savitskiy received his first award of Hero of the Soviet Union on 11 May 1944, for downing fifteen enemy aircraft, and his second award on 2 June 1945. He finished the war with a score of twenty-two personal and two shared kills. Savitskiy became a Marshal of Aviation in 1961 and in the middle 1960s was the deputy commander-in-chief of Soviet Air Defense Forces. In 1980 he joined the group of general inspectors of the Ministry of Defense. [JG]
11. The scores of these aces (except Reshetov, who was credited with thirty-six personal and eight shared kills) at the end of the war are shown in appendix B. [JG]

Over the Perekop

1. TsAMO RF, collection 20046, index 1, file 18, sheet 127.
2. Pokryshkin, *Poznat sebya v boyu*, 362–363.

3. TsAMO RF, collection 20046, index 1, file 18, sheet 126.

4. Ibid., sheet 130.

5. "Perekop" is the standard term used to refer to the narrow neck of land that connects the Crimean Peninsula with the mainland to the north. Throughout history it has been the scene of fiercely fought battles for the defense or capture of the peninsula. [JG]

6. TsAMO RF, collection 20046, index 1, file 18, sheets 126, 129; collection 16th Guards Fighter Regiment, index 143397, file 1, sheets 5, 6.

7. TsAMO RF, collection 20046, index 1, file 18a, sheet 56.

8. Ibid., file 18, sheet 126; collection 16th Guards Fighter Regiment, index 1433797, file 1, sheets 6, 7.

9. TsAMO RF, collection 20046, index 1, file 18, sheets 136, 138.

10. Ibid., sheet 135.

11. Ibid., file 18a, sheet 56.

12. Ibid.

Relocation to New Airfields

1. An airfield network is a group of active, reserve, and dummy airfields intended for the basing of an aviation unit. The location of the airfields and the main routes of supply and communications within the airfield network were selected to ensure the best sortie rate, ease of command and control, and material-technical support. Several airfield networks combined to form an airfield district.

2. TsAMO RF, collection 35, index 21578, file 7, sheets 47–48.

3. TsAMO RF, collection 311, index 4509, file 4, sheet 154.

4. Since one BAO was capable of supporting two single-engine regiments, when necessary the BAO was divided into two equally capable halves. One of these, removed from the basic structure of the BAO, was called an advance team (*komendatura* in Russian). A *komendatura* of a BAO serviced the aircraft on a single airfield. TsAMO RF, collection 35, index 226136, file 34, sheet 36.

5. TsAMO RF, collection 35, index 226136, file 34, sheet 36.

6. TsAMO RF, collection 20046, index 1, file 13, sheet 13.

7. Ibid., file 18, sheet 36.

8. Ibid., sheet 41.

9. Ibid., sheet 69.

10. Ibid., sheet 116.

11. TsAMO RF, collection 100th Guards Fighter Regiment, index 207599, file 1, sheet 24.

12. Ibid., sheet 25.

13. In accordance with Red Army regulations, air crews, technical personnel, and young specialists ate rations containing one of three different caloric contents. This was unlike the ground forces, where all categories of service personnel in a given unit ate the same rations.

14. TsAMO RF, collection 35, index 279157, file 3, sheets 3–4.

15. TsAMO RF, collection 20046, index 1, file 26, sheets 107–109.

16. In Russian, *aviatsionnaya korotkovolnovaya* (aviation short-wave). The transmitter operated in the 2,500 to 7,500 kHz range and the receiver in the

2,500 to 10,000 kHz range. This set was capable of telegraph and voice operation, with a range of 435 miles for telegraph and 220 miles for voice. It was transported on two 1.5-ton 6 × 4 GAZ trucks.

17. In Russian, *radiostantsiya batalonnaya-frontovaya* (battalion-*front* radio set). This radio set was used at all levels from battalion to *front*. The transmitter and receiver both operated in the 2,500 to 12,000 kHz range. This set was capable of telegraph and voice operation, with a range of 90 miles for telegraph and 45 miles for voice. It was transported on a single GAZ truck. The version of this set that was used at the lower tactical level (battalion and regiment) was man-carried, operated in voice mode on frequencies from 33,000 to 40,000 kHz, and had a range of 2.2 miles with a whip antenna.

18. TsAMO RF, collection 20046, index 1, file 26, sheets 110–111.

19. Ibid., sheets 107, 109, 185; file 29, sheets 69, 96–97.

20. The takeoff detail was a group of persons appointed from the aviation and aviation-technical units for each flying day to assist in the supervision of flight operations. They directed the movement of aircraft on the ground and in the air, maintained precise order on the airfield during flight operations, and carried out any and all measures for timely and uninterrupted support of flight operations. The takeoff detail consisted of an assistant flight operations officer, navigation duty officer, technical support duty officer, duty doctor (physician's assistant), weather duty officer, timekeeper duty officer, duty radioman (radio mechanic), and, when required, other personnel subordinated to the director of flight operations for the execution of these responsibilities. The takeoff detail command post was a place on the airfield equipped with communications means for controlling aircraft during takeoffs and landings. This was established at the discretion of the regiment commander no closer than 110 yards to the VPP, in a location that ensured unobstructed observation of the airstrip and the local airspace, especially for aircraft coming in to land.

21. TsAMO RF, collection 20046, index 1, file 39, sheets 82, 86, 125.

22. At the outbreak of the war in June 1941, the Red Army was equipped with over 104,000 trucks of this model. Produced in Moscow at the *zavod imeni Stalina* (plant named for Stalin), the two-wheel drive ZIS-5 had a carrying capacity of three tons.

23. Passengers waited at control-checkpoints that were located at intervals on main supply routes in the *front* zone and were picked up and dropped at their destinations by passing vehicles. This method of routine movement for passengers was widely employed throughout the war.

24. TsAMO RF, collection 20046, index 1, file 39, sheets 180, 184, 194.

The Airfield—the Aviators' Home

1. TsAMO RF, collection 302, index 4213, file 7, sheets 82–83.

2. TsAMO RF, collection 20046, index 1, file 18a, sheet 20.

3. Ibid., file 18, sheet 36. The word *kolkhoz* is a contraction of *kollektivnoye khozyaystvo* (collective farm). A *kolkhoz* was a group of farmers who worked together and who shared the produce of the farm according to the number of days each contributed to the group effort. The word *sovkhoz* is a contraction of *sovetskoye khozyaystvo* (Soviet farm). A *sovkhoz* was a group of farmers who

worked together and were paid a fixed wage by the owner of the farm, the government. [JG]

4. TsAMO RF, collection 20046, index 1, file 18, sheets 80, 84, 152.

5. Ibid., sheet 116.

6. Ibid., sheet 126.

7. TsAMO RF, 100th Guards Fighter Regiment collection, index 207599, file 1, sheets 3, 24.

8. See Loza, *Fighting for the Soviet Motherland,* 146–149. A *kolkhoz* field garden was a small plot of land, the produce from which the *kolkhoz* farmer was allowed to keep for personal use or sale.

9. TsAMO RF, 16th Guards Fighter Regiment collection, index 206874, file 2, sheets 11, 26.

10. Pursuant to the nonaggression pact signed between the two powers on 23 August 1939, Germany and the Soviet Union partitioned Poland and occupied their respective sectors in September.

11. Stepan Bandera (1909–1959) was the leader of the Ukrainian nationalist group OUN (Organizatsiya ukrainskykh natsionalistov). Although he himself was imprisoned by the German occupation regime in Ukraine in the summer of 1941, the large Ukrainian Insurgent Army (UPA, Ukrainskaya postanskaya armiya) swore allegiance to the OUN. In Soviet historiography, these Ukrainian anti-Soviet partisans are often referred to as *Banderovtsy* [Banderovs]. Bandera was assassinated in West Germany on 15 October 1959 by a Ukrainian national under the employ of the KGB. [JG]

12. TsAMO RF, collection 20046, index 1, file 26, sheets 108, 111.

13. TsAMO RF, 100th Guards Fighter Division collection, index 207597, file 3, sheets 63, 72.

14. TsAMO RF, collection 302, index 4213, file 7, sheets 82–83.

15. TsAMO RF, collection 20046, index 1, file 33, sheet 68.

16. Pokryshkin, *Nebo voyny,* 361.

17. TsAMO RF, collection 35, index 228603, file 1, sheets 3–5.

18. Ibid., index 558889, file 2, sheets 23–24.

Documents Tell the Story

1. TsAMO RF, collection 20046, index 1, file 13, sheet 116; file 77, sheet 151.

2. Ibid., file 22, sheets 7–8.

3. Ibid., sheets 15, 17–18.

4. Ibid., sheets 7–8.

5. Ibid., sheets 38–39.

Three Years Later

1. TsAMO RF, collection 20046, index 1, file 18a, sheet 58.

2. TsAMO RF, 16th Guards Fighter Regiment collection, index 206874, file 2, sheet 26.

3. The P-39's two oxygen tanks were located forward of the cockpit on the left side of the fuselage, in the aircraft's nose section. [JG]

4. The Henschel 129 was a twin-engined ground-attack aircraft armed with a mixture of forward-firing 20mm cannons and 7.9mm machine guns, and a 30mm cannon in a ventral pod. It had a top speed of approximately 250 mph. [JG]

5. Pokryshkin, *Nebo voyny*, 339–340.

6. TsAMO RF, 16th Guards Fighter Regiment collection, index 206874, file 2, sheets 3, 24.

7. Ibid., sheets 1, 2; file 3, sheet 23.

8. TsAMO RF, 104th Guards Fighter Regiment collection, index 20780, file 1, sheet 13.

9. TsAMO RF, 16th Guards Fighter Regiment collection, index 206874, file 2, sheet 39.

10. TsAMO RF, 100th Guards Fighter Regiment collection, index 207559, file 1, sheet 74.

11. TsAMO RF, 104th Guards Fighter Regiment collection, index 20780, file 1, sheet 15.

12. TsAMO RF, 100th Guards Fighter Regiment collection, index 207559, file 1, sheet 49.

He Flared Like a Comet

1. Nikolay Efimovich Lavitskiy was awarded the rank Hero of the Soviet Union on 24 August 1943. By this time he had flown 185 combat missions and participated in sixty-six aerial engagements. His score had reached twenty-two individual and two shared kills by the time of his death in this accident on 10 March 1944. [JG]

The Chase

1. TsAMO RF, 16th Guards Fighter Regiment collection, index 206874, file 2, sheets 25, 20.

Look, See, Find

1. TsAMO RF, 104th Guards Fighter Regiment collection, index 20780, file 1, sheet 6.

2. The Bf-110 was perhaps new on the Eastern front, but it had a long and not particularly good history in the west. With two engines of 1,100 horsepower each, it was capable of 340 mph with a range of 870 miles and a ceiling of 37,650 feet. Armed with a 20mm cannon and five 7.92mm machine guns, the aircraft had a two-man crew. Its most common role was as a night fighter. [JG]

3. TsAMO RF, 16th Guards Fighter Regiment collection, index 206874, file 2, sheet 113.

4. TsAMO RF, collection 20046, index 1, file 32, sheets 136–137.

At the Western Border

1. TsAMO RF, 16th Guards Fighter Regiment collection, index 206874, file 2, sheet 89.
2. TsAMO RF, 100th Guards Fighter Regiment collection, index 207597, file 3, sheet 10.
3. TsAMO RF, collection 20046, index 1, file 29, sheet 98.
4. Ibid., sheet 95.
5. TsAMO RF, 16th Guards Fighter Regiment collection, index 206874, file 2, sheet 104.
6. TsAMO RF, collection 20046, index 1, file 29, sheets 69, 70.
7. Ibid., sheet 103.
8. TsAMO RF, 16th Guards Fighter Regiment collection, index 206874, file 2, sheet 78; collection 20046, index 1, file 22, sheet 100.
9. TsAMO RF, collection 20046, index 1, file 33, sheet 13.
10. TsAMO RF, 100th Guards Fighter Regiment collection, index 207597, file 3, sheet 44.
11. Ibid., file 22, sheet 103.
12. TsAMO RF, collection 20046, index 1, file 22, sheet 111.
13. Ibid., file 29, sheets 71, 73.
14. TsAMO RF, 16th Guards Fighter Regiment collection, index 206874, file 2, sheet 83.

A Gift from the Bell Factory

1. TsAMO RF, collection 20046, index 1, file 32, sheet 3.
2. Ibid., index 2, file 2, sheet 27.
3. Pokryshkin, *Nebo voyny*, 290–291.
4. By the time of his death, Klubov had flown 457 combat missions, participated in ninety-five aerial engagements, and had a score of thirty-one personal and nineteen shared kills. [JG]

Flights from the Autobahn

1. For a complete description of the preparation of this autobahn for use as a takeoff and landing strip, see "Relocation to New Airfields."
2. TsAMO RF, collection 20046, index 1, file 39, sheet 126.
3. Ibid., file 32, sheet 70.
4. Ibid., file 3, sheet 136.
5. Ibid., sheet 141.
6. Ibid.
7. Ibid., file 39, sheet 230.
8. Ibid., sheet 208.
9. Ibid., sheet 193.
10. Ibid., sheet 201.
11. The number of ramming incidents fell steadily as the war progressed, from over 400 in 1941 and 1942, to approximately 200 in 1943 and 1944, to slightly over 20 in 1945. This sharp reduction in ramming incidents over time

was conditioned by two factors: the quantum improvement in the quality of aircraft and the skill of pilots on the Soviet side. The August 1944 publication of the order forbidding the use of this suicidal tactic does indicate, however, that even this late in the war many Soviet pilots still viewed the tactic as a legitimate means of taking down an enemy aircraft.

12. TsAMO RF, collection 35, index 78131, file 1, sheet 152.

13. TsAMO RF, collection 20046, index 1, file 36, sheet 213.

Mistletoe

1. An excellent description of this aircraft and its mission, with illustrations, is contained in P. W. Stahl, *KG 200: The True Story* (London: Jane's, 1981). Three chapters (pages 111–159) are devoted to this hybrid aircraft.

2. In fact, the nose section of the Ju-88 had been replaced with a 3,800-kilogram [8,380-pound] shaped-charge warhead. [JG]

3. TsAMO RF, collection 20046, index 1, file 39, sheets 202, 205–207; 100th Guards Fighter Regiment collection, index 207600, file 1, sheet 45.

4. TsAMO RF, 16th Guards Fighter Regiment collection, index 206869, file 3, sheets 123, 124.

The Airacobra as Shturmovik

1. TsAMO RF, collection 35, index 92665, file 55, sheet 5.

2. The USSR received 1,232,991 rounds of Shell, 37mm, fixed, M54 High Explosive, AC [aircraft] through Lend-Lease shipments during the war and no type-M80 armor-piercing rounds. This same source indicates that all of the 65,380 type-M80 armor-piercing rounds shipped via Lend-Lease went to Great Britain. See *Lend-Lease Shipments, World War II*, U. S. War Department, 31 December 1946, Section IV, Ordnance Ammunition and Explosives, 4. [JG]

3. *Voyennyy entsiklopedicheskiy slovar,* 322.

4. TsAMO RF, collection 20046, index 1, file 39, sheet 238.

5. The *panzerfaust* was a shoulder-fired, single-shot, recoilless antitank weapon that fired a shaped-charge round. [JG]

6. TsAMO RF, collection 20046, index 1, file 39, sheet 253.

7. Ibid., sheet 247.

The Last Combat Sorties

1. *Velikaya Otechestvennaya voyna 1941–1945,* 578.

2. The Dornier-217 was a twin-engined bomber with a crew of four. Depending on the model and engines, its top speed ranged from 320 to 350 mph. It could carry a maximum bomb load of approximately 8,000 pounds to a range of 1,700 miles. Defensive armaments included a variety of cannons and machine guns in various fixed and flexible mounts. [JG]

3. TsAMO RF, 100th Guards Fighter Regiment collection, index 207600, file 1, sheet 67.

4. TsAMO RF, 16th Guards Fighter Regiment collection, index 206869, file 3, sheet 124.

INDEX

Aeroproducts propellers, 124, 125, 127
Air army (numbered)
  2d, 128, 227, 229, 235, 301
  3d, 134
  4th, 27, 28, 30, 35, 36, 38, 43, 57, 58, 59, 79, 85, 97, 98, 99, 136, 221, 248
  5th, 36, 42, 227, 259
  8th, 36, 210, 212, 222, 223, 224, 225, 230, 231, 239
  16th, 132, 222
  17th, 36, 224, 225
Aircraft maintenance and repair, 117–128
Airfield basing district. See RAB
Airfield construction and rehabilitation
  airfield–engineer battalion ratio, 222–223
  autobahn, 134, 233–234, 301–311
  BAO participation in, 132, 222
  German airfields, 132, 242–243
  local materials used, 132, 133, 349n10
  local population used, 133, 223
  metallic landing mats, 133–134, 349n11
  unit resources expended, 132
Airfield service battalion. See BAO
Alert status. See Readiness levels
Allison engine
  booster coil failure, 125
  connecting rod bearing failure, 126
  distributor failure, 126, 348n27
  fuel requirements, 136, 349n16
  generator replacement, 121
  oil filter change, 123
  overcooling, 122
  overheating, 124, 226
  as powerplant of both P-39 and P-40, 22

removal and replacement of, 124, 126
seizure, 230, 285
sound, 169
spare engines, 128, 136
starter gear lockup, 125
V-1710-E4, 13
V-1710-83, 107, 122, 123, 124, 347n5
V-1710-85, 14, 107, 122, 123, 124, 347n5, 348n18
ALSIB (Alaska–Siberia ferry route), 14
Aviation repair facilities
  mobile, 119, 127, 131
  stationary, 119
  See also PARM

Banderovs, 241–242, 245, 353n7, 356n11
BAO (airfield service battalion)
  accommodations for personnel, 237
  advance teams sent out from, 222, 225, 226, 354n4
  airfield construction and rehabilitation, 132
  airfield defense role, 237, 243–245
  airfield relocation, 221, 224
  communication support for airfield relocation, 229
  maskirovka responsibilities, 133
  performance of, 123, 241
  purpose, mission, and structure explained, 131, 225
  ratio to serviced regiments, 131, 221–223, 354n4
  reliance on local food supply, 136
  relocation of, 221
  reserve battalions, 222
  Russian acronym spelled out, 348n14
  subordination to RAB, 131, 221

RAB, *continued*
    transportation assets used, 230, 231
    23d RAB, 230, 233
Radar (RUS-2)
    assigned to regiment command
        post, 213, 219, 239
    navigational aid, 152
    pilot communications with, 152,
        287
    received by 9th Guards Fighter
        Division, 146
    Russian acronym translated, 339n
    tactical employment, 147–148,
        149, 150, 198, 199, 207,
        213–214, 218, 219, 220, 245,
        286, 287, 303, 312, 314
    technical characteristics of, 146
Radio use
    in adjusting artillery fire, 193
    aircraft, 40, 45, 54, 63, 65, 66, 69,
        73, 77, 80, 93, 113, 180, 215,
        216, 262, 277, 294
    command and control use, 232
    deficiency in the Kuban, 142
    homing (beaconing) station,
        152, 153, 155, 156–157,
        289–290
    incentives for qualification, 144
    and poor discipline, 255
    Rechkalov remark about, 141
    transmissions restricted during
        relocation, 229
    VVS instructions for, 143
    See also Ground vectoring station
Rall, Guenther, 8, 9
Ramming incidents, 46, 47, 55, 168,
    311, 358n11
Readiness levels, 213, 345n10
Rechkalov, Grigoriy
    aerial engagement, 52, 55, 62, 64,
        74, 80–81, 110–112, 216,
        295–297
    ground attack, 206
    recipient of Bell gift watch, 299
    and remark on importance of ra-
        dio, 141
    renowned ace, 3, 9
    return to Moldavian airfield, 259

    as squadron commander, 166
Reserve of the Supreme High Com-
    mand (RVGK)
    Russian acronym spelled out,
        340n2
    216th Fighter Division a compo-
        nent of, 11

SMERSH, 176, 352n4
Soviet (Red) Air Force
    growth in 1942, 129
    growth in 1943, spring of, 35
    influence of operational art on
        postwar, 6
    medical support issues, 130–131
    mission briefing procedure, 184
    Operation Barbarossa losses, 1
    prewar and early war air combat
        tactics, 8, 25, 27–30
    reputation of 216th (9th Guards)
        fighter division in, 12
    subordination to Red Army, 11, 15
    tactical innovations in, 30–31
    use of radios monitored by
        Germans, 9
    See also VVS
Spitfire
    friendly fire incident, 79
    P-39, comparison to, 13
    use in Soviet Air Force, 26, 101,
        104, 122

"Tank buster" myth, 15–16
Tupolev, Andrey, 4

UTI-4 (two-seat version of P-39), 109,
    116, 153, 351n2

Vershinin, Konstantin
    as commander of 4th Air Army,
        7, 35, 57
    comment from memoirs, 98
VVS (*voyenno-vozdushnyye sily*)
    aerial photographic
        reconnaissance, 133
    airfield security, directive on,
        244–245
    air superiority in the Kuban, 35